LOVE MUST BE TOUGH

OTHER BOOKS BY DR. JAMES DOBSON

Life on the Edge

Children at Risk (with Gary L. Bauer)

What Wives Wish Their Husbands Knew about Women

The Strong-Willed Child

Emotions: Can You Trust Them?

Dr. Dobson Answers Your Questions

The New Hide or Seek

When God Doesn't Make Sense

Straight Talk to Men

Preparing for Adolescence

Love for a Lifetime

The New Dare to Discipline

Parenting Isn't for Cowards

Home with a Heart

Solid Answers

Coming Home

In the Arms of God

JAMES DOBSON

Love Must Be Tough

WORD PUBLISHING
NASHVILLE
A Thomas Nelson Company

WORD PUBLISHING
1996

Book design by Mark McGarry
Set in Electra

LIBRARY OF CONGRESS CATALOGING-IN-PUBLICATION DATA

Dobson, James C., 1936–
Love must be tough.
1. Marriage—Case studies
2. Problem families—Case studies. 3. Adultery—Case studies.
4. Interpersonal relations—Case studies. I. Title.
HQ734.D628 1983 646.7'8 83-21785
ISBN 0-8499-1341-1

6 7 8 9 0 BVG 5 4 3 2 1

Printed in the United Sates of America

This book is dedicated to every person who has been rejected and wounded by a husband or wife on whom everything depended. I pray that these words will begin the healing process and provide a basis for genuine forgiveness to thrive. For only in forgiveness can peace be found.

CONTENTS

PUBLISHER'S PREFACE

Everybody's talking about tough love these days. We seem to see or hear the term everyone we go. Over the last several months it has been used by investigative reporters, television news anchors, and soapbox orators, each pushing a particular agenda and a particular notion of what tough love is all about.

In January 1995, Rep. Marcy Kaptur (D, Ohio) used it on the floor of the House of Representatives in her stand against NAFTA, and later Rep. Luis Gutierrez (D, Illinois) used it in his proposal for retroactive term limits for his Republican opponents. In fact, one researcher recently found more than 100 references to "tough love" in the records of the 104th Congress. And that's just for starters.

But before the expression slides too quickly into the American vernacular, let us pause to remember that it was 1983, more than a decade ago, that Dr. James Dobson coined not only the term in his landmark book on marriage and parenthood, *Love Must Be Tough*, but also the concept that a mature love relationship is one that is built on mutual respect and genuine accountability.

Few books ever written have received the accolades, tributes, and fan mail that have descended upon *Love Must Be Tough*. A perennial favorite, winner of the prestigious Gold Medallion Award of the

Evangelical Christian Publisher's Association, and with more than a decade on the bestsellers lists, this book is still saving marriages and changing lives. Thousands of men, women, and children have been touched by the sensitive insights and wise counsel contained within these pages, and many of them write to say so.

In a note to Dr. Dobson, one grateful reader wrote, "your principles are absolutely correct. I am living proof!" Another said, "my life will never be the same," while still another made the stirring comment that, "your book saved my marriage, and my life." Letters like these have come to the offices of Focus on the Family from all over the world, expressing the heartfelt thanks of those who have gained a new outlook and a new context for their lives from this volume.

Today Focus on Family, the international ministry for families founded by Dr. Dobson, reaches millions of listeners each week through daily radio broadcasts on 1,951 affiliates in the United States and Canada and 2,000 more around the world. Through the efforts of a staff of some 1,200 men and women, Focus on the Family administers over sixty separate ministries, publishes ten magazines, distributes 130,000 tapes each month, and publishes an average of fifty books per year specifically addressing the principles of Christian Living.

At the heart of classic work, and in all areas of the ministry of Focus on the Family, is a dynamic commitment to Jesus Christ and the truth of Scripture. A licensed psychologist and former professor of pediatrics at the University of Southern California, Dr. Dobson has seen the stresses of modern life firsthand, and he brings years of experience to his analyses of the causes and cures of America's problems. He has served on national task force panels and commissions under three presidents, and his numerous books, film series, and daily radio broadcasts have helped to define the pro-family agenda in this country and to shape the debate over "family values."

It is with genuine pleasure that we introduce this new edition of *Love Must Be Tough*, not only in celebration of its ongoing success, but in the knowledge that the counsel and wisdom contained in these pages, seasoned with love and the blessings of God, will save other marriages and other lives in years to come.

INTRODUCTION

"Sit down, Carol. I have to talk to you about something very serious. I know what I'm going to say will come as a shock to you, but I can't withhold the truth any longer. You deserve to know that I've been involved in an affair with a woman at the office for nearly eighteen months. Her name is Brenda and she is very attractive. It started as an innocent flirtation, but quickly progressed into something more—much more. Now we are unable to pretend any longer. That's why I've made an appointment with an attorney, and I plan to divorce you as quickly as possible. I'm sorry! Honestly, I am. What more can I say? I never intended to hurt you. But I just don't love you any longer—and I *do* love Brenda—very deeply. So, Carol, I'm asking you to make it easy for both of us, and of course, for the kids. We'll all be better off as soon as this mess is settled."

With those words, the world falls off its axis for an unsuspecting woman and the children who can't understand why she cries. Suddenly, everything stable in their lives has been shattered. Rejection and insult are blended with pain and remorse. Self-esteem collapses like a grand old building scheduled for demolition. Security and confidence give way to fear and anxiety. The future loses its significance. But most disturbing of all, the woman who felt loved and respected a few hours before now feels utterly disdained and unlovable.

How common this set of circumstances has become in the Western world, not only for the Carols and Jeannies and Patricias around us, but also for the Robs and Toms and Carls. Whether for reasons of infidelity or because of one of the other great marriage killers, many husbands and wives find themselves being dragged relentlessly toward an unwanted divorce. For some, the realization does not come as a startling "announcement" like the one that shattered Carol. Rather, they watch helplessly as their marriages wither over a period of years, being consumed by an insidious cancer that gnaws at the soul of the relationship. They turn this way and that, searching desperately for answers—solutions—remedies. Unfortunately—and *this is the critical point*—the advice they are given by friends and even counselors is often disastrous in its effect.

The book you are about to read provides an alternative for those in the midst of family crises. My purpose in writing it has been to offer some practical tools—some understandings—which should be useful in drawing an apathetic husband or wife back in the direction of commitment. It may be surprising to learn that human conflict, *if properly managed*, can be the vehicle for transforming an unstable relationship into a vibrant, healthy marriage. On the other hand, the wrong response in moments of crisis can quickly smother the dying embers of love.

I should acknowledge at the outset that some of the principles I will offer may be controversial within Christian circles. It is my belief that the advice traditionally offered to victims of infidelity and other violations of trust has often been unbiblical and destructive. But obviously, not everyone will agree. To those who draw differing conclusions, I can only ask for charity as we seek to resolve the most difficult family problems with our limited knowledge and insight.

But that's enough for now. Let me offer one precaution before we proceed. If you are a husband or wife who is steadily losing the one you love—if you sense a growing disrespect and disdain from the most important person in your world—this book is intended for your eyes only. *Do not ask your partner to read it with you.* At least, you should review it first and then decide for yourself whether or not to reveal its message. It has been my experience that the principles of loving toughness are most effective when they are not discussed within the confines of a troubled marriage. I think you will soon understand why that is true.

Thank you for permitting me to share some new concepts with you. I hope you will find them helpful, even if you do not have a family in crisis.

CHAPTER ONE

With Love to the Victims

MORE THAN 100,000 LETTERS AND HUNDREDS OF TELEPHONE calls pour through our Focus on the Family offices each month, representing the full range of human circumstance and need. Every form of suffering and anguish, as well as many joys and triumphs, is shared with us in intimate detail from day to day. Included in that mail recently was a poignant letter from a man I'll call Roger.* His story moved me deeply.

> A few months ago, my wife, Norma, left to go to the grocery store in a nearby shopping center. She told our four children that she would be back in half an hour and warned them to behave themselves. That occurred on Saturday morning. Six hours later she had not returned, and I began a frantic search for her. I could imagine her being kidnapped or raped or even something worse. By Sunday morning I called the Detroit police, but they said they could not help until she had been gone 48 hours. The children and I were worried *sick*!
>
> We requested prayer from our church and Christian friends, especially for Norma's safety. She had left no notes or messages with friends, and she didn't call. We did find her car behind the shopping

*All the letters quoted in this book have been modified to protect the names and identities of the writers.

center, locked and empty. The police theorized that she had run away, but I didn't agree. That just wasn't like the woman I had lived with for fourteen years . . . the mother of my four children. We had been getting along quite well, actually, and had been planning to take a brief vacation over the Labor Day weekend.

On Tuesday, I obtained the services of a well-known police detective and asked him to help us locate my wife—or at least discover what had happened to her. Well, he began interviewing her friends and associates and the details unfolded. To my utter shock, it became clear that Norma had left of her own free will with a married man from her place of employment. I just couldn't believe it.

Then about two weeks later, I got a "Dear John" letter, saying she didn't love me anymore—that our marriage was finished. Just like that, it was over. She said she would be returning in a few months to fight for the children, and that they would be living with her in Kansas.

Dr. Dobson, I tell you truthfully that I have always been a faithful father and husband. Even since my wife left, I have taken good care of the kids. I did the best I could to pull our lives together and keep going . . . to try to make a decent home for these four bewildered youngsters. Nevertheless, the court ruled in my wife's favor last month, and now I am alone.

I built our house a few years ago with my own hands, and now it is empty! All I have to show for the family I lost is a stack of Norma's bills and the memories that were born in these walls. My kids will be raised in an un-Christian home, five hundred miles away, and I hardly have enough money to even visit them!

My life is a shambles now. I have nothing but free time to think about the woman I love . . . and the hurt and rejection I feel. It is an awful experience. Norma has destroyed me. I will never recover. I am lonely and depressed. I wake up in the night thinking about what might have been . . . and what *is*. Only God can help me now!

I wish this letter from Roger represented a rare tragedy that occurred only in the most unusual of circumstances. Unfortunately, variations on this theme are increasingly common today. Sexual intrigue has become a familiar pattern in today's marriages, not only outside the framework of the Christian church but within it as well. And, of course, the most vulnerable victims of family instability are the children who are too young to understand what has happened to their parents.

The most vulnerable victims of family instability are the children.

That tragic impact on the next generation was graphically illustrated to me in a recent conversation with a sixth-grade teacher in an upper middle-class California city. She was shocked to see the results of a creative writing task assigned to her students. They were asked to complete a sentence that began with the words "I wish." The teacher expected the boys and girls to express wishes for bicycles, dogs, television sets and trips to Hawaii. Instead, *twenty* of the thirty children made reference in their responses to their own disintegrating families. A few of their actual sentences were as follows:

> I wish my parents wouldn't fight and I wish my father would come back.
>
> I wish my mother didn't have a boyfriend.
>
> I wish I could get straight A's so my father would love me.
>
> I wish I had one mom and one dad so the kids wouldn't make fun of me. I have three moms and three dads and they botch up my life.
>
> I wish I had an M-1 rifle so I could shoot those who make fun of me.

I know it's hardly front page news to announce that the family is in trouble today, but it will always distress me to see little children like these struggling with such chaos at a time when simply growing up is a major undertaking. Millions of their peers are caught in the same snare. Consider the plight of Roger's children in the letter I shared. First, they lost their mother, then watched their father immersed in grief and agony, and finally found themselves jerked from familiar surroundings and transplanted into another state with a new guy who wanted to be called "Dad." They will never be the same! And why was this upheaval necessary? Because their mother cared more about her own happiness and welfare than she did about theirs. As a young woman, she had stood at an altar before God and man, solemnly promising to love and to cherish Roger—for better or worse, for richer or poorer, in sickness and health, forsaking all others, till separated by the hand of death. Unfortunately, Norma changed her mind.

The family is in trouble today.

The marriage is beyond repair. But could it have been saved?

It is apparent that the marriage between these former lovers is now beyond repair. But could it have been saved? Were there signs and symptoms that Roger failed to notice in the course of recent years? Would any advice by some profound "Solomon of psychology" have prevented the ultimate tragedy? Before attempting to answer these important questions, let's consider another troubled family that has not yet passed the point of no return. Their difficulties are summarized in the following letter from a wife and mother whom I'll call Linda. Please give careful attention to this letter, for I will be referring to it throughout the remainder of this book.

Dear Dr. Dobson:

I have a problem and it has become a terrible burden to me. It is affecting me both physically and spiritually. I grew up in a good Christian home, but married a man who was not a Christian. Paul and I have had a rough time—a lot of anger and fighting. He has refused to participate in the family as father of our three children—leaving everything up to me. He likes to bowl and watch football games on TV—and he sleeps all day Sunday. So things have always been rocky. But a much more serious problem arose a few years ago.

Paul began to get interested in a beautiful divorcee who works as his bookkeeper. At first it seemed innocent, as he helped her in various ways. But I began to notice our relationship was deteriorating. He always wanted this other woman along whenever we went anywhere, and he spent more and more time at her house. He said they were doing accounting work but I didn't believe it. I began to nag and complain, and it just made him more determined to be with her. Gradually, they fell in love with each other, and I didn't know what to do about it.

I bought a book about this time in which the author promised if I'd obey my sinner husband, God wouldn't allow any wrong to happen so long as I was submissive. Well, in my panic, I thought I would lose him forever, and I agreed to let the other woman come into our bedroom with us. I thought it would make Paul love me more, but it just made him fall deeper in love with her.

Now he is confused and doesn't know which one of us he wants. He doesn't want to lose me and says he still loves me and our three kids, but he can't give her up, either. I love Paul so dearly and I have begged him to turn our problem over to the Lord. I love the other woman too and know she is also hurting, but she doesn't believe God will punish this sin. I have experienced terrible jealousy and pain, but I always put the needs of my husband and his friend above my own. But what do I do now? Please help me. I'm on the bottom looking up.

Linda

Have you ever been presented with a problem of this nature by either friend or relative? If so, what counsel have you offered? Do you think Linda handled the crisis appropriately? Would *you* have permitted your husband or wife to bring another lover into your bedroom in a last ditch attempt to save your crumbling marriage? Linda's motives seem clear enough. She knows that her husband just might leave her if she doesn't accommodate him in every way possible, and perhaps his escapade with the "beautiful divorcee" will blow over and be forgotten if she can avoid antagonizing him. And after all, doesn't the Bible say that "Charity [love] suffereth long and is kind; charity envieth not; charity vaunteth not itself, is not puffed up; doth not behave itself unseemly, seeketh not her own, is not easily provoked" (1 Cor. 13:4, 5)? Love also "hopeth all things" and "*endureth all things*" (v. 7, KJV). Isn't it reasonable, therefore, for Linda to hold steady and "obey [her] sinner husband" in anticipation of a miracle? Would you have agreed with the wisdom of this approach? Or would you have told her to divorce the bum and get him out of her life? Is there a third alternative?

Based on my sixteen years of experience in marriage counseling, I am of the opinion that Linda's tolerance and longsuffering will probably be fatal to her marriage, and that her advisor has misinterpreted the Bible. If she deliberately set out to destroy what was left of her relationship with her husband, she could not do much more than has already been done. Though I empathize with her and intend no disrespect in this context, Linda has already made several fundamental mistakes that have contributed mightily to the present disaster in her home.

We must never underestimate the power of sexual chemistry.

Linda's first error occurred in not recognizing the threat imposed by a beautiful divorcee. We must never underestimate the power of sexual chemistry existing between an attractive, needy, available woman and virtually any man on the face of the earth. In the case of Linda's husband, he suddenly found himself hopscotching between their two houses to provide whatever service the gorgeous-one might desire, while his wife concluded, "It seemed innocent." Innocent indeed! That's like a farmer thinking the fox visited his henhouse because he enjoyed the company of chickens!

Linda's second error occurred after observing that her marriage was going downhill. That was an extremely important moment in their relationship when an appropriate reaction from Linda might have pulled her playboy husband back from the precipice. But alas, she was ill prepared for the task. She nagged and complained. How inadequate but how human! Her husband was rapidly falling head over heels in love with "the other woman," and Linda's only response was hand wringing and verbal abuse. That form of reproof is about as effective with a wayward spouse as it is with a disobedient toddler: he doesn't even *hear* it!

She nagged and complained. How inadequate but how human!

The key word in the next phase of this story is *panic*. Linda could see the handwriting on the wall. It scrawled the frightening word *divorce* and moved on. How terrifying to one whose entire life is her family! She could visualize herself as the mother of three fatherless children, struggling to survive financially and emotionally in a lonely, broken home. Furthermore, she was losing the man she loved with all her being. And as panic is irrational, so was her reaction to it. She brought the other woman into her bedroom in a desperate attempt to occupy even a crowded corner of her husband's heart. What an incredible error in judgment! She soon discovered the inevitable result: "It just made him fall deeper in love with her."

The best news I can give Linda is that it is still possible for her to save her marriage, but she hasn't a minute to waste. Her husband has admitted that a spark of love still glows under the smoldering ashes ("He doesn't want to lose me and says that he still loves me and our three kids"), but she must not smother it! One more bad move and he will be gone forever. He is in a state of confusion and can be swayed one way or the other, but how can Linda tug him in her direction? She's tried everything in her own playbook and nothing has worked. What does she do now? If she is like so many others in today's world, she will be baffled by the question.

It is still possible for her to save her marriage.

The frequency with which I have been confronted by problems similar to the plight of Linda and Roger has led me to write the book you are reading. I'm especially concerned about the person in an unsatisfying relationship whose mate could not seem to care less. Let me be more specific. In any apathetic or dying marriage, there is typically one partner who is relatively unconcerned about the distance between them, while the other is anxious or even panic-stricken over it. The detached spouse, whether husband or wife, may not realize how much danger the marriage is in or may not care. Therefore, that person resists any effort by his mate to entice him into counseling or compromises or even meaningful conversations to address their difficulties. "We have no serious problems," he contends.

In any apathetic or dying marriage, there is typically one partner who is relatively unconcerned.

The vulnerable partner, who could represent either sex but is more likely *initially* to be female, is aware that something precious is slipping away day by day. Everything of value is hanging in the balance, and she awakens in the midnight hours to contemplate the future. She thinks of the children—those beautiful kids who slumber unknowingly in their bedrooms—and wonders what will happen to them. She reaches for the affection and attention of her mate, and experiences depression when she doesn't get it.

I'm not implying, of course, that frail marriages can be blamed entirely on one spouse, and I'm accusing neither men nor women. Marital conflict *always* involves an interaction between two imperfect human beings who share the responsibility to one degree or another. Nevertheless, there is usually one partner who would do anything to hold the home together—and another who seems disinterested in the relationship.

Marital conflict always *involves an interaction between two imperfect human beings.*

The book you hold is dedicated, therefore, to that vulnerable member of the family who can be thought of as a victim in extreme cases. This is the only text of which I am aware whose primary purpose is to help a distressed person strengthen or preserve his or her marriage, *even in the absence of a willing spouse.* What advice can be offered to a woman like Linda whose husband is entangled in an affair, or a man like Roger whose wife seems to disrespect and hate him, or a wife whose husband is an alcoholic or drug abuser or child molester? And what about the woman who loves her husband and is loved by him in return, but worries about the total absence of romantic excitement between them? Is there any way she can heat up their relationship without nagging her husband incessantly?

We want to help one spouse maximize the chances of preserving the marriage.

Virtually every counseling program now in existence for such families is designed to bring together *two* people who can agree, at least, to discuss their problems. Or if therapy is offered for a single partner, it is directed at strengthening that individual to cope with the crisis and go it alone, if necessary. But our purpose here is unique: we want to help *one* spouse maximize the chances of preserving the marriage, as in Linda's case, and to survive till the long night is over. It's an ambitious undertaking.

In the process of reaching out to the hurting members of the family, it is my desire to accomplish much more. The principles I will describe are not only relevant to husbands and wives in a time of crisis; they are applicable to healthier marriages, too. Indeed, I wish they could be taught to every engaged or newlywed couple in the morning of their lives together. There would be fewer bitter divorces if young husbands and wives knew how to draw their drifting partners toward them, rather than relentlessly drive them away.

The concepts I will share are relevant to all *human relationships.*

But the concepts I will share have even broader applicability than the interaction between husbands and wives. As we will see, they are relevant to *all* human relationships, including employers and employees, parents and children, pastors and parishioners, business and labor, guards and prisoners, Americans and Russians, and all the other categories of people who share an interface from time to time. In other words, I will be describing in subsequent chapters what I consider to be some universal concepts that cut across cultures, sexes, races, and economic circumstances. And unless I have missed the mark, they will hit somewhere near your neck of the woods in one context or another.

Now isn't that just like an author to promise the moon to his readers? All writers have this tendency to overestimate the significance of their views. Books being published today offer everything from immeasurable wealth for men to instantly smooth thighs for women.

Unfortunately, these authors rarely deliver on their promises; they remind me of "Professor Miraculous" in the Old West who sold his Elixir of Life from the back of his covered wagon and then left town . . . fast.

Hoping not to fall into the same "cure-all" trap, let me tell you candidly how I feel about the concepts you are about to read. Genuine insights into human behavior are not everyday occurrences—at least not for me. Indeed, if one stumbles onto two or three fundamental principles in the course of a lifetime, he has done well. The pages that follow focus on one of my allotted few. I've called the concept *love must be tough*. It won't smooth out your thighs or make you wealthy, but it should help you cope better with the people around you.

Genuine insights into human behavior are not everyday occurrences.

CHAPTER TWO

Panic and Appeasement

ONLY THOSE WHO HAVE BEEN REJECTED BY A BELOVED spouse or lover can fully comprehend the tidal wave of sorrow that crashes into one's life when a loss is threatened. Nothing else matters. There are no consoling thoughts. The future is without interest or hope. Emotions swing wildly from despair to acceptance and back again. If one word must be selected to describe the entire experience, it would be something equivalent to *panic.*

Since panic is the characteristic response to rejection, imagine how much more distressing a loss is felt when a new and perhaps younger lover is brought into the picture! *Nothing* in human experience can compare with the agony of knowing that the person to whom you pledged eternal devotion has betrayed your trust and is now engaged in sexual intimacies with a "stranger" . . . a competitor . . . a more beautiful or handsome playmate. Death itself would be easier to tolerate than being tossed aside like an old shoe. Those who have experienced such a loss tell me that the most painful aspect is their own loneliness—knowing that their unfaithful partner is comforted in the embrace of another. How desperately Christian counsel is needed by those who awaken to the awful knowledge that adultery has taken residence in their homes!

Panic is the characteristic response to rejection.

In the absence of that guidance, a rejected man or woman often reacts in ways that make matters worse. Just as a drowning person exhausts himself in a desperate attempt to grasp anything that floats, including his rescuer, the panic-stricken lover typically tries to grab and hold the one who is attempting to escape. I have witnessed the scenario a thousand times. Supercharged emotions zip up and down a roller coaster of extremes.

Death itself would be easier to tolerate than being tossed aside like an old shoe.

Upon disclosure that the marriage (or premarital relationship) is over, the first reaction is almost sure to be one of utter shock and disbelief. That is followed by weeping and wailing and gnashing of teeth, giving way to begging and pleading for forgiveness and restoration. When that too is rejected, a bargaining period ensues. The person promises to be a better lover, to be more considerate, to quit work or to go to work or to bring flowers more often or to have a baby or whatever is perceived to be important to the disenchanted mate. Suggestions are made that they both seek counseling assistance, but the offer is almost always declined by the one whose mind is already settled. Then when all negotiations prove futile, an angry stage is often entered, perhaps eliciting every mean and hostile thought that the victim has harbored. A man may threaten to inflict bodily harm on his ex-lover during this phase, and sometimes succeeds in doing so. With or without violence, the hostility of this terrible ordeal is ventilated in a period of wrath, ending in physical and emotional exhaustion. Then a brief time of acceptance occurs, after which grief and sorrow return like an unwelcome visitor who so recently

The cycle repeats itself on a revolving merry-go-round of misery.

came to call. Finally, the cycle repeats itself on a revolving merry-go-round of misery.

With the reader's indulgence, I will continue to include letters that illustrate the circumstances I am attempting to describe. It is the best way I know to make the words come to life. These are the thoughts and feelings of real people who have been through the turbulent waters I have described. Faye is such a person whose panic has led her to plead and bargain with her husband. She wrote:

Dear Dr. Dobson:

I'm writing to you regarding my marriage. My husband gave me the bad news earlier this year, telling me he no longer loved me. He told me of his plans to leave soon. Well, I begged and pleaded with him to stay with me, and he did for a while. Then one night he became so cruel and said many mean things before walking out.

Ever since he left, for some odd reason, I humiliate myself every time I see him. I beg him to call the kids and me. He'll say, "I don't want to talk to you!" I tell him how much I love him, and he'll reply, "I have no love for you! I don't hate you, but I don't love you either." That hurts me so much!

I've asked Joe to see a counselor, but he said he doesn't need any help from anyone. He doesn't even care about the marriage. He only wants his freedom. He says he wants to go to Pennsylvania where he can get a better job in the mining business.

So what do you think the problem is? We've been married eleven years, and we have two beautiful children. The odd thing is that we never did fight or argue very much. It just seems that he slowly turned against me and changed his mind about being my husband. Have you ever seen cases such as this?

Now something awful has happened. I went to the doctor recently, and he told me I'm going to have to have surgery on my eye, and I could lose my vision. I'll be going into the hospital next week. I just couldn't help it, Dr. Dobson. I broke down and called my husband again, but he was indifferent to the news. He quietly asked me if I had made any arrangements for the kids and if I had someone to take me to the hospital. I asked if he would take me and then stay in the waiting room while I had the surgery. Joe hesitated and then said, "Well, I guess so."

What must I do to get Joe to love me again? He has told me over and over that nothing could make him care for me like before. I have cried and begged him to come home. I've told him how badly we need him. I've tried being nice. That doesn't help either. I've told him I'm afraid and I need him especially now, and he says, "I'm sorry. The timing is bad."

Is it likely that we will end up in a divorce? Joe has asked for one but I've refused. I still have hopes that we can get back together. I told him that and he said, "Can't you get it through your head that I'll never love you again?"

We used to do everything together, but now it's all over. I keep calling my husband because if I don't, he would never call me. Next Monday is a holiday; he didn't ask what the kids and I were doing, so I asked if he would spend the day with us. He acted so smart and said, "If I have *nothing* else to do . . . " Should I ignore him? If I do, I'll never see him again.

Dr. Dobson, please help me. Tell me what to do. I love Joe so much!

Faye

Though I understand the compulsion that drives Faye to plead for Joe's attention and love, she is systematically destroying the last glimmer of hope for a reconciliation. She has stripped herself of all dignity and self-respect, crawling on her belly like a subservient puppy before her master. The more Joe insults her and spurns her advances, the more intensely she seems to want and need him. That is, in fact, the way the system works.

The message Faye is giving her husband can be summarized thus: "Oh, Joe, I need you so badly. I can't make it without you. I spend my days waiting for you to call and am crushed when the phone doesn't ring. Won't you please, please, let me talk to you occasionally? You see, Joe, I'll take you any way I can have you, even if you want to walk all over me. I am desperate here without you."

She has stripped herself of all dignity and self-respect.

Linda, whose letter I shared in the first chapter, has given precisely the same message to her unfaithful husband. In her case, however, the panic even led her to invite the other woman into her bedroom. What a pitiful expression of low self-esteem and inadequacy. My heart aches for her and for the millions of others facing similar sorrows.

What a pitiful expression of low self-esteem and inadequacy.

Linda and Faye have brought us now to an extremely important and well-known principle of human relationships: *panic often leads to appeasement, which is virtually never successful in seeking to control the behavior of others.* In fact, it often leads directly to war, whether between husbands and wives or between antagonistic nations. Attempts by one side to "buy off" an aggressor or offender appear to represent peace proposals, but they merely precipitate further insult and conflict. World War II might have been prevented and fifty million lives saved if British Prime Minister Neville Chamberlain and other national leaders had understood the folly of appeasement in 1936-39. Every time they offered Adolph Hitler another Czechoslovakia to tranquilize his lust for dominion, they only fed his disdain for them and their armies. Hitler's interpretation of their yearning for "peace in our time" as evidence of weakness and fear enticed him to ever greater audacity. Finally, it became necessary to fight what Winston Churchill called the most *preventable* war in modern times. That is where appeasement leads, whether in affairs of state or affairs of the heart.

In Linda's case, her husband threatened to divorce her if she didn't allow him to engage in extramarital intimacies in their bedroom. Not only was this a cruel form of blackmail, it was also a test of her confidence and self-respect. She failed it.

Let me make it clear that my opposition to marital appeasement—this defenseless, pleading reaction—has nothing to do with pride, as such. If stripping oneself of dignity would preserve a marriage, I would enthusiastically endorse the behavior. Unfortunately, the opposite is true. *Nothing* destroys a romantic relationship more quickly than for a person to throw himself, weeping and clinging, on the back of the cool partner to beg for mercy. That infuses the wayward spouse with an even greater desire to escape from the leech that threatens to suck his life's blood. He may pity the wounded partner and wish that things were different, but he can rarely bring himself to love again under those circumstances.

> Nothing *destroys a romantic relationship more quickly than for a person to beg for mercy.*

Perhaps the reader can now understand why I disagree strongly with Christian leaders who recommend that rejected husbands and wives smile during a time of breakup or unfaithfulness and act as though nothing had happened. This advice is especially characteristic of those who write books for women today. They recommend, "Just keep lovin' your men, ladies, and sooner or later they'll come to their senses." As you will recall, that counsel was offered to Linda by some misguided author who promised, "God [won't] allow any wrong to happen so long as [you are] submissive." That is Pollyanna in the pulpit if I've ever heard it!

Please understand that I believe firmly in the biblical concept of submission, as described in the Book of Ephesians and elsewhere in Scripture. But there is a vast difference between being a confident, spiritually submissive woman and being a doormat. People wipe their feet on doormats, as we know. Furthermore, it is terribly destructive to one's internal organs to hold inside all the sadness and anxiety generated during a disintegrating marriage. Everything from hypertension to ulcers and even cancer can result from unventilated stress.

But there is a vast difference between being a confident, spiritually submissive woman and being a doormat.

Finally, successful marriages usually rest on a foundation of *accountability* between husbands and wives. They reinforce responsible behavior in one another by a divinely inspired system of checks and balances. In its absence, one party may gravitate toward abuse, insult, accusation, and ridicule of the other, while his or her victim placidly wipes away the tears and mutters with a smile, "Thanks, I needed that!" This passivity was the subject of a recent country song entitled "She's Got to Be a Saint." The words tell us what often happens to the appeaser who lacks the courage to confront a disrespectful partner.

> I'm out late ev'ry night, doin' things that ain't right,
>   And she'll cry for me.
> When I'm down in the dumps and she nurses my lumps,
>   How she cries for me.
> And she'll never complain, she keeps hiding the pain
>   But I know all the while:

She's not feeling too well 'cause I've put her thru hell;
  Still she forces a smile.
She's got to be a saint, Lord knows that I ain't.
I finally realized right before my eyes,
  Here is a saint.

There's a dress in the shop that'll make her eyes pop
  But she'll look away.
She'd-a gotten a lift if I bought her that gift
  For her birthday.
But her birthday has come and I feel like a bum
  'Cause I spent my last dime
On a worthless old friend on a drunken weekend.
  I've done it time after time.
She's got to be a saint, Lord knows that I ain't.
I finally realized right before my eyes,
  Here is a saint.

Should I stay, should I go? I really don't know,
  My mind's in a blur.
Soon it's gonna be dawn and if she finds me gone
  Would it be best for her?
I see her cry in her sleep so I kiss her wet cheek
  I kneel by her and pray.
And I'll turn off the light, step out in the night,
  and I'll go on my way.
She's got to be a saint, Lord knows that I ain't.
I finally realized right before my eyes,
  Here is a saint.*

Nice guy, huh? He's just the kind of jerk that every father fears is going to marry his daughter. (I can't help wondering what he said to

*"She's Got to Be a Saint," words and music by Joe Paulini and Mike DiNapoli. Copyright © 1970 Galleon Music Inc. Used by permission.

the Lord in that bedside prayer.) But let's take a closer look at him. What would motivate a man to be so cruel? Every elementary psychology book describes the yearning for affection that throbs within the breast of all mankind, males and females alike. Yet here we see a drunken bum who sneaks away from the caring, sharing, loving devotion of this marvelous woman. Why does he want to escape in the night? His wife would do anything to hold him, yet he prefers to spend the weekend weaving on some barstool with another wasted sot. How can such strange behavior be explained? Well, in addition to the effects of booze, this bleary-eyed crooner just can't handle an appeasing wife who gives him everything and requires nothing in return. Sober or not, *very few of us can!*

What would motivate a man to be so cruel?

It is even more important to understand the behavior of the woman represented in this song. Is she really some kind of superhuman saint? Of course not! She is merely a vulnerable female who has considered the alternatives and concluded that her only option is to keep her mouth shut. Perhaps in younger years she stood toe to toe with this beer-drinking bully and was hurt more than he by the brawl. Or maybe she is by temperament a peace-lovin' lady who just can't tolerate conflict. Either way, she knows that her husband is on the verge of leaving, and she wants to give him no excuse to split. Therefore, she has chosen to appease her man in the hope that he will clean up his act.

What passes for a "saint" to a half-drunk husband, then, is a normal woman who is carefully concealing what she really feels. You can be *certain* that she is in agony. She's like a duck who is calm and serene above the water but paddles like

Contented people do not cry themselves to sleep at night.

crazy below it. How can we be so sure that she is in secret pain? First, because contented people do not cry themselves to sleep at night, and second, because of the delicate psychological nature of human beings. Our emotional apparatus is like a finely tuned violin which can be distorted so easily. The woman in the song is being abused by the one she loves, and there is no doubt that she is experiencing agitation, resentment, low self-esteem and other disturbing emotions. These kinds of troubling feelings simply cannot be denied in most people, especially the female of the species.

If marriage is to last a lifetime, then it must not accumulate and preserve resentments that can eventually turn into hatred.

The question remains, what is she going to do with these negative emotions? Sending them downward into a secret holding tank is the psychological equivalent of storing TNT. Sooner or later, a spark will touch off a blast that will make Mount Saint Helens look like a popgun. (Helens was a saint, too, as you recall!) If marriage is to last a lifetime, then it must not accumulate and preserve resentments that can eventually turn into hatred. There must be a mechanism for releasing small tensions as they arise in everyday life. In the absence of that safety valve, what will happen to the saint in the course of time? Let's assume that her alcoholic husband stays with her but continues to take advantage of her passivity. A blowup is likely at some future moment. To illustrate the point, let's look in on our saint twenty years downstream, cleverly described in the lyrics of another country song entitled "To Daddy."*

*Written by Dolly Parton. Copyright © 1976 Velvet Apple Music, 8 Music Square West, Nashville, TN 37203. All rights administered by Tree Pub. Co., Inc. International copyright secured. All rights reserved. Used by permission.

Mama never seemed to miss the finer things in life.
If she did, she never did say so to Daddy.
She never wanted to be more than mother and a wife.
If she did, she never did say so to Daddy.
The only thing that seemed to be important in her life
Was to make our house a home and make us happy.
Mama never wanted any more than what she had.
If she did, she never did say so to Daddy.
He often left her all alone;
But she didn't mind the stayin' home.
If she did, she never did say so to Daddy.
And she never missed the flowers
And the cards he never sent her.
If she did, she never did say so to Daddy.
Being took for granted
Was a thing that she accepted,
And she didn't need those things to make her happy.
And she didn't seem to notice that he didn't kiss and hold her.
If she did, she never did say so to Daddy.
One morning we awoke, just to find a note
That mama carefully wrote and left to Daddy.
And as he began to read it,
Our ears could not believe it,
Words that she had written there to Daddy.
She said the kids are old enough, they don't need me very much,
And I've gone in search of love I need so badly.
I have needed you so long,
But I just can't keep holding on.
She never meant to come back home.
If she did, she never did say so to Daddy.
Good-bye to Daddy.

CHAPTER THREE

The Tender Trap

I HOPE WE HAVE SUCCEEDED IN DOCUMENTING THREE conclusions thus far:

1. Marital (and premarital) conflict typically involves one partner who cares a great deal about the relationship and the other who is much more independent and secure.
2. As a love affair begins to deteriorate, the vulnerable partner is inclined to panic. Characteristic responses include grieving, lashing out, begging, pleading, grabbing, and holding; or the reaction may be just the opposite, involving appeasement and passivity.
3. While these reactions are natural and understandable, they are rarely successful in repairing the damage that has occurred. In fact, such reactions are usually counterproductive, destroying the relationship the threatened person is trying so desperately to preserve.

In the previous chapter we explored the fears and sorrows reverberating in the mind of the rejected partner. Now let's take the next step by looking at the husband or wife who is drifting away. In order to pull that person back from the brink, we need to understand the forces operating within. What do you believe motivates a man or woman to terminate a marriage? What thoughts are typical of one who rejects the unconditional love offered at home? What secrets lie deep within the psyche of the woman who has an affair with her boss, or the man who chases the office flirt? Is desire for a new thrill the only enticement, or are more basic motivators operating below the surface?

It has been my observation that the lust for forbidden fruit is often incidental to the real cause of marital decay. Long before any decision is made to "fool around" or walk out on a partner, something basic has begun to change in the relationship. Many books on this subject lay the blame on the failure to communicate, but I disagree. The inability to talk to one another is a symptom of a deeper problem, but it is not the cause itself. The critical element is the way one spouse begins to perceive the other and their lives together. It is a subtle thing at first, often occurring without either partner being aware of the slippage. But as time passes, one individual begins to feel trapped. That's the key word, *trapped*.

But as time passes, one individual begins to feel trapped. That's the key word, trapped.

In its more advanced stages, a man considers his wife (gender is interchangeable throughout these discussions) and thinks these kinds of thoughts: "Look at Joan. She used to be rather pretty. Now with those fifteen extra pounds she doesn't even attract me anymore. Her lack of discipline bothers me in other areas, too—the house is a perpetual mess and she always seems totally disorganized. I hate to admit it, but I made an enormous mistake back there in my youth when I decided to marry her. Now I have to spend the rest of my life—can you believe it—all the years I have left—tied up with someone I'm disinterested in. Oh, I know Joanie is a good woman, and I wouldn't hurt her for anything, but man! Is this what they call living?"

Or Joanie may be doing some thinking of her own: "Michael,

Michael, how different you are than I first thought you to be. You seemed so exciting and energetic in those early days. How did you get to be such a bore? You work far too much and are so tired when you come home. I can't even get you to talk to me, much less sweep me into ecstasy. . . . Look at him, sleeping on the couch with his mouth hanging open. I wish his hair wasn't falling out. Am I really going to invest my entire lifetime in this aging man? Our friends don't respect him anymore, and he hasn't received a promotion at the plant for more than five years. He's going nowhere and he's taking me with him!"

If Joanie and Michael are both thinking these entrapment thoughts, it is obvious that their future together is in serious jeopardy. But my point is that the typical situation is unilateral. *One* partner begins to chafe at the bit without revealing to the other how his perception has evolved. A reasonably compassionate person simply does not sit down calmly and disclose these disturbing rumblings to someone who loves him. Instead, his behavior begins to change in inexplicable ways.

One partner begins to chafe at the bit without revealing to the other how this perception has evolved.

He may increase the frequency of his evening business meetings—anything to be away from home more often. He may become irritable or "deep in thought" or otherwise noncommunicative. He may retreat into televised sports or fishing trips or poker with the boys. He may provoke continuous fights over insignificant issues. And of course, he may move out or find someone younger to play with. A woman who feels trapped will reveal her disenchantment in similar indirect ways.

Let's examine a letter from a woman whose husband quite obviously feels locked into his marriage. He's never asked for a divorce, but we can sense what he is thinking from what his wife tells us.

Dear Dr. Dobson:

I have been married for twenty-one years, and the entire trip has been stormy. My husband cares about only one thing: getting ahead. He works two jobs, seven days a week. I know he loves our four kids, but he has no time for them, or else he's too exhausted to give them any attention.

Our relationship is stale! My husband has never (and I do mean never!) approached me physically with a hug, kiss, or embrace, but will "go along with it" if I am the initiator. I long to get inside his head and find out how he feels, but he simply won't talk about personal things.

We went to a marriage counselor a few years ago after almost splitting up, and I thought he was really helping us. Jack didn't agree. He called the counselor "worthless" and a "waste of money." Now he says he'll see a divorce attorney before he'll ever go back.

I've studied 1 Peter 3 (about submission) until I'm blue in the face. I've practiced those principles to the best of my ability. What has Jack done in response? He now expects me to always be cheerful and loving, regardless of how he treats me. *Am I to accept this non-affectionate man forever* [author's italics], or is there hope for change? He enjoys putting me down.

I love him, but sometimes I get so upset that I think I hate him. He just withdraws. Do you have any suggestions or books or tapes that could help me? Jack won't read anything I give him.

Thanks for your help.

Nancy

How could it be said any more clearly? Here we have a man who obviously disrespects his wife, treating her like an unwanted child. I would bet my shirt he's wishing there were an acceptable way out of his commitments and obligations. On the other side, we hear an emotionally deprived woman asking, "What's going on in this man's mind? Why is he so cold and unresponsive?" The answer? He feels trapped.

This intense desire to escape from a marriage can occur on the first day of the honeymoon or fifty years thereafter. For men, it is the primary ingredient of a midlife crisis. But these feelings of constraint are by no means unique to men. For women, they usually (but not always) occur in response to an unromantic relationship that refuses to be energized. A wife may "reach" for her husband for years, beg for his attention, nag him when he fails to notice, and then scream to herself, "Help! I'm suffocating in this loveless marriage! Somebody get me out!"

Here we have a man who obviously disrespects his wife.

How sad it is, furthermore, that this trapped partner who is fighting an impulse to run is rapidly sinking deeper and deeper into a form of marital quicksand. Why? Because the more he struggles to gain his freedom (or even secure a little breathing room), the more his panic-stricken spouse clutches his neck. Even the fluctuating emotions of the rejected party are interpreted as attempts to grab and hold him. For example:

The intense desire to escape from a marriage can occur on the first day of the honeymoon or fifty years thereafter.

The response of grief: "Please don't hurt me. Come and meet my needs."

The response of anger: "Get back in line, stupid! How dare you try to walk out on me!"

The response of blame: "How could you do this to me and the kids?"

The response of appeasement: "Name it and you can have it. Just don't leave me."

The response of servility (*the doormat*): "No matter what you do, I'll go on smiling 'cause you're mine."

The common denominator between these varied responses is one of entrapment. They each restrict the freedom of the less interested party. For someone in the trapped syndrome, love then becomes an *obligation* rather than an incredibly wonderful privilege. Perhaps it is now obvious why the natural reaction of the panic-stricken spouse typically drives the cool partner farther away; the more he pulls back from their relationship to gain desired space, the tighter the bonds close around him. He sometimes becomes almost claustrophobic in his desperate attempts to breathe—to get the noose off his neck. He may even resort to infidelity as a vehicle to escape from his partner's clutches.

For someone in the trapped syndrome, love then becomes an obligation.

If the reader will forgive the redundancy, I'll make a more graphic attempt to express this important concept. I have often explained it to those I have counseled by demonstrating with my hands, as follows:

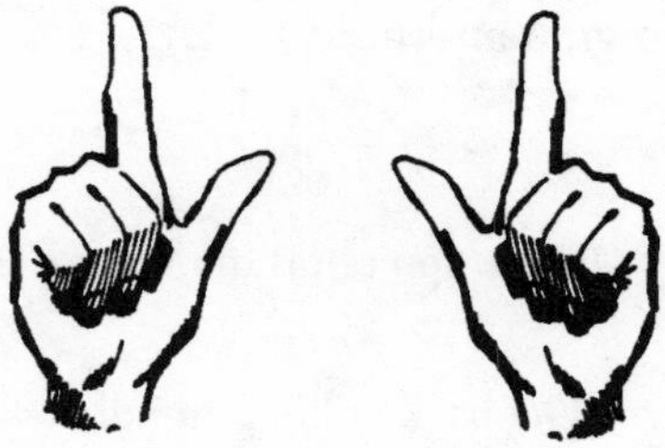

PARTNER A PARTNER B

Partners A and B decide to get married and live happily ever after. At some point along the way, however, Partner B begins to feel trapped in the relationship. His spouse offends or bores him in numerous ways, and he resents those five constraining words, "'til death do us part."

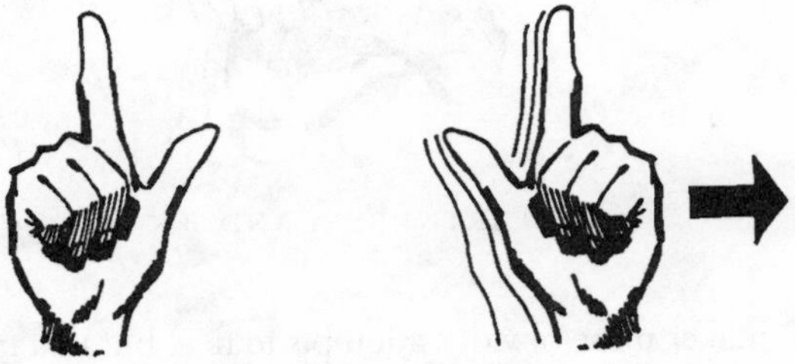

PARTNER A PARTNER B

In order to deal with this sense of containment—this restriction of freedom—Partner B moves gradually to the right, away from Partner A.

PARTNER A PARTNER B

Partner A observes Partner B's retreat and reacts with alarm. Her impulse is to pursue Partner B, closing the gap even tighter than before.

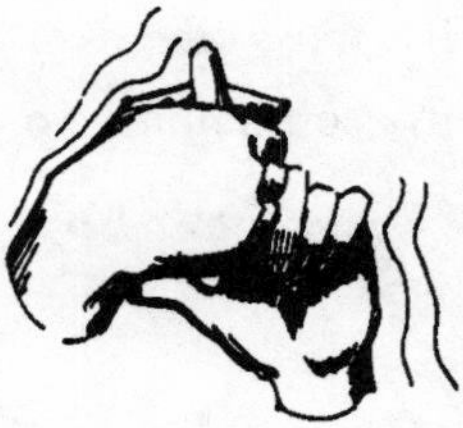

PARTNERS A AND B

Partner B makes more obvious attempts to flee, but in a moment of desperation, Partner A jumps on Partner B and clutches him with all her strength. Partner B struggles to escape and will surely run the moment he gains release.

PARTNER A

Partner A then droops in loneliness, wondering how something so beautiful became so sour.

INSTEAD . . .

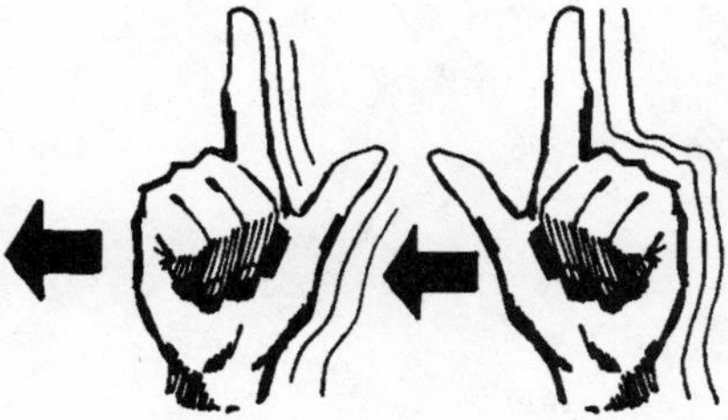

PARTNER A PARTNER B

Regardless of what common sense tells us to the contrary, Partner A's best chance of attracting and holding a suffocating lover is to pull backward slightly, conveying freedom for Partner B and respect for herself in the process. Curiously, Partner B often moves *toward* Partner A when this occurs.

We've all observed this need for "space" in human relationships, but the concept is still difficult to comprehend when it pertains to ourselves and our loved ones. The next chapter will explain why.

CHAPTER FOUR

Young Love, True Love

WE'VE BEEN DISCUSSING PSYCHOLOGICAL PRINCIPLES THAT may appear vague and esoteric when considered in adult terms. Grownups have a way of hiding their feelings, even from themselves. Perhaps these concepts will be more evident in the transparency of the very young. Do you remember during your dating days that the task of attracting a prize catch required a certain reserve —an appearance of indifference and poise? Those of our peers who were most successful in romantic pursuits were the cats who knew how to be coy—how to flirt without appearing to need the one they desired. And conversely, those who were eternally being dumped were desperate young men and women who inevitably became possessive and demanding—calling on the phone six straight times and parking the car in the shadows to spy on the lover, then complaining bitterly the next day about who the lover was with the night before. That was the beginning of the end, leading directly to what we used to call "the maroon harpoon."

The task of attracting a prize catch required a certain reserve.

Today's adolescents use different language to describe splintering romances, but the rules to the game have not changed. Lovers' quarrels typically involve one "clinging vine" who is being axed and an "oak tree" that stands confidently above the fray.

But who are these lady-killers and heartbreakers who seem so independent and secure? Do they take satisfaction in shredding their former boyfriends and girlfriends? Most do not. They are merely self-centered individuals who love to pursue but hate to be caught. They throw themselves into the chase with abandon as long as the affair is new and challenging. But their interest melts like hot ice cream the moment they achieve their goal and capture the prize. Suddenly, the tables are turned. They are needed—possessed—depended upon. Demands are made on them for loyalty and service and commitment. Thenceforth, their only passion is for escape and freedom.

But their interest melts like hot ice cream the moment they achieve their goal and capture the prize.

One reason I'm so familiar with these characteristics of young love is that I have such a good memory. It seems only yesterday that my wife, Shirley, and I were playing these cat-and-mouse games. In a subsequent chapter I will describe how I kept her guessing about my feelings for nearly two years, and even ended the relationship a time or two. If that seems cruel to a pretty little college sophomore, you should know that Shirley had broken more hearts than Bluebeard himself. As a teenager, she was interested in boys only until the moment she caught them. Then it was curtains. In her wake lay a trail of fallen adolescent heroes who made the mistake of trying to possess her—to hold her and demand her allegiance. They soon heard "the closing of the door" as she was on her way out.

One young man named Stan took his notice of termination quite hard. He and Shirley were sitting in his car at the edge of a park during their senior year of high school. After telling him that they were through, Stan sat staring at the angora dice hanging from his mirror for a few minutes. Then he bolted from the car and disappeared into the night. Shirley had no idea where he had gone or whether he would come back. Stan returned in about ten minutes with a bloody handkerchief wrapped around his hand, telling her that he had socked a tree in his anger. Oh, the joys and sorrows of adolescence!

Oh, the joys and sorrows of adolescence!

Teenage romance is often humorous to adults because its passions are so raw and undisguised. I suppose that's why I enjoy listening to the words of songs currently popular among the young. As with country and western music, the values of today's youth are clearly audible within the horrid lyrics of disco and rock.

Consider the following lament by a teenager whom I'll call Harry Highschool. His best friend has just snagged the last perfect woman on the face of the earth. Harry calls her "Jessie's Girl."

> Jessie is a friend
> Yeah, I know he's been a good friend of mine
> But lately something's changed
> It ain't hard to define.
> Jessie's got himself a girl,
> And I wanna make her mine.
> And she's watchin' him with those eyes,
> And she's loving him with that body
> I just know it.
> And, he's holding her in his arms late, late at night.
> You know I wish that I had Jessie's girl.
> I wish that I had Jessie's girl.
> When can I find a woman like that?
> I'll play along with the charade.
> There doesn't seem to be a reason to change.

You know I feel so dirty when they start talkin' cute.
I wanna tell her that I love her,
But the point is prob'ly moot.
And I'm looking in the mirror all the time.
Wonderin' what she don't see in me.
I've been funny.
I've been cool with the lines.
Ain't that the way love's supposed to be?
Tell me, when can I find a woman like that?
You know, I wish that I had Jessie's girl.
I wish that I had Jessie's girl.
I want Jessie's girl. *

Have you ever read lyrics that better reflected the adolescent mindset than these? Notice the depth of Harry's understanding of true love; he thinks it should flow like a river to any cool dude who's funny with the lines. He would like to tell Jessie's girl that he loves her, but admits he'd settle for any girl "like that." He's in love with an image—an illusion—not a woman. Observe his unconcealed sexual fantasies and jealousies and passions. When young love is viewed from this perspective, it's not surprising that 50 percent of all teenage marriages end in divorce within five years.

The most intense spasms of desire are felt by those who pursue sex objects that appear unreachable.

There is little doubt that adolescent romance is typically selfish and introspective; it blanches and buckles when asked to sacrifice or contribute or give. The most intense spasms of desire are felt by those who, like Harry, pursue sex objects that appear unreachable, unattain-

*"Jessie's Girl" written by Rick Springfield. Copyright © 1981 Vogue Music (c/o The Welk Music Group, Santa Monica, CA 90401). International copyright secured. All rights reserved. Used by permission.

able. We should ask what would happen if Harry should be so fortunate as to capture his elusive princess? What if she fell for him heart and soul, writing love letters every day and begging for his attention? What if she blasted Harry every time he looked longingly at a new, unattainable doll? I can tell you with great certainty that the bubble would soon burst. Harry would gladly give this complaining chick back to Jessie.

Harry will not always be so flighty in his sexual pursuits. Maturity should bring greater stability to his relationships with the opposite sex. But let me make this extremely important point, of relevance to us all: Adult romantic relationships continue to bear many of the characteristics of adolescent sexuality. We differ from the young only in degree, and will always reflect the rudiments of earlier sexual attitudes and values. Thus, grownups still love the thrill of the chase, the lure of the unattainable, the excitement of the new, and boredom with the old. Someone wrote, "Men love women in proportion to their strangeness to them." It is true. In committed love, of course, these immature impulses are controlled and minimized, but they exist nonetheless, especially in males. Furthermore, the desire for "breathing room" that was so typical during adolescence will be a lifelong characteristic, as will be the need to feel fortunate to have "captured" the one we married.

Adult romantic relationships continue to bear many of the characteristics of adolescent sexuality.

Conversely, in a marriage where the mystery and dignity have not been preserved in the relationship, or where one partner clings to the other in desperation, the couple is faced with a serious "balance of payments" deficit. All the emotional energy flows in one direction, which is certain to deplete reserves and resources. This is precisely what happens when an insecure spouse begins to smother the other. Even if infidelity and abandonment are never threatened, the pleading by one partner for the affection and attention of the other serves to short-circuit the electrical attraction between them. Once the process begins that says, "I own you!" the game is over. The home team loses.

Once the process begins that says, "I own you!" the game is over.

Human freedom is a precious thing, and we react decisively against those who would restrict it or take it from us. Not even a lover can deprive us of that God-given freedom *unless we surrender it voluntarily*. In fact, not even God will attempt to take it. If you ever come to Him in a love relationship, I guarantee that it will be of your own choice and through no coercion on His part. Not only *must love be tough*, it must be *free*, as well!

Country singer Tom T. Hall wrote a song in which he revealed surprising insight into this aspect of male-female relationships. He said, "If you hold love too loosely then it flies away; if you hold love too tightly, it'll die. It's one of the mysteries of life."* Hall's observation is accurate. If the commitment between a man and a woman is given insufficient importance in their lives, it will wither like a plant without water. The whole world knows that much. But fewer lovers seem to realize that extreme dependency can be just as deadly to a family. It has been said that the person who needs the other *least* will always be in control of the relationship. I believe that to be true.

Not only must love be tough—*it must be* free, *as well!*

Returning now to the letters from Linda and Faye, we can begin to

*"It's One Of The Mysteries Of Life." Written by Tom T. Hall. Published by Hallnote Music. Copyright 1977. All rights reserved. Used by permission

see what probably went wrong during their season of panic. Please understand that I'm not laying the blame for their husbands' departures on these women whose only crime was loving their men. But it is likely that they each played an unwitting part in the conflict, first by denying sufficient space to their self-centered husbands, and finally by choking their necks when they tried to leave. There *must* be a more effective way to draw cool lovers to the warmth of the hearth.

CHAPTER FIVE

Opening the Cage Door

WHEN MARRIED PERSONS FIND THEMSELVES HURTLING relentlessly toward a divorce, they sometimes turn to marriage counselors, ministers, psychologists and psychiatrists to stem the tide. The counsel they are subsequently given often involves changes in the way the two partners relate to one another from day to day. It may be proposed that they reserve an evening each week as "date night," or that they alter their sex habits or workaholic lifestyles. Such advice can be helpful in reestablishing communication and understanding between two wounded and disappointed people, but it may be inadequate to save a dying marriage. Why? Because the counsel is directed at *surface* issues.

> *Perceived worth is incorporated in the word* respect.

In most troubled marriages, a basic problem lies ominously below these relatively minor irritants. It involves the way one party has begun to perceive the other, as we have described. When expressed in materialistic terms, it is the value ascribed to one human being by another. That perceived worth is incorporated in the word *respect* and it is absolutely basic to all human relationships.

The way we behave from day to day is largely a function of how we respect or disrespect the people around us. The way employees perform is a product of how they respect the boss. The way children behave is an outgrowth of their respect for their parents. The way nations coexist is directly attributable to their respect for one another. And certainly, the way husbands and wives relate is a function of their mutual respect and admiration. That's why marital discord *almost always* emanates from seething disrespect somewhere in the relationship! That is the *bottom line* of romantic confrontation.

Marital discord almost always *emanates from seething disrespect.*

What I've been trying to describe are those gradual changes in perception—that subtle deterioration in attitude that precedes marital conflict. A starry-eyed young man and woman agree to wed because they hold one another in awe in deepest respect. And if they choose to remain for a lifetime, it will be because that positive attitude has been maintained, or in its absence, from the sheer power of commitment. Either way, the quality of their relationship will be a direct product of their mutual respect through the years.

Perhaps it is now apparent where the present line of reasoning is leading us. If there is hope for the dying marriages we have examined, and I certainly believe there is, then it is likely to be found in the reconstruction of *respect* between warring husbands and wives. Can there be any doubt that Linda's husband thoroughly disrespects his wife? Of all forms of disdain that one individual can show for another, there is none more profound than blatant infidelity. That is the *pits* in human affairs. And though Faye and Nancy are not yet victims of unfaithful-

If there is hope for the dying marriages, then it is likely to be found in the reconstruction of respect.

ness, they share the same basic problem. Their husbands feel trapped in suffocating relationships with women they clearly disrespect.

We return now to the question with which we began: What can be done to preserve these three marriages and the millions of others they represent? *The answer requires the vulnerable spouse to open the cage door and let the trapped partner out!* All the techniques of containment must end immediately, including manipulative grief, anger, guilt, and appeasement. Begging, pleading, crying, hand-wringing and playing the role of the doormat are equally destructive. There may be a time and place for strong feelings to be expressed, and there may be an occasion for quiet tolerance. But these responses must not be used as persuasive devices to hold the drifting partner against his or her will.

The answer requires the vulnerable spouse to open the cage door and let the trapped partner out!

To the reader who is desperately in need of this advice, please pay close attention at this point: I'm sure you would not have dreamed of using these coercive methods to convince your husband or wife to marry you during your dating days. You had to lure, attract, charm, encourage him or her. This subtle game of courtship had to take place one delicate step at a time. Can you imagine what would have occurred if you had wept violently and hung on the neck of your lover saying, "I think I'll die if you don't marry me! My entire life amounts to nothing without you. Please, please! Oh, please don't turn me down," etc.

This subtle game of courtship had to take place one delicate step at a time.

That approach to a potential marriage partner is about as disastrous as it would be for a used car salesman. What do you think he would accomplish by telling a potential customer through his tears, "Oh, please buy this car! I need the money so badly, and I've only had two sales so far today. If you turn me down, I think I'll go straight out and kill myself!"

This is a ridiculous analogy, of course, but there is linkage in it. When one has fallen in love with an eligible partner, he attempts to "sell himself" to the other. But like the car dealer, he must not deprive the buyer of free choice in the matter. Instead, he must convince the customer that the purchase is in his own interest. If a person would not buy an automobile to ease the pain of a salesman, how much more unlikely he is to devote his *entire being* to someone he doesn't love, simply for benevolent reasons. None of us is that unselfish. We are permitted by God to select only one person in the course of a lifetime with whom to invest everything we possess, and few of us are willing to squander that one shot on someone we merely pity! In fact, it is very difficult to love another person romantically and pity him or her at the same time.

It is very difficult to love another person romantically and pity him or her at the same time.

Let's apply this concept to married life. If begging and pleading are ineffective methods of attracting a member of the opposite sex during the dating days, why do victims of bad marriages use the same groveling techniques to hold a drifting spouse? They are only increasing the depth of disrespect by the one who is escaping. Instead, they should convey their own version of the following message when the right time affords itself:

> John, I've been through some very tough moments since you decided to leave, you know. My love for you is so profound that I just couldn't face the possibility of life without you. To a person like me

> who expected to marry only once and to remain committed for life, it is a severe shock to see our relationship begin to unravel. Nevertheless, I have done some intense soul searching, and I now realize that I have been attempting to hold you against your will. That simply can't be done. As I reflect on our courtship and early years together, I'm reminded that you married me of your own free choice. I did not blackmail you or twist your arm or offer you a bribe. It was a decision you made without pressure from me. Now you say you want out of the marriage and, obviously, I have to let you go. I'm aware that I can no more force you to stay today than I could have made you marry me in 1972 [or whenever]. You are free to go. If you never call me again, then I will accept your decision. I admit that this entire experience has been painful, but I'm going to make it. The Lord has been with me thus far, and He'll go with me in the future. You and I had some wonderful times together, John. You were my first real love, and I'll never forget the memories that we shared. I will pray for you and trust that God will guide you in the years ahead.

Slowly, unbelievably, the trapped spouse witnesses the cage door vibrate just a bit, and then start to rise. He can't believe it. This person to whom he has felt bound hand and foot for years has now set him free! It isn't necessary to fight off her advances—her grasping hands—anymore.

"But there must be a catch," he thinks. "It's too good to be true. Talk is cheap. This is just another trick to win me back. In a week or two she'll be crying on the phone again, begging me to come home. She's really weak, you know, and she'll crack under pressure."

It is my *strongest* recommendation that you, the rejected person, prove your partner wrong in this expectation. Let him marvel at your self-control in coming weeks. Only the passage of time will convince

Prove your partner wrong.

him that you are serious—that he *is* actually free. He may even test you during this period by expressions of great hostility or insult, or by flirtation with others. But one thing is certain: he will be watching for signs of weakness or strength. The vestiges of respect hang in the balance.

Every situation is unique.

If the more vulnerable spouse passes the initial test and convinces the partner that his freedom is secure, some interesting changes begin to occur in their relationship. Please understand that every situation is unique, and I am merely describing typical reactions, but these developments are extremely common in families I have seen. Most of the exceptions represent variations on the same theme. Three distinct consequences can be anticipated when a previously "grabby" lover begins to let go of the cool spouse:

1. The trapped partner no longer feels it necessary to fight off the other, and their relationship improves. It is not that the love affair is rekindled, necessarily, but the strain between the two partners is often eased.
2. As the cool spouse begins to feel free again, the question he has been asking himself changes. After having wondered for weeks or months, "How can I get out of this mess?" He now asks, "Do I really want to go?" Just knowing that he can have his way often makes him less anxious to achieve it. Sometimes it turns him around 180 degrees and brings him back home!

Let me illustate the effect of this second consequence in another way. Have you ever had something strike you funny at a formal banquet or church service or funeral, where it would have been humiliating to laugh out loud? Just the fact that you *couldn't* snicker made you jerk and snort to hold in the bellylaugh. This happened to me in a college chapel service many years ago. I was in a mischievous mood, and I put a small ball of aluminum foil on my knee. I intended to fire it twenty rows or more toward the front. Instead, I flipped it straight into the ear of a shy student sitting directly in front of me. He rose about six inches from his seat, and then settled down without ever looking back. His ear immediately began to glow and pulsate to the rhythm of his heart, which struck me funny. In fact, my roommate and I became hysterical, despite the seriousness of the service. He leaned to his left and covered his mouth, and I tilted to the right. We crowded extraneous thoughts through our heads in a desperate attempt to gain control. But just when we thought the crisis had passed, we would notice again the red spot spreading down the lad's neck in the direction of his shoulder. By this time one half of his head was crimson and the other white. That's all it took for the snorting and snuffing to begin again. It was awful. People all around us were disgusted with our irreverence, and who knows what the guy with the throbbing ear was thinking. But I'll tell you honestly, it was impossible to stop laughing.

My roommate and I became hysterical.

Finally, the speaker finished his heavy message, and the benediction was said. Everyone stood and the victim took his ear and walked out without making a comment. The pressure was over, and it was acceptable to laugh at last. But suddenly, there was nothing funny. The very fact that we could guffaw if we wished to removed the need even to smile. This is the way we humans

The very fact that we could guffaw if we wished to removed the need even to smile.

are constructed. And that's the way claustrophobic lovers feel when they are suddenly released. They often lose their need to escape.

3. The third change occurs not in the mind of the cool spouse but in the mind of the vulnerable one. Incredibly, he feels better—somehow more in control of the situation. There is no greater agony than journeying through a vale of tears, waiting in vain for the phone to ring or for a miracle to occur. Instead, the person has begun to respect himself and receive small evidences of respect in return. Even though it is difficult to let go once and for all, there are ample rewards for doing so. One of those advantages involves the feeling that he has a plan—a program—a definite course of action to follow. That is infinitely more comfortable than experiencing the utter despair of powerlessness that he felt before. And little by little, the healing process begins.

By this point in our discussion, some of my readers are undoubtedly beginning to ask a question that means more to me than any other aspect of the work we are doing: Is the advice offered herein consistent with Scripture? It is certainly different from what many Christian leaders would recommend.

Is the advice offered herein consistent with Scripture?

If I felt that my recommendations contradicted biblical teachings I would never utter them again. God's Word is the standard for all human behavior and values. And in this context, there are specific passages that support the psychological conclusions I have drawn. The most relevant is found in 1 Corinthians 7:12–15, NIV. Note especially the portion I have italicized.

> If any brother has a wife who is not a believer and she is willing to live with him, he must not divorce her. And if a woman has a husband who is not a believer and he is willing to live with her, she must not divorce him. For the unbelieving husband has been sanctified through his wife, and the unbelieving wife has been sanctified through her believing husband. Otherwise your children would be unclean, but as it is, they are holy. *But if the unbeliever leaves, let him do so. A believing man or woman is not bound in such circumstances; God has called us to live in peace.*

Those seem like very straightforward instructions to me. The Apostle Paul was talking to men and women who were married to unbelievers—some of whom who were undoubtedly involved in bad marriages. He was telling them unequivocally that divorce was not an option. Period. They were instructed to remain faithful and try to win their un-Christian spouses to the Lord. Good counsel! But Paul was also sensitive to those who had no choice in the matter. Like Linda and Faye, they were unable to hold their partners at home. In those instances they were advised to let the partners go. There is no blame in accepting a fate beyond their control. And just as I have indicated, this acceptance of the inevitable will result in "peace." Here we see the marvelous wisdom of the Creator as expressed through His servant in interpersonal and psychological dimensions.

Paul was also sensitive to those who had no choice in the matter.

CHAPTER SIX

The Tougher Questions

WE HAVE DEALT WITH THE MATTER OF LETTING GO OF a disenchanted lover. But in real-life situations, marital problems often involve complications and entanglements that make our task more difficult. Let's return, for example, to those men and women who know their spouses are being unfaithful. What should be the attitude of Linda and the other hurting people whose partners are fooling around? Whereas their infidelity would likely have been hidden a century ago, today it may be blatantly admitted and defended by the guilty. A recent popular song illustrates this justification of evil.

What should be the attitude of hurting people whose partners are fooling around?

*Torn Between Two Lovers**

There are times when a woman has to say what's on her mind,
Even though she knows how much it's gonna hurt.
Before I say another word, let me tell you, I love you.
Let me hold you close and say these words as gently as I can.

*© 1976 Muscle Shoals Sound Publishing Co., Inc. and Silver Dawn Music, Inc. Written by Phillip Jarrell and Peter Yarrow.

There's been another man that I've needed and I've loved.
But that doesn't mean I love you less. [*Oh, really?*]*
And he knows he can't possess me and he knows he never will.
There's just this empty place inside of me that only he can fill.
Torn between two lovers, feelin' like a fool.
Lovin' both of you is breaking all the rules.

You mustn't think you failed me just because there's someone else.
You were the first real love I ever had and all the things I ever said,
I swear they still are true. [*How about the marriage vows?*]**
For no one else can have the part of me I gave to you.
Couldn't really blame you if you turned and walked away.
But with everything I feel inside, I'm askin' you to stay.
Torn between two lovers, feelin' like a fool.
Lovin' both of you is breaking all the rules.

Isn't that sweet? This little darlin' is sleeping with two men and one of them is not her husband. That's bad enough. Then she has the utter audacity to tell the man she married that her affair will be continuing. He has two choices in the matter: live with it or shove off. He wasn't even asked for his opinion. She was determined to have her cake and ice cream too, or if her husband preferred, she'd settle for ice cream—with the other lover.

There is no shortage of husbands and wives who are torn between two (or more) lovers.

How about it, now? What would your answer be to this proposition? The question is highly relevant to our discussion. Linda's husband has confronted her with the same dilemma. She wrote, "He is confused and doesn't know which one of us he wants. He doesn't want to lose me and says he still loves me and our three kids, but he can't give her up either."

*Author's comment.
**Author's comment.

There is no shortage of husbands and wives who are torn between two (or more) lovers. I could fill the balance of this book with letters and living illustrations of men and women like Linda whose mates are openly engaged in sexual escapades. They, like the writer of the following letter, ask the same question: "What do I do now?"

Dear Dr. Dobson:

I heard your radio program today when you urged frustrated people not to get a divorce. It seemed like you were talking directly to me. But if I'm not going to get a divorce, then what can I do? Every day is worse than the one before and my husband and I are farther apart. I am more depressed than I've ever been.

My husband and I are thirty-four years old and we have four children. Chuck no longer cares about the things he used to love. He used to sing in the choir in church and work on a camper he was building for the family. Now he seems to be looking for a whole new way of life, spending his time dancing in bars and discos. He is involved with other women, spending money we can't afford, but nothing satisfies him for long. Tell me, what would you do if you were me?

My husband says I'm too old-fashioned, too moral. But I'm trying to live a Christian life. He says he would rather die than be a Christian. He makes me feel so dirty!

How do I continue this? I ask you. How?

A friend in Christ,
Mabel

Let's turn to the Christian literature to find answers to Mabel's question. Listed below are five suggestions which were paraphrased from *actual* books offering counsel to female victims of infidelity. This passive approach has been the "party line" for several decades, not only in books but also in the advice offered by Christian counselors, pastors, relatives, and friends. Let me ask you to put yourself in Mabel's situation as you read these recommendations.

1. After you learn of your husband's infidelity, go to him and tell him again how much you love him. Tell him you don't intend to let him go, and indeed, that you plan to fight for him. Your persistence will tell him that *there might be a chance that you will shape up*.
2. Tell your husband that you understand what he's done, and indicate that you realize you have given him some reason to fool around. Do not label his behavior sinful or immoral.
3. Ask God to reveal your specific failures that have led to your husband's unfaithfulness. When the answer comes, take this list of shortcomings to your husband and review it with him. Tell him specifically how you think you may have contributed to his need to find another lover and ask for his forgiveness.
4. Don't expect quick improvement in your relationship with your husband. Your marriage has taken years to get into the mess it's in, and it may take as long to recover. In the meantime, don't ask your husband to stop seeing the other lover.
5. Continue treating your husband as the man of the house. Remind him he is still your husband and the father of your children. If he is not living at home, encourage him to eat his meals with you and the children any time he wants to. Let him know you are ready to meet his sexual needs whenever he comes over.

Certainly, what is recommended here seems like the loving, nonjudgmental thing to do, and in fact, I agree that these suggestions will be entirely appropriate *after* a reconciliation has occurred. There will be a time for total forgiveness, no mention of the past, admission of personal flaws and shared responsibility for the problems that developed. Love demands nothing less. Furthermore, we must acknowledge that there *are* occasions when "unconditional acceptance," as described above, can be successful in winning back a wayward spouse. I have seen women who permitted their husbands to abuse them, betray them, deprive them and insult them, yet who returned such love and kindness that the marriage was saved. It *does* occur. The personality and temperament of the abusing partner is the critical factor here, of course.

A passive approach often leads to the dissolution of the relationship.

Nevertheless, I must report the facts as I see them. *A passive approach often leads to the dissolution of the relationship.* It is especially destructive in marriages where the unfaithful partner is desperate to escape from the wife he thoroughly disrespects, yet who won't let him go and instead announces her intention of fighting for him (see item 1 above) no matter what he does to gain his freedom.

Let me make one more attempt to explain why appeasement, even in the name of Christianity, can prove fatal to a marriage. Just as toddlers and teenagers will challenge the authority of their parents precisely for the purpose of testing their confidence and courage, a husband or wife will sometimes do the same. They, like children, want to feel the security of loving discipline which says, "Go this far and no farther." There is safety in defined limits for human beings of all ages.

There is safety in defined limits.

In other books I have described what happens when a parent collapses in response to consistent challenges from a child. Respect is lost when the question is asked, "How tough are you?" and the answer comes back, "I'm made of Jell-O!" Not only does the child begin to feel that the parent is unworthy of his respect, but he senses a lack of love in the relationship, too. Genuine love *demands* toughness in moments of crisis. It's true for grownups, too.

As indicated above, adults will occasionally challenge one another for the same reasons they challenged their parents as children. Unconsciously, perhaps, they are asking the question, "How much courage do you have, and do you love me enough to stop me from doing this foolish thing?" What they need in that moment is loving discipline that forces them to choose between good and bad alternatives. What they don't need, contrary to the suggestions offered above, is permissiveness, understanding, excuses, removal of guilt and buckets of tender loving care. To dole out that kind of smother-love at such a time is to reinforce irresponsibility and generate disrespect. It deprives the marriage of *mutual accountability*!

What they need in that moment is loving discipline.

Let's look at a couple of specific examples. Suppose a teenager comes home, stoned on amphetamines. He sits in his room for days at a time, popping pills while he deteriorates physically and emotionally. So what should his parents do? Does the adolescent need understanding and rationalization and never a word about his problem? Should his parents tell him how they've caused his addiction by their many failures? Is it best that they prop up his life and purchase his narcotics for him? Certainly not. *Love must be tough!* If they cannot reason with him and encourage him to get help, they should force the issue to a crisis that will save him from himself. By whatever method, including painful confrontation, they must break the cycle

Love must be tough!

of behavior that is destroying their son and get him to seek professional help.

How about the example of a wife whose husband is an alcoholic? Should she "cover" for his drunken condition, lying to his boss and concealing the problem from the neighbors? No, that is the *worst* course of action for a victim of alcoholism. The best approach is to force a crisis that will bring the matter to a head. Then it can be treated and resolved. (We will discuss this matter in greater detail in subsequent chapters.)

Perhaps my point has been made. Infidelity is an addiction that can destroy a life as quickly as drugs or alcohol. Once a man or woman is hooked on the thrills of sexual conquest, he or she becomes intoxicated with its lust for pleasure. This person needs every available reason to go straight—to clean up his life. He certainly does not need a spouse who says dreamily, "I understand why you need the other woman, David. My goodness! I am so riddled with flaws that it's no wonder you went looking for someone else. You should see the list of my own stupidities that I'm keeping. Let me propose a course of action: You just go on with your other friendships for a few years while I work on myself, and maybe you'll eventually feel like being a husband again. Spend our money foolishly if you wish, and I'll get along somehow. Maybe I can take in ironing or do some babysitting. In the meantime, drop over and I'll meet your needs anytime you wish. Bring your dirty clothes and a big appetite, too. The kids and I will try to keep the conversation from getting too heavy for you because we sure wouldn't want you to get the notion that you're doing something wrong. And David, why don't you bring your ladyfriend with you the next time you come. I'll bet she's a sweetheart."

Infidelity is an addiction that can destroy a life as quickly as drugs or alcohol.

That approach is like buying booze for the drunk and drugs for the junkie. It is *weak* love! It is disastrous!

I hope I've made the case for the use of loving toughness in response to blatant rebellion and sin. But the question remains, *how* is that discipline implemented? Does the offended party scream and cry and throw things? Does he or she run to the nearest telephone to call the attorney? Is it time to play dirty, spreading gossip that will embarrass and hurt the rascal? No! No! No! Those approaches may be tough, but they aren't loving!

I'll offer an alternative in the next chapter.

CHAPTER SEVEN

The Valley of the Shadow

ANYONE WHO HAS TRIED TO DIET OR STOP SMOKING OR maintain an exercise program for more than two weeks knows just how difficult it is to eliminate well-entrenched patterns of behavior. We can fight our persistent old habits tooth and nail, but they're always lurking out there somewhere, threatening to return and subject us again to their servitude. Many of these behavioral characteristics were cut during childhood in channels that run deep and wide. To change our ways of responding now, as adults, requires us to dam up the river, dig new basins and reroute the flow. It may be the most difficult thing a person is ever asked to do.

That is what the adulterer or the alcoholic or the child abuser is facing. When approached rationally, he will tell us that he dislikes what he has become and wishes he could change. But the old patterns persist, leading him to do tomorrow what he did yesterday. His promises and his declarations are not worth the gunpowder required to blow them up.

How, then, can we help turn him around? What can Linda do to make her husband abandon his female toys? She has tried nagging and begging and being sweet and being angry, but nothing has worked. What now?

Well, if Linda were sitting in my office, I would first suggest that we make her marital problems a matter of concerted prayer.

Any personal crisis should begin at that point, especially when it involves something so important as the stability of a family. Let me make it clear that the advice offered in this book or any other (except the Bible) is mere human wisdom, and is woefully inadequate without the direct leadership of the Holy Spirit. In almost every troubled marriage, there is a spiritual dimension that cannot be brushed aside by the application of psychological principles alone, regardless of how brilliant they sound.

I would first suggest that we make her marital problems a matter of concerted prayer.

Furthermore, in talking to hundreds of Christians who have seen their families torn apart, I have heard one comment with overwhelming consistency: "I would never have made it without the Lord!" They have then told me how the presence of Jesus Christ was never more real and compassionate than during the worst of the storm, when the winds of tragedy howled around them. It is my privilege, therefore, to direct Linda and all the multitudes who suffer into this harbor of God's infinite love. I have seen Him turn disaster into triumph, healing wounds and repairing hopelessly shattered relationships.

In almost every troubled marriage, there is a spiritual dimension that cannot be brushed aside.

But it is also true that God often uses pain and crisis to bring a sinful person to his senses. There is something about great stress that takes us back in the direction of responsibility. Remember that the rebellious prodigal son decided to go home to daddy only when his money ran out and he was eating with the pigs. A daily serving of slop does tend to make one hunger for the fatted calf. In the context of the present discussion, there is a place for a deliberately conceived confrontation in a troubled marriage that may take it literally to the door of death.

For purposes of illustration, let me return to Linda's situation. At the appropriate moment and armed with the prayer I have described, I would urge her to precipitate a crisis of major proportions. She must give Paul a reason for wanting to reroute his river. He is unlikely to make the investment of energy and self-control to accomplish that task until he absolutely must. It is only when he becomes miserable that he will accept the responsibility for change. It is only when he sees everything of value to him—his home, his children, his wife, his reputation—begin to slip away that his choices will become clear. It is only when the well runs dry that Paul will begin to miss the water.

There is a place for a deliberately conceived confrontation in a troubled marriage.

You see, Linda's husband needs her to be tough—but loving—at this moment, perhaps more than any other time in his life. He is wavering between responsibility and irresponsibility, admitting that he's confused as to which path he should pursue. He needs a strong excuse to do the right thing, and he almost seems to be asking Linda to give him that motivation. As long as he is permitted to be "torn between two lovers," he can postpone a commitment and play one "wife" against the other. That shatters everyone involved.

Linda's husband needs her to be tough—but loving.

Unfortunately, Linda is overdue in providing the motivation that Paul needs. It should have come like a clap of thunder the first time he fooled around. I stated earlier that it is not too late for her marriage to be saved, but I can't be certain of that fact. Linda's power to draw Paul back has been depleted by the missed opportunities she has squandered. Let me explain why. Whenever sexual indiscretion is occurring, a marital relationship necessarily deteriorates with the passage of time. It is inevitable! Therefore, the influence that a husband or wife holds with which to pull the partner back from the brink is rapidly seeping away. That's why in instances of infidelity, it is necessary to fire your biggest guns as early in the affair as possible.

The chances of saving a marriage will never again be as great as they are after the first indiscretion.

What I'm saying is that an early blowout is better than a slow leak! The chances of saving a marriage will never again be as great as they are after the first indiscretion. Remember that Linda's husband *gradually* fell in love with the other woman. That slowly developing love would not have been possible if Linda had said to him on the occasion of his third trip to the divorcee's house: "Paul, you are putting a severe strain on our marriage and I strongly suggest that you hear what I'm saying. If you persist in visiting this girl, you will come home and find me and the kids gone." If he paid no heed, she should deliver on the promise.

I can hear someone saying, "I thought you didn't recommend divorce." I don't, and I'm not. The choice will rest with the unfaithful partner. But it must be clear to him that he cannot have it both ways. It simply won't work. And, in fact, the best thing that can happen to a tomcat who prowls around at night is to come home after his first escapade to face reality. Right then, in the aftermath of his foolishness, he needs to feel the full impact of his sin. He should sit in an empty bedroom thinking, "What have I done? What in the world have I gone and done? I have violated the trust of this beautiful woman who has borne my children, devoted herself to my happiness, cared for me when I was ill, and loved me more than I ever deserved. And, in return, what does she get but a selfish cad who would sneak around behind her back and sleep with someone else? Will she ever forgive me? Will my children forgive me? Will *God* forgive me? Can I ever forgive myself?"

It would be naïve, of course, to assume that this contrite repentance is so easily achieved. It may be months before an affair is discovered, and even when loving toughness is applied, the confrontation between husband and wife is rarely a simple encounter. Games of bluff are played, skirmishes are fought, battles are won and lost. It can be a bloody engagement, even within the context of love. That is why I recommend that the victim—the one who is trying desperately to hold things together—never head for such a crisis without the guidance of a Christian professional who can help steer the course. Whenever I am assisting a vulnerable man or woman through these turbulent waters, I make myself available by phone both night and day to encourage them and help manage the conflict. I also request the prayerful support of every believer who knows and loves the family that is under fire.

Never head for such a crisis without the guidance of a Christian professional.

Even in these difficult relationships where the fury of hell itself is unleashed on the more responsible partner, there are rewards for hanging tough. Remember that the basic marital problem usually involves matters of respect, which are often generated during instances of confrontation. I can't explain why this is true of human nature, but I know that it is. I learned that lesson when I was in high school.

There are rewards for hanging tough.

I had just moved to a small Texas city in my junior year of high school and attended a football game the first Friday night. Since I knew no one, I sat among unfamiliar students in the stadium. I must have looked like an easy mark to an eleventh-grader named Ellis, who sat behind me and repeatedly hit me on the head with his rolled-up program. After two or three verbal exchanges between us, I turned around and jumped on his belly. I pounded him on the head and shoulders while he flailed at my body. It was a typical high school free-for-all with very little damage done to either of us. But believe it or not, that was the prelude to a deep and lasting friendship between Ellis and me. It was based on mutual respect. I overheard him telling another student in the hall later that year, "I wouldn't mess with Dobson. He doesn't look like a fighter, but he's tough as nails." My other bosom buddy from the same era was a 180-pound senior named Harlan with whom I slugged it out one Saturday morning. That fight ended in a bloody draw, but again, it precipitated genuine admiration between Harlan and me.

Applying this concept to romantic affairs now, the same characteristic is often evident. How frequently it happens that a dating couple will become engaged or will rush toward marriage shortly after recovering from the worst fight in their history together. I am not recommending that Linda, Faye, Nancy, Mabe,l and the others try to blow their husbands over with anger or hit them with frying pans. I am saying that by having the courage to stand up for themselves, they may regenerate a portion of the respect they have lost.

By making it clear that there are limits to what you can tolerate, you are showing self-respect and confidence.

Finally, let's return to the problem of the "trapped" syndrome. The person who is feeling smothered can find *instant* relief if you, his partner, will implement the advice I have given. By making it clear that there are limits to what you can tolerate, you are showing self-respect and confidence. Strangely, that often draws the partner toward you.

Some especially immature people absolutely have to feel there is a challenge in the relationship to be satisfied with it. Such individuals might even need to hear the door starting to close on the marriage before wanting to hustle back inside.

"Ridiculous!" you say. Of course it is. We only have one life to live so why spend it testing our loved ones and measuring the limits of their endurance? I don't know. But that's the way we are made. Why else will a toddler or a five year old or a teenager deliberately disobey his parents for no other reason than to determine how far Mom and Dad can be pushed? That same urge to test the limits causes students to harass teachers, employees to challenge bosses, privates to disobey sergeants, and so on. And regrettably, it leads some husbands and wives to test the ones they love, too. What is required in each instance is *discipline* and *self-respect* by the one on trial.

What is required in each instance is discipline *and* self-respect *by the one on trial.*

Now that I've presented the rationale for a period of confrontation in response to infidelity or other instances of blatant disrespect, I must hasten to explain what I mean by a crisis. I mentioned the possibility that Linda might separate from Paul to emphasize the seriousness of their situation. That is one way to heat things up, certainly, but moving out is not a step to take lightly. It may be the only method of getting a person's attention, but that is a decision requiring great individual wisdom and caution and prayer. The crisis of which I speak may or may not involve separation, but definitely encompasses much more.

The precipitated crisis, first, must be accompanied by an entire change of attitude. Instead of begging, pleading, wringing your hands and whimpering like an abused puppy, you as the vulnerable partner must appear strangely calm and assured. The key word is *confidence*, and it is of maximum importance. Your manner should say, "I believe in me. I'm no longer afraid. I can cope, regardless of the outcome. I know something I'm not talking about. I've had my day of sorrow, and I'm through crying. God and I can handle whatever life puts in the path."

The key word is confidence.

Not that you should say these things with words, of course.

In fact, the less said about your frame of mind, the better. It's your private business. One of the great errors made by the vulnerable lover when things begin to deteriorate is to talk too much. His secure partner is noncommunicative, evasive, deceptive, and mysterious. He will not sit down and explain his inner feelings to the one who desperately needs that information. Remember the words of Nancy in her letter: "I long to get inside [my husband's] head and find out how he feels, but he simply won't talk about personal things." That is typical.

I'm recommending that you, the one who has sought to hold the marriage together, now choose your words more carefully, too. It is as though you and your mate have been involved in a table game with him hiding his cards and you permitting yours to be seen. This has given the independent partner more information than he should have had, especially about the pain you are experiencing. It is time to be more discreet. No more should you reveal your every thought and plan. *Under no circumstances should this book be shared or discussed*. And certainly, never make such statements as, "I cried all night last night, Mindy. Oh, can't you see how much I need you!" *Crunch* goes the sound of the cage door coming back down. *Crack* goes the sound of respect starting to splinter again. *Slam* goes the sound of the door on Mindy's way out.

Under no circumstances should this book be shared or discussed.

It is also important during this time of crisis not to do the predictable things. Having lived with you for years, your partner has you analyzed to a tee. He knows what bugs you, what makes you laugh, and what makes you cry. He has memorized all your little "prerecorded" phrases that sprinkle your conversation. My advice is that you change these tapes. Don't offer him suggestions when you would typically do so. Don't make those inane remarks he's heard for twenty years. Don't be so predictable! Your purpose, you see, is to convince this man or woman that events are swirling out of control and may take him in directions he has not anticipated. The old rules don't apply. And why is this new mystery advantageous? Because one of the reasons your lover has lost interest in the relationship is that the "challenge" is gone. It's become so monotonous and routine. Hence, you would be wise to turn the whole thing upside down.

Don't be so predictable!

And by all means, unless there is business to be conducted, don't telephone a spouse who has separated. But if a call is necessary, state your reason for phoning after a few words of small talk and then get on with the matter at hand. When your business is finished, politely terminate the call and hang up. Do not, I repeat, do not get dragged into the usual verbal brawls. You don't want to appear to be an uptight crybaby merely covered by a thin veneer of poise. If you explode as you did in the past, it will be evident that you are, as he suspected, the weak old pushover he has come to disrespect. There may be a moment for anger if he insults you, but in that case keep your response crisp, controlled, and confident.

Curiosity infects the aloof party, and he begins to probe for details.

An interesting thing happens when this kind of quiet confidence suddenly replaces the tears and self-pity of earlier days. Curiosity infects the aloof party, and he begins to probe for details. For the first time in months, perhaps, he's coming your way. He's saying, "You seem different tonight," and, "I hope you're beginning to get over our problems." He's baiting you to find Out what's going on inside. It is uncomfortable for him to observe that changes are occurring which he neither controls nor understands. Tell him nothing. He *needs* to wonder.

Tell him nothing. He needs to wonder

Throughout these changes, you must be careful not to behave in unloving ways. Remember that with God's help, you are attempting to build new bridges to this disrespectful, trapped partner. Don't burn them before they reach the other shore. Don't call him names, except to label his harmful behavior for what it is. Don't try to hurt him with gossip or even embarrassing truth. Don't telephone his family and try to undermine his position with them. Don't inflame hatred in the children of your union. And don't forget that your purpose is to be tough, yes, but loving as well.

Though it may be obvious, perhaps I should take just a moment to explain why these changes in manner and response are so necessary. Some may think I'm recommending silly little cat-and-mouse games to people who are engaged in life-and-death struggles. Isn't it a bit childish, they may say, to pretend to be confident when you're dying inside? Not so. These are the conclusions I've drawn from a lifetime of counseling experience.

We must assume that a tug of war is going on inside.

The partner who is threatening to leave or chase another lover is rarely convinced beyond a shadow of a doubt that he's doing the right thing.

He's equipped with a God-given conscience, after all, that is hammering him with guilt. You can be quite certain of that. He may appear resolute and determined, but we must assume that a tug of war is going on inside. He feels terrible about hurting his kids, for one thing. Furthermore, a spark of love may exist for you as the woman of his youth, glowing somewhere beneath his cold exterior. While his manner is saying, "I don't care anymore," he may be engaged in these kinds of secret conversations in his mind: "Have I hurt the best friend I ever had? Maybe I should call off this whole affair. But I sure don't want my relationship with Sue to go back to what it used to be. I *do* think I could love her again." Round and round go the pros and cons.

We can assume that some degree of self-doubt exists in a majority of husbands and wives who are threatening to leave. It certainly appears to be characteristic of Linda's husband, Paul (see p. 15). He just can't decide which woman he wants. We know, therefore, that Linda is still in the running, and that's good news. But how can she protect and encourage the tiny spark that smolders in his heart? Clearly, she must not smother it! She should give it plenty of room to breathe, hoping it will grow into a small flame. That is accomplished by calling off the offensive. Instead of pressuring Paul to act a certain way and to come home, Linda needs to make him wonder if he could *get her back*. Freedom, you see, is the fuel of romantic fire!

Freedom, you see, is the fuel of romantic fire.

Now we come to the most important part of the crisis experience. I'm referring to a face-to-face encounter which must certainly occur soon. In fact, there will be several critical exchanges when you will be called upon to state your case. Don't blunder into those conversations unprepared. Carefully organize your thoughts and rehearse what you plan to convey. Talk this over with your counselor-advisor, seeking his perspectives on the issues. The central theme of the encounter should not focus on what you hope your partner will do, but on your own conclusions. If I were Linda, for example, I would say something like this:

> It's a curious thing, Paul, how a person loses all perspective when he's so close to a problem. It becomes difficult to see the issues clearly, and that has definitely happened to me in recent months. But in the past few weeks I've been able to pull back from our difficulties, and I now see everything in an entirely new light. It is incredible just how foolish I have been since you decided to leave. I have tolerated your unfaithfulness for almost a year and was even so naïve as to permit Susan to come into our bedroom. I can't believe now that I did that. I guess I just loved you so much that I was willing to do anything you demanded, just to keep you from leaving me.
>
> But I'll tell you, Paul, those days are over! If you want to go, you can certainly do so. In fact, that may be for the best. I doubt if I can ever trust you again or feel for you as I once did. I wasn't a perfect wife, to be sure, but no other man has touched me since I pledged myself to you. But you violated my trust—not once but repeatedly for all these months. I'm no longer special to you—I'm just one of a crowd. I can't live with that. I'd rather face life alone than as a member of your harem. If Susan is the one you want, I hope the two of you will be happy together. I'm still not sure how something so wonderful became so dirty and distorted, but that is between you and the Lord. We both have to answer to Him in our own way, and my conscience is clear.
>
> So where do we go from here, Paul? I've been doing some intensive thinking, and believe you should pack up and leave. It just won't work for you to hopscotch between Susan and me, sleeping with us both and trying to make it all seem so normal. You say you aren't sure which one you want? Well, that isn't very inspiring to me. You pledged eternal love and commitment to me on our wedding day, but now that

> could be gone with the toss of a coin. What we both need is some time apart. I think you should find another place to stay, perhaps with Susan if you wish. If in the future you decide you want to be my husband, then we'll talk about it. I make no promises, however. I'm doing everything possible to remove you from my heart, to spare myself any more pain. It's not going to be easy. You were my only love—the only one I ever wanted. But that was then and this is now. God bless you, Paul. The kids and I will miss you.

Can there be any doubt that Paul would be shocked by this candid approach? For over a year, he's been trying to get this nagging woman off his back. She has called him on the phone and begged him to come over—and inevitably, ended each conversation in tears. He has done everything to escape from Linda's cage, including insulting her, making ridiculous sexual demands and threatening a divorce. But nothing has worked. He wonders, "How in the world can the ol' lady keep her self-respect? I treat her like a dog, and she just keeps coming back!" Linda is obviously desperate.

Then, without warning, her entire demeanor begins to change. The next time they are together, Linda seems more confident, more in control. She asks for nothing and even appears rather bored with the conversation. "What's going on?" Paul wonders. "Has she found another man? Is some dude moving in on my territory? Is he going to be sleeping in my bed and expecting my kids to call him dad? Hold on a minute! Am I about to lose something very important to me?"

A letter becomes a permanent document to be read and reread in the days ahead.

Two weeks later, Linda delivers the speech I suggested. She feels uncomfortable trying to say it face to face, so she sits down and expresses her thoughts in writing. (This is recommended since words can be chosen more carefully without counter arguments and interruptions; also, a letter becomes a permanent document to be read and reread in the days ahead.)

Paul finds the envelope in his mailbox that evening when he gets home from work. “Here we go again,” he sighs. “I’ll bet Linda is begging me not to see Susan anymore.” Instead, she has granted him freedom to leave and even urged him to do so. His cage door springs open, and his wife suddenly takes on an aura of self-respect and dignity. For a certain percentage of people like Linda and Paul, that is the beginning of the healing process.

CHAPTER EIGHT

Three Women Who Tried It

I WISH THAT IT MIGHT BE POSSIBLE FOR YOU, THE reader, to get behind my eyes and perceive our subject as I see it. If only you could know intimately the brokenhearted husbands and wives I have counseled who floundered on a policy of appeasement and panic, and then with God's help, discovered the principles of self-respect and romantic freedom. But more important, I wish I could convey the broader applicability of these concepts to those with healthy marriages, to dating teenagers and unmarried adults, to employers and parents and governments. *Respect*, the critical ingredient in human affairs, is generated by quiet dignity, self-confidence, and common courtesy. It is assassinated by hand wringing, groveling in the dirt, and pleas for mercy.

> Respect, *the critical ingredient in human affairs, is generated by quiet dignity, self-confidence, and common courtesy.*

Given the limitations of language in attempting to convey these concepts, it seems advantageous to let my friends tell their own stories. In this chapter are letters from three women who have been where Roger, Linda, Faye, and Nancy are today.* They wrote to me in response to a series of radio programs devoted to the topic of this book. I think you will find their experience to be inspirational and enlightening.

We'll begin with an anonymous letter from a very intelligent lady who knows the meaning of pain.

Dear Dr. Dobson:

After listening to your radio series, *Love Must Be Tough*, I would like to tell you my own story. It is difficult to discuss the facts, even today, because my husband was a prominent minister serving a large congregation before he fell into sin.

It all started when a man from our church appeared at my front door, asking if he could talk to me. He brought with him a letter which proved unmistakably that my husband was involved with another woman. I never dreamed that anything was going on, and my shock was overwhelming. The man told me the full details, and after leaving, proceeded to tell the rest of the world. He reproduced the documents and circulated them throughout our church and all over town.

Dr. Dobson, never in my life have I felt so all alone as when this affair became public knowledge. I was treated like a "leper" by members of our congregation. My husband was immediately forced to resign, requiring us to move out of the parsonage. Suddenly, we had no home, no job, no money, and *very* few friends. We had given our lives to helping other people, but no one was there when we were down. I can't describe the anger and scorn that was hurled at us. We were subjected to physical threats, harassment by mail and by phone, damage to our property, incredible gossip, and false accusations. It was an awful time of our lives.

Not only had I lost everything overnight, but my marriage was

---

*Roger's letter appears on pp. 1–2; Linda's, pp. 5; Faye's, pp. 15–16; and Nancy's, pp. 28.

about gone, too. Before moving, I went into my bedroom and fell on my face before God, asking Him to take over. He was the only one I could talk to. A person simply does not discuss such matters with those who don't understand. Finally, the Lord directed me to a wise counselor who sat and listened to my story. I told him of my great guilt for the role I played in our problems and how terrible I felt. I'll never forget his reply.

He told me not to take the blame for my husband's affair, and that nothing I had done could justify his infidelity. He advised me to stand up and be firm with him, even though it would be difficult. It was, he said, the only way to save our marriage. We agreed that divorce was not the answer, even though I had scriptural grounds to leave him. I decided to pay the price to confront my husband.

A few months later the crisis came. I gave Milan an ultimatum—either go with the other woman or stay with me. He could not have both of us any longer. I put my hands on his shoulders and looked him straight in the eye and said, "You know you are to blame for what has happened to us. You committed adultery, I didn't." I told him if he loved the other woman more than me, then he should leave. I would accept it. I reminded him that he had a soul and would someday answer to God.

Milan not only broke off the affair, but he later thanked me for having the courage to stick it out with him through this difficult time. It was not easy but we worked it out and our family survived.

Since then, God has blessed us tremendously. The Lord helped me forgive Milan, reminding me that He had also forgiven so many of my sins. We are now back in the ministry in Oregon, and my husband is more effective for God than he has ever been. Our three children have adjusted well. I shielded them from hate for the church or disrespect for their father. They love their dad so much.

Yes, Dr. Dobson, *Love must be tough!* Had I given up and taken the easy way out, our story would not have had such a happy ending.

It took hard work, struggle, and prayer, but the Lord put our home back together. At first I thought I would never be able to smile again, but He has removed the clouds and brought us sunshine once more.

I know it isn't proper not to sign one's name, but under the circumstances, I feel it is better to remain anonymous. I would love to meet you and Shirley, sometime.

Isn't that an inspirational letter? It should be obvious why I wanted to share it in this context. Unfortunately, adultery among the clergy is becoming increasingly common. Ministers are usually busy men in high-pressure positions that limit the amount of time they can spend with their families. When that strain at home is combined with the natural access ministers have to admiring women, the temptations for indiscretion are apparent. The same condition prevails in my profession, as well. One study revealed that 25 percent of female students in secular schools of psychology have slept with their major professors during their graduate training. What an incredible commentary that is on the moral state of the so-called "helping sciences"! Let's turn now to another letter that came in response to the same series of broadcasts. It is representative of hundreds that were received.

Dear Dr. Dobson:

I listened to your radio program last week and was so glad to hear you tell a person how to handle adultery by a spouse. I went through this during the past two years. My first counselor told me to be kind, loving, etc., and to win him back by my pleasantness. It didn't work. Things got worse until I couldn't stand it anymore.

That's when I went to another counselor and also sought the advice of my pastor. They both advised me to be strong, as you suggested. It was so different and seemed unscriptural, yet the Lord used them to teach me how to cope with the situation. Gradually, I felt better about myself, and my self-respect returned. Then the Lord brought my husband back. It has been almost a year now since we started over and things are going well.

I want to encourage you to keep up the advice that *love must be tough.* It is hard to let go—especially when you are so confused and hurt. But it was only when I did turn loose that the Lord worked more in my husband's life.

If you ever print that series of messages, send me a copy please.

In Christ,
Lonna

Admittedly, these letters sound like phony Cinderella stories designed to support my particular biases. However, they represent real letters on file from living, breathing people who exist somewhere out there in the American culture. (I have changed some of the details to conceal the identities of the writers and to eliminate irrelevant comments.) The majority of the responses I received to the *Love Must Be Tough* broadcasts were like the ones I have shared—strong testimonials for the advice I've offered. Not every marriage was saved, of course. I am certainly no magician and the application of toughness does not remove the free will of a wayward spouse. But even when divorce was reported by those who wrote, the advantages of quiet self-respect as opposed to unbridled panic were usually apparent

The advantages of quiet self-respect as opposed to unbridled panic were usually apparent.

Finally, let's look at a letter from a woman who saw *herself* in the examples I gave. Her husband is holding her by force, and she is disrespecting him in return. I found this response interesting from one who represents the other side of the coin.

Dear Friend,

I listened in amazement to your radio program, *Love Must Be Tough*, and saw my own marriage in your discussion. I have known it was troubled but didn't understand why. Now it is clear.

You see, I have had many of the disrespectful attitudes toward my husband that you described (did you read my mind?). I have been embarrassed by him in public because he is not a good conversationalist and because he seems so dumb (although he is not). I was actually ashamed to be with him!

On the other hand, you described my husband correctly, too. He has had a stranglehold of control over me, resenting any friendships or commitments I've had outside the home.

I can see now that we were responding to each other's attitudes without a word being spoken about either. I was feeling stifled and he was feeling rejected.

Although I have not sought an extramarital affair, I can see now that I have been a prime candidate for one. I don't want that for myself or my family! Mixed in with my feelings is the low self-esteem you talked about, too.

We have a Christian counseling center here in St. Louis which I have consulted in the past. A counselor there told me some of the same things you said on the radio, but I was not ready to hear them. Now I am. I believe God used your comments to open my eyes to our problems so that He can heal them.

I thank God for the power and strength of your ministry and the way He is using it to speak to my needs. Facing oneself is not easy, but the growth that results is exciting. How many times that old adage, "Ignorance is bliss," has been shown to be so much nonsense in my life.

Love,
Charlotte

For all those readers who could not write positive and hopeful letters like those I've shared, I trust that God will use these pages to encourage you and begin the healing process. The Lord is, after all, in the business of performing miracles.

CHAPTER NINE

Questions and Answers

IT IS NEVER POSSIBLE TO COVER ALL ASPECTS OF A TOPIC so complex as the emotional interplay between human beings. Something important is certain to be left out of the text. In those instances, I have found it useful to toss in a section devoted to questions and answers. That permits me to gather up loose ends and elaborate on areas of confusion.

The following questions are obviously written for this purpose, therefore, but they represent actual inquiries I've heard from hundreds of people with a need to know.

Q. My wife has been involved in an affair with her boss for six months. I've known about it from the beginning but just haven't been able to confront her. Melanie acts like she doesn't love me anyway. If I give her an ultimatum I could lose her completely. Can you assure me that that won't happen? Have you ever offered the *love must be tough* advice and had it backfire, ending in divorce?

A. Yes, I have, and I certainly understand your caution. I wish I could guarantee how Melanie will react to a firmer approach. Unfortunately, life offers few certainties, even when all the probabilities point in one direction. Sometimes well-conditioned athletes drop dead from heart attacks. Some outstanding parents raise children who rebel and become drug addicts. Some of the most intelligent, cautious businessmen foolishly bankrupt themselves. Life is like that. Things happen every day that shouldn't have occurred. Nevertheless, we should go with the best information available to us. I read a sign on a wall this week that said, "The fastest horses don't always win, but you should still bet on them." Even as a nongambler, that makes sense to me.

Having offered that explanation, let me say that there is nothing risky about treating oneself with greater respect, exhibiting confidence and poise, pulling backward and releasing the door on the romantic trap. The positive benefits of that approach are often immediate and dramatic. Loving self-respect virtually never fails to have a salutary effect on a drifting lover, unless there is not the tiniest spark left to fan. Thus, in instances when opening the cage door results in a spouse's sudden departure, *the relationship was in the coffin already*. I'm reminded of the old proverb that says, "If you love something, set it free. If it comes back to you, it's yours. If it doesn't come back, it never was yours in the first place." There is great truth in that adage, and it applies to your relationship with your wife.

Now, obviously, it is risky to precipitate a period of crisis. When explosive individuals are involved in midlife turmoil or a passionate fling with a new lover, great acts and wisdom are required to know when and how to respond. That's why Christian professional counsel is vital before, during, and after the confrontation. It would be unthinkable of me to recommend that victims of affairs indiscriminately pose ultimatums with 24-hour deadlines, or that they push an independent partner into a corner. Great caution is needed in such delicate conflicts, and certainly, no move should be made without much prayer and supplication before the Lord.

In short, I suggest that you seek the assistance of a competent counselor who can help you deal with the problem of Melanie's affair.

Q. If you were the counselor who was helping someone manage a crisis situation like the one described above, you would obviously be making recommendations that could kill the marriage. Doesn't that make you nervous? Have you ever regretted taking a family in this direction?

A. To answer that question, you need to understand how I see my situation. My role is similar to that of a surgeon who tells a patient that he needs a coronary artery bypass operation. The man sits in his doctor's office, hearing the probabilities of success and failure. "If you undergo this operation," the doctor says, "you'll have—we'll say—a three percent chance of not surviving the surgery." Wow! three out of every hundred people who submit to the knife will die on the table! Why would anyone run that risk voluntarily? Because the chances of death are far greater without the surgery.

The *love must be tough* confrontations and ultimatum are like that. They may result in the sudden demise of a relationship. But, without the crisis, there is a much higher probability of a lingering death. Instead of bringing the matter to a head while there is a chance for healing, the alternative is to stand by while the marriage dies with a whimper. I'd rather take my chances today, before further damage is done. As I said, a blowout is better than a slow leak.

Q. My marriage seems beyond repair to me. My husband is just like Linda's; he's running around with other women and threatening to divorce me. Is there really any hope for us?

A. It's difficult to say without knowing the details, but I can tell you this. I've seen dozens of families who were in your fix but are now happy and whole. I taught a Sunday school class for young married couples for a number of years, and right there under my nose in a conservative church, infidelity was a surprisingly common event. There was one period of time during which I dealt with nineteen different couples where extramarital affairs had either occurred or were seriously threatening. These families are still known to me, and nine of them are apparently happily married today. Though this percentage may seem low, remember that these were families on the verge of divorce that have now survived ten years or longer. Loving toughness played a role in their recovery, although their commitment to the Christian faith was the significant factor. So yes, hope springs eternal, as well it should.

Let me give you one final word of encouragement. Nothing can seem so fixed but change so rapidly as human emotions. When it comes to romantic endeavors, feelings can turn upside down in a day or two. I've seen husbands or wives who expressed hatred for their spouses, saying, "I never want to see you again," only to fall weeping in the other person's arms some hours later.

Hang tough. God isn't through with you and your husband yet.

Q. You've referred to the case of Linda and Paul repeatedly throughout the book. Tell me what you would recommend to her if Paul came back asking her to forgive him and take him back. Should she just throw her arms open and pretend the affair never happened?

A. Well, she should certainly take him back. That's the point of everything I've written. But her power to negotiate needed changes will never be greater than in that moment, and she should not deal it away too quickly. I would suggest that she get Paul's written commitment to participate in counseling *immediately*, not even waiting two or three weeks to get started. Old patterns will persist if serious effort is not made to change them.

This family also has some deep wounds to work through and they're not likely to complete that healing process on their own. Linda must make it clear that *never* again—and I mean *never*—will she tolerate sexual unfaithfulness. Paul needs this motivation to go straight. He must know, and *believe*, that one more romp with another lover and the sky will surely fall. Linda must convince him that she means business. If he wavers, even slightly, she should give him another month or two to sit somewhere wishing he could come home. Better that they continue at the door of matrimonial death now than to go through the misery of infidelity again in a few years. Finally, Linda should insist on some major spiritual commitments within the family. This couple is going to need the healing powers of God and His grace if they are to rebuild what sin has eroded.

Then when Linda gets Paul home again, she should work like never before to make the man happy.

Q. How diffficult is it for people to implement the advice you are offering? I'm referring to the wounded and broken person who sees everything slipping away. Isn't it really tough for that man or woman to square up his or her shoulders and face the possibility of losing the one he/she loves?

A. Sure, it's hard. Some people have told me flatly that they couldn't do it. Others never quite comprehend what I've said. But to those who make even a small step in the direction of confidence, the rewards are instantaneous. For the person who has cried for days and lost a lot of weight and chewed the fingernails off both hands, you can't imagine what a relief it is to gain some self-respect again. Then when his partner also shows a measure of respect for the first time in months, the effect is exhilarating. As a bystander, I love it too!

Q. Several months ago my husband announced that he was divorcing me for another woman. Since then he has been seeing her regularly, but he hasn't left home and seems to be in a state of confusion. He's lost fifteen pounds and just looks terrible. What do you think is going on in his mind? He won't talk to me about his feelings, and he becomes angry when I ask him questions.

A. It is likely that your husband is experiencing intense guilt and conflict that often accompanies a selfish and sinful act such as infidelity. God has placed a little voice in the human soul that screams bloody murder at such moments, although some of us have learned to stuff a fist in its mouth. Even when we ignore its condemnation, the conscience is a formidable opponent of irresponsibility, and it will not permit gross violations of moral laws without a struggle. It is not uncommon for a person in this situation to experience a kind of internal war that can only be resolved in one of three ways: (1) the conscience wins and the person returns to the straight life; (2) the person rationalizes so effectively that his behavior begins to seem pure and holy; or (3) the conscience wins but the person persists in doing what he wants to do anyway.

People in this third category, which may include your husband, can be some of the most miserable men and women on the face of the earth. Their behavior has contradicted their personal code of ethics and all attempts to reconcile the two have been futile. Stated another way, these individuals are in a dog fight with their consciences, and the fur is flying in all directions. Not only psychological disorders but physical illness can result from such disharmony! A person who is going through this internal conflict often experiences depression, weight loss, sleepless nights, nail biting, etc. The ordeal is extremely uncomfortable to the sensitive individual.

If we are right about your husband's frame of mind, you can expect him to commit himself very quickly either to you or the other woman. It is simply too painful to remain in suspended animation between good and evil. I would advise you to seek professional counsel as to whether this is the proper moment to require your husband to make his choice. With the few facts I've been given, I would lean in that direction.

Q. It has always been my understanding that marriage was supposed to be based on *unconditional* love. That is, the commitment to one another should be independent of behavior, no matter how offensive or unfaithful. But your concept of accountability in marriage seems to be saying, "I will love you as long as you do what I want."

A. You've misunderstood my point. The limitations of language make it very diffficult to explain this concept adequately, but let me try again. I certainly believe in the validity of unconditional love, and, in fact, the mutual accountability I have recommended is an expression of that love! For example, if a husband (or wife) is behaving in ways that will harm himself, his children, his marriage, and the family of the "other woman," then confrontation with him becomes an act of love. The easiest response by the innocent partner would be to look the other way and pretend she doesn't notice. But from my perspective, that is tantamount to a parent's refusing to confront a fourteen year old who comes home drunk at 4:00 A.M. The mother or father has an obligation to create a crisis in response to destructive behavior. I'm trying to say that *unconditional love* is not synonymous with permissiveness, passivity, and weakness. Sometimes it requires toughness and discipline and accountability.

Q. When my wife left me for another man, I felt like the whole thing was my fault. I still feel that way. I had never even looked at another woman, yet here I am taking the blame for her affair. Rationally, I know I'm very unfair to myself, but I can't help it. Or can I?

A. It is *the* typical reaction of a victim, like yourself, to take the full responsibility for the behavior of an unfaithful spouse. I dealt with this situation in a prior book and feel it might be helpful to quote from that source here:

> It has always been surprising for me to observe how often the wounded marriage partner—the person who was clearly the victim of the other's irresponsibility—is the one who suffers the greatest pangs of guilt and feelings of inferiority. How strange that the one who tried to hold things together in the face of obvious rejection often finds herself wondering, "How did I fail him?—I just wasn't woman enough to hold my man . . . I am 'nothing' or he wouldn't have left . . . if only I had been more exciting as a sexual partner . . . I drove him to it . . . I wasn't pretty enough . . . I didn't deserve him in the first place."
>
> The blame for marital disintegration is seldom the fault of the husband or wife alone. It takes two to tangle, as they say, and there is always some measure of shared blame for a divorce. However, when one marriage partner makes up his mind to behave irresponsibly, to become involved extramaritally, or to run from his family commitments and obligations, he usually seeks to justify his behavior by magnifying the failures of his spouse. "You didn't meet my needs, so I had to satisfy them somewhere else," is the familiar accusation. By increasing the guilt of his partner in this way, he reduces his own culpability. For a husband or wife with low self-esteem, these charges and recriminations are accepted as fact when hurled his way. "Yes, it was my fault. I drove you to it!" Thus, the victim assumes the full responsibility for his partner's irresponsibility, and self-worth shatters.

I would not recommend that you sit around hating the memory of your husband. Bitterness and resentment are emotional cancers that rot us from within. However, I would encourage you to examine the facts carefully. Answers to these questions should be sought: "Despite my human frailties, did I value my marriage and try to preserve it? Did my husband decide to destroy it and then seek justification for his actions? Was I given a fair chance to resolve the areas of greatest irritation? Could I have held him, even if I had made all the changes he wanted? Is it reasonable that I should hate myself for this thing that has happened?"

You should know that social rejection breeds feelings of inferiority and self-pity in enormous proportions. And rejection by the one you love, particularly, is the most powerful destroyer of self-esteem in the entire realm of human experience. You might begin to see yourself as a victim of this process, rather than a worthless failure at the game of love.*

Q. My wife tried to make me feel guilty when she left. She angrily blamed me for the divorce, despite my desperate attempts to hold things together. In her mind, I failed so miserably as a husband that she was forced to run around with her boss! Are you saying that this transfer of responsibility is typical when one spouse has been unfaithful?

A. Yes, it often happens. Guilt is a very painful emotion, and the person who is willfully tearing up a home in pursuit of a new lover is in an uncomfortable position. He or she feels condemnation from four primary sources—from the rejected husband or wife, from the children, from friends and associates, and from God. In order to justify his behavior, he energetically constructs a verbal defense around those who would testify against him in a court of moral law. His purpose, of course, is to make adultery seem reasonable and downright godly. That takes some creativity!

**Dr Dobson Answers Your Questions* (Wheaton, IL: Tyndale House, 1982) pp. 306–7.

Ask any victim of an affair; he or she has probably heard a specialized version of the following rationalizations:

1. To resolve marital guilt . . . "I know that what I'm doing is difficult for you now, but someday you will understand that it is for the best. I never really loved you even when we were young. In fact, we should never have gotten married in the first place. Furthermore, this divorce is really your fault. You drove me to it by ——————— [insert grievances here, such as frigidity, in-law problems, nagging, overwork, or all the foregoing]."

This message has a transparent purpose. The first sentence marvelously purifies the motives of the unfaithful spouse. It says, in effect, "I'm really doing this for your good." The second sentence is also a beauty. It is designed to serve as an "annulment" to the marriage instead of a cruel abandonment of a loved one. By saying that they should never have gotten married, their union becomes an unfortunate mistake rather than a relationship which God Himself ordained and cemented. (Henry VIII used this approach to eject his first wife, Catherine of Aragon.) Then by putting the remaining responsibility on the other party, what was left of the blame is successfully transferred from the guilty to the innocent. So much for wedding vows. Now let's deal with the children.

2. To resolve parental guilt . . . "This will be hard on the kids for a while, but they'll be better off in the long run. It certainly isn't healthy for them to see us fight and argue like we've been doing. Besides, I will spend just as much time with them after things settle down as I do now."

Zap! Zap! Guilt over the children is also tucked away. Would you believe that Dad's escapade with another woman or Mom's flight with Don Juan is actually a constructive thing? Never mind what the children see and comprehend with their big, beautiful eyes. Pay no heed to the conclusions they draw about why Mommy or Daddy left, and why he or she doesn't love them anymore, and why God let it happen, and why the divorce may have been *their* fault, and why life is so painful and scary. Try to ignore the fact that everything stable has just come unstitched in the lives of some very impressionable and sensitive kids. Don't think about it, and maybe your rapidly beating heart will return to normal again. Guilt over the children can be the toughest to rationalize, but, fortunately, hundreds of books and tapes are available today that will help you silence your writhing conscience.

3. To resolve social guilt . . . "I'm sure our friends won't understand at first, and I can hardly wait to hear what your mother will have to say. But it's like I told the pastor last week, our divorce is really no one's fault. We've just outgrown each other. People change as the years go by, and relationships have to change to accommodate them." (If a woman is speaking she may say: "Besides, I am entitled to do what's best for *me* once in a while. I've given my entire life to everyone else—now it's time for me to think of myself. It's only fair that I fit into the picture at some point, and this is it. Anyway, what's right for me will prove best for you and the children, too.")

This line of reasoning has been provided for women today almost word for word by the more radical elements of the feminist movement. It is only one of many rationalizations by which selfishness can be purified and made to appear altruistic. Three down and one to go.

4. To resolve divine guilt . . . "I've prayed about this decision, and I am now certain that God approves of what I've chosen to do."

There it is, folks, in living color—the ultimate rationalization. If the Creator in His infinite wisdom has taken the matter under advisement and judged the divorce to be in the best interest of everyone, who can argue that point further? The conversation is over. Sin has been sanctified. Guilt is expunged. Self-respect is restored . . . and, alas, evil has prevailed. Having settled the "big four," every moral and spiritual obstacle is removed. The stage is set for separation and/or divorce.

Q. I know now that my husband is a "womanizer"—a guy who can't resist anything in a skirt. Will he always be like this? Can I change him?

A. It is difficult, if not impossible, to change anyone. It certainly cannot be accomplished by nagging and complaining and chastising. That only causes a person to dig in his heels and fight to the finish. What you can do is what I've suggested in this book: make it clear to your husband that he can't have you and a harem too, and that he must make a choice between his lust and his love. Unfortunately, merely putting these alternatives before him verbally will not force him to select one over the other. He would rather have *both* toys. That's why there will probably come a time for *loving toughness* when you back your words by firmness and definitive action. Remember in that difficult hour that God can change your husband, and that the crisis may be a divine vehicle to bring him to his senses.

Q. You implied earlier that the *love must be tough* philosophy has broad applicability. I understand its role in reconstructing a bad marriage. How would it function in a good relationship?

A. The best way of keeping a marriage healthy is to maintain a system of mutual accountability, within the context of love. Speaking personally, the secret of my beautiful relationship with Shirley for the past twenty-three years has involved a careful protection of the "line of respect" between us. This is a difficult concept to convey, and its function is different from one personality to another. Perhaps by explaining how it operates between Shirley and me, I can help the reader adapt the principle to his own circumstances.

Suppose I work in my office two hours longer than usual on a particular night, knowing Shirley is preparing a special candlelight dinner. The phone sits there on my desk, but I lack the concern to make a brief call to explain. As the evening wears on, Shirley wraps the cold food in foil and puts it in the refrigerator. Then suppose when I finally get home, I do not apologize. Instead, I sit down with a newspaper and abruptly tell Shirley to get my dinner ready. You can bet there'll be a few minutes of fireworks in the Dobson household. Shirley will rightfully interpret my behavior as insulting and will move to defend the "line of respect" between us. We will talk it out, and next time I'll be more considerate.

Let's put the shoe on the other foot. Suppose Shirley knows I need the car at 2:00 P.M. for some important purpose, but she deliberately keeps me waiting. Perhaps she sits in a restaurant with a lady friend, drinking coffee and talking. Meanwhile, I'm pacing the floor at home wondering where she is. It is very likely that my lovely wife will hear about my dissatisfaction when she gets home. The "line of respect" has been violated, even though the offense was minor.

This is what I mean by mutual accountability. Such minor conflict in a marriage plays a positive role in establishing what is and is not acceptable behavior. Some instances of disrespect are petty, like the two examples I gave, but when they are permitted to pass unnoticed, two things happen. First, the offender is unaware that he has stepped over the line and is likely to repeat the indiscretion later. In fact, he may go farther into the other person's territory the next time. Second, the person who felt insulted then internalizes the small irritation rather than spilling it out. As the interpretation of disrespect grows and the corresponding agitation accumulates in a storage tank, the stage is set for an eventual explosion, rather than a series of minor ventilations.

What I'm saying is that some things are worth fighting over, and at the top of the list is the "line of respect." Most of my conflicts with Shirley have occurred over some behavior that one of us interpreted as unhealthy to the relationship. Shirley may say to me, in effect, "Jim, what you did was selfish, and I can't let it pass." She is careful not to insult me in the confrontation, keeping her criticism focused on the behavior to which she objected.

A workable system of checks and balances of this nature helps a couple keep their marriage on course for a marathon rather than a sprint. And I can assure you, Shirley and I are going for the distance!

Q. That philosophy contradicts what I have been taught by Christian leaders who say as believers, "We have no rights." If I understand what they say, I should not even notice instances of disrespect because I have no rights to be defended. Do you disagree?

A. Perhaps. That "no rights" philosophy would be unbeatable if both partners were totally mature, unselfish, and loving. Unfortunately, we are all riddled with imperfection and self-serving desires. Therefore, we *need* reinforcement and accountability in order to do what is right. When only one member of the family buys the "no rights" concept and tries to implement it, a marriage can be blown apart. Why? Because the nonparticipating spouse begins to crawl all over the "line of respect." He gets the lion's share of everything—money, sex, power, fun and games, etc. Knowing the partner's spiritual obligation, he feels entitled by divine decree to do as he pleases.

The Christian spouse who is clinging desperately to this theological understanding is not made of steel. Nor is he blind. He sees instance after instance of disrespect and does his best to ignore them. But they go straight into a memory bank, whether he wishes to store them or not. That's the way he's made. Then one day when his resistance is down, perhaps when he is exhausted, or, in a woman's case, during the pressures of premenstrual tension, a hydrogen bomb can be detonated that may blow off the head of her startled husband. A "no rights" position would have carried that person through a short race; unfortunately, life is so *daily*, and the runner weakened on heartbreak hill.

I must hasten to offer an important disclaimer. *Any* recommendation can be carried to extremes, including defense of the "line of respect." There are millions of women, especially, who need nothing less than an excuse to harangue their spouses over perceived violations of one sort or another. They do that better than anything else in life. Their poor husbands live with a constant barrage of complaints and criticisms, knowing they can do *nothing* right. Then here comes Dobson advising, "Hold 'em accountable, ladies!"

That's not what I intended to say. Remember that 1 Corinthians 13:5 tells us love "is not easily provoked" KJV). That tolerance is certainly evident in good marriages. Husbands and wives must overlook a multitude of flaws in one another and not howl over the speck in a partner's eye when the accuser has a log sticking out of his own. Prolonged anger can kill a marriage—especially when it reflects perceived wrongs from the past that have never been forgiven.

Thus, the *love must be tough* concept *does* not suggest that people become touchy and picky; it does hold that genuine instances of disrespect should be acknowledged and handled within the context of love. And certainly, when major violations occur that threaten the relationship, such as Linda's husband running to see a sexy divorcee night after night, they should be met head-on. By confronting him when he got home, she would not have been fighting for her "rights" at all; she would have been defending her marriage! We've seen what happens when that defense is lacking.

Q. To be certain that I understand what you mean by the "line of respect" principle, could you discuss it further? Do you deal with this idea often in your marriage counseling?

A. In virtually every troubled family I see, the "line of respect" has crumbled. Sometimes the wife is trampling on the husband's territory; sometimes he is all over hers. Either way, within five minutes in my office it is apparent that there is an absence of fair play by one of two partners. Here's an extreme example as described in a letter from a woman whose line is now in shambles.

> My husband and I have three children, and I am with them day and night because I can't drive. My husband doesn't want me to go anywhere, anyway. He is very domineering. He dishes out the money and decides how every dollar will be spent.
>
> This past week was terrible. Mike wouldn't let the kids sing or talk in the car. He orders all of us to bed at a certain time and controls all TV and radio stations. I like to hear you on Christian radio, but he won't let me listen when he's home. He will change stations and then go downstairs. I sometimes tape your program secretly and play it after

Mike is gone. Mike's grandmother lives with us, too, and she thinks he is being mean to the whole family.

I would never get to go anywhere if it wasn't for good neighbors who take me to church functions. I just feel like I have no freedom at all and my nerves are beginning to act up. The kids are afraid of Mike too.

Anything you can do to help me would be *greatly* appreciated.

Fortunately, most cases are not as devoid of respect as this one, but it illustrates the problem. If I were working with this woman, my objective would be to teach her how to hold her own with her husband without blowing her marriage off the face of the earth. It would be a delicate task.

Q. I have a male physician friend who can't seem to resist the charms of his female patients. His marriage is in serious difficulty, even though I know he loves his wife. Would you explain the psychological dynamics in this kind of problem, and tell me what I should say to help my friend?

A. A similar question was addressed recently in an issue of the *Christian Medical Society Journal* where reference was made to an excellent article by Dr. Merville Vincent entitled "The Physician's Own Well-Being."* Dr. Vincent discussed twelve hazardous assumptions that can ruin a physician's career. One of those assumptions, quoted below, is the belief by the male doctor that he is God's gift to women.

Some patients fall in love with their doctor. The scenario often goes something like this. The patient is a young lady with a minor illness and is unhappily married or divorced. She comes to her

*Vincent, M. O., "The Physician's Own Well-Being," *Annals Royal College of Physicians and Surgeons of Canada* 1981, vol. 14, 4, 277–81

physician not only with her specific complaints, but at a time when she is feeling frightened and helpless. In his office, the doctor seems strong, confident, calm, and caring. He knows what to do and does it. He helps her with her presenting problem. She then is relieved and gains strength from his confidence. She begins to think, "Isn't he wonderful, he'd be so nice to have around the house." Meanwhile, back in the doctor's home, his wife is also thinking, "He'd be so nice to have around the house" or less kindly, "If patients could only see him like I do."

Next our patient communicates to the doctor that he's wonderful. He immediately agrees and, after careful thought, concludes that she is a genius and wishes his wife was smart this way also. He says to himself "excellent judge of men, that girl."

The problem is he mistakes her needs for his assets. Typically, the situation involves two people with unmet needs. The physician at risk is one whose needs to be cared for are not being met at home. Sometimes this has been due to his business; sometimes because he denied any such needs. Often his wife is tired of giving of herself with little apparent attempt by her husband to meet her various needs for a husband and father of her children. She is now putting demands on her husband to do something at home. She is tired of feeling she is nothing but his housekeeper and sexual partner. He often responds to these demands by feeling unappreciated and nothing but the breadwinner. At such a time, he is a sitting duck for a relationship with a young lady with needs that also make her vulnerable. The affair at first not only boosts sagging self-esteem for both, but seems to offer the doctor a relationship in which he may receive much more admiration than he gets at home and with much less responsibility. She, who has no right to this man, can be warm and accepting at first. Meanwhile, his wife, who feels she has a right to him, is becoming more angry and frustrated about his absence from the house. Later the young lady begins to feel jealous. Now our emotionally and physically depleted doctor feels he has two demanding women and still no one to look after him.

How may such a predicament be prevented? First, realize it happens, and it starts primarily because of the role of the two people in the situation. Realize it begins because of her needs, not your assets. Realize that when you meet dependent needs with an erotic response, you become part of the problem, not part of the solution. The best prevention is to be sure that your own needs to be cared for (dependent needs) are being met. These are best met in a marriage where there is reciprocity of mutual need-meeting. Perhaps the early warning signal is when you begin to feel that your patients appreciate you and love you more than your wife and family do. The next step may be to spend even more time with patients and less with your spouse.

Q. My husband is a very attractive man, and he's the president of his own company at a young age. I know that women are out to get him, especially some divorced secretaries who constantly flirt with him. I'm raising these kids here at home, and I have to admit that I worry about holding Dwight. I believe he's been faithful to me, but I wonder if he will always turn down the opportunities around him? I mean, he comes home, and tells me what these women do and say, and I can't believe it! They practically proposition him. What can I do to hang onto my husband?

A. Twenty years ago, your question would have seemed unnecessarily anxious and even a bit silly. But it makes plenty of sense today—the world has changed that much. There has always been hanky-panky going on, but never has it been so blatant and never have males and females been so bold in their pursuit of one another. More to the point of your concern, it is no longer considered taboo for an available woman to consciously lure a married man—even one with several children at home. He's fair game to anyone who can entice him away from his family. A woman told me recently that her nice-looking husband reports that girls deliberately brush against him in the subway and make risqué comments. Men are just as audacious in their pursuit of women, whether those women are married or not. Thus, the concern expressed in your question has a basis in reality.

Nevertheless, the solution is *not* to "hang onto" Dwight. You must not build a cage around him in an attempt to reduce your anxieties. That would only add unnecessary stresses to your relationship. Dwight must stay with you of his own free will—the same reason for which he married you in the first place. *Love must be free*, even in a world of sexual intrigue and disloyalty.

Perhaps it would be helpful for me to offer a couple of perspectives that may not have occurred to you. First, Dwight is primarily responsible for the insecurity you feel, one way or the other. He could allay your fears if he wished. It's a fairly simple task for a man to let his wife know he is committed to her for life. Instead, Dwight is regularly telling you about the sexy women who hang onto him and beg for his favors. *That's* the source of your butterflies. Indeed, most instances of "competition anxiety" among homemakers can be attributed to husbands like Dwight who subtly create insecurities in their wives.

Why would a man do such a thing? What can be gained by dangling a partner in suspense over something so basic as a marital commitment? Well, the male ego enjoys being desired by women—lots of women. That's why a married man will flirt with female employees, even when he has no intention of being unfaithful. Furthermore, he will tell his wife about these admirers in order to gain "power" in their relationship. Whether consciously or not, he is saying by these disclosures, "You'd better treat me right because there are plenty of other women out there just waiting to get their hands on me."

At some point in your conversation with Dwight, these dynamics should be discussed. I'm not suggesting that you hammer him with accusations or complaints, but an opportunity may come to verbalize your feelings and put the matter of competition in proper perspective. The healthiest families are those that can discuss this kind of sensitive subject in an atmosphere of openness and acceptance.

Before that conversation ensues, however, I think you should look at a related issue. The way you stated your question implies that your own self-esteem is none too high. Why do I get the feeling that you see yourself as a lowly homemaker in a world of women lawyers and athletes and congresswomen? Do you feel inferior to women in the business world? Is it possible that you feel fortunate to have "captured" your good-looking, successful man and wonder how long the illusion will last? If these are secret weaknesses in your self-concept, they will be reflected in your relationship with your husband. He will sense your fearfulness—your unhealthy dependence—your "unworthiness" of his love. You must believe that you bring as much to the family as your husband does and that, not only are you fortunate to be married to Dwight, but he's a pretty lucky guy, too.

* * *

All right, now it's final examination time. You have sat in my course on *love must be tough* for an entire semester, and the time has come to demonstrate what you've learned. Provided below is a test—a prototype letter drawn from thousands I receive. Read it and answer the questions that follow as you think I would, and then express your own views on the issues.

> Dear Dr. Dobson:
>
> I hope you can take a few minutes and try to help me. I feel really desperate, and I'm praying that you have some answer for me.

My husband and I were married very young, and after about four years he started running around. That lasted for a couple of years before he became a Christian. Then for six years things were fine. He is an insurance salesman and did quite well financially. But then he had an affair with a woman in our church. It only lasted a short time—and the other members did not find out about it. We moved to another town to get away from her. From then on, it was one woman after another, ending with my next-door neighbor. He moved in and out of the house on four occasions. He settled back in last September and hasn't left since, although the affair with my neighbor didn't end. We have been trying to get our marriage back together since then, but I'm finding it's getting harder instead of easier for me. My mind is in a turmoil.

I cannot accept it when he says to me, "I love you." (He does not know any of these feelings and does not seem willing to discuss anything either.) I'm torn. I don't know what to do. For years, my great fear has been, "When will it happen again?" And very soon, it does. Would I be better off with him or without him? The other woman is the total opposite of me spiritually. She and her three children have now moved in my house to stay, which I sometimes find unbearable. (This other woman's husband divorced her.)

Dr. Dobson, my mind is so full of questions, and I guess one of the main problems is, "What are his true feelings for this woman?" Sometimes he just sits so quietly, and, of course, I think his mind is on her. He's thirty-eight now, and if I truly believed his problems were the "change of life," I could probably handle it better. But I see it more as a lifelong pattern.

Sex is super important to my husband, I think to a fault. He tells me he has "no complaints" where I'm concerned. One remark he made once was, "I always come back to you; that should tell you something."

He will not allow me to work (I may look at someone else), and he does not believe in counseling and would be furious if he knew I was writing to you.

I'm so torn I don't know what to do. Our whole family has been devastated by this, and I feel like Satan has made a real bid for all of us.

What should I do to straighten out my marriage?

Mary

Final Examination

1. List the mistakes Mary has made; underline the *first* and most serious one.
2. What is her husband probably thinking now?
3. How does he see his wife?
4. Mary's husband said, "I always come back to you; that should tell you something." What does it tell her?
5. Mary is not permitted to work for fear she will find another man. What does this say about the power she possesses with her husband?
6. Will her husband continue to cheat?
7. Why do you suppose Mary has permitted her husband to behave as he wished?
8. Can this marriage be saved?
9. What would you advise Mary to do?

Dobson's Answers

1. Mary made seven mistakes by my count:
   a. *She apparently failed to create a crisis when her husband's first act of infidelity occurred, permitting it to continue for two years.*

b. She cooperated in the concealment of his second affair with a church member. If he had repented, it would have been best to keep the affair a secret. In the absence of that contrition, perhaps the pastor should have been approached.
c. She permitted him to move in and out of the house like a yo-yo, allowing him to return without any commitment to be faithful. Indeed, his affair with a neighbor continued without interruption.
d. She concealed her own feelings about his phony concept of love. Neither did she tell him about her great fears of his continued unfaithfulness. Why? Because she was appeasing her husband. He might have left if she dared to complain. This woman could easily be the "saint" we read about earlier in the song "She's Got to be a Saint."
e. Alas, she allowed the other woman and her three children to move into her house permanently!
f. She continued to meet her husband's sexual needs as though nothing had happened. He was joyfully jumping from one bed to the other, apparently.
g. She permitted this unfaithful, disrespectful man to continue as her leader ("He will not allow me to work"). She should have been preparing herself for economic survival if he decided to abandon her.

By the foregoing measures, Mary demonstrated *weak* love. What she desperately needed was loving toughness!

2. He's trying to decide whether or not to leave his wife.
3. He sees her as a good woman, but as a pathetic pushover who will let him escape with murder. He disrespects her profoundly.
4. It tells her (1) that he still cares for her, in a manner of speaking, and (2) that he disrespects her. His statement puts him in

the position of a master tossing a bone to a grateful dog. She should tell him, "Who needs it?"

5. This statement is *the* most important line in the letter. If I were counseling Mary, I would build an entire strategy on the implications of those words. What it says, in effect, is that this man cares enough about Mary to be jealous of her. He doesn't want anyone else to even know her! This should give her the confidence to call his bluff and lay the relationship on the line. I believe he would yield in a crisis.
6. Yes, unless Mary takes his toys away.
7. She is terrified—of loneliness, rejection, divorce, financial ruin, single parenthood, embarrassment, physical violence, and the unknown. She also suffers from massive low self-esteem which keeps her immobilized.
8. More than likely, it *can* be saved. Much depends on Mary's courage.
9. Mary should ask her loose lover to leave and take his girlfriend (and her three kids) with him. Let him play with his harem until he's sick of life on the road. She should get a job and prepare for a long winter. When (and if) he comes home with a desire to reconcile, I would advise them to completely reconstruct their relationship with the help of a Christian counselor. And of course, Mary should pray without ceasing.

CHAPTER TEN

Victims of Affairs: A Dialogue

SINCE OUR PURPOSE HEREIN IS TO DISCOVER THE FUNDAMENTAL causes of marital erosion and divorce, it seems appropriate that we continue to look closely at families that have experienced this tragedy. If a medical scientist wishes to understand the effects of typhus or emphysema or ulcers, he carefully examines patients who are afflicted with those diseases. Accordingly, we must focus our attention on marriages that have been invaded by the "bacteria" of interpersonal conflict—the most infectious disease of our time.

Toward that end, I invited four intelligent, highly verbal people into our radio studio to talk about their experiences with infidelity. The program, "Focus on the Family," is heard daily on 450 U.S. radio stations and more than 250 overseas. Each in his or her own way is a victim of an affair, having been betrayed by an unfaithful spouse. What follows in this chapter are portions of the transcript from that intense two-hour conversation involving three women and a man. Their stories are symbolic of millions in the Western world today and will serve to illustrate the principles I've tried to address.

May I suggest as you read these personal accounts that you attempt to correlate the details with our discussion to this point? Our purpose is not to embarrass the anonymous participants, of course, who have graciously given me permission to present their cases. Rather, we want to learn from them. Therefore, I hope you will look for common mistakes and errors in judgment, especially in the early stages of infidelity. Watch for panic and appeasement as the participants weave their way through their stories. Ask yourself if long-suffering and tolerance were successful in healing relationships. And finally, postulate your recommendations for those who are currently enduring a trial by fire. I will provide a commentary on the discussions in the following chapter.*

DOBSON: I'd like to begin by paying special tribute to the four of you who've joined us in the studio today. It won't be easy to talk about the break-up of your families, but we can profit from what you learned as victims of infidelity. It goes without saying that this topic is a heavy one. Only this morning I heard about a woman whose husband left her. She cried almost incessantly for twelve months, and last Thursday, her thirteen-year-old daughter tried to commit suicide. That is where infidelity sometimes leads. But then, who would know that better than the four of you?

Let me begin by introducing you to our radio listeners. You've asked that I not use your real names, so we'll call you Sue, Jean, Mary Ann, and Mike. And I'm going to ask you, Mary Ann, to begin by telling us your story.

MARY ANN: All right. Shortly after George and I were married, we lived at the beach, and I taught school. My husband was unemployed and had too much free time on his hands. He obviously had a lot of female friends I didn't know, because in the evening he would get phone calls from these other women. I would ask him about the callers, but he would never respond. Of course, I was feeling so much pain because we were married but not living in a marital relationship. We were living as roommates, due to, I'm sure, the guilt he had over his affairs.

*The comments have been edited for clarity and grammatical accuracy.

DOBSON: How long had you been married?

MARY ANN: We had been married for about six months when this began. Our divorce occurred after three and one-half years. It was very painful.

DOBSON: Do I understand that you tolerated what you knew to be blatant infidelity for that period of time?

MARY ANN: I knew it in my heart but—

DOBSON: You didn't really want to know it.

MARY ANN: Yes, right, exactly. I made a decision to say, "No, it's not really happening."

DOBSON: Was your husband unemployed by choice?

MARY ANN: It was by choice. The beach was too alluring. And the beautiful girls out there were, I'm sure, even more alluring to him.

DOBSON: Just how obvious was the infidelity? Did he ever bring women home with him?

MARY ANN: No, he didn't. He was very discreet. It was just that he didn't want to touch me or have anything to do with me. That was very painful. When your husband shows no interest, you feel like you have no worth and that you're very unattractive.

DOBSON: Did you and your husband share the same values before you were married? Did you think he was a Christian?

MARY ANN: My former husband and I dated eight years before we married!

DOBSON: Eight years!

MARY ANN: Yes. My parents had been divorced, and I wanted to make sure that I was not getting into a bad marriage.

DOBSON: And you still got a surprise?

MARY ANN: I was—

DOBSON: Blind?

MARY ANN: Very blind, I guess. You know, I really believed that he loved the Lord. Now I know that he was living a double life during all those years we dated. But I had no knowledge of it. He was the first person who really loved me, I thought. I didn't get love from my home. I was twenty-four years old and I was educated and had my profession, so I really felt like I knew what I was doing. I really thought I knew this person. But, a month after we were married, it all came apart. The difficult thing, of course, is to try to go back and relive that decision. We had met at a Christian college, and I believed in him. He believed in himself. There certainly wasn't any suggestion of danger then, nor did anyone else perceive it. Then when the affairs began, I would go back in my dreams at night, what little I could sleep, and re-examine my decision to marry. I was committed to God; I wasn't out of fellowship with Him. Despite my caution, I made an enormous mistake.

DOBSON: Sue, I understand you thought you married a Christian, too?

SUE: Oh, I would have staked my life on it. And in fact, I did. We had been married, let's see, probably fifteen years before I ever knew he was playing around. At that time he was an administrator in a Christian college where I was teaching. He was also chairman of a moral action committee in our church, which is very ironic. When I learned he was involved in an affair, I could say nothing to anyone because our pastor, our college president, his colleagues . . . were all my friends, too. I just couldn't ruin his reputation with them. It was a terrible time.

DOBSON: How long were the affairs going on before you knew?

SUE: I'm not sure. I was very spaced out until I finally faced reality. After that, the affairs were continuous until finally the marriage was dissolved. That was a period of six years.

DOBSON: Like Mary Ann, you knowingly tolerated your husband's infidelity for six years?

SUE: Yes. As a Christian I just committed myself more strongly to the marriage; I was determined that if there were any way to make it work, with God's help, I was going to do that.

DOBSON: But you lost it anyway?

SUE: Yes.

DOBSON: Looking back on the experience, would there have been any way to have saved your home?

SUE: I don't think so. And, of course, by being patient I was able to give my children their father for six more years. They loved him best of anyone in the world and still have a good image of him. I wouldn't change that.

DOBSON: Mike, tell me your story.

MIKE: Well, I had a very successful marriage until my wife had a severe accident and a concussion which left her totally incapable of functioning from January to the end of that school year. She was a teacher, and during that lengthy period of time where she could not function, I took over most of the responsibilities of the home. The next year the doctors felt that for her own self-image, she needed to return to teaching, which she really wanted to do. But she was not emotionally or physically ready. She needed somebody to lean on. That somebody happened to teach next door. Their friendship just evolved from there.

DOBSON: Could you see it coming?

MIKE: At first I couldn't, but during the next two years, I sensed that she was drawing away from me. When we would try to talk about it, we just went around in circles and never seemed to come to a conclusion. I couldn't figure out what I was dealing with. I had trusted her implicitly for seventeen years. We had had a happy marriage and to even imagine that she was unfaithful was unthinkable.

SUE: It's almost impossible to believe you've been betrayed when you've committed your life to another person.

DOBSON: Especially in the Christian context.

MARY ANN: Absolutely.

DOBSON: You all were involved in church-going families—

SUE: Yes. In fact, the worst part of the experience for me was the loss of my spiritual leader. I could handle the rejection and the treachery better than I could deal with the implications of James's sin.

DOBSON: Jean, let's hear your story.

JEAN: I identify with what Sue just said. That loss of the person that I looked up to spiritually was the hardest part for me, too. My husband was a career churchman, so I not only lost my mate and the father of my children, but I felt like I lost my spiritual leader.

DOBSON: That's interesting. Both you and Sue experienced the same thing.

JEAN: Oh, it was my whole lifestyle. Divorce is different than just losing a person; you lose your way of life.

DOBSON: How did it happen to you, Jean?

JEAN: Well, I feel like the senior member here. We lost our marriage after thirty-two years, which is really a tragedy. In fact, that's why I'm here today. If you go through a tragedy, you ought to be able to use it to help someone else, and I hope my story will do that. The reason I was so attracted to Maury (and, in fact, I still am) was that he was the most moral, sincere kind of boy that I had ever dated. We married when we were both nineteen, and we had children right away. He had his first affair, a short little one, when we had two children. I was very upset about it, naturally. I confronted him, and we decided to treat this like modern people would do. So the four of us, two husbands and two wives, sat down and talked about it. Maury was terribly sorry about the whole thing. He really was. It was not the kind of thing that a man with his background would want to do. And so, all was forgiven and the matter ended. He also had another little encounter, just a little kind of an evening thing, at a party one night, but that blew over, too. Right after that, Maury began his career, and we went along as a very normal, happy family. Then about ten or fifteen years ago, I guess, I found out that he was involved in an affair with someone else. I was ill at the time, and Maury is a very sensitive man. He said he was lonely and needed another woman to do what I couldn't do for him at the time.

DOBSON: Did you buy that?

JEAN: At the time I did. Yes and no. I wanted to believe him because he really was such a good man. But his extramarital activity continued. He had a long-term affair where he saw a woman regularly for nearly two years. It was not a sexual affair. But it was just as painful to me.

DOBSON: An emotional affair?

JEAN: That's right. I felt a greater sense of disloyalty over that, picturing him sharing himself, than I would have if he had been sleeping with her. He had other affairs as the years went by—some occasionally with women of the street. I'm not sure you would call that kind of thing an affair.

DOBSON: You knew about each involvement?

JEAN: Yes. Sometimes a long period of time would go by before I found out. But I always found out.

DOBSON: Mary Ann, didn't you tell me earlier that God revealed your husband's infidelity to you?

MARY ANN: Yes, he did. I had attended a Christian seminar, and on the way home, I experienced a horrible grip of fear. I just knew I was going to go home and find my husband in bed with another girl. Then I said to myself, "Mary Ann! What in the world is wrong with you? That's ridiculous!"

DOBSON: You had never caught him before?

MARY ANN: No. That's why I condemned myself. Nevertheless, I confronted my husband when I got home. He became very angry and made me feel like I was really off the wall. But he was involved at the time, and it was God's way of preparing me for what was to come. The Lord is so gentle in the way He deals with His children.

DOBSON: Looking back on the first revelation, the moment when each of you first became aware that you had serious problems on your hands, how wisely do you feel you handled the situation? Was there anything you could have done that would have helped? Is there anything you'd do differently if you had those years to live over?

MARY ANN: What I did wrong was that I didn't pray about the very thing I wanted so desperately. I reacted with anger. Instead of saying, "Lord, show me what kind of wife George needs," I was always so spiritually dogmatic that my husband *had* to be the way he was. You know it takes two to make a marriage work, and some of my actions didn't help accomplish that. My husband probably ran from the very thing I wanted him to do because I was so strong.

DOBSON: How is that?

MARY ANN: I was a very self-righteous Christian at that point, who loved the Lord with all her heart, soul, strength, and mind.

DOBSON: How can you blame yourself for that, Mary Ann?

MARY ANN: Well, nothing is wrong with that, but I handled it wrong. I would say to him, "Please read the Bible to me." You know, sometimes I'd be into the Word of God, and really wanting to seek after Truth, and he'd try to distract me. I remember making a comment I'll never forget. It's the worst thing a woman can do. I said, "You're a tool of Satan!" It was horrible. So there were many things I did wrong that God has revealed to me over the years. I thank the Lord that He only revealed them to me very gradually.

SUE: The main mistake I made was becoming very cold, sexually. My husband was so cruel and rough, and I had gotten to where I just couldn't respond. But the moment his infidelity was revealed, I was able to be warm and loving again. I asked his forgiveness immediately. That was my first response when I got the news. I think that's why I became suicidal. I felt so guilty; I knew I had caused the affairs. But then when I did everything I could to make up for those mistakes and the infidelity continued, then I didn't feel as guilty.

But that first year after learning about his unfaithfulness was awful. I cried every day for twelve months. I'm sure I was a wonderful blessing to my husband during that time. By then we had five little children, and it was so hard to manage the home and be a professional person as he wanted me to be. I wish I could have stopped crying, but I didn't know what else to do. And there was no one in our environment to whom I could turn. The church counselors were his friends. There was no one. I couldn't talk to his parents or mine. It was terrible.

DOBSON: Sue, that says so much about your character . . . about who you are. Your primary concern was for his reputation, even when your own pain took you to the threshold of suicide. You had every right to seek counsel from someone!

SUE: Yes, but I was afraid that whoever I talked to would come back to the school and then his reputation would be ruined.

DOBSON: Well, that shows the extent of your courage. But I would not have advised it.

SUE: I did call his mother a few times that spring, but my husband said, "Don't you ever talk to Mom about this again." So I honored his orders. I said I would not.

DOBSON: Jean, what mistakes did you make during the time of crisis?

JEAN: I was angry and my ego was hurt and I handled it terribly. There were many confrontations and demands that the affairs stop. But it was all wrong. After Maury and I became Christians (we were baptized holding hands), our marriage stabilized and there was a long period of time, maybe fifteen years or so, before there was any other instance of infidelity. I always thought it would never happen again, you know, because he was so sorry. We would talk about his unfaithfulness, and he would be so sorry. Usually, he would only get in trouble during times when his career was at a really low point. I felt I understood why he did it. I didn't like it, but

I understood him; I concluded that he was a man who wasn't very verbal, and he couldn't talk about the pain he felt about his career and where he fit into the world.

SUE: My ex-husband had that problem too.

JEAN: So I felt that he went and looked for another woman to kind of give him a little boost.

SUE: That's exactly my experience too. My husband could be open with me when he was emotionally up, but in those low times he needed to go find someone else to get high with, I think, because he was so nonverbal and it was very hard for him to open up.

DOBSON: Mike, looking back on your trials, what mistakes did you make?

MIKE: Well, finally when I found out about the affair, it did not come as a surprise. I confronted my wife and she denied it. Then I got in touch with the wife of the man that she was involved with, and it was confirmed.

DOBSON: How did you react?

MIKE: I waited six days before confronting her. Then I said that I knew what she had told me the previous week had not been true.

DOBSON: Why did you wait so long to confront her?

MIKE: A friend advised me not to react the night I got the news. He told me to think it over and seek God's guidance about how I should deal with the problem. It's probably the best advice I got. I'm convinced that that is the best thing I could have done because I got myself ready to accept and face whatever I needed to deal with, realizing I loved her. But my mistake was in not recognizing sooner what was going on. When I would say, "I love you," and I did not get a loving response back, that should have been my clue. I should have asked her if she loved me.

DOBSON: If she wouldn't admit her involvement when she was knee deep in an affair, would she have confessed no matter what you said or did?

MIKE: At one point she might have. I remember I told her I loved her, and she looked at me and said, "Mike, you have a very confused wife." I dropped the subject. I felt like she didn't want to talk about it, but I should have pursued it with her.

JEAN: It is hard to know what would be helpful.

MIKE: That's it. You question everything.

Note the next comment. It is significant to our discussion.

SUE: Another mistake I made was in not knowing how to confront. I now think I understand what might have been a better approach. My sister went through a similar experience. Neither she nor her husband was a Christian. She had been very soft-spoken and passive, but she became stronger overnight. She asked her husband to move out and get an apartment, which he did. Within a year he decided his family was most important and he came home. I looked at that and wished I could have found a biblical basis to do something similar.

DOBSON: Sue, I have seen that happen more times than I can count, where loving toughness and confrontation brought responsibility in marriage in the same way that they do between a parent and a child or in any other relationship in life. There is a place in marriage for one partner to say to the other, "Rick, I love you. We married one another of our own free will; no one forced us to become husband and wife. We dedicated ourselves to one another exclusively, and it must continue to be that way. If you can't be faithful to me for life, then I'd rather separate right now. I cannot be one of many lovers. It must be all or nothing. If you choose to leave me I will be severely hurt, because my love for you is very deep. Let me say it one more time so you will understand exactly how I feel. I want you as my husband more than anything in the world, and if you can pledge yourself to me for the rest of our lives together, I'll do my best to forgive and forget. But if not, then there's no better time than right now for you to leave with one of your girlfriends." Do you understand the wisdom of a firm stance like that? Does it make sense to you?

JEAN: Oh, yes, I understand it now. At one point toward the latter years of our marriage, Maury got involved with yet another woman that he didn't tell me about. She called our home and I found out they were meeting. I was a stronger person at that time than I was when I was younger, and I said to Maury, "All right, I will give you a divorce, and you can pursue the relationship." He said, "No, I don't want you to divorce me; I just want some freedom to see where this relationship is going." I said, "No, that won't work. If you go with this woman, I will divorce you." He said, "I don't want that," and he cut off the relationship.

DOBSON: That is precisely my point. If when you were younger, you had been able to apply that kind of toughness after the first act of unfaithfulness, instead of years later when the damage had been done, you might have saved your marriage.

MIKE: Later on I realized that I should have been tougher. But I struggled with guilt for a long time. My father-in-law is a minister and I love him very dearly, but he contributed to my self-condemnation. He wanted so badly to see the marriage continue because of his own pain. He wrote to me listing all the Scriptures that said divorce was wrong. I agreed, but I had no choice in the matter! I eventually saw that it wasn't my fault.

SUE: Oh, I felt so guilty, too. I felt that maybe it was all my fault, and if I had been a better wife, he wouldn't have looked somewhere else. If I had been more understanding, if I had been more perceptive—all of these things. So I forgave him time after time. I have to say I still feel married; I feel like a married single. I don't know whether time will dispel that or not.

DOBSON: Did all of you deal with bitterness?

MARY ANN: Oh, definitely.

SUE: I was bitter initially, but I forgave immediately. Then James got involved again. So I thought, okay, if I am like Christ and absolutely sacrificial in my love, perhaps that will be attractive to him. But it wasn't. I mean I can say I was absolutely sacrificial for six years!

DOBSON: Let me ask an important question. It has been my observation in dealing with people who have been through what you have experienced that the unfaithful partner typically tries to expunge his guilt by refusing the blame. He tells his spouse that their marriage should never have occurred . . . that he didn't love her even in the beginning . . . that the divorce is really an act of kindness . . . that it wouldn't have happened if his spouse hadn't caused the problems . . . that their breakup is actually in the best interest of the kids . . . and that God Himself has approved of the divorce. Did your partners give you these phony messages?

SUE: Oh, all of them, especially the one about God's approval. My ex-husband's present wife, the one with whom he had an affair, is also a Christian college teacher. I felt the Lord wanted me to go to her and ask her forgiveness for my bad attitude. She had been my friend for twenty years, and it was extremely difficult to approach her, but I did and I told her I had forgiven her for what had happened. She then told me that she and my ex-husband had prayed about their marriage and received assurance from God that it was right.

DOBSON: That is the ultimate rationalization. It makes blatant sin sound sanctified, but only for a time. A day of accountability is coming.

SUE: Yes, I suggested to my friend that she look a little closer at what the Scripture says about keeping the marriage bed undefiled, and other passages. She said, "Oh, no, I don't believe in reading the Bible too closely because it is subject to so many *interpretations.*"

JEAN: The real crusher is when your unfaithful husband says, "But I really love you, I really do. This affair is something that has happened outside of our relationship. It is irrelevant. We still love one another and shouldn't let this problem affect us." You feel at times like you are almost going insane because these contradictory messages are given back to back.

SUE: That is what caused me to have a serious breakdown.

DOBSON: You said you were suicidal, Sue. Were you, Mary Ann?

MARY ANN: Yes, I was.

DOBSON: Did anybody else think of suicide?

MIKE: Yes.

SUE: I had been a Christian since I was a preschooler, but I still was suicidal when all of this happened. My husband said, "You think God is so great; why isn't He helping you?" I had sense enough to say that I knew He would if I could let Him, but I was hurting so badly I couldn't stop shouting. I later read a book by C. S. Lewis called *A Grief Observed*, and he experienced the same inability to accept God's grace when he went through the death of his wife. That really ministered to me. A number of books have helped me.

JEAN: Can I tell you something wonderful that happened to me? During my period of suicidal tendencies, my older daughter died from a terminal illness. She left a supply of her medication, and I looked at those pills and knew there were enough to take my life. I was at the end of my rope, and I was counting the pills when the phone rang. It was a friend who offered to come over. I didn't want to see him and said I wouldn't let him in. He asked what he could do for me, and I said, "Nothing, there is no reason to go any further." He talked to me and prayed with me, but you know, I was so distressed that I couldn't hear him. I couldn't even hear the Scripture he read. After I hung up the phone, he began calling different people, some who knew me and some who didn't. Those people called me all night long. They either prayed with me or just talked with me every hour. That's how I got through the night. . . .

MIKE: That is wonderful!

JEAN: It was at the same time the worst and best night of my life.

DOBSON: In listening to the four of you share your individual pain, I am impressed again by the willingness of loving people to blame themselves for things they couldn't help. Each of you did the best you could to cope with irresponsibility and unfaithfulness in your spouses. Even though you made mistakes and were imperfect marriage partners, you were the ones who did everything you could to hold things together. Nevertheless, you blamed yourselves, felt incredible guilt, suffered low self-esteem, and even wanted to die for your failures. Doesn't that seem a bit unfair to yourselves?

SUE: Yes, but that's the way I felt. I had to work through it.

JEAN: Yes!

MIKE: I definitely felt like that. Another thing that makes you feel so terrible is that you are alone, but your unfaithful spouse is in the arms of another lover. You walk into the church you have attended for years with her, and you sit in the pew where the two of you used to worship. The building begins to close in on you, even though you are surrounded by people. You feel a kind of panic sweeping over you.

DOBSON: Mike, did you deal with bitterness?

MIKE: Oh, yes! I didn't realize just how bitter I was. That's why I couldn't talk to my boys about what was going on. They had never heard their mom or me fight, and they didn't know until the night before she left that she was leaving. Now I know why I couldn't sit down and explain everything to them. I would have conveyed my bitterness to them. Then after my wife had been gone for about four months, I knew it was time to tell the boys the whole story. I was afraid someone at church would tell them if I didn't. It needed to come from me.

DOBSON: How did they take it?

MIKE: Well, it was more difficult for the younger one. He had always turned to his mother. In fact, he had really been her favorite.

DOBSON: Did it make him bitter?

MIKE: Very bitter. It was extremely difficult to deal with. He did not know how to handle it. He went through one very, very bad year in school. But he has come to me since then and said, "I am sorry that the divorce took place, but at least it helped me get to know you." And I am glad for that.

DOBSON: Did he cry himself to sleep in the early days?

MIKE: Yes.

DOBSON: Did he bite his nails? Did he wake up in the middle of the night? Did he have an upset stomach? Did he have headaches? What were the other symptoms?

MIKE: There were headaches; there were days when he didn't feel like going to school; there were attendance problems. There were other stresses we *all* had to deal with. Finally, we talked one night and I said, "Guys, I think right now we need to recognize that we are all going through some terrible times, and so when we are down, let's just be honest and say, 'Hey, today I am in the pits. Don't bug me; just leave me alone. I really need your support today.'" The three of us learned to do this. It was amazing how, when we began to pull together, God helped us love one another and survive the crisis.

SUE: It has been eight years for my children, and my boy was a special problem. He ran away from home and got into the gay scene. It was terrible for a time. But now he's married and has two little kids. But all our children went through some depression. One of our girls had epileptic seizures until we found out it was caused by depression, and then she was able to control it. All of them are still suffering from some of these things.

DOBSON: Mary Ann, you didn't have children when all this took place, did you?

MARY ANN: No. I was married at twenty-four, but I chose not to be a mother. I never wanted to have children. I love kids, but some of my background from my own family had frightened me. Now I have two little girls with my second husband, and I love them to pieces.

DOBSON: Jean, how did your five children make it?

JEAN: My oldest daughter died just before we separated.

DOBSON: So you went through the divorce and the death at almost the same time. How did you handle that?

JEAN: I think I handled the death fine. That may sound strange, but it is a wonderful memory. My daughter had cancer of the brain, but she went into remission during the summer months—as though God gave us an unexpected gift. My husband and I were very close during that time. We supported each other well against death; we just couldn't face life. . . .

DOBSON: What happened after your daughter's death?

JEAN: He filed for divorce. Once she was gone, there was very little to hold us together.

DOBSON: What was the effect of the divorce on the rest of your kids?

JEAN: There have been lasting effects. I have a son, a fine young man who was engaged to be married to a lovely girl this past year. But three days before the wedding, they canceled their plans. They were both scared. They both came from divorced families. They love each other and are still very close; in fact, they are still engaged to be married. But they are afraid to take that step. And, of course, my other teenage son just could not handle the divorce at all. He is still having counseling and—

DOBSON: Is he bitter at his father?

JEAN: No, he is not bitter. All of my children were very protective of their father. Their father was a very fragile man, and they didn't know about any of the uglier part of our marriage. They just knew that we didn't get along and that we led rather separate lives toward the end. I think I made a big mistake, I have to say, in a moment of bitterness and certainly in poor judgment. I told the whole story about the affair to my oldest daughter who is twenty-eight. It only made her angry at me.

DOBSON: At you?

JEAN: At me. She did not want to hear that. She didn't want her boat rocked, you know, and it has taken us a long time to mend.

SUE: My son blamed me at first, but he sees now that it wasn't my fault. The girls were very shocked, but they supported me.

MARY ANN: I was the child of a broken marriage where infidelity had occurred. My mother tried to get my support by putting my father down and telling me some truths that were too painful for me to receive. I immediately went to my father's side.

JEAN: It is awful to place immature children in that vise!

SUE: That's why I always sought ways to honor their father and tried to figure out ways to do that. I admit it was difficult at times.

MIKE: My younger son finally said, "You know, if mom is going to get back into the proper relationship with God, it may only come through my brother or me."

SUE: Yes, my girls have said the same thing.

DOBSON: Each of you has talked about feeling bitterness, guilt, low self-esteem, and other negative emotions. It is surprising, though, that very little has been said about anger. Mary Ann, did you harbor a great deal of hostility over your husband's unfaithfulness?

MARY ANN: Well, as a Christian I didn't feel that anger was right, so I wanted to suppress it as long as I possibly could until my husband finally asked me to leave. And I said, "God, could this really be your will, having him ask me to leave again?" I mean, I'm a glutton for punishment, obviously, but I wanted to know for sure.

DOBSON: Now let's get it straight. Your husband was having multiple affairs with his beach friends. He was unemployed, not even looking for a job. You were paying the bills and bailing him out of jail and getting calls from his girlfriends. Yet he asked *you* to get out!

MARY ANN: That's right. When he asked me to leave the first time, I remember just running out of the house in tears. I had no place to go. I didn't care if I lived or died. I was extremely angry at God. I'll never forget shaking my fist at Him and saying, "God! You said in Your Word that You would work all things together for those who love You and are called according to Your purpose, and I love You! But this is *not* good in my life and I can't stand it!"

DOBSON: And so your anger was directed not at your husband but at God?

MARY ANN: That's right. I realize now when I look back that most of us have to deal with anger in some way. I did it in my closet, so to speak.

DOBSON: You didn't tell anybody?

MARY ANN: No one. Not even my parents.

DOBSON: How do you think God received your anger at that time?

MARY ANN: Very lovingly. He wrapped His arms around me and let me cry and express my anger like a child.

DOBSON: I'm sure He did, Mary Ann. He saw you as a frightened little girl who'd been terribly hurt. You thought you had found a man to love you and go through life with, but suddenly you were thrown out into the night with no place to go and no one even to talk to. The loving God we serve must have felt immeasurable compassion and tenderness toward you at that moment.

MARY ANN: I know He did. The verse that He gave me was in Psalm 30:5. "Weeping comes in the evening but joy comes in the morning." I would have never known the extent of God's love if I had not gone through this trial.

DOBSON: As a matter of fact, you told me God wrote you a love letter at that time.

MARY ANN: Yes, he directed me to a second passage in Isaiah 54 that became His love letter to me. I was angry at God, not only because of the pain He permitted me to experience, but because I was embarrassed in front of my students. They knew I was a Christian, and yet I had to admit to them that I had gotten a divorce. I wanted to run—to escape to Australia or somewhere. Then the Lord assured me that it was His reputation at stake, and He would take care of it. He then gave me this beautiful passage of Scripture.

> "Do not be afraid; you will not suffer shame.
>   Do not fear disgrace; you will not be humiliated.
> You will forget the shame of your youth
>   and remember no more the reproach of your widowhood.
> For your Maker is your husband—
>   the LORD Almighty is his name—
> the Holy One of Israel is your Redeemer;
>   he is called the God of all the earth.
> The LORD will call you back
>   as if you were a wife deserted and distressed in spirit—
>   a wife who married young,
>   only to be rejected," says your God.
> "For a brief moment I abandoned you,
>   but with deep compassion I will bring you back.
> In a surge of anger
> I hid my face from you for a moment,
>   but with everlasting kindness
> I will have compassion on you,"
>   says the Lord your Redeemer.
>
> Isaiah 54:4–8, NIV

That Scripture was so relevant to my need that it could easily have begun with the words, "Dear Mary Ann." I was that young and rejected wife who felt forsaken by God. But He gathered me and embraced me in His everlasting love.

DOBSON: That is beautiful, Mary Ann. Do you still believe all things work together for good to them that love God?

MARY ANN: Oh, yes!

DOBSON: Even for those whose spouses get into affairs?

MARY ANN: You know, I can say this honestly. If I had to do it over again I'd do it the same way, because I love who I am today. When I was rejected and left alone, I was able to love myself for the very first time because I knew I was loved by God.

SUE: I had a pastor say to me, "How can you stand all of this?" And I said, "Because I really like myself. I know what I am in God's sight." And that was the thing that sustained me!

JEAN: No one wants to suffer and have her foundations crumble, but God made me strong through these things. He held me and let me grow in strength, and you know, I've lost a child—had a lot of tragedy in our family. I've had a breakdown, I've had a divorce, I've had a suicidal child, but God has been there as my rock.

SUE: That's exactly the way I feel. It's been eight years and I still have to lean on the Lord. All I can say is, "I am content in my circumstances this day." I had a friend who said, "But I don't have the gift of celibacy." I just laughed. To someone who's been married twenty years, that was hilarious. Who *does* have the gift of celibacy? But God is giving me the grace to cope with single parenting and all the other stresses. You know, I wasn't cut out for this role. I'm not a good president; I'm a good vice president, a helper. But my family is doing fine and I'm in one piece. I don't understand the tragedy in my life, but I'm stronger than I would have been without it.

MIKE: I went through a divorce the same year I was demoted in my work. I had been a counselor in a junior high school for fifteen years. Then my job was eliminated at the end of that term, and I was sent back to the classroom. That was embarrassing. Suddenly, every prop that we call "success" was literally knocked out from under me, and my trust for the first time had to be totally on the Lord. I had trusted Him before, but now I was powerless to do anything else. Like the rest of you, I became a very strong person during this time of challenge. I continue to be amazed at how much God loves us and seeks us out wherever we are.

JEAN: You know, my children are proud of me, too. All of my married life I was a homemaker. I never felt I had a choice to have a career. I was a wife and a mother and that was my role in life. When the divorce occurred, I had never worked a day outside the home. I didn't have any skills or any great talent. I didn't have a college education! But I took hold and God kept saying, "You can do it! You can do it!" It looked impossible. I didn't know how to get a job or how to support myself. I didn't even know how to balance the checkbook. But God was there, and I'm proud of what I've accomplished. He let me be a bigger person than I used to be.

DOBSON: I'm sure the four of you realize you are talking to many people by means of radio today who are going through the agony you experienced in the past. Someone is listening who has recently discovered that a beloved husband or wife is involved in an affair. That person feels like life is over, but what you're saying is, "You can make it, and even though it feels like God is unconcerned, He really does care!"

JEAN: That's why I accepted your invitation to be here today. I wanted to help someone who is suffering the way I did.

DOBSON: You have all done that during these broadcasts, and I've learned to love each of you through our conversations. On behalf of our listeners, I thank you for opening these old wounds and letting us feel your pain. Your faith and courage have been an inspiration to us all.

CHAPTER ELEVEN

Discussion of the Dialogue

I'M SURE THE READER WAS IMPRESSED, AS WAS I, BY the ability of Mary Ann, Sue, Jean, and Mike to articulate their experiences and feelings. I respect each of them highly and have profited from their insights and observations. Nevertheless, it is surprising to me that these four intelligent people still have very little comprehension of the forces that destroyed their marriages (although I have seen the same "blindness" in many others who have faced similar circumstances.)

A key ingredient in the erosion of their homes was a kind of marital permissiveness which proved to be fatal. Upon learning that their spouses were involved in affairs, their instinctive reaction was to understand, to explain, to forgive, or to ignore the adultery occurring under their noses. These good people were motivated by committed love in its purest form, and I admire them for their compassion under the most awful pressure. Nevertheless, they each found "excuses" for the unfaithfulness of their partners, which permitted the disloyal behavior to continue unchecked.

A key ingredient in the erosion of their homes was a kind of marital permissiveness.

Mary Ann felt she was too righteous, saying, "I was so spiritually dogmatic that my husband *had* to be the way he was." Sue blamed James's infidelity on her own sexual unresponsiveness. (May I ask, who wouldn't be cooled off by his "cruel and rough" treatment?) Jean attributed one of Maury's affairs to her illness. Mike thought his wife's car wreck was the key factor. Then they agreed that business reverses, low self-esteem, and communicative problems were instrumental. Perhaps they are right—perhaps there were mitigating circumstances in each case. But no one labeled the behavior for what it was: selfishness and sin!

Therein lies a fundamental problem. These loving, gracious people inadvertently shielded their wayward spouses from the consequences of infidelity. If there is *anything* that an adulterer does not need, it is a guilt-ridden mate who understands his indiscretion and assumes the blame for it. Such a person needs to be called to *accountability,* not excused by rationalization! That's why being married to a tolerant, compassionate husband or wife who instantly forgives and forgets can give an infidel a one-way ticket to hell! And I mean that literally.

> *If there is* anything *that an adulterer does not need, it is a guilt-ridden mate.*

I want to be careful not to imply condemnation and criticism of the four members of our discussion group. They are admirable people who are made out of better stuff than I am. I sat in awe as I observed the tenacity with which they faced their problems. I ached for each of them as they groped to explain what had gone wrong, and how the blame somehow always managed to bounce back in their faces. But I disagreed with many of their conclusions, and in fact, believe their early tolerance played a role in the divorces that subsequently occurred.

Not only did these four victims (they dislike that name, but I don't know how else to label them) fail to confront their spouses with loving toughness, but they also shielded them from emotional pain. That is unfortunate. Just as a rebellious preschooler can profit from a well-timed spanking, the psychological consequences of sinful behavior should be experienced by the guilty. There's nothing quite like a dose of reality to awaken a dreamer from his fantasies. Nevertheless, the four infidels were protected from those important consequences.

The psychological consequences of sinful behavior should be experienced by the guilty.

Remember that each of the victims diligently concealed the truth to preserve his or her partner's reputation. Though each case must be considered individually, especially where children are concerned, the degree of secrecy maintained in those instances seems unwarranted to me. It was almost masochistic of Sue and Mary Ann to tell *no one*, not a living soul, about the agony they were suffering in silence. Mike and Jean guarded their secrets as well. All four of them were taken to the brink of suicide.

Because of this concealment, other natural consequences of infidelity were avoided. The adulterer was under no gentle pressure from fellow Christians who would have reinforced responsible behavior; none of the offenders had to justify his conduct to his older children; none was asked to move into new and inconvenient living quarters; none, apparently, was denied sexual privileges from the rejected spouse (Sue even became warmer at the time of disclosure and immediately asked for forgiveness); none had to pay a marriage counselor; none had to support a lawyer (or two of them); none faced the financial pressures of maintaining two residences; and, alas, none had to look himself in the mirror each morning and ask, "Why does everyone seem to think it's *my* fault?"

Under the circumstances, we should not be surprised that the affairs involving the three husbands continued through the years. (Mike's wife was in a different situation, but she still needed discovery and confrontation.) It should have been expected. The lure of infidelity is an *addiction* to an individual who has a chink in his moral armor. While some people are chemically dependent on alcohol or heroin or cocaine, this kind of infidel is hooked on illicit sex. Psychologically, he needs the thrill of the chase, the clandestine meetings, the forbidden fruit, the flattery, the sexual conquest, the proof of manhood or womanhood, and in some cases, the discovery. And like the drug abuser, he is constantly attempting to reform. He promises with sincerity never again to yield to his habit. But unless his entire social milieu acts to support that commitment, he is likely to forget it. In the case of the husbands of our three female guests, they were cradled in a forgiving and protective environment that encouraged and supported their folly. What they needed were wives who were committed to the concept that *love must be tough*.

The lure of infidelity is an addiction to an individual who has a chink in his moral armor.

There are other lessons to be learned from the experiences of the dialogue participants. Let's return to a question-and-answer format which will permit us to tease out those kernels of understanding.

Q. How can you say that the four victims of affairs failed to confront their unfaithful partners, when it is obvious from the dialogue that they had some incredible battles? Mary Ann described those conflicts as "horrible." Jean said she handled them "terribly," making many demands that Maury stop his infidelity. Isn't that what you mean by *confronting* the problem?

A. Unfortunately, it is not. Simply becoming angry and throwing temper tantrums is no more effective with a spouse than it is with a rebellious teenager. Screaming and accusing and berating are rarely successful in changing the behavior of human beings of *any* age. What is required is a course of action—an ultimatum that demands a specific response and results in a consequence. That is what didn't occur in the four homes we've heard described. None of the victims recognized the difference between expressions of anger and loving toughness. It is a common misunderstanding.

Q. I'm interested in Sue's comment that by tolerating her husband's infidelity, she permitted her children to have their father for six more years. At face value, that would imply that a victim of an affair should hold it all inside for the sake of the kids. This is different from your advice, of course. But what would you say to Sue? She *did* give her children their father for six more valuable years.

A. Again, I want to be gentle to Sue whom I admire greatly. Nevertheless, I feel her perspective was shortsighted. In the process of giving her children their father for a while longer, she also gave them a severely depressed, suicidal mother, and eventually, a family breakup. Her children continue to suffer today, as she indicated. Perhaps—perhaps if she had been tougher when the first affair occurred, she might have given the children their father for a lifetime. We'll never know, of course, but it could have happened.

Q. Sue also said she would have separated from her unfaithful husband if she could have found a biblical basis to do so. Since you have recommended separation in response to some instances of infidelity, I wonder what scriptural support you have for that position.

A. At the end of this chapter I have provided a theological understanding of divorce and remarriage, as quoted from the writings of Dr. Chuck Swindoll. He refers to a passage in Matthew wherein Jesus made an exception to the permanence of the marital bond in instances of infidelity: "And I say to you, whoever divorces his wife, except for immorality, and marries another woman commits adultery" (19:9, RSV). I will leave it to Dr. Swindoll to explain that understanding. For our purposes here, let's accept it as stated, that is, divorce is permissible (but not mandatory) in instances of continued, unrepented, flagrant infidelity. If that is true, then a *separation* that is intended not to kill the marriage but to rescue it must also be lawful. If a person has biblical grounds for divorce, he certainly would not be judged guilty for attempting to salvage the relationship through a painful process of separation. In this context, I believe that living apart for a period of time can clear the air for some families and permit the healing process to begin, especially where one partner is desperately in need of accountability. On the other hand, separation can destroy a marriage if done for the wrong reasons and in the wrong spirit.

Q. What about separation for reasons other than infidelity?

A. Again, I find no biblical prohibition against couples living apart for a time, if their purpose is not to seek divorce and remarriage. As implied above, husbands and wives often trample on one another's nerves and desperately need some time alone to reorient their outlook. From my point of view, the rightness or wrongness of their separation depends entirely on *intent*, which only God can judge. For example, a wife whose alcoholic husband needs to experience life without the support of his family may find temporary separation to be the only method of forcing him to seek professional help. This crisis of loneliness may be the last hope to jar the man to his senses, and his wife could be doing a loving thing by making him more miserable! If this is the desire that motivates the more responsible partner to separate, then I find no scriptural condemnation of it. But please be warned! This understanding can also provide an open door to rationalization for those who are unhappy in marriage and are seeking an easy way out. I am certainly not sanctioning that maneuver.

Q. Since almost every couple fights from time to time, what distinguishes a *healthy* marriage in conflict from one that is in serious trouble? I'm asking how a husband and wife can know when their interpersonal struggles are within normal limits and when they are symptoms of more ominous problems.

A. It is true that conflict occurs in virtually all marriages. That is how resentment and frustration are ventilated. The difference between stable families and those in serious trouble reflects what the battles accomplish. In healthy relationships, a period of confrontation ends in forgiveness—in drawing together—in deeper respect and understanding—and sometimes in sexual satisfaction. But in unstable marriages a period of conflict produces greater pain and anger that persists until the next fight. When that occurs, one unresolved issue is compounded by another and another. That accumulation of resentment is an ominous circumstance in any marriage. Isn't this why the Apostle Paul admonished us not to let the sun go down on our wrath (Eph. 4:26)?

Q. Is it harder for a man or for a woman to recover from an affair by a spouse?

A. I have not observed any appreciable difference between the sexes at the time of disclosure. Both husbands and wives suffer incalculable anguish when a mate is unfaithful. Men do seem to have a cultural advantage after the crisis is over, however. Their work is a better diversion and their economic consequences are less severe. They also find it easier to find someone new, as a rule. But no one wins in illicit affairs of the heart.

Q. You referred above to a kind of "blindness" that occurs when a victim of an affair denies the truth. Mary Ann said she didn't notice her husband's infidelity because she didn't want to see it. I think I did the same thing when my husband was fooling around with my best friend. The affair went on for two years before I could acknowledge it to myself. But why would I deny the truth? Why do victims "choose" to be blind?

A. The psychological process is called *denial*, and it is designed to protect the mind from an unacceptable thought or reality. You see, once a person admits to himself that his beloved spouse has been unfaithful, then he is obligated to deal with that circumstance. The extremely painful experiences of grief, anxiety, and insomnia become inevitable once the truth has been faced. Furthermore, the injured person fears that a confrontation with the unfaithful partner might drive him into the arms of the new lover. Given these concerns, the unconscious mind apparently chooses not to notice the affair in the hope that it will blow over and be forgotten. Obviously, there is ample motivation for a vulnerable person to deny what his eyes tell him.

When the evidence of unfaithfulness becomes overwhelming, a man or woman will sometimes "ask" the guilty spouse to assist with the denial. This is done by making accusations in the hope of being proven wrong. For example, a wife will say, "Are you and Donna seeing one another?"

"No, I've told you a thousand times that nothing is going on," he lies.

"But where were you until 2:00 A.M. last night?"

"I had car trouble. Now will you get off my back?"

This wife knows her husband's story is phony, but she continually asks him to lie to her. And interestingly, she does not feel obligated to "blow the whistle" on him until he *admits* his involvement . . . which may never happen. These tacit agreements help her maintain the illusion that "all is well."

Denial has many applications and uses in human experience.

It will permit a woman to ignore a suspicious lump in her breast, or the drugs in her son's bedroom, or the debt that the family is accumulating. Through this process the mind is protected for a time, but it often permits even greater disasters to gain a foothold in our lives.

Q. How should a person respond to someone who is in denial? I have a very good friend whose wife is cheating on him, but he chooses not to see it. Should I make him face reality?

A. I am uncomfortable in giving a blanket answer to that question, in view of all the thousands of specific situations to which it could be applied. There *are* times when denial is the only link to sanity or stability, and that must be preserved. On other occasions, it can be a loving thing to break the bubble of illusion. Either way, it is risky to awaken a dreamer, as Jean discovered when she tried to inform her daughter of her father's misbehavior. The girl couldn't accept what she was hearing. If the need for denial is intense, the individual will often lash out at the one who threatens its validity.

Q. What surprises me most about the dialogue we've heard is that all four of the unfaithful spouses called themselves Christians. In fact, Jean's husband was a career churchman and a teacher in a Christian college, and Sue's husband was chairman of a "moral action committee." These were seasoned believers—not merely babes in Christ. How could they cheat on their spouses? What goes on in the mind of someone who violates his own standard of morality in so blatant a manner?

A. Like you, I'm amazed at the audacity of those who pursue affairs while calling themselves Christians. You talk about moral gymnastics! Such people can cite the Seventh Commandment by heart ("Thou shalt not commit adultery"), and they fully understand God's promise to punish sinful behavior, yet somehow they expect to break His laws with impunity! Not only is their behavior forbidden by God, but it's also in violation of every moral code in the civilized world. If that isn't heavy enough, an unfaithful spouse has to deal with the responsibility for crushing his or her wife or husband, and for warping the children of their union— those innocent and unsuspecting kids who are about to be shredded by one parent's selfishness and shame. All told, it's enough to cool off some of the most passionate playboys and playgirls. In fact, millions have come right to the door of an affair, and, having seen what lies just over the threshold, have retreated to the arms of a relieved spouse.

Q. It would appear to me that more Christians are involved in divorces now than ever before, and that disturbs me. Some are saying that the Bible has been misunderstood on this subject and that there *is* justification for the dissolution of marriage within Scripture. Do you agree with these reinterpretations?

A. Like you, I am aware of a loosening attitude toward divorce and remarriage within Christian circles and by religious leaders. There has always been pressure on those in positions of authority to "modernize" the Bible and make it seem to endorse the behaviors that make us feel guilty. But any attempt to tamper with eternal truths makes me very uneasy. For example, a recent publication by an evangelical theologian completely reversed the meaning of Jesus' teachings by providing readers with a complicated mumbo jumbo about context and background. Lo and behold, it turns out that Jesus didn't mean it when He said, "I tell you that anyone who divorces his wife, except for marital unfaithfulness, and marries another woman commits adultery" (Matt. 19:9, NIV). This statement would have been much easier to explain away if Jesus hadn't been so explicit in His response!

Returning to your question, I do not want to sound uncharitable or dogmatic in response to the views of fellow Christians. But I admit I am concerned by what appears to be an effort to squeeze the Bible into a twenty-first century mold. It just won't fit!

Q. What, then, is *your* theological position on the subject of divorce? Is remarriage ever permissible for Christians?

A. Although it is evident that I have very strong personal convictions on that subject, I recognize my inadequacies to answer your question as a biblical authority. I am not a theologian and I prefer to quote a writer who is. Therefore, I have chosen to respond to your question by quoting what my good friend Dr. Chuck Swindoll had to say in his book *Strike the Original Match*. I agree with the explanation he has offered therein. For purposes of brevity, I have omitted sections of his discussion and urge the reader to consult Dr. Swindoll's book for further extrapolation and biblical support.

DIVORCE AND REMARRIAGE: A CONTROVERSIAL SUBJECT

I'm convinced that there is no way any group of Christians picked at random would ever come to unanimity on the subject [of divorce and remarriage]. I'll go further. I don't believe a busload of American evangelical theologians would be in unanimous agreement on divorce and remarriage even if they toured the United States an entire summer! It's a controversial issue, for sure. Therefore, no matter what I may conclude, I am confident some very reliable, competent, and equally sincere people will disagree. So save your cards and letters!

The question everyone wants answered is this: When is divorce permissible? Because of limited time and space, I will spare you a lot of verbiage and supportive quotations. Suffice it to say, I will answer the question with remarriage in mind. In other words, my answers assume that we are really asking, "Are there any biblical grounds for remarriage?"

I believe there are. I have searched the Scriptures, read everything I can get my hands on, and discussed this issue with my wife, my friends, fellow staff, church board members, pastors, many theological professors, and other serious students of the Bible. I have talked with numerous divorced people, single persons, married couples, publishers, authors on the subject, and authorities in the field—both Christian and non-Christian. Here are my conclusions, simplified for the sake of clarity.

I believe the Christian has biblical grounds for remarriage when the divorce transpired under one of the three situations described as follows:

1. *When the marriage and divorce occurred prior to salvation.*

In 2 Corinthians 5:17 we read these words: "Therefore if any man is in Christ, he is a new creature; the old things passed away; behold, new things have come."

I take this literally. I even take it to the extreme! I think "new" means "new" . . . so when God promises the believing sinner that he is "a new creature," then I take that to mean exactly that. A brand new, fresh creation. Unlike before. When God promises the passing away of "old things," it surely includes divorce prior to salvation. After all, being alienated from God and at enmity with Him, how could any unbeliever possibly know His will regarding the choice of a lifetime mate? Having thought through this very carefully, I believe it falls within the context of God's superabundant grace to wipe our slate clean when we turn, by faith, to Christ the Lord.

When the marriage and divorce occurred prior to salvation, I believe God grants His "new creation" the freedom to remarry.

2. *When one's mate is guilty of sexual immorality and is unwilling to repent and live faithfully with the marriage partner.*

Much has been written on this particular issue, I realize. I repeat, I have read everything I can get my hands on, so I do not write these words hurriedly or superficially. I am fully aware of the difficulties connected with determining who is really the guilty party when it comes to sexual promiscuity. I also acknowledge the subjectivity involved in identifying "sexual immorality." Such matters must be carefully determined, usually with the help of a qualified counselor who can provide objectivity and wisdom in matters this serious. Each case must be considered independently.

Nevertheless, we cannot ignore or deny what Christ said in Matthew 19:9: "And I say to you, whoever divorces his wife, except for immorality, and marries another woman commits adultery."

All sorts of interpretations have been suggested to explain what our Lord was saying. Frankly, having examined every one of the suggestions and theories (some of them are incredibly forced and complicated), I return to the verse and accept it at face value.

Throughout my Christian life I have operated under a very simple—yet reliable—principle of interpretation: If the normal sense makes good sense, seek no other sense. Let's do that here.

When a spouse is guilty of immoral sexual conduct with another person and is unwilling to remain faithful to the innocent partner, the option is there for the faithful mate to divorce and remarry.

Before moving on to the third reason, let me ask you to reread that last sentence. I want to amplify it for a few moments. Two thoughts need to be emphasized. First, this is not simply a case of quickie sex on the sly—a one-time-only experience. This is *porneia*. I take this to mean an immorality that suggests a sustained unwillingness to remain faithful. I hesitate to use the term lest I be misinterpreted—but I think of the idea of an immoral lifestyle, an obvious determination to practice a promiscuous relationship outside the bonds of marriage.

Second, the faithful mate has the option to leave . . . but such is not mandatory. I have seen numerous marriages rebuilt rather than ended because the faithful partner had no inner peace pursuing a divorce. How much better to look for ways to make the marriage work rather than anxiously anticipate evidence that is needed to break off the relationship. But there are occasions when every attempt has been made to keep the marriage together . . . but sustained sexual infidelity won't allow it. It is in such cases our Lord grants freedom from that miserable and unbearable bond.

3. *When one of the mates is an unbeliever and willfully and permanently deserts the believing partner.*

You probably don't need to be told that all sorts of suggestions have been made by sincere and qualified students of Scripture to explain what constitutes desertion . . . and to spell out what "not under bondage" really means. Because I promised to spare you numerous quotations and tedious pages of verbiage, I'll not attempt to represent all the opinions that range from unbelievably conservative to downright crazy (in my opinion!). But perhaps a word of caution is needed.

When we read of the departure of the unbelieving partner, obviously Paul is not referring to a temporary, quick decision to chuck it all and bail out . . . only to return in a little while. No, leaving means leaving. Permanence is definitely in mind. It implies a determined and willful decision that results in leaving the relationship with no desire to return, no interest in cultivating that home, no plan to bear the responsibilities, and no commitment to the vows once taken. That's "leaving." And the one being left has little doubt in such cases. The marriage is over. Finished. Ended.

A *Summary and a Warning*

I agree with John R. W. Stott: [Divorce was] a divine concession to human weaknesses.* No Christian should aggressively seek the disso-

*John R. W. Stott, *Christian Counter-Culture* (Downers Grove, IL: Intervarsity Press, 1978), p. 95

lution of his or her marriage bond. Some of the very best things God has to teach His children are learned while working through marital difficulties.

Endless stories could be told of how God honored the perseverance of abused and ignored partners as they refused to give up.

But in certain extreme cases, against the wishes and efforts of the committed mate, the marriage bond is destroyed beyond any human ability to restore it. Scripture teaches that God's "divine concession to human weakness" is occasionally justified, allowing the Christian divorced person the right and freedom to remarry in the Lord.

Before closing the chapter, a warning must be sounded. Being human and sinful and weak, we are all equipped with a remarkable ability to rationalize. Unless we consciously guard against it, when we experience marital difficulties, we'll begin to search for a way out instead of a way through. Given sufficient time in the crucible, divorce will seem our only option, our long-awaited and much-deserved utopia. And we will begin to push in that direction, at times ignoring the inner voice of God's Spirit and at other times violating the written principles of God's Word. Either is a grievous act.

I warn all of us against such thought and actions. To carry out that carnal procedure is to short-circuit the better plan God has arranged for His people and, worse than that, is to twist the glorious grace of God into a guilt-relieving excuse for giving us what we have devised instead of accepting what He has designed.

Where God permits divorce and remarriage, humbly let us accept it without fear or guilt. Let us not call "unclean" what He now calls clean. But neither let us put words in His mouth and make Him say what He, in fact, has not said. No matter how miserable we may be.

There is something much worse than living with a mate in disharmony. It's living with God in disobedience.*

---

*Taken from the book *Strike the Original Match* by Charles R. Swindoll, copyright © 1980 by Multnomah Press, Portland, Oregon 97266. Used by permission.

CHAPTER TWELVE

Anatomy of Adultery

BECAUSE THE PREVIOUS CHAPTERS, AND PERHAPS THE entire book, have left the impression that infidelity is typically committed by self-centered males who betray their devoted wives, I feel I should present the other side of that coin. At least one secular poll reportedly found that among those under twenty-nine years of age, "significantly more married women are having affairs than married men." The same study also indicated that teenage girls lose their virginity earlier than boys, on the average. I have no way of assessing the accuracy of those conclusions, but I do know that sexual experimentation among women is becoming increasingly common today. It is apparent in the world around us.

Shirley and I used to enjoy jogging in the park near our home during early morning hours. Every day we noticed two cars parked side by side in a remote section of the lot, with one car empty and two people sitting close together in the other. The windows were always very steamy. It didn't take a detective to figure out what was going on. We surmised that these secret lovers had made their spouses think they were at work instead of kissing and cuddling in the park. Somewhere near my home are two unidentified families, and perhaps two sets of children, that unknowingly await the tragic moment of disclosure.

It has been my observation that when wives engage in extramarital sexual activity, a unique pattern of circumstances often precedes it.

Women are much less likely to be involved in the multiple, casual relationships that characterized the men described in chapter 10. Instead, unfaithful women often take the pathway pursued by Mike's wife. A vulnerable lady may find herself involved in an entanglement which she neither sought nor expected. It just seemed to "happen" when she and another needy person were thrown together at the right (or wrong) time. Yet the consequences of unexpected disloyalty are just as deadly as infidelity in the first degree.

To brace my female readers against this deceptive sin, and to help their husbands avoid the precipitating circumstances, let me describe what I have called an "anatomy of adultery." It reflects the most common pathway to *female* indiscretion (though not the only one), and it can be divided into eleven distinct stages or steps. I wrote it after counseling yet another family in the throes of divorce.

ANATOMY OF ADULTERY

Wife's Perspective	*Husband's Perspective*
STAGE ONE	
The wife is in a state of emotional need. She is lonely, suffers from low self-esteem, and has had difficulty making female friends. She reaches for the romantic involvement of her husband but he fails to notice. She resorts to nagging and complaining, which puts a greater wedge between them.	The husband has made business commitments that he must meet. He's in a highly competitive and satisfying position, and his emotional energies are drained by the time he comes home. He loves his wife but doesn't have much time to "carry her," psychologically.

Wife's Perspective	*Husband's Perspective*
STAGE TWO	
She experiences greater frustration and depression, which gradually give way to anger. She begins to "bludgeon" her bewildered husband for his failures in the home.	He makes some feeble attempts to relate to his wife, especially after emotional explosions have occurred between them. But this leopard finds it difficult to change his spots. He is still overcommitted at work, whether he likes it or not, and he constantly falls back into familiar patterns.
STAGE THREE	
This needy woman is now in a dangerous position. She is vulnerable to any attractive, available man who comes into her life. Inevitably, it seems, such an encounter occurs. A casual introduction to a flirtatious man sets the wheels in motion, and he quickly becomes the object of her fantasies, hopes, and dreams. He appears to be so compassionate compared to her husband, so much more dignified, so much more in touch with her feelings, so much more worthy of respect. Nothing illicit has occurred at this point, but she's spending a great deal of time thinking about an affair with this specific man. Jesus once said, "As a man (or woman) thinketh in his heart, so is he!" Alas, this woman is becoming an adulteress in her mind.	The husband continues in ignorance of what his wife is experiencing. His mind is elsewhere. He wishes she would be happier because he *does* love her and the kids, but he has no idea how her unhappiness relates to him.

Wife's Perspective

Husband's Perspective

STAGE FOUR

Wife's Perspective: An extramarital relationship gradually begins to heat up. It's no sudden romp in the grass. Rather, the affair grows slowly, an escalating friendship. She feels guilty, of course, but the excitement is incredible. Anyway, her husband doesn't seem to care. Finally it happens; a sexual experience occurs.

Husband's Perspective: The man of the house is still not aware of any unfaithfulness. He may notice some coolness and a lessened demand for his attention, but his suspicions are not aroused. Her hostility to him may increase during this time, but he has already become accustomed to that attitude in her.

STAGE FIVE

Wife's Perspective: More illicit sexual activity now transpires, with all the guilt, fear and raw passions that accompany this way of life. Her spiritual life rapidly deteriorates as she lies and rationalizes and lives a double standard. It is a tough assignment to play-act the role of a faithful wife when she's giving her all to someone else. Bible reading and church attendance become less frequent or even nonexistent. She loses all sexual interest in her husband.

Husband's Perspective: The man may now begin to worry about the deteriorating relationship for the first time. He doesn't yet have much evidence on which to base his suspicions, but he knows intuitively that something has changed. His reaction is still one of confusion at this stage.

STAGE SIX

Wife's Perspective: For the wife, the affair continues hot and heavy. Every minute that can be spent with her new lover is grabbed.

Husband's Perspective: Somehow discovery occurs, usually by "accident." Perhaps a tiny lie is betrayed, or an anonymous phone call is received. His first reaction is one of *utter* shock! He can't believe what has happened. He confronts his wife in one of the most emotional and unpleasant encounters in their lives.

Wife's Perspective

Husband's Perspective

STAGE SEVEN

Her feelings of guilt and embarrassment are concealed behind rationalizations and recriminations against her husband. She is going to admit nothing that she doesn't have to disclose. Depending on the quality of her husband's evidence, she may continue to lie and deny at this stage. In the other hand, some women will break emotionally, weeping profusely and begging for forgiveness. Either way, this stage is characterized by wildly fluctuating emotions from day to day.

For the first time, enormous pain is felt by the husband. Whereas he could hardly give his wife the time of day a few weeks before, his unfaithful partner suddenly becomes the *only* important thing in his life. This guy who would rather go to a football game with his male friends than be with his wife—the man who hid behind the newspaper every night after work—now finds himself pleading for her favors. He crawls. He cries. He bargains. I've known men in this fix who called me from a phone booth near a freeway where they had been driving eighty miles an hour, looking for a place to crash their cars. A pitiful sight!

STAGE EIGHT

We come now to a critical juncture. When confronted by the spiritual implications of their behavior, some women decide not to sacrifice their families, but to reconcile with their husbands. Others are determined to have their own way and go with the new lover, who is infinitely more exciting and alluring. Such a woman may pity her mate and desire not to hurt him, but she finds him boring and disdainful.

The pain experienced by the husband is intensified. He had never known such stress in his entire life. Jealousy burns through his mind as he imagines what his wife and her lover have done together. At alternating times he feels rage, guilt, remorse, love, hate, despair, etc. He makes all the mistakes described in the early chapters of this book, including appeasement, entrapment, panic, threats of violence, and self-debasement. Now *he* is dealing with the low self-esteem which his wife experienced some years ago.

Note: Since the classic pattern can go in several directions at this point, depending on the reaction of the woman, we will follow the one where her affair continues.

Wife's Perspective

STAGE NINE

It has been said, "A woman wants a man she can look up to, but one who won't look down on her." It is true. Women need to hold their husbands in a certain awe, or at least in modest respect, if their relationship is to be healthy. The Apostle Paul instructed men to *love* their wives, but he told women to *respect* their husbands. Those are the conditions needed respectively shown by each sex. Nevertheless, this woman begins to experience a tug of war in her mind. The welfare of her children weighs heavily in her thoughts, and she knows they are hurting. She sees the flaws and faults of her new lover for the first time, and the romantic dream fades just a bit. Sex with him is still exciting, but it no longer thrills her as it did. All the ugly realities of divorce stare her in the face. Is that what she wants? Still, she remembers her prior state of loneliness and low self-esteem. "I can't go back to that!" she says to herself. It is this motivation, more than any other, that may push her over the edge.

Husband's Perspective

The agitation of stage 8 continues unabated, especially as the husband contemplates the details of what his wife and her lover are experiencing together. He doesn't think he can stand it, and that sense of panic is evident in everything he does. His work suffers and his face reveals the strain he is under. Unfortunately, the behavior now being shown by the rejected lover serves to assassinate respect and put a severe strain on a relationship already stretched to the breaking point.

STAGE TEN

Wife's Perspective

The decision to divorce is made; lawyers are consulted; papers are filed; hearings are held and property is divided. The children are caught between the parents and become the object of struggle and contest. A bloody custody battle is fought with numerous casualties on both sides. Harsh words are exchanged. Tears are shed. Then they are dried; life goes on: people learn to cope. But every now and then, just before the woman goes to sleep at night or perhaps in a moment of quietness, she asks herself, "What have I done?"

Husband's Perspective

The human mind cannot tolerate agitated depression and grief indefinitely. The healthy personality will act to protect itself in time, throwing off the despair

and groping for stability. One method by which this is accomplished is by turning pain into anger. Thus, the husband may harbor a deep but quiet hostility toward his wife—the one who shattered his home, took half his money and hurt his kids. He no longer accepts the blame for what has happened, feeling instead that he was betrayed. He would not take his wife back now under any circumstances. He begins to brace himself for whatever may come.

STAGE ELEVEN

As events unfold, she weds her new lover and life is exciting for a time. But eventually, it becomes more like her first marriage. The great thrill is gone, the relationship having been "too hot not to cool down." Daily living is routine once more. The dating and laughter and the walks and talks give way to doing laundry and fixing meals and going to work. The marriage may be successful or it may not. The probabilities of another divorce are higher than for first marriages, *perhaps because both partners have demonstrated a willingness to fool*

The man gradually works his way through bitterness to a state of apathy. Life returns to normal except that his wife is gone. He will probably remarry, since divorced men are in much greater demand than divorced women in our society. He again loses himself in work and slams the door in the past. Except . . . when he thinks of the kids . . . he feels guilty.

Wife's Perspective | *Husband's Perspective*

around with married lovers! If there is no divorce, the new husband and wife plod on through the years, moving inexorably toward the Great Day of Accountability when their lives will be laid bare before their Maker. These two people have convinced themselves they did the right thing—except . . . when they think of the children . . . they feel guilty.

> But every man is tempted, when he is drawn away of his own lust, and enticed. Then when lust hath conceived, it bringeth forth sin: and sin, when it is finished, bringeth forth death.
>
> James 1:14–15, KJV

I know I've painted a very dark picture on my canvas, but it represents reality as I perceive it. Adultery is not pleasant either to read or to write about, but I feel that someone must describe the sordid side of this sin. Night after night on television we see beautiful people jumping into bed with strangers and it all looks so exciting. Popular magazines tell us that sex, lots of sex with a variety of partners, is not only healthy but everyone is doing it. Ridiculous books like *Open Marriage* make extramarital affairs sound like a tonic guaranteed to revitalize tired relationships. Alas, at times it seems like the entire world of entertainment is organized for the sole purpose of propagating that one enormous lie, and no one is effectively refuting it.

What I am about to write will sound phony but, so help me, it is true. I have secluded myself with my family to write this book, and few others know I am in this city. Nevertheless, my telephone rang immediately after I completed the paragraph above. The caller was a distressed woman asking for consultation regarding her marital problems. She told me that her husband (who claims to be a Christian believer) ran off with a young girl and is now living with her in a nearby city. There it is again—another outbreak of the epidemic that sweeps the Western world. That's why I've felt compelled to write this difficult book. Infidelity and marital conflict are cancers that gnaw on the soul of mankind, twisting and warping innocent family members who can only stand and watch.

But let the record show that the guilty suffer severely, too. God has not forbidden indiscriminate sexuality just to deprive us of fun. In His ultimate wisdom, He has attempted to protect us from the devastation of sin. Herpes and syphilis and Acquired Immune Deficiency Syndrome (AIDS) and gonorrhea are not the only consequences of unbridled passion. The greater pain is experienced in the soul of mankind. Consider the following letter from Florence.

Dear Dr. Dobson:

We heard your radio program during which you discussed the consequences of adultery. This has happened in our family, and we would like to share our story with you.

My husband has been unfaithful to me through the years, even though I had never known or wanted any other man. Finally, his loose attitude toward the marriage began to affect my commitment, and I got entangled in an affair. It lasted for nine months before my husband found out about my involvement. He has been devastated ever since.

Bill is experiencing such guilt and anger toward himself now, because he feels that this would never have happened if he had not been unfaithful. He says he has lost something more precious than gold when he lost this part of me. His emotions do strange things. First, he is deeply angry at me for doing this to him; then he's mad because I told him about it. His anger and hate then turn onto the other man—sometimes to the point of his wanting to do something destructive to him. At other times he goes through the mental torture of imagining what "took place" between me and the other man. This angry stage occurs about one-third of the time. Another third is spent weeping and hating himself, and a final third in loving me so much that nothing matters so long as we are together.

We've spent endless hours in prayer that God would take the anger and pain away, or help us cope with it. All we want now is to be happy and make up for what we've done to each other. We feel a greater love for one another than ever before, and we want to serve the Lord throughout our remaining years together. But Bill and I need for this torment to go away! Can you help us?

Florence

Bill has discovered one of the eternal principles on which the universe is founded: we are all governed by a moral code that cannot be violated without inevitable consequences. It has been true throughout human history. In fact, Bill's remorse reminds me of the turmoil King David experienced from a similar sin more than three thousand years ago. As you will recall, David had fallen into an adulterous relationship with Bathsheba while her husband was away at war. God was very angry at the king for this sinful act and vowed that his punishment would involve rebellion and sexual indiscretion within his own family.

That curse was manifested in the life of David's son, Absalom, who tried to overthrow the king. As a deliberate insult, the defiant young man had sexual intercourse publicly with his father's wives. Civil war resulted and Absalom was executed after his hair was caught in the thistles of a tree.

Adultery always produces this kind of devastation.

When David learned of the death

of his son, he knew that his own sin with Bathsheba had led to this tragic climax. His agony is described in one of the most pathetic scenes of the Bible: "And the king was much moved, and went up to the chamber over the gate, and wept: and as he went, thus he said, O my son Absalom, my son, my son Absalom! would God I had died for thee, O Absalom, my son, my son!" (2 Sam. 18:33, KJV).

What a tragic moment, as David paced the floor in guilt and regret. Adultery always produces this kind of devastation—both for the innocent spouse and for the guilty, to say nothing of the young "Absaloms" in the family. It is an inevitable law of God! Solomon, another of David's sons, said it best:

> Can a man scoop fire into his lap without his clothes being burned?
> Can a man walk on hot coals without his feet being scorched?
> So is he who sleeps with another man's wife;
> no one who touches her will go unpunished.
> Men do not despise a thief if he steals to satisfy his hunger when he is starving.
> Yet if he is caught, he must pay sevenfold,
> though it costs him all the wealth of his house.
> But a man who commits adultery lacks judgment;
> whoever does so destroys himself.
> Blows and disgrace are his lot,
> and his shame will never be wiped away.
>
> Proverbs 6:27–33, NIV

Why have I bothered to repeat what every Christian must surely know—that sexual promiscuity is forbidden by God and is destructive to marriage? I suppose these words serve to express my own frustration at the permissiveness of the age, when we have become so blasé concerning evil in all its varieties. This disease of sin is more deadly, more virulent, than any illness known to mankind, yet the family is gripped by its fever. At a moment when the Christian church is desperately needed to call the nation to repentance, so much of its emphasis is placed on the supposed benefits of Christian "enlistment"—health, wealth, and business wisdom. "Something good is going to happen to you today," we sing. Perhaps. Perhaps not.

I sit in churches and listen to this positive rhetoric that tickles our ears, while all around me are people who have been in my office at one time or another. Every form of rebellion against God is represented behind their glassy eyes, while the disease that afflicts mankind goes undiagnosed and undetected. I thank God for ministers who still have the courage to call sin by its name and to urge their congregations toward repentance and obedience to the Lord of Hosts.

No sin *is beyond the forgiveness of God*.

I am also thankful that *no sin* is beyond the forgiveness of God. Even the most selfish, evil sinner on the face of the earth can obtain total cleansing at the cross. All that is required is for him to repent of his sins and believe on the name of the Lord Jesus Christ. He is then baptized into the fellowship of believers. Henceforth, he is promised that his misdeeds will be separated as far as the east is from the west, and remembered against him no more throughout eternity. That is the greatest proposition ever offered in the long history of mankind.

CHAPTER THIRTEEN

Loving Toughness in Other Settings

NOW THAT I'VE TOLD YOU MORE THAN YOU EVER WANTED to know about adultery, it is time to apply the *love must be tough* philosophy to other difficult family problems. As indicated, this approach to interpersonal relationships is certainly not confined to illicit love affairs or even to the framework of marriage. It has its place wherever two or more people come into contact with one another. Let's take a brief look, then, at some of the thorny situations that confront today's families in the context of our theme, again referring to letters received in response to the "Focus on the Family" radio series.

1. THE WIFE OF A VIOLENT SPOUSE

Dear Dr. Dobson:

This is an extremely difficult letter to write, but I must have help. My husband and I have been married for twelve years, and throughout most of this time, he has had a secret problem. Only I know that he has a violent temper that is absolutely terrifying to me. He is a leader in our church and is a very prominent lawyer in our city. Everyone respects him highly. But when he is at home, he is a different person.

At least once or twice a month he explodes over something the Kids or I have done to irritate him, and he becomes furious. He yells, throws things, threatens me, and makes an awful scene. If I say the wrong thing or if I say *anything*, he beats me with his fists.

Last week he loosened three of my teeth and cut the inside of my lip. I really thought he was going to kill me! This happened because I failed to do some errands he asked me to get done. What bothers me is that the beatings are becoming more frequent and more violent as time goes by.

After each fight is over, my husband refuses to take any blame for what happened. He steadfastly insists that I am at fault for deliberately provoking him. He interprets everything as a personal insult. The only way I can keep him calm is to do *everything* he asks and to hold inside every thought that might make him angry.

I don't know what to do. I really do love my husband. He's a fine man when he isn't mad about something. He never shows this side of himself in public, even when he is frustrated. No one has any idea he is a wife abuser. I haven't told anyone, and my husband would blow straight up if I asked him to go *with* me for counseling. No telling what he'd do if he knew I was consulting *you!*

So what can I do? I don't believe in divorce. I am trying to be gentle and cautious at all times, but inevitably I step on his toes and he explodes again. I'm so tired of being beaten and then having to stay home for days to hide my bruises.

How do I deal with this situations?

Laura

The problem of wife abuse is reaching epidemic proportions in today's families. The violence that is characteristic of the culture around us is being translated into husband-wife relationships and to parent-child interactions. Entire volumes have been addressed to this problem, and I am not likely to add to that understanding in the time and space allotted here. I can, however, offer Laura a condensed answer which would be the basis for our work if I were counseling her personally.

As I see it, Laura only has four alternatives in response to her circumstance. They are:

1. *Remain silent at home, walk on cracked eggs, and be the eternal conciliator*. She is taking this approach now, but it is not succeeding. No matter how passive she becomes, she will eventually trigger the anger of her uptight husband. Furthermore, she'll pay a terrible price emotionally for living on a powder keg year in and year out. For the long term, this is not the answer.
2. *Divorce her husband*. As a Christian, I agree with Laura that divorce is not the solution to this problem. Our purpose should be to change her husband's behavior, not kill the marriage.
3. *Proceed with an "emotional divorce," remaining married but keeping herself detached and independent from her husband*. This form of "emotional isolation" will shield Laura from psychological pain, but it will make for a terrible relationship. I don't favor it.
4. *The love-must-be-tough response*. This is risky and psychologically expensive, but it is my choice and my recommendation. In essence, Laura is being emotionally blackmailed by her husband. He is saying by his behavior, "Do what I wish or I'll beat you." She must break out of that tyranny while she's still young enough to cope with the consequences. This might be accomplished by forcing the matter to a crisis. Change of behavior does not occur when waters are smooth, as we have seen; it sometimes happens after a storm. I would suggest that Laura choose the most absurd demand her husband makes, and then refuse to consent to it. Let him rage if he must rage. She should prearrange a place to go and ask friends or relatives to step in for assistance at that critical moment. Separate

living quarters may be necessary until her husband settles down. He should be made to think that he has lost his wife over this issue, and in Act, I would recommend that she not return until there is reason to believe that he is willing to change. If that takes a year, so be it. When (and if) her husband acknowledges that he has a severe problem and promises to deal with it if she'll come home, a period of negotiations should follow. One of the conditions for reconciliation is competent Christian counseling for the psychological problem that is now apparent to everyone but the husband. By all means, Laura will need the support of Christian friends and counselors, especially during the time of crisis. And it goes without saying that the entire matter must be bathed in prayer from the beginning. I can offer no guarantees that this advice will resolve Laura's problem with her violent husband. But I believe it represents the best possibility for success. Let me ask those of you who disagree, what would you advise? Counselors suggesting that this frightened woman remain passive and submissive despite the abuse should have to look into Laura's eyes and tell her that in person. I don't believe anyone should be required to live in that kind of terror, and in fact, to do so is to tolerate a behavior which could eventually prove fatal to the marriage, anyway.

Related Question

Q. Are you suggesting that *any* woman who is being beaten should take the same course of action? My husband has only hit me once in a big fight we had. Should I separate from him?

A. I am not offering blanket advice to every wife who has had a violent encounter with her husband. As in your case, a man can become so enraged that he does something he is immediately sorry for and would never do again. That is very different from the repetitive, pathological situation Laura is in. Let me offer another word of caution which is likely to be misunderstood by those who *want* to misunderstand. It deals with a very volatile subject that angels would fear to touch, but I feel it must be addressed. I have seen marital relationships where the woman deliberately "baited" her husband until he hit her. This is not true in *most* cases of domestic violence, but it does occur. Why, one may ask, would *any* woman want to be hit? Because females are just as capable of hatred and anger as males, and a woman can devastate a man by enticing him to strike her. It is a potent weapon. Once he has lost control and lashed out at his tormentor, she then sports undeniable evidence of his cruelty. She can show her wounds to her friends who gasp at the viciousness of that man. She can press charges against him in some cases and have him thrown in jail. She can embarrass him at his work or in the church. In short, by taking a beating, she instantly achieves a moral advantage in the eyes of neighbors, friends, and the law. It may even help her justify a divorce, or if one comes, to gain custody of her children. Remember what the Japanese sneak attack on Pearl Harbor did to American morale and unity? It solidified our forces and gave us a cause worth fighting for. There are those who believe President Roosevelt ignored warnings of the Pearl Harbor invasion for the precise purpose of unifying our resolve against a rising Japanese imperialism. In that same spirit, I have seen women belittle and berate their husbands until they set them aflame with rage. Some wives are more verbal than their husbands and can win a war of words any day of the week. Finally, the men reach a point of such frustration that they explode, doing precisely what their wives were begging them to do in the first place.

I remember one woman who came to church with a huge black eye contributed by her husband. She walked to the front of the auditorium before a crowd of five hundred people and made a routine announcement about an upcoming event. Everyone in attendance was thinking about her eye and the cad who did this to her. That was precisely what she wanted. I happened to know that her noncommunicative husband had been verbally antagonized by his wife until he finally gave her the prize she sought. Then she brought it to church to show it off. It *does* happen.

It is obvious why this analysis is inflammatory to women like Laura who are victims in the true sense of the word. They may think I am suggesting that they are responsible for their husband's violence. Not so! But domestic violence has more than one source of motivation, and that fact should be admitted.

2. THE HUSBAND OR WIFE OF A CHILD ABUSER

My friend Paul Powers was one of the most pathetic victims of child abuse I've ever known. Both his mother and father were alcoholics who produced or adopted twelve children, despite their inability to care for them. When Paul was seven years old, his mother came home from a party in a drunken stupor and collapsed before she reached the front door. The children found her the next morning lying in the snow. She contracted pneumonia and grew gravely ill. Two weeks later when Paul came home from school, his mother called him to her bedside and reached out to take his hand, but died before she could convey her thoughts. Seeing that she was gone, the child ran sobbing to his drunken father who pushed him away and began beating him with his fists. The man screamed, "Shut

> *Paul's nose and two ribs were broken, and his teeth were knocked out.*

up! Boys don't cry like babies!" Paul's nose and two ribs were broken, and his teeth were knocked out. Even today, he bears a two-inch scar on the inside of his lower lip from the beating his father gave him that day. Paul didn't cry again until he was twenty-two years old.

That was typical of Paul's developmental years. Especially after the death of his mother, he and his siblings were subjected to cruel and vicious beatings on a regular basis. The father's abuse was reported to local authorities on numerous occasions, and each time a social worker visited the home. As soon as she had left, Paul and several of his brothers were taken to the basement, stripped, and beaten until they could not get up from the floor.

At twelve years of age, Paul committed his first murder in a robbery attempt.

It is not surprising that Paul and every one of his eleven siblings have spent time in prison. At twelve years of age, Paul committed his first murder in a robbery attempt. He shot a female carnival worker who refused to give him her money. The judge asked Paul's father what he wanted done with the boy and he said, "Send him to hell!" Paul was confined in prison for this and related crimes and was filled with hatred and bitterness. But there in prison five years later, the most significant event in Paul's life occurred. He was seventeen years of age when he saw a Billy Graham film and began to be acquainted with the Lord Jesus Christ! Sometime later he repented of his sins and was marvelously converted. Can you imagine what it must have been like for this young man who had never known love, who had experienced nothing but pain and suffering and sorrow, to be made clean and to know he was loved by the Creator Himself? His entire life was changed on that incredible day.

He repented of his sins and was marvelously converted.

Paul was eventually released from prison, married a Christian woman, and became the father of a little girl. He felt God wanted him to distribute Christian films, since he had found the Lord through this medium. But times were rough. Paul and his wife were struggling to survive financially in their little ministry. It was Christmastime, and they lacked money even for groceries.

He resorted to the behavior he had seen as a child.

By contacting churches that had shown his films, Paul managed to collect a few dollars that were owed to him. His wife took $8.00 to the grocery store to buy food, and when she returned, he was furious to learn that she had foolishly spent $1.00 for wrapping paper and tape. While Paul and his wife argued with one another, their three-year-old daughter was quietly rummaging through the sack of groceries. When she found the wrapping paper, she took it into the living room and used it to cover a shoe box.

Paul finally realized the child was gone and went looking for her. He found her sitting on the floor with the box covered by crooked paper and half a roll of tape. When Paul saw that the child had wasted the valuable materials, his temper blew again. He resorted to the behavior he had seen as a child, grabbing the toddler by one arm and flailing her violently. Then he sent her sobbing to her room, literally terrorized. He cannot talk about the event today without crying.

The next day when gifts were exchanged, the little girl ran behind the tree and retrieved her gold box. She handed it to Paul and said, "Daddy, this is for you!" He was embarrassed that he had spanked her unmercifully for something she perceived as a gift. He slowly began unwrapping the paper and lifted the lid to find the box completely empty.

Paul's anger flared once more and he said, "What have you done? There's nothing in this box. Why did you give me an empty box?

When you give someone a present you're supposed to put a gift inside it!"

The three year old looked up at her father innocently and said, "Oh, no, Daddy. The box is not empty! It is full of love and kisses for you. I stood there and blew kisses in there for my daddy, and I put love in there too. And it is for you!"

Paul was broken. He wrapped his arms around his little girl and begged her to forgive him. Then he got on his knees before the Lord, repenting and pleading for God to purge the violent temper he had learned as a child. Never again did this remarkable man abuse any of his sons or daughters. He kept that gold box beside his bed for years, and whenever he would be hurt or discouraged, he would reach into the box and lift out an imaginary kiss from his child. Then he would place it on his cheek and say, "Thank you, Lord."

Never again did this remarkable man abuse any of his sons or daughters.

I must share a more recent chapter in Paul's story which also moved me to tears. Paul and his father had gone their separate ways in 1956 and rarely saw each other in the two decades that followed. All of Paul's attempts to make contact had been rejected. Then one day, Paul received a call from his father, who was at the Union Train Station in their town, asking if Paul could come see him. He said he would be there for only one hour. Paul and his wife jumped into the car and drove through rush hour traffic to get to the station on time. They arrived just three minutes before the train was to leave. Paul climbed aboard the train, wondering what he would say to the old man. They had been mortal enemies

For the first time in his life, this 79-year-old man told his boy that he loved him.

when they last parted company. Paul searched frantically for his father, and when they saw each other, they paused and then embraced affectionately. For the first time in his life, this 79-year-old man told his boy that he loved him. The conductor then shouted, "All aboard!" and Paul had to hurry from the train. They had only time enough to agree that they would meet soon in a nearby city.

Paul got off the train in a state of shock. His father had *never* hugged him in his life, and, in fact, had seemed totally incapable of love. "But more than that," Paul told his wife, "there was a different look about him! I saw it in his eyes. He was not the same man! I can't explain it, but that man is different!" He anticipated the time when they could talk leisurely and heal the wounds they had inflicted on one another in earlier years.

Unfortunately, the rendezvous was never held because the old man suffered a heart attack and died the following Monday. As with his mother so many years before, Paul was deprived of his father's last words. But a local pastor filled in the details at the funeral. Paul's father had indeed experienced an encounter with Jesus Christ, and had become a born-again Christian in the closing months of his life. In fact, his train journey had been a last desperate attempt to reach out to several of his children and reestablish relationships that had been ruptured for years.

Paul's father had indeed experienced an encounter with Jesus Christ.

I have shared Paul's story in this context for two reasons. First, because it touched me deeply and will, I know, be inspirational to others. Languishing in prison for the crime of murder, aware that no one had ever loved or needed him in his life, this young man came face to face with the compassion of God! Instead of being condemned for his sins and crimes, he was given an unconditional pardon and the record was obliterated. That is thrilling to me because I also experienced that incredible forgiveness!

But Paul's background will also help us understand the problem of child abuse. His case is characteristic of the majority of offenders today who also experienced abusive childhoods. We parents develop our child-rearing styles primarily from watching our own mothers and fathers who served as role models. Even when we disliked what they did to us, we were influenced by the standard they set. "This is how the job is done," they seemed to say. Thus, when we are grown and have children of our own, our tendency during times of frustration and stress is to imitate what we learned at home. More than 60 percent of abusive parents were themselves abused as children; that's why they need our love and understanding, not our condemnation.

We parents develop our child-rearing styles primarily from watching our own mothers and fathers.

Even though we understand its cause, child abuse cannot be tolerated. Its effect on a developing youngster can be devastating. That's why I recommend loving toughness when one parent observes consistent violence being inflicted on a boy or girl by the spouse. Of course, I could list an entire page of qualifiers behind that statement. What one permissive parent may interpret as child abuse may be, in fact, good discipline by the other spouse. The ideal approach is for mothers and fathers who disagree on techniques of discipline to discuss the matter with a wise, neutral counselor who can mediate the conflict.

I recommend loving toughness when one parent observes consistent violence being inflicted on a boy or girl by the spouse.

But let's be realistic. There are hundreds of thousands of homes today where one parent is aware of injustice and cruelty on the part of the other. Perhaps the father overreacts in response to routine childishness, beating the kids in anger or vindictiveness. Or maybe a mother is thrashing a colicky infant or punishing an older child too severely. What is a concerned parent to do under those circumstances? If he goes to the authorities, he threatens to destroy his home and incur the wrath of his spouse. Furthermore, the family's reputation in the community will be tarnished and their friendships undermined. Often, the price is too great and the mother or father chooses not to pay it. Therefore, their little children suffer the brunt of this injustice without advocacy.

Worse yet, I have become aware in recent years that many mothers knowingly permit their husbands to abuse their daughters sexually for the same reasons! I have seen numerous situations where a little girl was expected to relieve the sexual pressure on her mother by satisfying the father's passions. Unbelievable, you say! Hardly! It is estimated that 20 to 25 percent of all females in this country were sexually abused as children, most of them in their own homes. I have talked to these individuals after they've grown to be women. Virtually every one of them bears scars that will never be healed. They feel utter disgust and revulsion, not for their fathers, but for themselves! "I feel so dirty!" is the typical comment. It is as though they have taken the entire blame for the exploitation they suffered.

Every child deserves a chance to grow up with a healthy mind and body.

Mothers and fathers, if this is going on in your home, you simply must come to the rescue of your child! You can't deny it another day. Nothing can make it right. Even at the risk of damaging or destroying your marriage, that little girl or boy who is being subjected to sexual exploitation or physical violence must be protected. Every child deserves a chance to grow up with a healthy mind and body. I urge you to seek professional help, today. If you don't know who to consult, talk to your pediatrician or call the toll-free Childhelp hotline to talk anonymously to a counselor. They will direct you to a local agency that can help you. Their numbers are 1-800-422-4453 and 1-800-4ACHILD. If all else fails and the abuse continues, get the child out of the house in which it is occurring. That is loving toughness under fire! Then let the Lord lead as you seek to reconcile and heal your marriage.

Finally, if you are the abuser, don't wait another day to seek professional consultation. Most cities have organizations that help parents with this problem. Sure, it will be painful to admit that you have hurt your children, but if you'll act now, there may still be time for your son or daughter to recover and live a normal life during the critical developmental years. You will never regret dealing with this terrible problem before it is too late. Don't be like Paul Powers's father who was in his final days on earth before showing love to his son. The same Lord who touched his life wants to do a miracle in yours, too.

3. WIFE IN FINANCIAL STRESS

Q. What do you say to the woman who tolerates infidelity in her husband because she has no financial resources? What if she is afraid to confront him because he could leave her in poverty?

A. I have no simple answers for that lady. Life can place us between rocks and hard places where problems seem almost unsolvable! Such is the plight of mothers raising children with little or no financial help from their ex-husbands. According to the Department of Health and Human Services, this is the primary source of poverty in America today. Almost half of all people living below the poverty line are divorced women with children, according to the 1980 census. The same survey revealed that half of the divorced mothers do not receive the court-ordered amount of child support from their ex-husbands. I must say that I don't understand the laissez-faire enforcement of the law in this regard. Oh, I know the courts instruct men to do their duty, but little is done to prod those who resist. In a society that is regulated to death with laws and ordinances for virtually every human activity, it does seem that we could put the squeeze on men who won't care for their kids. Even in the administration of justice, you see, *love must be tough.*

Millions of divorced men do pay child support, of course, and many exceed the minimum amount established by the courts. Let me share an encouraging letter I received recently from a mother who faced the problem described in the question above, but overcame it with prayer.

Dear Dr. Dobson:

I have appreciated your broadcasts this week on the subject *love must be tough.*

I am going through the very situation you talked about, an unfaithful husband after fifteen years of what I thought was a good marriage. Yes, I experienced all the emotions you mentioned plus one that I think many women face. My problem was financial insecurity.

You see, I never had worked outside the home, and I was scared about how I would manage to pay the bills. It costs so much to keep kids in clothes and all the other needs today. My husband works for a Ford dealership and he's made a decent living, but we've never been able to save any money.

My husband was unfaithful and I was miserable, but because of this fear, I never confronted him with it. Finally I just confessed this fear to the Lord and told Him I was depending upon Him for my finances and security. Praise the Lord, He worked it out beautifully!

I told my husband to either straighten up or leave. Well, he left, but he decided to continue with the same financial arrangements as before. Sure it hurts, but not like before when I knew he was with someone else and playing games with my emotions.

Since I confronted him with this, I have evidently taken the fun out of his relationship with this woman. I honestly believe he enjoyed the secretiveness of playing around. He treats me better now than he has for years.

The Bible says that God will make even our enemies to be at peace with us when we obey Him. This has certainly been true in my case.

Your advice is correct. The only thing I would add is for the person to ask God to give him the courage and strength to carry it out. I put up with infidelity for nine years because I didn't have that confidence.

God bless you,
Marvella

Thank you, Marvella. *Your* advice is correct, also.

4. HUSBAND OF A "NEW WOMAN"

Since the so-called "women's movement" has been a major force in Western thought for three decades, it is now possible to evaluate its effect on the self-concept of women and on their marriages. Despite many concerns I have expressed in the past, the picture definitely has its positive elements. There is no doubt in my mind that the movement has brought greater respect and dignity for females, especially in the business world.

The movement has brought greater respect and dignity for females.

Prior to 1965, it was not uncommon for an attractive young woman in the work force to be treated like a piece of flesh, a toy to be used by men. Sexual innuendoes spoken about her and within her hearing were almost expected as proof of male virility. That disrespect, and other forms of it, still occur in everyday life, but it is less common today, and women know that they are entitled to better treatment. In this and many related ways, the elevated self-concept of women has been a healthy phenomenon in our culture.

But there have been casualties, too, especially when the philosophy of radical feminism is adopted uncritically by former traditionalists. I'm referring to the role reversal and change in lifestyle that often occurs when a loving wife and mother suddenly becomes a "new woman." You've seen it happen—probably within your circle of friends. One day she is raising a family, maintaining a home, doing her best to live on a budget, undergirding her husband in his career, helping out at the church or the PTA or the hospital, and trying to serve God to the best of her ability. Then overnight, or so it would seem, she makes a 90-degree turn and becomes somebody else.

But there have been casualties, too.

Her new attitude can best be described as deeply angry. She is tired of being abused and taken for granted and disrespected. From now on, you'd better believe, she is not going to be pushed by anyone. Her new system of values has been programmed for her by feminist organizations and publications, almost as though a computer software package were keypunched into her brain. From that day forward, her primary concern is *herself!* The children will make it fine, she feels, with far less mothering. Her own career

From that day forward, her primary concern is herself.

becomes all-consuming to her, and if it conflicts with her husband's work, then he'll just have to compromise. She bristles when her new beliefs are challenged or contradicted. These very words I'm writing, in fact, would make her furious. Her attitude toward God is likely to be revised, too. If He's not an antifeminist, then in her opinion, most of His people are. She just may throw overboard everything she believed before her rebirth as a "new woman."

The saddest chapter in the life of the new woman occurs when she runs—runs from her children—runs to establish a new identity—runs to the arms of another man. I remember one young woman whom I had watched with interest during her childhood and adolescence. I saw her as a high school homecoming queen, as a college coed, as a bride, and then as a mother. But the babies came too fast for her. She couldn't handle the stresses of raising toddlers and changing diapers and wiping runny noses. I'll never forget the look in her eyes when she told me, "They're driving me crazy!" But I underestimated her frustration until the day she disappeared. She left behind three beautiful kids and a bewildered, wounded husband. Her behavior changed, her faith evaporated, her morals crumbled, and her former loves perished. And five people in that little family will never be the same.

> *What should the husband of a "new woman" do?*

What should the husband of a "new woman" do? How can he deal with her anger and spiritual rebellion? Again, at the risk of providing simplistic answers to extremely complex questions, let me list some approaches that have succeeded with others:

1. First, this hostile woman may have (and most certainly does have) some legitimate complaints that should be addressed. The loving part of our prescription (*love must be tough*)

dictates that these irritants be given a full hearing. There will undoubtedly be places for compromise and compassion and concern. It is even possible that a man who is willing to listen to his wife may prevent the "new woman" transformation from occurring.

2. Once the storm begins to howl, it resembles the turmoil of adolescence. By that I mean that the great anger of those years will not continue at the same level of intensity forever but will dissipate in time. Until then, the purpose of the more responsible party is to get through the crisis without killing relationships and crushing families.
3. The particularly hostile "new woman" needs space during her discontent, and it should be given to her. If she would separate from her family, let her go. If she doesn't call, leave her to her solitude. Let her feel that she is free, in the spirit I have described. Open the door to her domestic cage, but make *her* do the flying. As a responsible and faithful husband in this context, I would not voluntarily leave the family to accommodate her. If she obtains a court order to force my departure, then the responsibility rests on her shoulders.
4. At some point, especially if infidelity is involved, it will be appropriate to apply the principles of loving toughness described herein. Great wisdom and tact are required to know how and when to say, "That's enough; now make your choice. I'll accept either decision."
5. Pray consistently and seek the best counsel available.

5. WIFE OF A HOMOSEXUAL

Dear Dr. Dobson:

I am plagued by a problem with a thousand things that worry me. It scares me half to death. My husband and I have been married for twelve years, and I've known for the past eight that he is a practicing homosexual. We have one little girl but she was kind of a miracle. We rarely have sexual relations. He has no interest in me, he says.

Warren told me he's known he was gay since he was nineteen years old and now he's thirty-eight. He was raised in an alcoholic's home, and I guess his childhood was pretty rough. I didn't know about his problem before I married him or else I never would have. Now it is terrible living with him. I never know when he's out with a guy. He works as a dancer here in Vegas, and he gets off at 2:00 A.M. But he doesn't come home until dawn. Whenever I ask where he went after work he gives me some phony story.

I am not a nagging wife, but I've about reached my limit. I usually find out later that Warren has lied to me, and he's been out with a man again. I believe that's all he cares about. A counselor told me that homosexuals are very self-centered people who think mainly of themselves. Even in their sexual activities, their main purpose is to please themselves. I can see that in our intimate times together, too.

I'll tell you what really scares me now. I'm starting to really not care for him anymore. Even when I learn he's made love to a guy, I just feel nothing. It happens so often that I have come to expect it. What I really want now is a divorce, and I want to know if I have a right to get one on scriptural grounds. I've heard so many answers to that question from Christians I've talked to, but in watching your films, I thought you seemed like the kind of person who understands different situations and how to handle them.

I just don't know which way to turn. I want the kind of family that God describes in the Bible. I don't think my husband has a right to continue in the gay life and then stay married to me. Does he? Thank you for helping me.

Vickie

My heart goes out to you, Vickie. If there is anything more painful than knowing your mate has had an affair, it is the awareness that your spouse is involved in a gay lifestyle. I don't blame you for feeling betrayed by the man who promised to "love and cherish" you for life.

As to whether you have scriptural grounds for a divorce, I believe you do. Keep in mind that I am *not* a theologian, and there are great differences of opinion on the interpretation of Scripture. You've already heard those conflicting viewpoints from your Christian counselors. But I see *no* differences between heterosexual unfaithfulness and the homosexual variety. They both are condemned in the Bible and should be considered in the same classification, morally. It is difficult to miss the intent of inspired writers who described a time when men would "burn with lust" for one another. Homosexuality is always included in lists of the most heinous sins, as seen in the following Scriptures.

I see no difference between hetrosexual unfaithfulness and the homosexual variety

> Do you not know that the wicked will not inherit the kingdom of God? Do not be deceived: Neither the sexually immoral nor idolaters nor adulterers nor male prostitutes nor homosexual offenders nor thieves nor the greedy nor drunkards nor slanderers nor swindlers will inherit the kingdom of God.
>
> 1 Corinthians 6:9–10, NIV

> Because of this, God gave them over to shameful lusts. Even their women exchanged natural relations for unnatural ones. In the same way the men also abandoned natural relations with women and were inflamed with lust for one another. Men committed indecent acts with other men, and received in themselves the due penalty for their perversion.
>
> Romans 1:26–27, NIV

God in His wisdom would not have condemned this perversion if it had represented just another lifestyle chosen by gays. (A further discussion appears in the next section).

On the other hand, Vickie, I can't say that God wants you to divorce your husband. He loves Warren as much as he does you and me, and He would much rather help him turn from his sin. He would also like to heal your marriage if you and Warren will permit Him to do so. We must always distinguish between the sin—*any* sin—which God hates, and the sinner, whom He loves!

We must always distinguish between the sin—any sin—which God hates, and the sinner, whom He loves.

My advice to you, therefore, is that you apply the recommendations offered throughout this book. Prayerfully establish a point of crisis with Warren, and force him to choose between good and evil—between committed love and a life of homosexuality. If he wants to preserve his relationship with you, then he will need competent counseling to cope with his problem. And contrary to what you've heard, homosexuality *can* be treated successfully when the individual desperately wants to change. It isn't easy to conquer, but the majority of gays can become comfortable and reasonably satisfied in an exclusively heterosexual world.

Homosexuality can be treated successfully.

I pray that Warren will be one of those fortunate people, with the help of God.

Caution: Sensitive Information Follows

I permitted a friend to read a preliminary draft of this book, and he said he felt my discussion of homosexuality was inadequate. He asked me to describe the gay lifestyle for those who are not informed. Reluctantly, I agreed to do so.

If you have a weak stomach or don't wish to know the more unpleasant facts about homosexuality, I encourage you to skip the remainder of this section. The description I'm about to write will be very disturbing to most of my readers. My purpose is not to shock, but to dispel a carefully constructed myth. I repeat—don't read if you don't want to know!

Gay propaganda would have us see homosexuality as just another lifestyle being very similar to that of heterosexuals. They picture two young men or women holding hands and strolling serenely through the park, as though their perversion were merely another expression of human love. Unfortunately, the actual gay experience is another matter! It can be incredibly sordid and perverse in its most extreme context.

Many homosexuals (but not all) prefer a group experience.

It is apparent from the discussions in the recent spate of articles, interviews, and books on the subject that homosexuality has become a major health hazard in the Western world. Whereas heterosexuals typically engage each other one on one, many homosexuals (but not all) prefer a group experience. Their orgies occur in "gay baths," among other places, made legal by antisodomy laws struck down by the courts in recent years. There are between 200 and 400 of these so-called bathhouses in existence in the U.S. today. (The success of these businesses has been severely affected by the AIDS phenomenon, but they are still in operation at the date of this writing.)

If you were to follow a gay man into such an establishment, this is what you would typically observe: For the next hour and a half, that individual would have oral-anal contact with ten to thirty partners, ingesting small amounts of fecal matter from each one; he would have oral-genital sex with five to ten more; he would be penetrated orally by five to ten men and would be the object of oral-genital contact by the same number. These men would all swallow fecal matter from one another, passed around from anus to genitalia to mouth to anus, etc. This is not exaggeration or overstatement. According to the second Kinsey Survey conducted in San Francisco, 83 percent of homosexuals report they practice oral-anal sex. The Gay Report, written for and by homosexuals, places the incidence at 89 percent. Likewise, 23 percent admit they routinely urinate on one another during their sexual encounters. There are other activities and characteristics of this "alternate lifestyle" that I would not even write in a frank discussion of this nature! That is the gay experience when expressed at its worst. The accuracy of this description was reviewed and verified by my friend Dr. Donald Tweedie, a Christian psychotherapist who has specialized for twenty-five years in the treatment of homosexual patients. Not all gays and lesbians participate in bathhouse behavior, of course, but according to Dr. Tweedie, even those who claim to be committed to monogamous relationships are often promiscuous. In other words, homosexual encounters with *multiple* partners are common, even for those who reject the orgiastic activities I have described.

> *Homosexual encounters with* multiple *partners are common.*

Is it any wonder that so many homosexuals have hepatitis and other diseases? It certainly appears to explain the recent discovery of the incurable illness called AIDS, mentioned earlier, which is spreading unchecked through the gay community. According to the Center for Disease Control in Atlanta, Georgia, 100 percent of all patients diagnosed with the classical symptoms of AIDS in 1980 or before are now dead, and the number is doubling every six months. These developments carry ominous implications for the health of the nation, since homosexuals can be found in every profession and occupation. They drill our teeth, perform our surgeries, serve our food, teach our children, and provide their blood for our hospitals. Any major health hazard affecting up to 2 percent of the population must be considered relevant to the totality. Yet our government is busily banning cyclamates and saccharin and ignoring the more obvious dangers that are politically volatile.

I have chosen to offer this graphic description of homosexuality, not only to set the record straight, but to explain my understanding of the biblical perspective on this lifestyle. It seems unreasonable to think that God, in His infinite wisdom, would forbid premarital or extramarital sex between a man and woman, but then wink approvingly at homosexual orgies and perversions. What nonsense! To the churches that have whitewashed the gay experience and absolved it of divine sanction, I can only say I'm glad I won't be the one to explain that stance on the Great Judgment Day!

I'll conclude this statement by repeating what I said earlier concerning the homosexual *himself* as opposed to his problem:

> I believe our obligation is to despise the sin but love the sinner. Many men and women who experience homosexual passions have not sought their way of life; it occurred for reasons which they can neither recall nor explain. Some were victims of early traumatic sexual encounters by adults who exploited them. I remember one homosexual teenager whose drunken father forced him to sleep with his mother after a wild New Year's Eve party. His disgust for heterosexual sex was easy to trace. Such individuals need acceptance and love from the Christian community, as they seek to redirect their impulses,*

**Dr. Dobson Answers Your Questions* (Wheaton, IL: Tyndale House Publishers, 1982), p. 452.

6. HUSBAND OR WIFE OF AN ALCOHOLIC

A government survey form was reportedly sent to the president of a small company and asked, "How many employees do you have, broken down by sex?" He replied, "None that I know of. Our big problem here is alcohol."

Since we are dealing in rapid succession with the most difficult marital crises facing us today, we must not fail to address the pervasive problem of alcoholism. One out of every three Americans is a close family member of an alcoholic, and the incidence seems to be rising. It is not a white man's disease or a black man's problem or an Indian weakness. It is a *human* condition, affecting all races, nationalities, and both sexes. The French, who pride themselves in their low rate of alcoholism, have a higher incidence of cirrhosis of the liver than any country in the world. *Mother* Russia has 22 million alcoholics among its citizens. Problem drinkers can be found among Protestants, Catholics, and Jews. Some are down-and-outers, sprawled on skid-row streets; others have been at the pinnacle of public popularity and power, such as Betty Ford, Sid Caesar, Senators Wilbur Mills and Harold Hughes. We rub elbows every day with people whose lives are dominated by the bottle, the flask and the glass.

One out of every three Americans is a close family member of an alcoholic.

The saddest dimension of alcoholism is its effects on innocent family members, especially children who are too young to understand what is happening to their parents. The National Institute on Alcohol and Alcohol Abuse estimates that half of the problem drinkers in this

The saddest dimension of alcoholism is its effects on innocent family members, especially children.

country are women, many being "closet alcoholics" who successfully hide their addiction behind the doors of their homes. But they can't hide it from their kids. I shudder to contemplate how many toddlers will wander aimlessly through their homes today wondering why mommy "sleeps" so long on the floor. How many kids like little Paul Powers will be unjustly punished or made to go hungry or otherwise abused by a parent who is too drunk to care? It is difficult to overestimate the effect of alcoholism on the stability of today's families.

In the view of the vastness of this problem, I felt it should be given more than cursory attention here. Thus, I invited four authorities to my office to give us an up-to-date look at alcoholism and current methods of treatment. Included were a physician and a marriage, family, and child therapist with twenty-five years of counseling experience, whose own father committed suicide during one of his drunken binges. Also with me were "Bob," a recovered alcoholic, and his wife "Pauline," who preferred that we withhold their real names.

I did not ask these four individuals for a detailed analysis of the *problem;* we already know how serious it is. Rather, I wanted them to provide us with practical suggestions as to how family members can recognize the disease and then how they can help. The answers they gave were most encouraging and enlightening.

The physician was asked whether alcoholism can be treated successfully, today. Is it a hopeless condition, or is there a way out for the victim and his family? This was his reply:

> I specialized in the field of internal medicine for many years, but found it to be depressing work. I could help my patients with chronic lung disease and severe diabetes and heart disease, but in reality, my efforts were just a delaying action. Over time, the conditions worsened and the diseases progressed. I made my rounds in intensive care each day and watched people losing their battle for life, whereas my alcoholic patients were getting well. That's why I deal almost exclusively

with alcoholics now and find it to be extremely rewarding work. I see people who come in with more horrible problems than you can imagine, but they get into a recovery program, and in a few months, the difference is like going from night to day. So yes, not only is alcoholism treatable, but the medical community does better with this disorder than any other chronic disease. Alcoholics emerge from treatment programs more functionally integrated, more capable, and more effective than before they "caught" the disease.

That was the theme of the entire discussion: there is *hope* for the alcoholic! But before treatment can occur, the problem has to be identified and acknowledged. My guest was then asked to describe the early characteristics of the disease for family members who need to be able to recognize the symptoms. He said:

The first red flag is a "tolerance" to alcohol. The persons find he has to drink more to achieve the same result. He calls this being able to "hold his liquor"—a status symbol around the world. In reality, it is a danger signal indicating that a chemical adjustment has been made. Secondly, the person reaches a place where he doesn't want to talk about his drinking anymore. He knows he is consuming more alcohol than other people and he wants to avoid all reference to it. This begins a process of denial that may be with him for years to come. Thirdly, the person begins to experience blackouts. By that I mean that he has brief periods of amnesia that lengthen as time goes by. What is happening is that the brain's recording cells aren't remembering what is being said and done. Furthermore, it's a low dose phenomenon: It happens after one or two drinks. I'm not referring to the process of becoming stone drunk from the anesthetic effect of great quantities of alcohol. Instead, the person thinks back on the previous night and says, "Gee! I can't remember a doggone thing after the second drink." It's a scary experience. Fourth, the person begins to notice that he can't consistently predict how much he's going to drink once he starts. To me, this is the key feature of alcoholism and constitutes the definition of the disease. It occurs when an individual is constantly drinking more than he intended because he can't help it. He sits down to have a beer and wakes up the next afternoon. It may be hard for people to believe, but alcoholics don't intend to get drunk. They merely want to have a drink or two. That's why they can swear they'll never get drunk again, and *mean* it. They have no intention of breaking that promise. Nevertheless, they sit down to have a drink with a friend and bingo, it's morning.

At this point in our discussion, we heard from Pauline who shared her personal experience:

I couldn't count the times Bob promised he would never drink again. That must be the most frustrating part of the experience—having Bob look me straight in the eye and tell me he's through—really done with binging. He'd say, "I've seen how it hurts you and the kids and I've had it. I promise you that I'll never do it again!" Then in a day or two he was dead-drunk. I thought he was lying to me. How could he love me and lie so many times to my face? But he wasn't lying. He *couldn't* keep his promise. Bob thought he could whip this problem with willpower, but you can't conquer a physiological problem with willpower. It's like trying to stop diarrhea by making up your mind to do so.

We asked Bob to express what he was feeling during this time of repeated failure. He said he was confused by his inability to overcome his habit.

I thought the problem might be vodka, so I switched to scotch, and then bourbon. Then I tried meditation. Nothing worked. I tried a dozen approaches to control my drinking, but I always went back to it. Then I tried covering it up. I carried a bottle of Binaca in my pocket and always had a green tongue. I drank for six months without Pauline ever knowing it. Every Saturday morning she would wash her hair and then sit under a noisy dryer for a half hour. I could hardly wait for her to get preoccupied because I had a fifth of vodka in the cupboard. I would race in and get a can of Fresca from the refrigerator, pour half of it down the drain, and fill the other half with my vodka. Then I'd drink it in front of the television set with a halo around my head. You really have to be calculating to hide a drinking problem from those you live with. This went on for months. You see, I was addicted to a drug and was completely unaware of it.

I'm sure this pattern sounds familiar to many of my readers who live with an alcoholic. The critical question is, what can they do to help? Let's begin by describing the harmful approaches to avoid, and then we'll consider the recommendations of our panel.

1. Do not nag, complain, scream, cry, beg, plead, embarrass, label or berate the victim. He has a *disease* which he can't control. It is not within his power to overcome it alone.
2. Do not keep the alcoholic's life together by lying to his boss, covering for his irresponsibilities, bailing him out of jail and paying his bills. Such a rescuer is called an *enabler*, and he may actually prolong and worsen the problem.
3. Though opinions differ, most authorities do not look on alcoholism as a character weakness or a moral problem. It *was* a moral problem during earlier days when the person *chose* to drink excessively. But later, it was not his desire to hurt his family, stay in a drunken stupor, waste his money, etc. The alcoholic has long since lost his capacity for voluntary action.
4. Do not perpetuate the alcoholic's problem for your own

selfish reasons. It is not uncommon for family members to resist any treatment for what may be unconscious motives. For example, a woman whose husband is usually drunk has *power* over her family. She is the unrivaled boss—the one who controls the money and makes all the family's decisions. As her alcoholic husband begins to recover, she may realize she is losing that power and move to sabotage his rehabilitation. Guard against these subtle forces that may undermine recovery in your homes.

We come now to the most important part of our discussion. What can family members do to help themselves and their addicted loved ones? First, it is virtually impossible to resolve this problem without outside help. In a very real sense, the entire family shares the sickness of the alcoholic. They are affected by rage, depression, disillusionment, despair, financial fear, denial, low self-esteem, and myriad other emotions that accompany this illness. They are wounded in spirit and need the loving concern of those who have been there. As Jerry Butler said, "If the alcoholic does manage to recover, he is almost certain to regress unless his family has been treated, too.

But where can that outside assistance be found? Our panel was unanimous in their recommendations of Alanon, a support program for the families of alcoholics. Pauline credits them with saving her family and perhaps her life. She said, "After refusing to attend for a year I went to Alanon in desperation and finally began to get the answers I needed. I'll never forget the first night. They gave no sympathy and no advice. They just shared their experience, their strength, and their hope. I latched onto it with everything I had, and within a few weeks, things began to change for me. Alanon directed me toward God and helped me get my eyes off myself and on Him. Then they taught me how to deal with Bob."

I asked Bob what changes he began to notice at home and he was emphatic in his reply.

> If you really want to mess up an alcoholic's drinking fun, just get his spouse involved in Alanon. Pauline changed her approach in three ways and it bugged me like crazy: (1) Whereas she previously poured my booze down the drain, she stopped doing that or anything else to keep me from drinking. I really wondered if she loved me anymore. (2) On Mondays, I would ask her to call the office and tell them that I had the flu. She had always done that for me. But after going to Alanon, she would simply smile and say, "No, you'll have to do that yourself." (3) She seemed to be calmer, more in control. Before, I would come home from drinking with the guys and look for an excuse to leave again. All I had to do was pick a fight with Pauline and then say, "All right, if that's the way you're gonna act, I'll just take off." Now, she gets in this Alanon thing and instead of trying to hold me at home, she smiles and says, "So long. I'm going to a meeting."

Getting help for the family is only the first step in recovery, of course. The second stage is tougher. How on earth can husbands or wives of problem drinkers get them to Alcoholics Anonymous or to a similar treatment program? That person is steeped in denial and his thought processes are blurred by booze. You simply can't expect him to make a rational decision, even to save his life. Begging him to cooperate is equally nonproductive. Are we blocked, therefore? Do we come down to the old, insurmountable barrier that has stood for centuries—the unwillingness of the alcoholic to seek help? No, not according to our panel.

You simply can't expect him to make a rational decision, even to save his life.

Jerry Butler made it clear that there is a way around the resistance of the drinker. In fact, if you wait until he admits his need for help, he'll be dead first. Thousands die every year while denying they have a problem. That's why Alanon teaches family members how to confront in love. They learn how to remove the support systems that prop up the disease and permit it to thrive. They are shown how and when to impose ultimatums that force the alcoholic to admit his need for help. And sometimes, they recommend separation until the victim is so miserable that his denial will no longer hold up. In essence, Alanon teaches its own version of the *love must be tough* philosophy to family members who must implement it.

Alanon teaches its own version of the love must be tough *philosophy.*

I asked Bob if he was forced to attend Alcoholics Anonymous—the program that put him on the road to recovery. He said,

> Let me put it this way. No one goes to AA just because they've got nothing better to do that evening. Everyone there has been forced to attend initially. You just don't say, "On Monday night we watched a football game and on Tuesday we went to the movies. So what do you do on Wednesday? How about going over to an AA meeting?" It doesn't work that way. Yes, I was forced—forced by my own misery. Pauline allowed me to be miserable for my own good. It was loving duress that moved me to attend.

Though it may sound easy to achieve, the loving confrontation that brought Bob to his senses was a delicate maneuver. I must reemphasize that families should not attempt to implement it on their own initiative. Without the training and assistance of professional support groups, that encounter could degenerate into a hateful, vindictive, name-calling battle that would serve only to solidify the drinker's position. My purpose, therefore, has been to introduce my readers to the philosophy of loving toughness as applied to alcoholism, and to direct them to the organizations that will fill in the details.

Alanon Family Groups and Alcoholics Anonymous are both listed in local phone books. Also to be found there is the number of the Council on Alcoholism, which can provide further guidance. Finally, there are neighborhood or regional alcoholism programs provided by hospitals, governmental agencies, and private organizations. They can help you. Most will not assault your faith as a Christian, and, in fact, may well strengthen your dependence on God.

If you or a family member is struggling with the disease of alcoholism, you do not have to fight it alone. Call for help today.

7. DAUGHTER OF AN ALCOHOLIC

Dear Dr. Dobson:

Hi. My name is Karen and I am fourteen years old. I really enjoy your radio programs. I thought it was sad when you talked about your father. My dad and I don't get along so well. He used to be a policeman but not any more. He lost his job because he is an alcoholic. He's been to doctors and he's so far gone he can't be helped.

Dad always gets drunk and takes out his problems on the rest of the family. He's always sitting in taverns, somewhere. Living with an alcoholic is like living in hell. One night I was talking to a friend next door on the telephone and my dad heard me. He had come home drunk as usual. He came to my door, threw it open and yelled, "If you don't get off that phone I'm going to kill you." I knew he meant it.

I hung up the phone and sneaked out the back door. I went to a friend's house and spent the night there. Then I came home and crawled in a window at 6:00 A.M. so no one would notice I was gone. I was really scared.

> I hate living with an alcoholic. I get very angry at my dad. I've had to put up with his drinking since I was born. I always have problems at home. Please help me!
>
> Karen

I feel your pain, Karen, and I have some advice that will help you. First, your father is *not* too far gone. He can still be helped. There are no hopeless alcoholics—just alcoholics without hope. I'm sure your dad hates what he has become even more than you do, but he doesn't know how to overcome the disease he has.

Believe it or not, you can help him. Listed in your phone book is an organization called Alateen. It is for young people whose parents are afflicted with alcoholism. You can go there without your parents' permission or knowledge, and it's absolutely free. You will meet friends your age there who have the same problem you face. You will also meet grownups who'll show you how to handle it. I hope you'll give Alateen a call.

There are no hopeless alcoholics—just alcoholics without hope.

God loves you, Karen. I trust that He will help you get through this difficult time of your life, and then you'll learn how wonderful a family can be when drinking does not occur. Until then, keep your faith. Thanks for writing me.

CHAPTER FOURTEEN

Angry Women and Passive Men

THERE IS ANOTHER CLASSIC PATTERN OF MARITAL DISHARMONY occurring so commonly today that I feel I should devote an entire chapter to its cause and effect. Many of you will find yourselves described on the next few pages. Others will recognize parents, friends, or perhaps that divorced couple that used to live next door.

The problem has its origins in childhood, long before a young man and woman stand at the altar to say, "I do." For her part, the girl is taught subtly by her culture that marriage is a lifelong romantic experience; that loving husbands are entirely responsible for the happiness of their wives; that a good relationship between a man and woman should be sufficient to meet all needs and desires; and that any sadness or depression that a woman might encounter is her husband's fault. At least, he has the power to eradicate it if he cares enough. In other words, many American women come into marriage with unrealistically romantic expectations which are certain to be dashed. Not only does this orientation set up a bride for disappointment and agitation in the future, it also places enormous pressure on her husband to deliver the impossible.

Many American women come into marriage with unrealistically romantic expectations.

Unfortunately, the man of the house was taught some misconceptions in his formative years, too. He learned, perhaps from his father, that his only responsibility is to provide materially for his family. He must enter a business or profession and succeed at all costs, climbing the ladder of success and achieving an ever-increasing standard of living as proof of manhood. It never occurs to him that he is supposed to "carry" his wife emotionally. For Pete's sake! If he pays his family's bills and is a loyal husband, what more could any woman ask for? He simply doesn't understand what she wants.

It never occurs to him that he is supposed to "carry" his wife emotionally.

Inevitably, these differing assumptions collide head-on during the early years of marriage. Young John is out there competing like crazy in the marketplace, thinking his successes are automatically appreciated by the lady at home. To his shock, she not only fails to notice, but even seems to resent the work that takes him from her. "I'm doing it for you, babe!" he says. Diane isn't convinced.

What gradually develops from that misunderstanding is a deep, abiding anger on Diane's part, and a bewildered disgust from John. This pattern has been responsible for a million divorces in the past decade. The wife is convinced that her low self-esteem and her unhappiness are the result of her husband's romantic failures. With every year that passes, she becomes more bitter and hostile at him for giving so little of himself to his family. She attacks him viciously for what she considers to be his deliberate insults, and bludgeons him for refusing to change.

The wife is convinced that her low self-esteem and her unhappiness are the result of her husband's romantic failures.

John, on the other hand, does not have it within him to satisfy her needs. He didn't see it modeled by his father and his masculine, competitive temperament is not given to romantic endeavors. Besides, his work takes every ounce of energy in his body. It is a total impasse. There seems to be no way around it.

In the early years, John tries to accommodate Diane occasionally. At other times, he becomes angry and they slug it out in a verbal brawl. The following morning, he feels terrible about those fights. Gradually, his personality begins to change. He hates conflict with his wife and withdraws as a means of avoidance. What he needs most from his home (*like the majority of men*) is tranquility. Thus, he finds ways of escaping. He reads the paper, watches television, works in his shop, goes fishing, cuts the grass, plays golf, works at his desk, goes to a ball game—anything to stay out of the way of his hostile wife. Does this pacify her? Hardly! It is even more infuriating to have one's anger ignored.

He hates conflict with his wife and withdraws as a means of avoidance.

Here she is, screaming for attention and venting her hostility for his husbandly failures. And what does he do in return? He hides. He becomes more silent. He runs. The cycle has become a vicious one. The more anger she displays for his uninvolvement, the more detached he becomes. This inflames his wife with even greater hostility. She has said everything there is to say and it produced no response. Now she feels powerless and disrespected. Every morning he goes off to work where he can socialize with his friends, but she is stuck in this state of emotional deprivation.

She feels powerless and disrespected.

When a relationship has deteriorated to this point, the wife often resorts to some very unfortunate tactics. She begins to look for ways to hurt her husband in return. She embarrasses him by telling his business associates what a cad he is at home. She refuses to attend office functions or provide any other support for his occupation. She tells stories about him to their church associates. She shuts him down sexually and undermines his relationship with the children. To be sure, she can be a formidable opponent in the art of infighting. No one on the face of the earth could hurt John more deeply than his own wife.

Let me make it clear that I'm not condemning this woman out of hand. She has a good case against her husband. He doesn't meet her needs properly and he's an inveterate workaholic. To that extent, the man is guilty as charged. I attempted to express this feminine perspective in my book *What Wives Wish Their Husbands Knew About Women*, because I believe it is valid.

But every story has two sides, and John's version should also be told. His wife is wrong to believe that her contentment is exclusively his burden. No one should be expected to carry another person emotionally. Only Diane can make herself happy! She has no right to lay that total load on John. A good marriage is one in which the dominant needs are met within the relationship, but where each spouse develops individual identity, interests, and friendships. This may be the most delicate tightrope act in marriage. Extreme independence is as destructive to a relationship as total dependence.

No one should be expected to carry another person emotionally.

To summarize my concern, American women tend to be more unrealistic about marriage than their sisters around the world. Movies and television have made them feel that romantic excitement is not only a birthright, but the most important aspect of marriage. When this "feeling" component of the relationship is missing, the family is doomed. It'll just have to be scrapped. Not even the welfare of the children is important enough to preserve the marriage, and that is tragic.

Let me speak directly and boldly to the women who have seen themselves in this chapter. With all due respect, my most difficult task may be to help you recognize yourselves as part of the problem. The angry women I've counseled in the past have been so consumed by their husbands' disrespect and failures that they couldn't acknowledge their role in his inability to respond. But certainly, they had helped to make him what he was.

Look at it this way. Verbal bludgeoning never made anyone more loving or sensitive. You simply can't tear a guy to pieces and then expect him to meet your emotional needs. He's not made that way. Rather than attacking an unresponsive man and driving him away, there is a method of drawing him in your direction. It is accomplished by taking the pressure off him—by pulling backward a bit—by avoiding the worn-out accusations and complaints—by appearing to need him less—by showing appreciation for what he does right and for being fun to be with. Happiness is a marvelous magnet to the human personality.

Happiness is a marvelous magnet to the human personality.

Sometimes it is necessary to interject a challenge into the relationship in order to motivate a disengaged spouse. According to the *love must be tough* philosophy, a demeanor of self-confidence, mysterious quietness, and independence is far more effective in getting attention than a frontal assault.

I remember counseling a bright young lady whom I'll call Janet. She came to me because she seemed to be losing the affection of her husband. Frank appeared bored when he was at home, and he refused to take her out with him. On weekends, he went sailing with his friends despite the bitter protests of his wife. She had begged for his attention for months, but the slippage continued.

I hypothesized that Janet was invading Frank's territory and needed to recapture the challenge that made him want to marry her. Thus, I suggested that she retreat into her own world—stop "reaching" for him when he was at home—schedule some personal activities independently of his availability, etc. Simultaneously, I urged her to give him vague explanations about why her personality had changed. She was instructed not to display anger or discontent, allowing Frank to draw his own conclusions about what she was thinking. My purpose was to change his frame of reference. Instead of his thinking, "How can I escape from this woman who is driving me crazy," I wanted him to wonder, "What's going on? Am I losing Janet? Have I pushed her too far? Has she found someone else?"

I wanted him to wonder, "What's going on? Am I losing Janet?"

The results were dramatic. About a week after the change of manner was instituted, Janet and Frank were at home together one evening. After several hours of uninspired conversation and yawns, Janet told her husband that she was rather tired and wanted to go to bed. She said goodnight matter-of-factly and went to her bedroom. About thirty minutes later, Frank threw open the door and turned on the light. He proceeded to make passionate love to her, later saying that he couldn't stand the barrier that had come between them. It was precisely that barrier which Janet had complained about for months. Her approach had been so overbearing that she was driving him away from her. When she changed her direction, Frank also threw his truck in reverse. It often happens that way.

Having raised the subject of sex, let me ask you an interesting question. Which marriage is likely to enjoy the greatest physical attraction, the steady-as-a-rock relationship or the one that runs hot and cold?

Surprisingly, it is the one that varies from time to time. The highest voltage does not occur in the static marriage that is characterized by overfamiliarity, overexposure, and demystification. According to Kinsey researchers, the healthiest relationship is one that "breathes"—one that drifts from a time of closeness and tenderness to a more distant posture. That sets up another exciting reunion as the cycle continues. Couples that work or play together day after day are at a disadvantage compared to husbands and wives whose lifestyle takes them apart briefly and then brings them back together.

The healthiest relationship is one that "breathes."

Do you see the relevance to our discussion? Those individuals who constantly hover over their partners, drawing their complete reason for existence from that one person, actually handicap the relationship. They interfere with the natural "breathing" that proves to be so healthy over the years.

I'll conclude with an enlightening interview with my good friend Jean Lush, respected marriage, family, and child counselor. She spoke these words on our radio program, "Focus on the Family."

LUSH: Over-closeness can cause a marriage to become very dry. When a couple becomes tied to one another in this way, when they feed off each other exclusively, they lose some of the magic. You see, I feel a woman should preserve what I call the "mystique" that is uniquely hers. There should always be a bit of "mystery" in her personality.

DOBSON: Do you think it is possible for a husband and wife to destroy this sense of mystery by overcommunicating?

LUSH: I certainly do. I have counseled couples that complained about not loving each other anymore, even though they communicated beautifully. When they told me *how* they communicated, I then understood why love had died. They had destroyed the mystique and left only the bare ugliness. That's why I hate to see absolute honesty in marriage.

DOBSON: Explain what you mean by that.

LUSH: Well, let's consider what happens to a woman throughout the menstrual cycle. She can have some pretty depressing days, especially during the premenstrual stage. Speaking personally, I had a very biting, vicious tongue at that time, and that is not unusual. Now, if a woman believes she has a right— even an obligation—to be totally honest even when she knows her perception is distorted, she can say some horrid things that she doesn't really mean. That can be very hard on a marriage. It is simply not healthy to dump all the ugliness on your partner. We need to exercise some discipline in what we say to one another.

DOBSON: When you say you are opposed to total honesty in a marriage, you're not suggesting that husbands and wives be *dishonest* with one another, are you?

LUSH: No. But I am saying we don't have to verbalize every thought that comes in our heads. Love is a delicate flower that must be nurtured. It doesn't like heat, and it doesn't like cold. Remember that husbands and wives live in fleshly bodies; we are not saints, and too much ugly reality can take the edge off our affection for one another.

DOBSON: You also worry about women who lean too heavily on their husbands in their thirties, expecting them to carry them emotionally—

LUSH: I know of no better way to set up a midlife crisis ten years later than for a woman to demand more of her husband than he can give in his thirties.

I couldn't have said it better myself!

CHAPTER FIFTEEN

Loving Toughness for Singles

AN ENTIRE BOOK COULD BE WRITTEN ON THE LOVE MUST be tough principles as related to unmarried men and women. The problem, quite frankly, is that many singles want so desperately to be married that they violate the laws of freedom and respect in romantic relationships. That is like turning a firehose on a flickering flame. All that remains is black smoke and ashes.

Many singles violate the laws of freedom and respect in romantic relationships.

I heard of one young man who was determined to win the affection of a girl who refused to even see him. He decided that the way to her heart was through the mail, so he began writing her a love letter every day. When she did not respond, he increased his output to three notes every twenty-four hours. In all, he wrote her more than seven hundred letters, and she married the postman.

That is the way the system works. Romantic love is one of those rare human endeavors that succeeds best when it requires the least effort. Those who work the hardest at it are the most likely to fail. And speaking of people who try harder, no one beats a dude named Keith Ruff whose story was told in the *Los Angles Times*, February 21, 1982, by

Betty Cuniberti. The headline read, "Man Spends $20,000 Trying to Win Hand of Girl Who Can Say No."

> A love-struck man holed up in a $200-a-day Washington hotel has spent, at latest estimate, close to $20,000 demonstrating to his beloved that he won't take "no" for an answer to his marriage proposal.
>
> On bended knee on Christmas Day, 35-year-old Keith Ruff, once a stockbroker in Beverly Hills, proposed marriage to 20-year-old Karine Bolstein, a cocktail waitress at a Washington restaurant. He met her in a shoe store last summer. The pair had gone out a few times over a two-month period before the proposal.
>
> To his proposal, she looked down and said, "No."
>
> Since then, Ruff has remained in Washington and demonstrated his wish that she reconsider by sending her everything but a partridge in a pear tree.
>
> That may be next.
>
> He is, he thinks, "close to spending all of my money. I'm not an Arab sheik."

Shower of Gifts

The tokens of his affection include:

—A Learjet, placed on standby at the airport, "in case she wanted to ride around."

—Between 3,000 and 5,000 flowers.

—A limousine equipped with a bar and television, parked outside her door.

—A gold ring.

—$200 worth of champagne.

—Catered lobster dinners.

—Musicians to serenade her.

—A clown to amuse her younger brother.

—A man dressed as Prince Charming, bearing a glass slipper.

—Cookies, candy, and perfume.

—Sandwich-sign wearers walking around her home and the restaurant where Bolstein works, conveying the message "Mr. Dennis Keith Ruff LOVES Ms. Karine Bolstein."

—Balloons, which she promptly popped. "What else would she do?" said the undaunted Ruff. "The house was so full of flowers there was no room to walk around."

—For her father, a basket of nuts and $300 worth of cigars "to pass out to his friends at the Labor Department. It may sound goofy, but I like him."

—For her mother, flowers at the French Embassy, where she works. "I don't think her mother likes me. She called the police," Ruff said. "But I'll keep sending gifts to her also. How could anyone be so mad?"

—For both her parents, a stepladder, "so they might look at the relationship from a different angle."

Unsurprisingly, Ruff said he has "a very, very strange monetary situation."

He has not worked in some time, describing himself as being of independent means.

"I don't care how many job offers I get. I'm not interested in any of them," Ruff said. "I'd rather think about her than sit at a job."

He said he will spend his last dime and will beg for money if he has to, that he will "keep on trying for 10 years, 20 years. I'll ask her to marry me 50,000 times."

Nothing Stops Him

"It doesn't matter how many times she says no. I will do everything in my power that's not absurd or against a reasonable law. I wouldn't stop if she became a nun.

"I've never felt this way before!"

Bolstein, meanwhile, said she is flattered, but too young to get married. She also said the house looks like a funeral parlor.

Ruff said, "I don't want to force her to love me, but I can't stop.

"Maybe this makes her nervous, but at least she gets to smile along with being nervous. Anybody would like it somewhat."

Ruff said many people he talks to are skeptical.

"People would say my love is strange," he said, "but our whole society is falling apart because of the way people love. What is dating? Some guy putting his paws all over you?

"My friends in L.A. know how many women I've gone out with. I didn't like being a womanizer. I believe in the old values. I found the woman I love."

Ruff said he spends a lot of time in his hotel room planning what to do next and occasionally crying. Bolstein, meanwhile, has been getting asked for her autograph where she works and has had a drink there named after her, a concoction of gin, vodka and rum entitled She Won't.

Ruff said Bolstein called him once. "But I hung up on her. I didn't like what she said.

"Reality, to me, is disturbing," Ruff said. "I'd rather close my eyes and see her face.

"Fantasy is where I'm living. I'm living with hope.

"And some very big bills."*

There are several things ol' Ruff needs to know about women, assuming Miss Bolstein hasn't gotten the message across by now. He could cry in his hotel room for the next fifty years without generating the tiniest bit of sympathy from her. And that jet airplane doesn't mean a hill of beans to her either. Very few women are attracted to sniveling men who crawl, who bribe, who whine, and make donkeys of themselves in view of the whole world. Tell me, who wants to

---

*Man Spends $20,000 Trying to Win Hand of Girl Who Can Say No" by Betty Cuniberti, copyright, 1982, *Los Angeles Times*. Reprinted by permission.

marry an unambitious weirdo who grovels in the dirt like a whipped puppy? Goodbye, romance! Hello, poorhouse.

On a much smaller scale, of course, the same mistake is made by singles in other places. They reveal their hopes and dreams too early in the game and scare the socks off potential lovers. Divorcees fall into the same trap—especially single women who need a man to support them and their children. Male candidates for that assignment are rarities and are sometimes recruited like All-American athletes. I've seen no better illustration than the following item, also appearing in the *Los Angeles Times*. It was submitted to Virginia Doody Klein for use in her column "Living with Divorce":

Very few women are attracted to sniveling men who crawl, who bribe, who whine.

> Q. I am a recently divorced, professional man with an unusual problem. I hope you can help me. A woman I dated once called me before I even had a chance to make a second date with her and wanted to know why I hadn't called her again. After our second date she began to call almost daily with offers for dinner, something funny she'd read and thought I'd enjoy, etc. The crazy part is that this same routine has started with another woman I'm just beginning to ask out. If such behavior is typical, maybe I should have stayed married! How do I extricate myself from this frenzied dating and have a nice, quiet social life?*

Isn't it obvious what is occurring here? The women being dated by this "professional man" are chasing him like a hound after a rabbit. And predictably, his natural impulse is to run. If they are interested in

*"*Los Angeles Times*, April 12, 1982. The above excerpt is from the nationally syndicated column LIVING WITH DIVORCE by Virginia Doody Klein © 1982 Sun Features Inc.

pulling him toward them, they simply must not invade his territory. Instead, they should maintain a sense of decorum in their responses to him.

I attempted to explain the "how to" of this recommendation during the midseventies when I was writing *What Wives Wish Their Husbands Knew About Women*. The concepts I was formulating then have withstood intensive scrutiny since that time and provide the foundation for the book you are reading. This is what I wrote:

> It is of highest priority to maintain a distinct element of dignity and self-respect in all romantic encounters. I have observed that many relationships suffer from a failure to recognize a universal characteristic of human nature. We value that which we are fortunate to get; we discredit that with which we are stuck! We lust for the very thing which is beyond our grasp; we disdain that same item when it becomes a permanent possession. No toy is ever as much fun to play with as it appeared to a wide-eyed child in a store. Seldom does an expensive automobile provide the satisfaction anticipated by the man who dreamed of its ownership. This principle is even more dramatically accurate in romantic affairs, particularly with reference to men. Let's look at the extreme case of a Don Juan, the perpetual lover who buzzes from one feminine flower to another.
>
> His heart throbs and pants after the elusive princess who drops her glass slipper as she flees. Every ounce of energy is focused on her capture. However, the intensity of his desire is dependent on her unavailability. The moment his passionate dreams materialize, he begins to ask himself, "Is this what I really want?" Farther down the line as the relationship progresses toward the routine circumstances of everyday life, he is attracted by new princesses and begins to wonder how he can escape the older model.
>
> Now, I would not imply that all men, or even the majority of them, are as exploitative and impermanent as the gadabout I described. But

to a lesser degree, most men and women are impelled by the same urges. How many times have I seen a bored, tired relationship become a torrent of desire and longing the moment one partner rejects the other and walks out. After years of apathy, the "dumpee" suddenly burns with romantic desire and desperate hope.

This principle hits even closer to home for me at this moment. Right now, as I am writing these words, I am sitting in the waiting room of a large hospital while my wife is undergoing major abdominal surgery. I am writing to ease my tension and anxiety. While I have always been close to Shirley, my appreciation and tender love for her are maximal this morning. Less than five minutes ago, a surgeon emerged from the operating room with a grim face, informing the man near me that his wife is consumed with cancer. He spoke in unguarded terms of the unfavorable pathological report and the malignant infestation. I will be speaking to Shirley's surgeon within the hour and my vulnerability is keenly felt. While my love for my wife has never flagged through our fourteen years together, it has rarely been as intense as in this moment of threat. You see, not only are our emotions affected by the challenge of pursuit, but also by the possibility of irrevocable loss. (The surgeon arrived as I was writing the sentence above, saying my wife came through the operation with no complications, and the pathologist recognized no abnormal tissue. I am indeed a grateful man! My deepest sympathy is with the less fortunate family whose tragedy I witnessed today.)

A better example of fickle emotions is illustrated by my early relationship with Shirley. When we first met, she was a lowly sophomore in college and I was a lofty senior. I viewed myself as a big man on campus, and my relationship with this young coed mattered little to me. She, in turn, had been very successful with boys, and was greatly challenged by the independence I demonstrated. She wanted to win me primarily because she wasn't sure she could, but her enthusiasm inhibited my own interest in return. After graduation, we had one of those lengthy conversations well known to lovers the world over, when I said I wanted her to date other fellows while I was in the Army because I didn't plan to get married soon. I'll never forget her reaction. I expected Shirley to cry and hold on to me. Instead, she said, "I've been thinking the same thoughts, and I would like to date other guys. Why don't we just go our separate ways for now?" Her answer rocked me. For the first time in our relationship, she was moving away from me. What I didn't know was that Shirley stoically closed her front door and then cried all night.

I went away to the Army and returned to the University of Southern California for my graduate training. By this time, Shirley was an exalted senior and I was a collegiate has-been. She was homecoming queen, senior class president, a member of *Who's Who in American Colleges and Universities,* and one of the most popular girls in her class. And as might be expected, she suddenly looked very attractive to me. I began to call several times a day, complain about who she was spending her time with, and try to find ways to please my dream girl. However, the moment Shirley saw my enthusiasm and anxiety, her affection began to die. Gone was the challenge which had attracted her two years before. Instead, I had become just another fellow pounding on her door and asking for favors.

One day after a particularly uninspiring date, I sat down at a desk and spent two solid hours thinking about what was happening. And during the course of the introspection, I realized the mistake I was making. A light flashed in my head and I grabbed a pen and wrote ten changes I was going to make in our relationship. First, I was determined to demonstrate self-respect and dignity, even if I lost the one I now loved so deeply. Second, I decided to convey this attitude every time I got the chance: "I am going somewhere in life, and I'm anxious to get there. I love you and hope you choose to go with me. If you do, I'll give myself to you and try to make you happy. However, if you choose not to make the journey with me, then I can't force my will on you. The decision is yours and I'll accept it." There were other elements to my new manner, but they all centered on self-confidence and independence.

The first night that I applied the new formula was one of the most thrilling experiences of my life. The girl who is now my wife saw me starting to slip away on that evening, and she reacted with alarm. We were riding in silence in my car, and Shirley asked me to pull over to the curb and stop. When I did she put her arms around my neck and said, "I'm afraid I'm losing you and I don't know why. Do you still love me?" I noticed by the reflected light of the moon that she had tears in her eyes. She obviously didn't hear my thumping heart as I made a little speech about my solitary journey in life. You see, I had reestablished the challenge for Shirley, and she responded beautifully.

The psychological force which produced our see-saw relationship is an important one, since it is almost universal in human nature. Forgive the redundancy, but I must restate the principle: we crave that which we can't attain, but we disrespect that which we can't escape. This axiom is particularly relevant in romantic matters, and has probably influenced your love life, too.*

Given that background, let me get very specific with those of you who are single but wish not to be. (No insult is intended to those who are single by design and wish to remain unmarried. That is a legitimate choice which should be respected by friends and family, alike.) Listed below are sixteen suggestions that will help you conform to the principles of loving toughness in matters of the heart.

1. Don't let the relationship move too fast in its infancy. The phrase "too hot not to cool down" has validity. Take it one step at a time.

**What Wives Wish Their Husbands Knew About Women*, (Wheaton, IL: Tyndale House, 1975), pp. 78–82.

2. Don't discuss your personal inadequacies and flaws in great detail when the relationship is new. No matter how warm and accepting your friend may be, any great revelation of low self-esteem or embarrassing weaknesses can be fatal when interpersonal "valleys" occur. And they *will* occur.
3. Remember that respect precedes love. Build it stone upon stone.
4. Don't call too often on the phone or give the other person an opportunity to get tired of you.
5. Don't be too quick to reveal your desire to get married—or that you think you've just found Mr. Wonderful or Miss Marvelous. If your partner has not arrived at the same conclusion, you'll throw him or her into panic.
6. *Most important*. Relationships are constantly being "tested" by cautious lovers who like to nibble at the bait before swallowing the hook. This testing procedure takes many forms, but it usually involves pulling backward from the other person to see what will happen. Perhaps a foolish fight is initiated. Maybe two weeks will pass without a phone call. Or sometimes flirtation occurs with a rival. In each instance, the question being asked is, "How important am I to you, and what would you do if you lost me?" An even more basic issue lies below that one. It wants to know, "How free am I to leave if I want to?" It is incredibly important in these instances to appear poised, secure and equally independent. Do not grasp the other person and beg for mercy. Some people remain single throughout life because they cannot resist the temptation to grovel when the test occurs.
7. Extending the same concept, keep in mind that virtually every dating relationship that continues for a year or more and seems to be moving toward marriage will be given the ultimate test. A breakup will occur, motivated by only one of the lovers. The rejected individual should know that their

future together depends on the skill with which he/she handles that crisis. If the hurting individual can remain calm, as Shirley did with me, the next two steps may be reconciliation and marriage. It often happens that way. If not, then no amount of pleading will change anything.

8. Do not expect anyone to meet *all* your emotional needs. Maintain interests and activities outside that romantic relationship, even after marriage.
9. Guard against selfishness in your love affair. Neither the man nor the woman should do all the giving. I once broke up with a girl because she let me take her to nice places, bring her flowers, buy her lunch, etc. I wanted to do these things, but expected her to reciprocate in some way. She didn't.
10. Beware of blindness to obvious warning signs that tell you that your potential husband or wife is basically disloyal, hateful, spiritually uncommitted, hooked on drugs or alcohol, given to selfishness, etc. Believe me, a bad marriage is far worse than the most lonely instance of singleness.
11. Don't marry the person you think you can live with; marry only the individual you think you can't live without.
12. Be careful to defend the "line of respect," even during a dating relationship. A man should open doors for a woman on a formal evening; a woman *should* speak respectfully of her escort when in public, etc. If you don't preserve this delicate line when the foundations of marriage are being laid, it will be virtually impossible to construct them later.
13. Do not equate human worth with flawless beauty or handsomeness! If you require physical perfection in your mate, he or she may make the same demands of you. Don't let love escape you because of the false values of your culture. In the same vein, be careful not to *compare* yourself with others—which is the root of all inferiority.
14. If genuine love has escaped you thus far, don't begin

believing "no one would ever want me." That is a deadly trap that can destroy you emotionally! Millions of people are looking for someone to love. The problem is finding one another!

15. Regardless of how brilliant the love affair has been, take time to "check your assumptions" with your partner before committing yourself to marriage. It is surprising how often men and women plunge toward matrimony without ever becoming aware of major differences in expectation between them. For example:

    a. Do you want to have children? How soon? How many?
    b. Where will you live?
    c. Will the wife work? How soon? How about after children are born?
    d. Who will lead in the relationship? What does that reach mean?
    e. How will you relate to your in-laws?
    f. How will money be spent?
    g. Where will you attend church?

    These and dozens of other "assumptions" should be discussed item by item, perhaps with the help of a premarital counselor. Many future struggles can be avoided by coming to terms with potential areas of disagreement. If the differences are great enough, it is even possible that the marriage should never occur.

16. Finally, sexual familiarity can be deadly to a relationship. In addition to the many moral, spiritual, and physical reasons for remaining virgins until marriage, there are numerous psychological and interpersonal advantages to the exercise of self-control and discipline. Though it's an old-fashioned notion, perhaps, it is still true that men do not respect "easy" women and often become bored with those who have held nothing in reserve. Likewise, women often disrespect men

who have only one thing on their minds. Both sexes need to remember how to use a very ancient word. It's pronounced "NO!"

These sixteen suggestions are not guaranteed to win the hand of a lover, of course, but they will certainly beat the approach of Mr. Keith Ruff. And you'll save $20,000 in the process!

CHAPTER SIXTEEN

Components of a Good Marriage

PERHAPS WE HAVE SAID ENOUGH ABOUT DETERIORATING human relationships and why homes are falling apart today. I have devoted the large measure of fifteen chapters to the concept of loving toughness and how it can draw families back together, even when they have been on the brink of disintegration. But there are limitations to this approach, directly related to the inherent strength of the foundation upon which the troubled marriage was built. For the injured partner to show self-respect and poise in a period of crisis will bring about no more than a temporary respite *unless there is a foundation of authentic love upon which to rebuild.*

It is appropriate, therefore, that we turn our attention now to the foundation itself. What are the mysterious ingredients that almost all good marriages have in common? What accounts for the marvelous blending of personalities when two separate and distinct individuals establish a young family and then live together in love and in harmony for the next fifty or sixty years? Is anything of significance known about these long-term marriages that will help others achieve stability in a world of impermanence?

> *The healthiest marriages are those where a proper "bonding" has occurred between a husband and a wife.*

Fortunately, Dr. Desmond Morris has provided an intelligent answer to those questions in his book *Intimate Behavior.* It was brought to my attention by Dr. Donald Joy, who interpreted the findings for our radio listeners. Dr. Joy said research now verifies that the healthiest marriages are those where a proper "bonding" has occurred between a husband and wife. Bonding refers to the emotional covenant that links a man and woman together for life and makes them intensely valuable to one another. It is the specialness that sets those two lovers apart from every other person on the face of the earth. It is God's gift of companionship to those who have experienced it.

But how does this bonding occur, and why is it missing in so many relationships? According to Drs. Joy and Morris, bonding is most likely to develop among those who have moved systematically and slowly through twelve steps during their courtship and early marriage. These stages, described below,* represent a progression of physical intimacy from which a permanent commitment often evolves.

1. *Eye to body.* A glance reveals much about a person—sex, size, shape, age, personality, and status. The importance people place on these criteria determines whether or not they will be attracted to each other.
2. *Eye to eye.* When the man and woman who are strangers to each other exchange glances, their most natural reaction is to look away, usually with embarrassment. If their eyes meet again, they may smile, which signals that they might like to become better acquainted.
3. *Voice to voice.* Their initial conversations are trivial and include questions like, "What is your name?" or "What do you do for a living?" During this long stage the two people learn much about each other's opinions, pastimes, activities,

---

**Intimate Behavior* by Desmond Morris, chap. 3, "Sexual Intimacy" (New York: Random House, 1971), esp. pp. 73–78. Used by permission.

habits, hobbies, likes and dislikes. If they're compatible, they become friends.

4. *Hand to hand.* The first instance of physical contact between the couple is usually on nonromantic occasions such as when the man helps the woman descend a high step or aids her across an obstacle. At this point, either of the individuals can withdraw from the relationship without rejecting the other. However, if continued, hand-to-hand contact will eventually become an evidence of the couple's romantic attachment to each other.
5. *Hand to shoulder.* This affectionate embrace is still noncommittal. It is a "buddy" type position in which the man and woman are side by side. They are more concerned with the world in front of them than they are with each other. The hand-to-shoulder contact reveals a relationship that is more than a close friendship, but probably not real love.
6. *Hand to waist.* Because this is something two people of the same sex would not ordinarily do, it is clearly romantic. They are close enough to be sharing secrets or intimate language with each other. Yet, as they walk side by side with hand to waist, they are still facing forward.
7. *Face to face.* This level of contact involves gazing into one another's eyes, hugging, and kissing. If none of the previous steps were skipped, the man and woman will have developed a special code from experience that enables them to engage in deep communication with very few words. At this point, sexual desire becomes an important factor in the relationship.
8. *Hand to head.* This is an extension of the previous stage. The man and woman tend to cradle or stroke each other's head while kissing or talking. Rarely do individuals in our culture touch the head of another person unless they are either

romantically involved or unless they are family members. It is a designation of emotional closeness.

9–12. *The final steps.* The last four levels of involvement are distinctly sexual and private. They are (9) *hand to body,* (10) *mouth to breast,* (11 *touching below the waist,* and (12) *intercourse.* Obviously, the final acts of physical contact should be reserved for the marital relationship, since they are progressively sexual and intensely personal.

What Joy and Morris are saying is that intimacy must proceed slowly if a male-female relationship is to achieve its full potential. When two people love each other deeply and are committed for life, they have usually developed a great volume of understandings between them that would be considered insignificant to anyone else. They share countless private memories unknown to the rest of the world. That is, in large measure, where their sense of specialness to one another originates. Furthermore, the critical factor is that they have taken these steps in *sequence.* When later stages are reached prematurely, such as when couples kiss passionately on the first date or have sexual intercourse before marriage, something precious is lost from the relationship. Instead, their courtship should be nurtured through leisurely walks and talks and "lovers' secrets" that lay the foundation for mutual intimacy. Now we can see how the present environment of sexual permissiveness and lust serves to weaken the institution of marriage and undermine the stability of the family. *

Intimacy must proceed slowly.

*If you have further interest, let me suggest that you consult Joy's extended work linking pair bonding to Genesis 2 and to Jesus' words in Matthew 19. See "Basic Life Intimacies: Pair Bonding" and

At the risk of trivializing a beautiful concept, let me share the words of a recent popular song that illustrates this shared intimacy. Though the lyrics were apparently intended to be humorous, they speak clearly about the voice-to-voice stage of courtship from which bonded relationships develop.**

> I'm the official historian on Shirley Jean Berrell,
> I've known her since Lord only knows and I won't tell;
> I caught her the first time she stumbled and fell,
> And Shirley, she knows me just as well.
> I can tell you her birthday and her daddy's middle name,
> The uncles on her momma's side and ones they don't claim;
> What she's got for Christmas since nineteen fifty-two,
> And that's only the beginning of the things I could tell you.
> I can tell you her fav'rite song and where she'd like to park,
> And why to this very day she's scared of the dark;
> How she got her nickname and that scar behind her knee,
> If there's anything you need to know 'bout Shirley, just ask me.
> I know where she's ticklish and her every little quirk,
> The funnies she don't read, and her number at work;
> I know what she stands for and what she won't allow,
> The only thing that I don't know is where she is right now.
> Ole Shirley, she knows me just as well.

It would appear that Shirley Jean Berrell and her singing boyfriend are well on their way toward a bonded relationship. I hope they will be happy together.

"Jesus: What God Joins Together," Tape 8341 in the series *Discipleship Development in the Home* 1983. This is one of sixteen tapes in the series. Write to Center for the Study of Children, Conscience, and the Family, Wilmore, KY 40390.

**Title: The Official Historian on Shirley Jean Berrell. Written by: Don Reid and Harold Reid. As recorded by The Statler Brothers. Copyright © 1978 by American Cowboy Music Company. Used by permission.

Before we tuck away this understanding of bonded commitments, let me emphasize that this concept applies not only to courtship experiences. The most successful marriages are those wherein husbands and wives journey through the twelve steps regularly in their daily lives. Touching and talking and holding hands and gazing into one another's eyes and building memories are as important to partners in their midlife years as to rambunctious twenty year olds. Indeed, the best way to invigorate a tired sex life is to walk through the twelve steps of courtship, regularly and with gusto! Conversely, when sexual intercourse is experienced without the stages of intimacy that should have preceded it in prior days, the woman is likely to feel used and abused.

Successful marriages are those wherein husbands and wives journey through the twelve steps regularly.

For couples that have found it difficult to maintain the kind of intimacy and closeness I have described, I would like to offer the strongest endorsement for a program called Marriage Encounter. While not intended for marriages in serious jeopardy, this program is the best I've seen for improving the quality of communication within the family. The principles on which it is based are valid and effective.

I would like to offer the strongest endorsement for a program called Marriage Encounter.

Shirley and I had heard about Marriage Encounter for years but had never found time to participate. Finally, at the urging of a pediatrician friend, we decided to experience ME for ourselves. Frankly, I attended for professional reasons, not expecting to get anything relevant to my wife and me. If there is anything I felt Shirley and I didn't need it was help in communicating. I have rarely been so wrong.

The beauty of Marriage Encounter is that it has the ability to *float* to wherever the need is greatest. In our case, the need had little to do with communication in the classic sense. Instead, we discovered a secret source of tension that Shirley had not verbalized and I didn't know existed. It had to do with the recent deaths of eight senior members of our small family, six of whom were males. My wife had watched as the survivors struggled to cope with life alone and the awesome implications of sudden widowhood. Because Shirley and I were in our midforties, she was quietly worrying about the possibility of losing me—and was wanting to know where we were going from here. My loving wife was also saying to herself, "I know Jim needed me when we were younger and he was struggling to establish himself professionally. But do I *still* have a prominent place in his heart?"

One simply does not sit down to discuss such delicate matters, voice to voice, in the rush and hubbub of everyday life. They are held inside until (and if) an opportunity to express them is provided. For Shirley and me, that occurred throughout the Marriage Encounter program. In the early part of the weekend, we worked through the possibility of my death; then on the final morning, the issue of my continued love for her was laid to rest.

One simply does not sit down to discuss such delicate matters, voice to voice, in the rush and hubbub of everyday life.

Shirley was alone in our hotel room, expressing her private concern in a written statement to me. And by divine leadership I'm sure, I was in another room addressing the same issue, even though we had not discussed it. When we came together and renewed our commitment for the future, whatever it might hold, Shirley and I experienced one of the most emotional moments of our lives. It was a highlight of our twenty-one years together, and neither of us will ever forget it.

Although it will require me to share an intensely personal statement between my wife and me, I would like to conclude with a portion of the letter I wrote to her on that memorable morning. I will skip the more intimate details, quoting only the memories that "bonded" me to my bride.

Who else shares the memory of my youth during which the foundations of love were laid? I ask you, who else could occupy the place that is reserved for the only woman who was *there* when I graduated from college and went to the Army and returned as a student at USC and bought my first decent car (and promptly wrecked it) and picked out an inexpensive wedding ring with you (and paid for it with Savings Bonds), and we prayed and thanked God for what we had. Then we said the wedding vows and my dad prayed, "Lord, you gave us Jimmy and Shirley as infants to love and cherish and raise for a season, and tonight, we give them back to you after our labor of love—not as two separate individuals, but as one!" And everyone cried. Then we left for the honeymoon and spent all our money and came home to an apartment full of rice and a bell on the bed, and we had only just begun. You taught the second grade and I taught (and fell in love with) a bunch of sixth graders, and especially a kid named Norbert, and I earned a masters degree and passed the comprehensive exams for a doctorate. and we bought our first little home and remodeled it and I dug up all the grass and buried it in a 10-foot hole which later sank and looked like two graves in the front yard—and while spreading the dirt to make a new lawn, I accidentally "planted" eight million ash seeds from our tree and discovered two weeks later that we had a forest growing between our house and the street. Then alas, you delivered our very own baby, and we loved her half to death and named her Danae Ann and built a room on our little bungalow and gradually filled it with furniture. Then I joined the staff of Children's Hospital, and I did well there, but still didn't have enough money to pay our USC tuition and other expenses, so we sold (and ate) a Volkswagen. Then I earned a Ph.D. and we cried and thanked God for what we had. In 1970, we brought home a little boy and named him James Ryan and loved him half to death and didn't sleep for six months. And I labored over a manuscript titled "Dare To" something or other and then reeled backward under a flood of favorable responses and a few not so favorable responses and received a small royalty check and thought it was a fortune and I joined the faculty at USC School of Medicine and did well there. Soon I found myself pacing the halls of Huntington Memorial Hospital as a team of grim faced neurologists examined your nervous system for evidence of a hypothalamic tumor and I prayed and begged God to let me complete my life with my best friend, and He finally said, "Yes—for now," and we cried and thanked Him for what we had. And we bought a new house and promptly tore it to shreds and went skiing in Vail, Colorado, and tore your leg to shreds, and I called your mom to report the accident, and she tore me to shreds and our toddler, Ryan, tore the whole town of Arcadia to shreds. And the construction on the house seemed to go on forever and you stood in the shattered living room and cried every Saturday night because so little had been accomplished. Then during the worst of the mess, 100 friends gave us a surprise house warming and they slopped through the debris and mud and sawdust and cereal bowls and sandwich parts—and the next morning you groaned and asked, "Did it really happen?" And I published a new book called *Hide or Seek* (What?) and everyone called it Hide *and* Seek, and the publisher sent us to Hawaii and we stood on the balcony overlooking the bay and thanked God for what we had. And I published *What Wives Wish* and people liked it and the honors rolled in and the speaking requests arrived by the hundreds. Then you underwent risky surgery and I said, "Lord, not now!" And the doctor said, "No cancer!" and we cried and thanked God for what we had. Then I started a radio program and took a leave of absence from Children's Hospital and opened a little office in Arcadia called Focus on the Family, which a three-year-old radio listener later called

"Poke Us in the Family," and we got more visible. Then we went to Kansas City for a family vacation and my dad prayed on the last day and said, "Lord, we know it can't always be the wonderful way it is now, but we thank you for the love we enjoy today." A month later he experienced his heart attack and in December I said goodbye to my gentle friend and you put your arm around me and said, "I'm hurting with you!" and I cried and said "I love you!" And we invited my mother to spend six weeks with us during her recuperation period and the three of us endured the loneliest Christmas of our lives as the empty chair and missing place setting reminded us of his red sweater and dominoes and apples and a stack of sophisticated books and a little dog named Benji who always sat on his lap. But life went on. My mother staggered to get herself back together and couldn't and lost fifteen pounds and moved to California and still ached for her missing friend. And more books were written and more honors arrived and we became better known and our influence spread and we thanked God for what we had. And our daughter went into adolescence and this great authority on children knew he was inadequate and found himself asking God to help him with the awesome task of parenting, and He did and we thanked Him for sharing His wisdom with us. And then a little dog named Siggie who was sort of a dachshund grew old and toothless and we had to let the vet do his thing, and a fifteen-year love affair between man and dog ended with a whimper. But a pup named Mindy showed up at the front door and life went on. Then a series of films were produced in San Antonio, Texas, and our world turned upside down as we were thrust into the fishbowl and "Poke us in the Family" expanded in new directions and life got busier and more hectic and time became more precious, and then someone invited us to a Marriage Encounter weekend where I sit at this moment.

So I ask you! Who's gonna take your place in my life? You have become me and I have become you. We are inseparable. I've now spent 46 percent of my life with you, and I can't even remember much of the first 54! Not one of the experiences I've listed can be comprehended by anyone but the woman who lived through them with me. Those days are gone, but their aroma lingers on in our minds. And with every event during these twenty-one years, our lives have become more intertwined—blending eventually into this incredible affection that I bear for you today.

Is it any wonder that I can read your face like a book when we are in a crowd? The slightest narrowing of your eyes speaks volumes to me about the thoughts that are running through your conscious experience. As you open Christmas presents, I know instantly if you like the color or style of the gift, because your feelings cannot be hidden from me.

I love you, S.M.D. (remember the monogrammed shirt)? I love the girl who believed in me before I believed in myself. I love the girl who never complained about huge school bills and books and hot apartments and rented junky furniture and no vacations and humble little Volkswagens. You have been *with* me—encouraging me, loving me, and supporting me since August 27, 1960. And the status you have given me in our home is beyond what I have deserved.

So why do I want to go on living? It's because I have you to take that journey with. Otherwise, why make the trip? The half-life that lies ahead promises to be tougher than the years behind us. It is in the nature of things that my mom will someday join my father and then she will be laid to rest beside him in Olathe, Kansas, overlooking a wind-swept hill from whence he walked with Benji and recorded a cassette tape for me describing the beauty of that spot. Then we'll have to say goodbye to your mom and dad. Gone will be the table games we played and the Ping-Pong and lawn darts and Joe's laughter and Alma's wonderful ham dinners and her underlined birthday cards and the little yellow house in Long Beach. Everything within me screams "No!" But my dad's final prayer is still valid—"We know it can't always be the way it is now." When that time comes, our childhoods will then be severed—cut off by the passing of the beloved parents who bore us.

What then, my sweet wife? To whom will I turn for solace and comfort? To whom can I say, "I'm hurting!" and know that I am understood in more than an abstract manner? To whom can I turn when the summer leaves begin to change colors and fall to the ground? How much I have enjoyed the springtime and the warmth of the summer sun. The flowers and the green grass and the blue sky and the dear streams have been savored to their fullest. But alas, autumn is coming. Even now, I can feel a little nip in the air—and I try not to look at a distant, lone cloud that passes near the horizon. I must face the fact that winter lies ahead—with its ice and sleet and snow to pierce us through. But in this instance, winter will not be followed by springtime, except in the glory of the life to come. With whom, then, will I spend that final season of my life?

None but you, Shirls. The only joy of the future will be in experiencing it as we have the past twenty-one years—hand in hand with the one I love . . . a young miss named Shirley Deere, who gave me everything she had—including her heart.

Thank you, babe, for making this journey with me. Let's finish it—together!

Your Jim

That is known as marital bonding!

CHAPTER SEVENTEEN

With More Love to the Victims

I BEGAN THIS BOOK WITH AN EXPRESSION OF LOVE AND empathy for the men and women who have gone through severe family crises and personal suffering. I would like to conclude my comments by speaking directly to those same individuals who desperately need the advice I've offered. I know this has not been an easy book for you to read. Frankly, I found it difficult to write. I have taken no pleasure in describing the sordid details of infidelity, child and wife abuse, homosexuality, alcoholism, marital conflict, and divorce. But this is reality! Half the American couples over forty years of age have experienced extramarital affairs at some point,* and more divorces are occurring than marriages at this time. That translates into millions of people who have experienced the same emotional trauma that you've encountered. And that's why I wrote this book. I hoped to provide some practical tools and philosophies with which to draw your partner back in the direction of commitment and responsibility. I pray that will happen!

But now I must offer one final word of advice, equal in importance to anything I have written. Surprisingly, my greatest concern is reserved for those families that have pulled themselves back from the brink of divorce with God's help and seem to be on the road to

---

*According to *Psychology Today*, 1983

recovery. At that moment of celebration, a new peril often emerges that can be more deadly than the first. Just when the battle appears to have been won, everything can be lost for reasons that did not exist in the beginning. That's why I urge you to read this final chapter carefully and heed its warning.

At that moment of celebration, a new peril often emerges that can be more deadly than the first.

In order to explain, let's return to the plight of Linda, whose husband is involved with another woman. As you recall, she has suffered untold agonies over Paul's blatant infidelity and rejection, being wounded almost to the point of death. Indeed, suicide has undoubtedly been her option many times in the early hours of the morning or on a lonely afternoon.

But then a quiet transformation begins to occur. Let's suppose Linda stumbles across the principles of loving toughness and gradually learns to set her husband free. She realizes for the first time that the guilt she feels is not entirely valid, and the dynamics of their conflict come into clearer focus. Her self-esteem slowly returns, and the long bleak winter starts to thaw.

Linda may no longer want Paul back when she finally learns she can have him. It often happens just that way!

You can't imagine how good it feels for her to escape the pain of the past! Relief, blessed relief, occurs after months of unrelenting depression and sorrow. But beware! Therein lies the danger! It is very easy in that moment for Linda to forget her original desire to draw Paul back to her, permanently sealing him out of her heart. When the selfishness of what he has done is fully realized, her depression can turn to anger or profound apathy. She could also fear that once Paul has returned and the crisis is over, her original problems will recur and life will be no different from their darkest hours. For these and other reasons, Linda may no longer want Paul back when she finally learns she can have him. It often happens just that way! When it does, the unfaithful spouse sometimes goes through the same agonies that besieged his wife a few months earlier. The entire relationship can turn upside down.

There is no place for hatred in the heart of one who has himself been forgiven.

To all those who find yourselves in Linda's situation today, I urge you to remain open to the will of the Lord, even though it means loving and forgiving the one who caused so much grief! I know it is easier to talk about forgiveness than to exercise it, especially when the hurt was inflicted by a marital partner. Nevertheless, that is what we as Christians are required to do in time. There is no place for hatred in the heart of one who has himself been forgiven of so many sins.

I must stress this point. The toughness I have recommended in response to irresponsibility can be destructive and vicious unless it is characterized by genuine love and compassion. Our purpose must never be to hurt or punish the other person, even when retribution is deserved by him or her. Vengeance is the exclusive prerogative of the Lord (Rom. 12:19). Furthermore, resentment is a dangerous emotion. It can be a malignancy that consumes the spirit and warps the mind, leaving us bitter and disappointed with life. I'll say it again: no matter how badly we have been mistreated or how selfish our partners have seemed, we are called upon to release them from accountability. That is the meaning of true forgiveness. According to psychologist Archibald Hart, "Forgiveness is surrendering my right to hurt you for hurting me."

Some of the most dramatic moments in my counseling experience have involved outright forgiveness by one spouse for the devastating wrongs of the other. I'll never forget the day Janelle walked into my office. She brought an air of depression and sadness with her as she sat head downward in a chair. Her husband, Lonny, had asked for my help after Janelle attempted suicide in the middle of the night. He had gotten up at 3:00 A.M. to go to the bathroom and found her in the process of taking her life. If he had not awakened, she would have been gone.

I'll never forget the day Janelle walked into my office.

Lonny had no idea why Janelle attempted to kill herself or why she was so depressed. She wouldn't tell him. He knew she was dealing with something awesome, but he could not make her reveal it. Even after the suicide episode, she held everything inside, moping around the house in depression. Finally, she agreed to talk to me, and Lonny brought her to my office.

Lonny sat outside while Janelle and I talked. At first she threw a smokescreen around her emotions, but eventually the story broke. She was deeply involved in an affair with a business acquaintance and the guilt was tearing her to pieces.

I said, "Janelle, you know that the only way you will ever settle this matter is to confess the affair to Lonny. You can't keep this enormous secret between you forever. It will be a barrier that will destroy what's left of your marriage. I think you should tell Lonny the truth and seek his help in ending the affair."

She was deeply involved in an affair.

She looked at me sadly and said, "I know that's right, but I can't tell him! I've tried and I just can't do it!"

I said, "Do you want *me* to do it?"

Janelle nodded through the tears, and I said, "Go to the waiting room and ask Lonny to come in. You stay there and I'll call for you in about an hour."

Lonny arrived with an anxious look on his face. He was worried about his wife, yet he had no idea what to expect. That was, I believe, one of the toughest assignments I've ever had—to tell a loving, faithful husband that he had been betrayed by his wife. As might be expected, the news hit him like a blow from a hammer. His anger and anguish were intertwined with compassion and remorse. We continued talking for a while, and then I invited Janelle back into my office.

These two wounded people sat in depression as I attempted to ease communication between them. But the atmosphere was extremely heavy. Finally, I prayed and asked them to leave and come back at 10:00 A.M. the next day.

Janelle and Lonny had a bad night. They didn't fight, but they were both so hurt and disturbed that they couldn't sleep. Nor could they talk to one another. They arrived back in my office the next morning in the same state in which they had left. I talked to them about forgiveness, about divine healing of memories, and about their present situation. I don't know how it happened even today, but a spirit of love began to permeate that office. We prayed together and suddenly, Janelle and Lonny fell into each other's arms, weeping and asking for forgiveness and *granting* that forgiveness. It was an unbelievable moment of joy for all three of us, and it happened because a man who had been deceived and betrayed was willing to say, "I hold nothing against you!"

A spirit of love began to permeate that office.

Though this kind of forgiveness is difficult to either give or receive, I can assure you that divorce is even more difficult. It leaves scars on its victims that will last a lifetime. This is why God hates divorce (Mal. 2:16). He knows the devastation that it inflicts, not only on adults, but even more severely on young children! That is, of course, the soft spot in my heart. I have a special tenderness for kids who hurt, especially those who ache for the arms of a departed parent. It is an everyday occurrence among children in the United States. Over half of the boys and girls under eighteen years of age have one or both parents missing. Within three years of the divorce, half of the fathers never see their children. One of those kids, Lisa Castro, a friend of my daughter, wrote the following poem and addressed it to her father. She said,

God hates divorce.

Father, I wonder . . .
Did you want to leave us?
I've always wondered why.
Did you ever wonder how it *could* have been?
Did it ever make you cry?
I sit at home and think of you—and how our lives could be.
I've always wished, so very much, that you were here with me.
I feel like a part of me has somehow never grown.
Do you ever think of me? My father? My own?

I don't know the circumstance which caused Lisa's father to leave, but often the motive for family disintegration is nothing more substantial than unbridled selfishness. In those instances, I must ask what sexual thrills—what romantic extravaganzas, what conflict—could justify the pain of a child like Lisa? It will be remembered for a lifetime! Comedian Jonathan Winters referred to his parents' divorce forty years earlier when he said, "All of my humor is a response to sorrow!"

Divorce is also devastating to parents who want to be with the children they lost in a custody hearing. That is Martin's situation, as he described it in an emotional letter to me:

Dear Dr. Dobson:

I watched your film on the subject of fathering last night. Those around me were in tears when it was over and I could not find the strength to leave. You see, I am the father of a 3-year-old son named Bradley. Two years ago his mother decided to divorce me and she got a court order to force me out of the house. A staff psychologist testified that I would make a better parent than my wife, but she got custody of the child and the judge gave her almost everything we had. The one thing I wanted—the one thing I really cared about—was little Bradley. He needed me!

Bradley was still in diapers when my wife and I separated and the only words he could say were, "My daddy!" But he knew what they meant. When I would come for my visitation day, he would cling to me saying those words. He would sleep for three hours within a few minutes after I picked him up. Then when I returned him to his mother, Bradley would stretch his arms toward me screaming, "My daddy! My daddy!"

I have cherished my times with Bradley these past two years. He and I watch television together, and he lies on my stomach and goes to sleep. Sometimes he sits on the floor beside me and puts his little legs on top of me because Daddy puts his feet on the couch. I taught Bradley to brush his teeth and how to use the potty chair. If he's had a bad dream he will tell me about it. In earlier days when his mother washed his hair, Bradley would scream. But now I tell him what I expect and assure him that I will not get soap in his eyes, and he doesn't cry. He trusts me. I feel so close to my son. If I go to the garage and do some work, Bradley goes with me. Daddy is so proud to have his little boy with him that he doesn't even care when his son dumps nails all over the floor. I taught him to pray.

Now that Bradley is three and a half, he can express his feelings to me. Yesterday he asked if I had to take him back to be with his mommy. When I told him, "Not right now, son, but yes, this is the day," he started crying. He said, "Daddy, I really miss you." Yes, I cried then, too. And I am crying now.

Bradley's mother tells him I am no good and he should forget me. She criticizes the meals I fix and tries to convince him that I can't cook. She curses me and calls me names in Bradley's presence. These are minor offenses compared to other things she has done. But the most painful thing to me is that my child has a daddy to teach him only four days a month. Four lousy, stinking, rotten days! How can I mold his developing personality and teach him my values in four short days?

Bradley, I love you. My prayers for you and those like you never cease. I'll take my four days with you now and pray for the time I can see you more.

You can understand, Dr. Dobson, why I was screaming inside when I saw your movie tonight. I wanted you to keep saying it. Tell the people what they are doing to their kids! Show them how to resolve their differences. Save the families.

It doesn't seem quite right for a 6'2", 205-pound Black Belt in karate to cry, but that's all I seem to do anymore.

Thanks for your time,

Martin

It almost seems as though Singer Tom T. Hall had a father like Martin in mind when he wrote the lyrics to his song, "I Left You Some Kisses on the Door."

Your mom says I can't see you; the judge says that it's right.
We can't be together, 'cause me and Mommy fight.
But you're my little girl and Daddy loves you more and more.
And I left you some kisses on the door.

I came by to see you but Mommy just said no.
I knocked but Mommy saw me as she peeked through the hole.
I only want to hold you, honey; Mommy thinks it's war.
But I left you some kisses on the door.

You know your Daddy worries, honey, but it's not Mama's fault.
You do what your Mommy says; you know she's the boss.
No matter what I gave you, Mommy thought you needed more,
But I left you some kisses on the door.

Hey, you're my little angel, babe, and it don't make much sense
To only get to watch you play through that old schoolyard fence.
Someday you'll come to me, sweetheart, that's all I'm waiting for,
'Cause I left you some kisses on the door.*

Come on, America. Enough is enough! We've had our dance with divorce, and we have a million broken homes to show for it. We've tried the me-philosophy and the new morality and unbridled hedonism. They didn't work. Now it's time to get back to some old-fashioned values, like commitment and sacrifice and responsibility and purity and love and the straight life. Not only will our children benefit from our self-discipline and perseverance, but we adults will live in a less neurotic world, too!

Now it's time to get back to some old-fashioned values.

But I can hear someone saying, "Okay, so divorce is not the answer. I have done everything I can to forgive my mate, but I still don't think I can ever feel affectionate toward this person who deliberately broke my heart." Let me assure you that romantic love and tenderness can be nurtured back to health, even when the relationship seems beyond the grave. I've seen the Author of

Romantic love and tenderness can be nurtured back to health.

*Written by Tom T. Hall. Published by Hallnote Music. Copyright 1979. All rights reserved. Used by permission.

Love "restore the years the locusts have eaten" for those who have tried to obey Him. I'll conclude with a letter from Jacque, who has been where *you*, the reader, may be today.

Dear Dr. Dobson:

I was married to a nonbeliever for fourteen years in what proved to be a living hell on earth. There's no way I can describe how terrible Brent treated me during that time. I considered running away or anything that might help me cope. It seemed that my prayers and my church work were useless in bringing me peace of mind. Gradually, I gave in to the advances of another church member.

He was also unhappily married and, inevitably, we became deeply involved in an affair.

This man's wife then died of heart disease, and I intended to divorce my husband to marry him. But when Brent saw that he was losing me with no hope of reconciliation, he quietly gave up all the terrible treatment of me and became kind almost overnight. He even changed occupations to give him more time at home.

That put me in a very difficult situation. I loved the other man and felt I couldn't live without him, and yet I knew it was wrong to divorce my husband. By an act of sheer faith, I broke off the relationship with the other man and did what I believed to be right in the eyes of God. For three years, I did not feel anything for my husband. I claimed the scriptures and believed that if I would do what they said, the Lord would give me what I had never had. I admit that I went through a terrible struggle with my emotions at this time.

During the last two years, however, God has poured out a blessing on us that you can't believe! I am so committed to my husband that I find myself loving the man that I hated for fourteen years. God has given me this intense affection for him. Now, something else has happened. Our children have grown so close to us and love each other as never before. We love to look in the Scriptures for things to obey and then we make a commitment to do what we've read. First it included a daily study of the Word and now it involves church work—together. We are a witness to all those who see this incredible change in our family.

I said all that to say this. It is worth everything to follow God's will, even when it contradicts our desires. Oh, there's always the temptation to chuck it from time to time. But I'd rather spend five minutes in real fellowship with the Lord than a lifetime in fun and games. I can truly say, it works!

Thank you,
Jacque

It will work in your family, too. Thanks for reading my book. I pray that the Lord will bless your home with love and warmth and every good thing.

Straight Talk

Other Books by Dr. Dobson

Love Must Be Tough
What Wives Wish Their Husbands Knew about Women
The New Dare to Discipline
The New Hide or Seek
The Strong-Willed Child
Preparing for Adolescence
Emotions: Can You Trust Them?
Dr. Dobson Answers Your Questions
Love for a Lifetime
Parenting Isn't for Cowards
Life on the Edge
When God Doesn't Make Sense
Home with a Heart
Solid Answers
Coming Home
In the Arms of God
Children at Risk (with Gary L. Bauer)

Dr. James C. Dobson

Straight Talk

WORD PUBLISHING
NASHVILLE
A Thomas Nelson Company

The drawing on the following page is by Ray Craighead, a student of James Dobson, Sr.

Library of Congress Cataloging in Publication Data

Dobson, James C., 1936–
Straight talk : what men need to know, what women should understand / James C. Dobson. —Rev. and exp. ed.
p. cm.
Includes bibliographical references.
1. Men—United States. 2. Fathers—United States. 3. Men—Psychology. I. Title.
HQ1090.3.D6 1991
305.3—dc20 91–20334
CIP

ISBN 0-8499-0905-8 (Hardcover)
ISBN 0-8499-3858-9 (Trade Paper)

Printed in the United States of America.

9 BVG 9 8 7 6 5 4 3 2 1

This book is affectionately dedicated to the memory of my father, James Dobson, Sr., for reasons which will be understood as these pages are read.

James Dobson, Sr.
1911–1977

"Yet we have this assurance: Those who belong to God shall live again. Their bodies shall rise again! Those who dwell in the dust shall awake and sing for joy! For God's light of life will fall like dew upon them!"—Isaiah 26:19, TLB

Contents

Introduction

1

A Man Looks Back

The first edition of the book you are about to read was written approximately ten years ago. It has sold more than a million copies since its publication and continues to represent my best understanding of what it means to be a man . . . God's man . . . in today's topsy-turvy world. Still, I have felt a need in recent months to revisit the topic, to update the context, and to add the perspective afforded by another decade of living.

I was forty-four years old when *Straight Talk to Men and Their Wives* was first published, and indeed, several experiences in my personal life were highly relevant to its content. My father had died recently (as you will read in Chapter 3) confronting me with my own mortality. My own unexpected heart attack some years later served to emphasize the point. Our children were still at home and our house was fairly crackling with adolescent activity. Most importantly, I was knee-deep in the infamous mid-life years as I sat down to write.

As it turned out, I never did go through what is commonly known as a classic mid-life crisis (as described in Chapter 16), but I did do my share of critical thinking during that era. By contrast, many of my friends and associates *did* struggle through a troubling experience in their forties. Some even went a little crazy when they realized that youth was gone and life was rapidly passing them by. Although sympathetic to their distress, I found it somewhat amusing to watch these men trying desperately to hold on to what was already long gone.

Ten years ago, and to some degree today, men in mid-life crisis wore their self-doubt like a walking billboard for the whole world to see. Suit coats and ties were replaced by garish silk shirts, which were always left unbuttoned down in the direction of the navel. A bushy array of grey chest hair was usually on display. It had been carefully blow-dried. A gold medallion on a chain was usually nestled in the curly crop, presumably as a testimonial to youthful vigor. The men also did weird things with their hair, attempting to make a little look like a lot. (The frustrating thing about aging is that hair won't grow on the top, but it sprouts abundantly in the nose and ears.) In serious cases of baldness, this meant whipping the sideburns over the top and then cementing everything in place with super glue. Sharp-pointed Italian type shoes finished off the garb, accompanied by Rolex watches (probably fake) and heavy jewelry on both hands. So much for the appropriate uniform.

Men in mid-life crisis then sought to beef up their image with racy automobiles. Their cars had to be sleek, fast, and hot. A Porsche or a Ferrari conveyed the proper message, but a guy with financial problems might have to settle for a Volkswagen with mag wheels. Thus outfitted, the aging gentleman and his shaky ego set out to conquer worlds unknown.

Sexual conquest was, and still is, the ultimate proof of virility for the over-the-hill gang. These men often try their luck with younger . . . hopefully gorgeous . . . ladies. They flirt with their secretaries and make passes at every skirt that passes by. They are also frustrated by their wives' age, because it reminds them of their own.

I heard of one such man who came in one night and asked his wife what she was smearing on her face.

> "Cold cream," she replied.
> "What's it for?" he asked naively.
> "Wrinkles," came the response.
> He thought for a moment and then said, "Well the stuff is working. You got a whole raft of 'em."

An article that appeared in a local newspaper described another man with a similar attitude who abandoned his wife and ran off with another woman. This is what it said,

> A young man spotted a Mercedes for sale in a newspaper. He telephoned to inquire, assuming the figure must be a typographical error. A woman answered the phone and told him the figure was correct. He asked whether or not the car was damaged. "No, it's in perfect condition," she told him. Then why was she selling it at such a ridiculously low price? "Well, my husband just phoned me from Las Vegas. He's there with his secretary. He told me he's leaving me and that he went broke gambling. He asked me to sell the Mercedes and send him half of what I got for it. That's just what I'm going to do!"

This playboy is only beginning to realize what his fun and games will cost him. The consequences of infidelity usually reverberate for a lifetime and touch every member of the family. I'm thankful, as I indicated earlier, that I did not experience these same pressures that brought the roof down on some of my friends. Shirley and I have now been married for thirty-one years and I couldn't be happier about that fact. I own no silk shirts, and we drive a station wagon and a four-door sedan. Nevertheless, I *was* confronted during the forties by some of the same unsettling thoughts that gnaw at the souls of other men in the mid-life years.

It is almost impossible to bridge the awesome gap between the thirties and the fifties without wandering for a time through a dark valley. My journey was no exception. For at least seven years, I went through a period best described as a time of "contemplative reassessment." I was busily dealing in that decade with the many disturbing thoughts that echo through the mind of a man who realizes suddenly that he will not live forever. Whether he is a Christian, an atheist, an agnostic, or a New Ager, he *must* come to terms with these kinds of questions: "Who am I, *really?*" and "What am I doing here?" and "Is this the way I want to spend the rest of my life?" and "What really matters to me?" and "Who put me here?" and "What did He have in mind for me to accomplish?" and "Is Someone keeping score?" and "Is there life after death?" and "What will it be like to die?" These and many related questions seem to descend on men in rapid succession in mid-life.

As a deeply committed believer in Jesus Christ, I had already answered the questions related to my faith and my relationship with my Maker. Nevertheless, I needed to transform my beliefs from a youthful abstraction to a personal reality. I also needed to get a new fix on my circumstances and objectives. Have you arrived at that point in life? Have you ever felt like you were running so fast and were so involved and entangled with the task of living that you were failing to notice about 90 percent of what was happening around you? That's what was going on in my mind. By the time I had paid my taxes, fixed the leak in the roof, changed the tires on the car, raised my kids, and done my job and all the other stuff expected of me, an entire decade had gone by and it was only a blur in my memory. There are times like these for all of us when we need to pull back and say, "Just a minute, here, I need to do some thinking. Stop shouting at me, world, until I can get myself together."

That process of re-evaluation took about seven years to complete. I emerged from it with a stronger dedication to the fundamentals of what I had been taught . . . and to a determination to "stay the course." Specifically, there were two conclusions that jumped out at me and which now serve as centerpieces of my system of values. Neither is new or particularly unique, but perhaps my readers will find it helpful to review the basics on which family and spiritual stability are grounded.

The first realization that has shaped my attitude toward everything else has already been mentioned. I came face to face with the breath-taking brevity of life. The passage of time seemed like a well-greased string that was sliding through my taut fingers. I was but a short-term visitor on this planet. It is a tremendous shock to the system when it first sinks in that you are simply "passin' through."

I remember sitting in church one day when I was forty-eight years old, and I was thinking about what it would be like to be fifty. Then I thought of my father's death at sixty-six. "Wow," I said to myself. "I may only have eighteen years left." Then I began calculating the meaning of those figures. (The sermon that morning must have been uninspiring.) I quickly realized that if I had lived forty-eight years and had eighteen to go, I had already "burned" 72 percent of my allotted time. What a stomach-grabber for a man who still thought of himself as Joe College! Nine years earlier, I had been in my thirties . . . still considered youthful . . . but two years hence I would be in my fifties . . . with only 24 percent of a lifetime left. Furthermore, there was not the slightest guarantee that I would be granted even one more hour.

I thought again about the meaning of the term "mid-life." It is a seductive lie for most of us; the middle *thirties* are the mid-life years and the forties are the "two-thirds" years. In my case, I had hit the three-fourths years by age forty-eight. A humorous notion, perhaps, but a hammer blow to this guy who thought of himself as a very young man.

There were other insults. In an incident that has now become almost a "trademark" for me, I went to the YMCA one day to play basketball. I was an out-of-towner and unfamiliar with the guys who routinely played there in Dallas. I must have looked eighty years old to the teenagers on the court that day. They couldn't figure why a decrepit dude like me would think he could play a young man's game. But what could they do? I was there and they had to include me.

We divided the troops that day into a four-on-four arrangement, and I was assigned to guard a seventeen-year-old black athlete. This kid was loaded with natural talent, and he knew it. He was as smooth as silk. Despite the mismatch, however, I rose to the challenge. I reached back about twenty years and pulled up some moves long forgotten. Adrenalin surged through my body, and the old thrill came back. Through luck and pluck, I scored about three quick baskets in the face of this young hotshot. With that, he took a step back, put his hands on his hips, and said, "Man! You must have been sompin' in yo' prime!"

His words stuck in my heart. "My prime?! I couldn't even remember my prime!" I soon grabbed my warm-up jacket and headed back to the hotel. My self-concept wobbled violently for a few days.

Many writers have attempted to describe this emotional impact of comprehending life's brevity for the first time. One of my favorites is a lady named Erma Bombeck. I saw her as a guest on the "Phil Donahue Show" when she was asked if she was sensitive about her age.

"Not at all," she replied.

"Then how old are you?" Phil asked.

"I'm somewhere between estrogen and death," she answered.

Erma went on to say that her next-door neighbor wore a pacemaker, and every time he sneezed, her garage door opened.

Some of Mrs. Bombeck's pronouncements are not intended to be funny, however. In fact, they contain striking observations about life. One such statement about the aging process appeared in her book, *If Life Is a Bowl of Cherries, What Am I Doing in the Pits?* Included in that collection of writings was a short piece entitled, "When Does the Mother Become the Daughter and the Daughter Become the Mother?" It focused on her relationship with her own mom, which underwent a radical role reversal with the passage of time. Her mother had always been so strong, so independent and secure. Erma admired her and attempted to model herself after the one who had brought her into the world. But in recent years, the mother was undeniably becoming more childlike.

Erma first noticed the change when they were riding in a car one day. She was driving, and her mom was sitting near the right front door. Suddenly, an emergency occurred causing Erma to slam on the brakes. Instinctively, she reached out to keep her mother from hitting the windshield. When the crisis had passed, the two women sat looking at one another. Each realized that something had changed in their relationship . . . for in prior years Mom would have attempted to protect Erma.

Then there was the following Thanksgiving when Erma baked the turkey and her mother set the table. Clearly, the mother was becoming the daughter and the daughter was becoming the mother. As time passed, the transformation became more dramatic. When the two women were going shopping, it was Erma who said, "My goodness, don't you look nice in that new dress" and, "Don't forget to wear your sweater so you won't be cold in the department stores." Echoing in her mind was the advice of a concerned mother, "Button up your coat, Erma. Wear you galoshes, stay warm, take care of yourself."

Erma understood the new role she was asked to play, but resisted it vigorously. She didn't want to see this strong, noble woman become dependent . . . childlike . . . insecure. Nevertheless, the inexorable march of time could not be resisted. She had to get her mother up at night to take her to the bathroom and to care for most of her physical needs. How different the relationship had become. When Erma was a kindergartner, she had made a plaster-of-paris "hand" which decorated the kitchen for years. Forty years later, mom was sent to a senior citizen's crafts class where she made a macrame. It eventually hung in her room in the Bombeck home.

As senility began to creep in, Erma found her own frustration rising to a crescendo. She said, "Mom! Will you *please* quit talking about seeing Dad last night. You *know* he's been gone for ten years." But Mom couldn't help it because she was no longer mentally competent. That completed the transformation. The mother had become the daughter and the daughter became the mother.

Shortly thereafter, Erma and her own daughter were riding in a car one day. There was a sudden stacking of cars and the illumination of brake lights. Instinctively, the daughter reached out to protect Erma from hitting the windshield. They looked at each other for a moment, and Erma said, "My Lord! How quickly!!"

How quickly, indeed! One of the most wrenching experiences of the forties for me was watching my mother become my daughter and beginning to look at me as her father. She and my dad had been best friends, and his loss was devastating to her. She never fully recovered from his sudden death. It was as though she had been cut in half.

I remember making a fatherly visit to see my mother one day in her little condo. After leaving, I wrote down a portion of our conversation as a reminder of that period of her life. This is the exact interchange that took place:

> "How you doing today?"
>
> "I'm holding my own."
>
> "Are you missing dad today?"
>
> (pause) "I miss him every day."
>
> "I know. What do you suppose he's doing right now?"
>
> "I wish I knew. He's probably off on Mars or Jupiter learning about how they're made."
>
> "You loved him, didn't you, Mom?"
>
> "I loved him, Jim."
>
> "Mom, I worry about you staying in this condo too much. You really need to get out and mix with people—get involved in something."
>
> "No, I'm all right. I just don't have any desire to go anymore."

"I love you, Mom."
"I love you, Jim."

The son was becoming the father and the mother was becoming the daughter. Her mind then began to slip and many of the experiences of Erma Bombeck became my own. Mom was soon afflicted with Parkinson's disease and slowly began a long descent toward her death in 1988. Another conversation occurred twenty-one months before her passing that proved to be historic. I recorded the following comments on a pocket dictaphone immediately after a remarkable encounter had transpired.

> Shirley and I just visited my mother in the nursing home where she resides. She has been rather deeply into senility in recent weeks and has been unable to either understand what we say or communicate with us. Yet today the Lord granted us a brief reprieve. She was asleep when we arrived and we gently sat on her bedside and awakened her. She instantly recognized us, and for the first time in weeks she was able to express her thoughts and understand the love that we gave to her. I took that opportunity, not knowing if it would return, to stroke her forehead and pat her hand and thank her for being a good mother. I thanked her for being a good wife to my father—a good pastor's wife, even though it was he who was called to the ministry. I thanked her for living according to the principles of Christianity and staying true to the Christ whom she accepted when she was twenty years old. I stroked her face and thanked her for sacrificing to help me through college, doing without things that she needed. I thanked her for coming to our house when we were on our honeymoon and putting twenty dollars worth of groceries and staples in our cupboard when I knew she didn't have those same items in hers. I told her how she was loved, not only by us, but by the Lord Himself. She smiled—she understood. She took my hand and said, "You know I've been thinking." And I said, "What have you been thinking about?" And she said, "That it's almost over. I've almost made it. It's almost done." I said, "Mom, when you make that crossing, you know my dad is

going to be waiting for you on the other side." She smiled and understood. Then I said, "Jesus is waiting for you, too. And He's going to say, 'Well done! Thou good and faithful servant.'" Then I prayed for her and thanked the Lord for the influence of a good woman, and for her love in my life. She returned our love and we said good-bye. At this stage of life, we never know when the last opportunity to communicate soul to soul has occurred. If this proves to be that last window of opportunity, I am grateful for the Lord's presence in that room today.

As it turned out, that *was* the final rational conversation I had with my mother. I will always be thankful for those concluding moments at the close of her time on earth.

This rapid passage of time that we have discussed is not just relevant to those in the mid-life years, although it becomes more apparent as we get older. For those who are younger, let me suggest that you conduct your own investigation. Look carefully at your family, and especially at the changing relationships with your own children. It is there, up close and personal, that the pace of life will come into focus. If you were riding on a passenger train and wished to judge the speed at which you and it were traveling, the distant mountains would be of little help. You'd get a better approximation by looking at the ground nearest the train. Likewise, those loved ones closest to you are the best measure of the dramatic changes in process. Children remain children for a brief moment, and hardly a day is the same as the next. It is in their growth and development that the dynamic nature of living is seen.

I can almost hear your thoughts as I write, "What morbid ideas! Why would anyone want to contemplate the passage of time and focus on the brevity of life?" The answer comes directly from scripture. The temporary quality of this life is a very important biblical concept! King David said, "As for man, his days are as grass: as a flower of the field, so he flourisheth, for the wind passeth over it, and it is gone: and the place thereof shall know it no more" (Ps. 103:15–16, KJV).

Moses shared that perspective and said, "So teach us to number our days, that we may apply our hearts unto wisdom" (Ps. 90:12, KJV). Wisdom, you see, comes from understanding the temporary nature of this life. Jesus, on the other hand, referred to a rich man who thought he had years to live and called him a "fool." We would also be foolish to assume that things will always be as they are, or that eternal matters can be dealt with later. For all we know, "This night thy soul shall be required of thee" (Luke 12:20, KJV). If that is the nature of this human existence, then we would do well to acknowledge it and live our lives accordingly. *That* fact hit me hard during my own mid-life years!

Let's move now to the second major conclusion that emerged from the discomfort of my own mid-life years. It was this: The *only* true source of meaning in life is found in love for God and His son Jesus Christ, and love for mankind, beginning with our own families. Compared to this fundamental system of values, everything else is puny and insignificant. Certainly, there *must* be a more valid reason for living than the mere pursuit of money and possessions!

Shirley and I have seen the material world from the bottom up, to be sure. We had absolutely nothing when we were married and it looked for about ten years like we were destined to keep it. We didn't have any financial problems because we had no finances. I finally clawed my way through the doctoral program at the University of Southern California and escaped the oppressive tuition that had strangled us. After graduation, I immediately joined the faculty of the USC School of Medicine and began earning a livable salary. Then I wrote my first book, and we were finally able to purchase and furnish the house in which we still live.

I would not be truthful if I denied the satisfaction derived from this establishment of a home and a "place" for our kids. During the mid-life years, however, we realized how temporary and how empty those things can be if not kept in proper perspective. The Lord seemed to use some everyday object lessons to emphasize this truth to Shirley and me. On one occasion it was a simple table game that caught my attention. I had been a dedicated game player as a kid, and especially loved Monopoly by Parker Brothers. I could wheel and deal with the best of 'em! But those days were gone and almost forgotten by the time our sixteen-year-old daughter came home raving about "a new game called Monopoly." She begged Shirley and me to take her on, and we consented.

We sat down to play one evening after Ryan had gone to bed, and very quickly I caught the old excitement of the game. And why not? I began prospering almost from the beginning. Before long I owned Boardwalk and Park Place, Illinois, Kentucky, Indiana, and even Baltic and Mediterranean. I started putting little green houses everywhere, and soon they were traded in for big red hotels. It was wonderful. My family was squirming like crazy and I was loving it. I had $500 bills stuffed in my pockets, under the board, and even in my shoe. What I was experiencing was green-eyed greed, pure and simple.

The game ended precipitously when Shirley and Danae landed on my hotels in quick succession and suffered irreversible financial collapse. Suddenly, it was over. I had won. My family was pretty disgusted with my unsportsmanlike conduct by that point, so they went off to bed in a huff and left me to put away the game. There I was sitting alone in the family room around midnight, feeling strangely empty and unfulfilled. All of my earlier excitement and competitive energy were left with nowhere to go. I had won the game. So what? I began sorting all my money and laboriously putting it back in the box. My beautiful $500 bills were begrudgingly returned to the "bank." Then I stacked and replaced my coveted property . . . Boardwalk and Park Place included. My amassed fortune was disappearing in front of my eyes.

That's when it seemed that the Lord spoke to me. No, it was not an audible voice, but these were my thoughts in the family room on that night:

> "Jim, pay attention now. I'm about to teach you a lesson. That's not just the game of Monopoly you've been playing. It's very

much like the game of life. You sweat and struggle to acquire things . . . to build and grow . . . to get bank accounts, property, retirement programs, and a piece of the rock. You spend a lifetime *accumulating* . . . in search of security. Then one day, it suddenly ends. You're going along minding your own business, when a strange pain develops gradually in your chest and then extends down your left arm. 'Could this be . . . ?' you ask yourself. Or you're taking a morning shower and inadvertently discover a protrusion in the area of you abdomen. 'I've never noticed a bump there before. Maybe I ought to check it out.' Or you're driving your car and make a sudden lane change without looking in your rearview mirror. Just that quickly, the great quest for security and possessions is over. The game ends and everything must be returned to the box. The rules specify that *nothing* can be taken with you. Not one dime. There are no U-Haul trailers that follow the hearse to the cemetery. We come into the world with a clenched fist, and we die with an open hand. That's what life does to us. Each person must then answer the question asked of the rich fool, 'Whose shall those things be, which thou hast provided?' (Luke 12:20, KJV)."

Since antiquity, men have tried desperately to beat the game and achieve some measure of earthly immortality. The Egyptians built pyramids and filled them with material wealth they hoped to take along to the next world. Sorry, Pharaoh. Grave-robbers reaped the benefit of that miscalculation a few centuries later. A thousand years hence, Spaniards hunted for the "fountain of youth" to reverse the ravages of time. It was a nice thought.

The search continues today. Some of the ways modern man seeks to "live" beyond the grave are as follows:

1. *Through art.* Rembrandt, Picasso, Mozart, Bach, Beethoven, and Frank Lloyd Wright achieved some remembrance beyond their passing.
2. *Through philanthropy.* Carnegie, Rockefeller, and Huntington secured their place in the culture by building libraries, concert halls, and hospitals in their memory.

3. *Through business.* Ford, Krup, Getty, and the Warner Brothers immortalized their names . . . at least to this point.
4. *Through children.* Henry VIII was desperate for an heir, so that his bloodline and legacy might survive his death.
5. *Through literature.* Plato, Shakespeare, Dostoevsky, and Steinbeck will be remembered for centuries.
6. *Through politics and history.* Washington, Lincoln, Churchill, and Roosevelt have secured their place in history.
7. *Through conquest.* Alexander the Great, Julius Caesar, Adolph Hitler, Joseph Stalin, and Mao Tse Tung are notable examples.
8. *Through science.* Galileo, Newton, Einstein, Edison, and Hubble made the grade here.
9. *Through cryonics.* A more recent effort has led people to arrange to have their bodies freeze-dried in hopes some future medical technology will bring them back alive. Lots of luck!

There are other approaches to the pall that hangs over the entire human race . . . the nagging specter of death. All of them have a basic flaw, however. They permit only a person's *memory* to escape the grim reaper. Sooner or later, even those who achieve cultural immortality will die like the rest of us. Like John Brown in the Civil War ballad: "His body lies a'molderin' in the grave."

True eternal life is available from only one source. It is a free gift to those who believe in the Lord Jesus Christ and accept His forgiveness for sin. Only through this Gate can we escape the sting of death and the "victory" of the grave.

"True enough," a critic might reply, "but I'm not trying to accumulate wealth for my own use. My goal is to pass it along to my children and future generations. I want them to have it easier than I did . . . to enjoy a head start that only money can give."

Shirley and I have spent many hours thinking and talking about that objective with reference to our own children. Even it if were possible for us to leave them a large estate, would that be a wise thing to do? I think not. It takes a steady hand to hold a full cup, and many young people have been destroyed by money that burned its way through their lives.

In a sociological study published under the title *Rich Kids,* we read the case histories of individuals who inherited large trust funds. The findings were consistent: wealth passed to the second and third generations has typically wreaked havoc in the lives of the recipients. They fought each other to control it. They lost their incentives to work. They lived profligate lives. They shamefully wasted their resources. Some even committed suicide. When the Apostle Paul said "the love of money is the root of all evil," he spoke the truth.

Should it be our desire, then, to inflict this "evil" on our precious children? Not to excess, certainly. It makes sense to help the next generation get started or perhaps to assist with the purchase of their first homes. But if our objective is to generate *wealth* for those who will not earn it, we are putting our beloved children at high risk for satanic mischief. Likewise, we must not get so busy attempting to give our kids what we didn't have as children that we fail to give them what we *did* have as kids.

Perhaps it is clear now why I emerged from the mid-life years with some concepts firmly in place. My children (and other people) are the *only* things I can take to heaven with me. That's why I left the medical school back in 1977 and declined almost all speaking invitations that came my way. It became clear to me that Danae and Ryan were temporary residents in our home . . . that they would soon be grown and on their own. Parenthood is a short-term affair, and the opportunity to lead and influence them was a "now or never" proposition. Thus, I retooled my professional responsibilities and focused heavily on my own family I've made some bad decisions in my life and a few rather good ones, but this was my most brilliant moment. The empty nest did indeed come quickly, and I thank God I have not squandered my most precious privilege of participating in the lives of my children.

Let me leave you with a letter I wrote the day our son Ryan went off to college. Perhaps it will serve to punctuate this update on one of the most important topics I've ever addressed. Incorporated in this letter are all the primary conclusions I drew during the mid-life years and which I wish I had understood fully when I first entered manhood.

> Twenty-three precious years have come and gone since the morning of October 6, 1965, when our first child came into the world. An instant and irrational love affair was born that day between this new dad and his baby daughter, Danae Ann, who took center stage in the Dobson household. How deeply I love that little girl! She would stand in the doorway each morning and cry as I left for work, and then run giggling and breathless to meet me at the end of the day. You would have thought we had been separated for months. Could I ever love another child as much as this one? I wondered.
>
> Then five years later a little lad named James Ryan made his grand entrance, and it all happened again. He was my boy—the only son I would ever be privileged to raise. What a joy it was to watch him grow and develop and learn. How proud I was to be his father—to be trusted with the well-being of his soul. I put him to bed every night when he was small, and we laughed and we played and we talked about Jesus. I would hide his sister's stuffed animals around the house, and then we would turn out the lights and hunt them with flashlights and a toy rifle. He never tired of that simple game. But the day for games has passed.
>
> This morning, you see, marked the official beginning of the "empty nest" for Shirley and me. Danae graduated from college a year ago and is now building an exciting life of her own. It was difficult for us to let her go, back in 1983, but we took comfort in Ryan's six remaining years at home. How quickly those months have flown, and today, our formal years of parenthood came suddenly to an end. We took Ryan to the airport and sent him off to Colorado for a five-week summer program.

Then in August, he plans to enter his freshman year at a college in the Midwest. Though he will be home periodically for years to come, our relationship will not be the same. It might be even better, but it will certainly be different. And I have never like irreversible change.

Though for many years I knew this moment was coming, and though I had helped others cope with similar experiences, I admit freely that Ryan's departure hit me hard. For the past two weeks, we have worked our way through a massive accumulation of junk in his room. Ryan is a collector of things no one else would want—old street signs, broken models, and favorite fishing rods. The entire family took tetanus shots, and we plunged into the debris. Finally last night, Shirley and Ryan packed the remaining boxes and emptied the last drawer. The job was finished. His suitcases were packed. Our son was ready to go.

Ryan came into my study about midnight, and we sat down for another of the late-night chats that I have cherished. He has always liked to talk at the end of the day. I won't tell you what we said in that final conversation. It is too personal to share with anyone. I can only say that the morning came too quickly, and we drove as a family to the airport. There I was, driving down the freeway, when an unexpected wave of grief swept over me. I thought I couldn't stand to see him go. It was not that I dreaded or didn't look forward to what the future held. No, I mourned the end of an era—a precious time of my life when our children were young and their voices rang in the halls of our house. I couldn't hide the tears as we hugged good-bye at Gate 18. Then Shirley and I drove alone to our house, where a beloved son and daughter had grown from babies to young adults. There I lost it again!

The house that we had left three hours earlier in a whirlwind of activity had been transformed in our absence. It had become a monastery—a morgue—a museum. The silence was deafening to us both. Every corner of it held a memory that wafted through the air. I meandered to Ryan's room and sat on the floor by his bed. His crib had once stood on that spot. Though many years had passed, I could almost see him as toddler—running and jumping to my open arms. What a happy time that was in my life. The ghost of a kindergartner was there, too, with his brand-new cowboy clothes and his

Snoopy lunch pail. Those images are vivid in my mind today. Then a seven-year-old boy appeared before me. He was smiling, and I noticed that his front teeth were missing. His room was filled with bugs and toads and a tarantula named Pebber. As I reached out to hug him, he quietly disappeared. Then a gangly teenager strolled through the door and threw his books on his desk. He looked at me as if to say, "Come on, Dad. Pull yourself together!"

My own words now come back to mind. I remember saying in my second film series, *Turn Your Heart Toward Home*, that the day was coming soon when "the bicycle tires would be flat, the skateboard would be warped and standing in the garage, the swing set would be still, and the beds would not be slept in. We will go through Christmas with no stockings hanging by the fireplace, and the halls will be very quiet. I know those times will soon be here, and I realize it has to be so. I accept it. I wouldn't for anything try to hold back out son or daughter when it comes time to go. But that will also be a very sad day because the precious experience of parenting will have ended for me." Alas, the day that I anticipated has just arrived.

If you're thinking that I am hopelessly sentimental about my kids, you're right. The greatest thrill of my life has been the privilege of raising them day by day in the service of the Lord. Still, I did not expect such intense pain at the time of Ryan's departure. I thought I was prepared to handle the moment, but I quickly realized just how vulnerable I am to the people I love.

In a large sense, however, it is not merely the end of formal parenting that has shaken my world today. I grieve for the human condition itself. When Ryan boarded that plane in Los Angeles, I comprehended anew the brevity of life and the temporary nature of all things. As I sat on the floor in his room, I heard not only Ryan's voice but the voices of my mother and father who laughed and loved in that place. Now they are gone. One day Shirley and I will join them. First one and then the other. We are just "passing through," as the gospel songwriters used to say. All of life boils down to a series of happy "hellos" and sad "good-byes." Nothing is really permanent, not even the relationships that blossom in a healthy home. In time, we must release our grip on everything we hold dear. Yes. I felt the chilly breeze of change blowing through my home this morning, and I understood its meaning.

If we really grasped the brevity of our lives on this earth, we would surely be motivated to invest ourselves in eternal values. Would a fifty-year-old man pursue an adulterous affair if he knew how quickly he would stand before his God? Would a woman make herself sick from in-law conflict or other petty frustrations if she knew how little time was left to her? Would men and women devote their lives to the pursuit of wealth and symbols of status if they realized how soon their possessions would be torn from their trembling hands? It is the illusion of permanence, you see, that distorts our perception and shapes our selfish behavior. When eternal values come in view, our greatest desire is to please the Lord and influence as many of our loved ones for Him as possible.

I ask each of my readers this important question. If we fully understood that the eternal souls of our children hung in the balance today—that only by winning them for Christ could we spend eternity together in heaven—would we change the way this day is lived? Would we ignore and neglect so great an opportunity if our eyes were fully opened to this awesome responsibility? I think not. I pray not.

Addressing myself now to the mothers and fathers of young children, I urge you to keep this eternal perspective in view as you race through the days of your lives. Don't permit yourselves to become discouraged with the responsibilities of parenting. Yes, it is an exhausting and difficult assignment, and there are times when you will feel like throwing in the towel. But I beg you to stay the course! Get on your knees before the Lord and ask for His strength and wisdom. Finish the job to which He has called you! There is no more important task in living, and you will understand that assignment more clearly when you stand where Shirley and I are today. In the blink of an eye, you will be hugging your children good-bye and returning to an empty house. That is the way the system works.

God bless you all. I love you in the name of Christ.

2

A Man and His Sexual Identity

Before returning to the edited original text of *Straight Talk to Men and Their Wives,* we need to restate the issue that motivated its writing in the first place. Our purpose was to redefine the meaning of manhood in a world gone slightly crazy. Traditional concepts of masculinity and femininity have been battered and ridiculed for more than twenty years, creating confusion for both men and women. These revisions of age-old behavior patterns have produced awkwardness in the relationships between the sexes. Should a man stand when a woman enters the room? Will he please her by opening the door for her? Should he give her his seat on a crowded bus or subway? Have all the rules changed? Is there anything predictable and certain in the new order?

While these questions of social etiquette may seem superficial at first, they are hardly trivial. They reflect much deeper attitudes that have far-reaching implications. We are, after all, sexual beings. Everything we do is influenced by our gender assignment. The first element of self-identity as toddlers comes from our identification as boys and girls. Any confusion at that point . . . or in the relationship between the sexes . . . must be seen as threatening to the stability of society, itself.

Dr. Charles Winick at City University of New York studied more than two thousand cultures that have existed in world history. He found only fifty-five where masculinity and femininity were blurred. Not one of those unisexual societies survived for more than a few years. Why not? Because a society can be no stronger than the vitality of its families, and its families are a function of the way the sexes relate to each other. Maleness and femaleness are not merely social niceties that have evolved through time. While customs vary from one culture to another, the linkage between the sexes is a function of powerful forces deep within the human spirit. That attraction must not be tampered with by social engineers with an agenda of their own.

Social engineers love to tamper, however, and they've been tinkering with sex role definitions since at least 1968. Everything understood to identify womanhood for thousands of years has been held up to ridicule and disdain. It was remarkable, in fact, how effectively a very small number of radical feminists (remember the early bra burners?) were able to redefine the role of women and reorder the relationship between the sexes. These firebrands have long since been discredited, but never underestimate the changes in social attitude that they inspired. In a single decade, for example, the term "housewife" became a symbol of exploitation, oppression, and . . . pardon the insult . . . stupidity. How strange!

Since the beginning of human existence, women in most cultures have identified themselves with child-rearing responsibilities. It was an honorable occupation that required no apology. How has it happened, then, that homemaking has fallen on such lean times in the Western world? Why do women who remain at home in the company of little children feel such disrespect from the society in which they live? A partial answer can be found in the incessant bombardment by the media on all traditional Judeo-Christian values. Radio, television, the press, and the entertainment industry have literally (and deliberately) changed the way America thinks.

Many years have passed since Barbara Walters and Tom Snyder hosted a three-hour television special on the subject of women. I refer to it now because the program was so typical of the fare served up to the public in that day. The broadcast was aired on NBC in prime time and captured the attention of the country for one full evening. (What fantastic power for social change has been wrought by the tube!) I watched Walters and Snyder carefully on that occasion and, in fact, taped the program for future reference. Their stated purpose was to evaluate the world of women at that time, examining the many activities and involvement of the feminine gender. What resulted, however, was a powerful propaganda piece for what was then the new way of thinking. Women were depicted in numerous work situations, from business ownership to blue collar jobs. Not once in the three-hour program, however, was the role of the homemaker mentioned, except to refer indirectly to this outmoded responsibility in vaguely derogatory terms. Perhaps 14 million homemakers lived and breathed in this country, at that time, yet they were not referenced once in a program dedicated to the world of women. I'm sure the viewers got the message.

The effort to reorder the role of women proceeded on a broad scale, touching every dimension of society. For example, I received a letter about that time from a mother who was curious to learn why her local library had removed hundreds of books from its shelves. Upon investigation, she was shocked to discover that each volume depicting males and females in a traditional context was eliminated. If a woman was shown cooking dinner and a father was working in a factory, the book had to go. Obviously, no stone was left unturned in the campaign to revolutionize our ideas, though none dared call it censorship.

The courts also played a major role during that era. I remember receiving a call from a physician who was consulting with a major law firm. He asked if I would serve as an expert witness on behalf of Sav-On Drug Company in California. I learned that a suit had been brought against the pharmaceutical chain by a feminist attorney who represented the family of a young girl. The suit charged Sav-On with inflicting great psychological damage on the child because . . . are you ready for this? . . . toys in their stores were separated by probable gender interest. Ten feet above the floor were signs identifying "Toys for Girls," and in another place, "Toys for Boys." The attorney claimed, apparently with a straight face, that the girl had been emotionally damaged by being "denied access" to toys designated for males. A psychiatrist actually submitted a statement to the court, indicating the great degree to which the child had been wounded by Sav-On Drug Company. *That's* how far the nonsense went.

This campaign to revolutionize our thinking has lost most of its fire today and the world has moved on. But make no mistake. The case against traditional womanhood has been heard, and it will never be the same. The female students at Wellesley College may not be familiar with the history I have described, since some of them were not yet born when the movement began. Nevertheless, they are recipients of its legacy. When they voted not to invite the First Lady, Barbara Bush, to speak at their Commencement in 1990 because she hadn't done anything but raise a family and support her husband, they demonstrated how effectively feminist ideology has been ingrained in the attitudes of the young . . . especially those under the influence of liberal professors on university campuses.

Not only has there been a revolution in female sex role identity, but maleness has been turned upside down, too. Apart from the elements of social etiquette mentioned earlier, much deeper questions have been raised. What does it really mean to be a man today? We know it is unacceptable to be "macho," whatever that is, but we're not sure how we're expected to perform. Consider how a young husband might look upon his new role at the beginning of married life. Is he supposed to earn a living for his wife? Well, probably not. She may bring in more money than he. Is he expected to provide benevolent leadership for his family in the major decisions? Even raising that issue in some circles is a sure way to start an argument. Is he supposed to be stoic and strong, or tender, sensitive, and emotional? Alas, is there *anything* that distinguishes his role from his wife's, and where can he go to find out what is expected of him?

Historically, married men were not so uncertain; they understood intuitively that two family responsibilities exceeded all others in significance. They were expected to *protect* and *provide* for their wives and children. You can be sure they felt strongly about that obligation. If you insulted a woman in the nineteenth century or before, you would have dealt shortly with her angry husband. He would not have hesitated to lay down his life for her, if necessary. He was the defender of her honor, and she felt secure in his care. He took great satisfaction in what he contributed, materially and otherwise, to the welfare of his family. It was this masculine identity that linked him to his wife and children and gave him a sense of pride and accomplishment in his manhood.

One of the greatest threats to the institution of the family today is the undermining of this role as protector and provider. This is the contribution for which men were designed, physically and emotionally. If it is taken away, their commitment to their wives and children is jeopardized. Let me personalize the concept. Within a lifetime of responsibilities and professional assignments, I have drawn the greatest satisfaction from the fact that I have cared for each member of my family for more than thirty years. I have worked hard to provide the necessities and a few luxuries for them. I have watched over them in times of danger, and I have dedicated myself to their welfare. My identity is inextricably linked with that family commitment. If my role as protector and provider had been taken from me, much of the joy in family life would have gone with it.

Permit me a contrivance to illustrate how far we have drifted in our understanding of this traditional concept of masculinity. Imagine, by some magic, a delegation of yesterday's husbands and fathers being transported through time to visit our day and witness the conditions that Western men have come to tolerate. The conversation between then (perhaps 1870) and now might go something like this:

Today's representative speaks first. He says,

> "Our purpose, gentlemen, will be to show you the features of our culture in the 1990s which differ most radically from yours. And in some instances, the picture will not be a pretty one. Ours is a very violent society, for example. In the United States alone, more than ninety thousand women are brutally raped every year. One in three adult females living in certain cities will be ravaged during their lifetime. One in every five college women is raped on campus . . . usually by someone they know. This is a disgrace in our time."
>
> "What?" They would reply in disbelief. "That is worse than a wartime experience. What is being done to stop it?"
>
> "Very little, I'm afraid."
>
> "What punishment befalls those who are apprehended?"
>
> "Well, most offenders are never caught. Of those who are, many are never convicted. Only 16 percent will serve time in prison."
>
> "What do you do with those who are proved guilty? Do you shoot or hang them?"
>
> "Oh no, some spend less than a year in jail and then they are set free. Others may be incarcerated for as long as fifteen years before being released."
>
> "Released?! What's to keep them from harming women again?"
>
> "Unfortunately, many do just that."
>
> "Why do so many men want to rape and kill women?"
>
> "There are many reasons. Some boys grow up very angry at women. But also, we live in a provocative society. Are you familiar with the pornography that is available widely today?"

"No, does it show women partially clothed?"

"Far worse, I'm afraid. It depicts nude women being brutalized in every imaginable way. They are shown being violated with blunt instruments, hanging from trees, and being murdered with knives, guns, ropes, etc. Every immodesty is depicted in color and bloody realism."

"I can't breathe! How could such things be? And you say this material is legal and widely disseminated?"

"Yes, teenagers are the most frequent buyers of it. And in some countries . . . Australia, for example . . . the same type material focusing on *children* is legal."

"You don't mean the public would tolerate such things?"

"I'm afraid so. Australians don't seem offended by it, or by the knowledge that real children are abused by the photographers. A brisk child pornography business goes on in North America too, although it is technically illegal. It was largely ignored in the United States until 1983, but it still generates millions of dollars in sales under the counter."

"Why? Tell us why?"

"Obviously, it's not a high priority matter with our legislatures and court system."

"And most of those people are men?"

"Yes, the overwhelming majority are men. They are determined to protect the civil rights of the pornographers."

"What about the civil rights of your women and children? What kind of men would permit such abuse? What has happened to manhood? We would give our lives to protect our loved ones."

"Yes, we've read about your commitment in our history books. Surprisingly, not everyone admires your approach to family life. Some refer to you as chauvinists. That means you are patronizing to women . . . that you don't really respect them. One advertisement tells women they've come a long way since the oppression of your day."

"Oh, really? But your men *do* respect women, is that right?"

"Yes, but times have changed. The fierce protective spirit toward family life is less intense today. For example, a female minor who is secretly pregnant out of wedlock can receive a legal abortion without parental knowledge."

"Let me sit down. You're telling me that a mother and father would not even be told when their child was violated in that way?"

"That's right. In fact, abortion is not seen as a violation. Even at thirteen or fourteen years of age, a girl can be transported legally by her teacher or counselor to an agency that terminates pregnancies. There the baby is drawn from her uterus by a suction device. Not only is parental permission not needed to perform this procedure; they aren't even informed that evening when the young lady comes home. They will never know unless she chooses to tell them."

"But how can parents in that situation care for the girl's health? She's but a child. What if she develops complications from this procedure?"

"If problems develop, the parents may be the last to be told."

"I can't believe fathers would permit someone to assault their daughters in this way. If that happened in our day, someone would be shot over it. What is wrong with the men who accept such outrage?"

"Well, attitudes have changed. Many people today believe the State is really responsible for its children. Parents have a lesser role than in your day. There is a point of view with international adherents, for example, called the 'Children's Rights Movement.' Our position is that boys and girls are entitled at any age to do anything, see anything, decide anything that adults might choose. And when I say anything, I mean just that."

"Anything? You mean, a child could decide to have sexual relations with an adult, and the parents could not intervene?"

"Yes. In Sweden today, it is illegal for a parent to spank a child for disobedience . . . but it is legal for a father to have intercourse with his daughter or a homosexual experience with his son."

"That is sickening. Who would do such a terrible thing?"

"Not many, perhaps. Yet it illustrates how far the children's rights advocates have gone. According to its philosophy, the child is on equal footing with adults. Those who promote this movement want to see boys or girls given the right to vote, travel, choose their own faith, have a guaranteed income, and generally operate independently of their parents."

"Surely, that notion hasn't caught on."

"Not universally, but Western society moves farther in that direction every year."

"We think you modernists are a little crazy."

"Oh, by the way, you'll be interested to know that women are very active in the military today."

"Yes, that was true in our time, too. They served as nurses in the great Civil War and they rolled bandages and performed other functions."

"No, that's not what I mean. Women today are full-fledged members of the armed forces. When a general mobilization is called, those who have volunteered are required to participate. They don't yet fight in combat, at least not technically, but they are near the battle zone, and they actually help to prosecute the war. Furthermore, many people feel it's only a matter of time before women will be obligated to serve, just as men do in times of national crises. It's all part of the equality thing. If women are truly equal to men in the eyes of the law, then they must be willing to fight and die like their male counterparts.

"What if the women have babies?"

"If they're in the military, they have to go. Babies are left behind. When both husbands and wives serve in the armed forces, their children are farmed out to relatives or to someone who will care for them."

"Do you mean a mother of a tiny baby is expected to fight to defend the country while any able-bodied men stay at home?"

"Yes, millions of male students and others who have not joined the military are exempt. It was the woman's choice to enlist. She must do her duty."

"It is incomprehensible that a man could let a young mother do his fighting for him. But then, your people make no sense anyway. Who would have thought that little more than one century of "progress" would produce such foolish ideas. The folks back in our day will never believe what we've heard. We will pray for you."

"Thank you."

Yep. You've come a *very* long way, baby!

It is probably best that no such direct contact between people then and now is actually possible. Past generations would hold us in utter disdain for our failure to preserve and propagate the wisdom of the ages. Consider that final issue of women in the military, for example. There is a *reason* why men have fought the wars to this point. It has to do with children and society's acknowledgment of their dependence on their mothers. The image of babies being handed to stay-at-home fathers so their wives could be deployed overseas should be shocking to all of us. Specifically, there is no more dramatic evidence of the crisis in masculinity today than the fact that men would tolerate even the *possibility* that their wives, sisters, and daughters would do their fighting for them. Isn't that like a man staying in bed with the covers over his head while his wife goes to confront an intruder? Is there no dignity left in modern manhood?

I wish it were possible for me to emphasize just how critical this masculine understanding is to family stability. Sociologist George Gilder said it best in his excellent book, *Sexual Suicide.* He makes it clear that single men (as a class) are often a threat to society. Until they accept the responsibility for families, their sexual aggression is largely unbridled and potentially destructive. He writes:

> Men commit over 90 percent of major crimes of violence, 100 percent of the rapes, 95 percent of the burglaries. They comprise

> 94 percent of our drunken drivers, 70 percent of suicides, 91 percent of offenders against family and children. Single men comprise between 80 and 90 percent of most of the categories of social pathology, and on the average they make less money than any other group in the society—yes, less than single women or working women. As any insurance actuary will tell you, single men are also less responsible about their bills, their driving, and other personal conduct. Together with the disintegration of the family, they constitute our leading social problem.*

Gilder goes on to say that women, by contrast, are naturally more motivated to achieve long-term stability. Their maternal inclinations (they do exist and are evident in every culture throughout the world) influence them to desire stable homes and a steady source of income. They want security for themselves and their children.

Suddenly, we see the beauty of the divine plan. When a man falls in love with a woman, dedicating himself to care for her and protect her and support her, he suddenly becomes the mainstay of social order. Instead of using his energies to pursue his own lusts and desires, he sweats to build a home and save for the future and seek the best job available. His selfish impulses are inhibited. His sexual passions are channeled. He discovers a sense of pride—yes, masculine pride—because he is needed by his wife and children. Everyone benefits from the relationship.

When a society is composed of millions of individual families that are established on this plan, then the nation is strong and stable. It is the great contribution marriage makes to a civilization. But in its absence, ruination is inevitable. When men have no reason to harness their energies in support of the home, then drug abuse, alcoholism, sexual intrigue, job instability, and aggressive behavior can be expected to run unchecked throughout the culture. That is precisely what has happened to many inner-city black families. The government

*George Gilder, *Sexual Suicide* (New York: Quadrangle/The New York Times Book Co., 1973), 7.

pays the bills. Who needs the man? He procreates and disappears. His masculinity has been assaulted, and he takes out his hostilities on the culture which rejected him. It all begins with an unhealthy relationship between the sexes that undermines families and leaves broken lives in its wake.

We must not abandon the biblical concept of masculinity and femininity at this delicate stage of our national history. Not that every woman must become a mother, mind you, or even a homemaker. But those who do must be honored and respected and supported. There should be a clear delineation between maleness and femaleness, exemplified by clothing, customs, and function. Men should be encouraged to provide for and protect their families, even laying down their lives for them if necessary. Children must be valued as our most priceless possession. Their relationship with their mothers is the most important association in their lives, and it must be given the highest social priority. Boys and girls should be taught that the sexes are equal in worth but very different from one another. Girls should know they are girls, and boys should know they are boys. And for the rest of us, self-awareness begins with an understanding of our sexual identity. It must not be blurred by those with an avant-garde agenda of their own.

A Final Thought

I'll conclude this part of our discussion with an illustration of manhood at its best. After all, how else can we get a handle on the ephemeral qualities of character and strength in a man of God? It is understood most readily by observing a good *model,* and I crossed paths momentarily with one of the finest a few years ago.

My family had joined me at Mammoth, California, for a weekend ski outing. The kids were still young, and I was working frantically to teach them the fundamentals of the sport. That's a tough assignment, as every skiing father knows. You can guess who gets to carry *all* the skis, boots, and poles, and then park the car, stand in line to buy the lift tickets, herd the clan toward the ski slopes, and get everyone zipped up and ready to go. At that precise moment, inevitably, one of the children announces that he or she has to go to the bathroom. Upon hearing that important news, dad clomps back down the hill with his child in tow, and then goes through the zippety-zip process twice more. Then he trudges back up the mountain. That is how the system works on a *good* day.

On a bad morning, some of the most frustrating experiences in living can occur. Children are fully capable of announcing this need to visit the "john" one at a time, sending dad up and down the mountain like a yo-yo. By the time he and the last child get back, the first one has to go again. Kids seem to delight in losing valuable equipment, too, such as leather gloves, designer wool hats, ski jackets, etc. They're also good at bickering, which drives their harried parents crazy.

On the particular day in question, it was a *bad* morning for my family. Our children did everything wrong. There we were on a family vacation to produce a little togetherness, but I couldn't stand either one of my kids. They complained and dawdled and spread clothes all over the city of Mammoth. Maybe it will make other families feel better to know that the Dobsons have nerve-wracking days like that. By the time I transported the family to the ski lodge, I was well on my way to total irritation. Danae and Ryan climbed out of the car with a grumble, and I headed toward a parking lot a mile or so away. On the way down the hill I muttered a brief prayer. Actually, it was more an expression of exasperation than anything else.

"What am I going to do with these kids you've given to me?" I said to the Lord, as though it were His fault. He did not reply.

I parked the car and walked back to an assembly area where a flatbed truck comes by every ten minutes to pick up passengers. About fifteen skiers stood awaiting a ride up the mountain, and I quietly joined them. Then I noticed a "different" young lady standing with the others. She turned to look at me, and I observed the unmistakable appearance of mental retardation in her eyes. This late teenager was behaving in a very strange way. She stood facing the mountain, quoting the word "Whomever" over and over. "Whomever!" she said in a loud voice. A few seconds later, she repeated the word nonsensically.

Having worked with developmentally disabled individuals for years, I felt an instant empathy for this girl. It was apparent, however, that the other skiers didn't share my concern. They were young, attractive, and beautifully outfitted. I watched them glance in the direction of the girl and then take a step or two backward. They rolled their eyes at each other as if to say, "Who's the 'crazy' we have with us?"

About that time the truck arrived, and all of us began climbing onto its bed. As the driver took us toward the ski lodge, the retarded girl continued to face the mountain and say the word "Whomever." By this time she stood alone as the "in crowd" left her isolated at the center of the bed. She was alone, that is, except for a big man who stood nearby. Suddenly, I realized that he was her father.

It was at that point that this man with the kind face did something I will never forget. He walked over to his daughter and wrapped his arms around her. He put his big hand on the back of her head and gently pressed it to his chest. Then he looked down at her lovingly and said, "Yeah, babe. Whomever."

I must admit that I had to turn my head to conceal the moisture in my eyes. You see, that father had seen the same rejection from the beautiful people that I had observed. He saw their smiles . . . their scorn. His act of love to the girl was only partially done for her benefit. The father was actually speaking to all of us.

He was saying, "Yes, it's true. My daughter is retarded. We can't hide that fact. She is very limited in ability. She won't sing the songs. She won't write the books. In fact, she's already out of school. We've done the best we could for her. But I want you all to know something. This young lady is my girl, and I love her. She's the whole world to me. And I'm not ashamed to be identified with her. 'Yeah, babe. Whomever!'"

The selfless love and tenderness of that father flooded out from his soul and engulfed mine. Instantly, I felt compassion and love for our two children.

"All right, Lord!" I said. "I get the message."

Two weeks later, I was a guest on a national television show, and the moderator gave me four and a half minutes to answer such questions as "How did the institution of the family get into such a mess, and how can we correct the problem?"

I couldn't have answered the question in four and a half hours . . . but I can say this: One of the solutions to family disintegration has something to do with what that father was feeling for his handicapped girl, there in the back of that flatbed truck. That kind of unconditional love will heal a troubled home. It will resolve conflicts between parent and child. It will even help us cope with a tragedy like mental retardation.

What we desperately need as a framework on which to rebuild the quaking family is a generation of men who have the capacity to love like the father of the retarded girl . . .

> men who know who they are . . .
>
> men who know where they're going . . .
>
> men who know in Whom they believe . . .
>
> men who will put the best interests of their wives and children above their own selfish desires and pursuits . . .
>
> men who will fight for what they believe . . .
>
> men like my father and grandfather, who modeled these qualities for me during my impressionable years.

Let's turn back the clock in the next few chapters to look specifically at these influential members of my family and the way they lived their lives. Perhaps their example will speak loudly to younger men in search of worthy role models.

WHAT IS A MAN?

3

My Father

Who could have suspected on such a pleasant afternoon that my father, at sixty-six years of age, was enjoying his final moments on this earth? He held the baby and chatted amiably with members of the family. A Sunday dinner was then placed on the table and Dad was asked to bless the food. This good man, James Dobson, Sr., bowed his head one last time and thanked the Lord for his generosity and love. It was to be his own benediction, for, minutes later, God beckoned his soul across the chilly waters of death. There was no struggle, no pain, no agonizing "good-byes." He simply paused, then leaned toward my mother and was gone.

An hour later, my wife reached me by telephone to break the news. I was speaking twelve hundred miles to the west, and had devoted my remarks that day to the importance of Christian fatherhood. In fact, I talked throughout the morning about my dad and the beautiful example he had set before me. Then came Shirley's call. We shared an incredible sense of grief and loss in that moment. Only those who "have been there" will fully comprehend such an experience.

The funeral was held three days later, at which time I delivered a tribute to my father. Somehow I managed to express the following words from my heart on that cold December day.

The Tribute

To our friends and loved ones, I want to express appreciation on behalf of our family for each of you being here today. We appreciate your coming to honor the man whom we loved so dearly—the man whose name I share.

I asked my mother for this privilege of paying tribute to my dad, although quite honestly, this is the most difficult moment of my life. This man whose body lies before me was not only my father and my friend, but he was also the source of great inspiration for me. Few people realize that most of my writings are actually an expression of his views and his teachings. Whenever we were together, he would talk and I usually took notes. That's the kind of relationship we had, and his loss is devastating to me.

So I don't apologize for the grief that overwhelms me in this hour. These are not tears of guilt or remorse or regret. I have no bitter memories . . . there were no harsh words that I wish I could retrieve . . . we had no conflicts or struggles or strife. The emotion that you see reflects only the love of a son who has suddenly lost his father and gentle friend.

Some of you are aware that my dad had a very serious heart attack in September of this year. Shirley and I had traveled to San Antonio, Texas, where I was to speak to the Texas Pediatric Society on Friday. When we arrived at the hotel on Thursday night, we received a message from Dr. Paul Cunningham, indicating that my dad was in intensive care in a Kansas City hospital. On Friday morning, Dr. Cunningham called again to say that my father's condition had worsened and he was not expected to live through the night. He also informed me that my uncle, Dr. James McGraw, had died in the same hospital at 10:30 that morning. It is impossible to describe the sorrow that Shirley and I felt as we flew to Kansas City that afternoon. We never expected to see my dad alive again and went through all the agonies of his loss. But when we arrived at the airport, we learned that my dad had made a remarkable improvement and was anticipating our visit at the hospital. How thankful I will always be that God answered our prayers and granted us seventy-nine more days—beautiful, golden days—before He took my dad to heaven on December 4, 1977.

May I share with you what thoughts went through my troubled mind on that endless plane trip from San Antonio to Kansas City? I journeyed backward in time, experiencing a kaleidoscope of early memories. I thought about the very happiest days of my life, occurring when I was between ten and thirteen years of age. My dad and I would arise very early before the sun came up on a wintry morning. We would put on our hunting clothes and heavy boots, and drive twenty miles from the little town where we lived. After parking the car and climbing over a fence, we entered a wooded area which I called the "big woods" because the trees seemed so large to me. We would slip down to the creek bed and follow that winding stream several miles back into the forest.

Then my dad would hide me under a fallen tree which made a little room with its branches. He would find a similar shelter for himself around a bend in the creek. Then we would await the arrival of the sun and the awakening of the animal world. Little squirrels and birds and chipmunks would scurry back and forth, not knowing they were being observed. My dad and I then watched as the breathtaking panorama of the morning unfolded, which spoke so eloquently of the God who made all things.

But most importantly, there was something dramatic that occurred out there in the forest between my dad and me. An intense love and affection was generated on those mornings that set the tone for a lifetime of fellowship. There was a closeness and a oneness that made me want to be like that man . . . that made me choose his values as my values, his dreams as my dreams, his God as my God.

These were among the memories that surged through my mind on that lonely plane trip in September. Then another flood of emotion came over me, as I thought about my own children. I wondered what memories will predominate in their minds when I lie at the point of death, a moment or two from now. What will they remember to be the happiest experiences of their lives? Will they recall a busy father who was preoccupied with writing books and catching planes and answering mail and talking on the telephone and being a "big man"? Or will they recall a patient dad who took time to love them and teach them and enjoy the beauty of God's world with them? I pray that the Lord will help me keep my little family at the top of my list of priorities during the precious primetime years.

James Dobson was a man of many intense loves. His greatest passion was expressed in his love for Jesus Christ. His every thought and deed were motivated or influenced by his desire to serve his Lord. And I can truthfully say that we were never together without my being drawn closer to God by being in his presence. Not because he warned me or chastised me . . . but because his love for the Lord penetrated and shaped my own attitudes.

The last conversation I ever held with my dad reflected my confidence in his faith. Exactly five days before his death, I telephoned him from Los Angeles at 11:27 A.M.

I said, "Dad, I have an appointment at 11:30 and can only talk for three minutes. I am calling because I face some decisions this afternoon which are very important to me professionally, and I want you to pray for me." His final words were, "I *will* pray about it, Jim." You can be sure that he did!

My dad also loved my mother with great intensity. This fact was beautifully illustrated last year when my parents came to visit us in California. Dad and I took a walk in a nearby park one morning, and as usual, he was talking and I was writing. He then reached into his pocket and retrieved a crumpled sheet of paper which looked very old.

He said, "You might be interested in reading this statement. These are words I expressed to your mother before we were married, forty-two years ago. They were not read to her, but I later wrote down the thoughts I had communicated."

This message was written on the paper.

> I want you to understand and be fully aware of my feelings concerning the marriage covenant which we are about to enter. I have been taught at my mother's knee, and in harmony with the Word of God, that the marriage vows are inviolable, and by entering into them, I am binding myself absolutely and for life. The idea of estrangement from you through divorce for any reason at all (although God allows one—infidelity) will never at any time be permitted to enter into my thinking. I'm not naive in this. On the contrary, I'm fully aware of the possibility, unlikely as it now appears, that mutual incompatibility or other unforeseen circumstances, could result in extreme mental suffering. If such becomes the case, I am resolved for my part to accept it as a consequence of the commitment I am now making, and to bear it, if necessary, to the end of our lives together.
>
> I have loved you dearly as a sweetheart and will continue to love you as my wife. But over and above that, I love you with a Christian love that demands that I never react in any way toward you that would jeopardize our prospects of entering heaven, which is the supreme objective of both our lives. And I pray that God Himself will make our affection for one another perfect and eternal.

Isn't that a beautiful way to say "I love you"? How badly America needs husbands and fathers who are committed to their families—men who are *determined* to succeed in this important responsibility. My father was such a man, and his devotion to my mother grew steadily through their forty-three years of marriage. They were *mutually dependent* in the way God intended. It is fitting, therefore, that in his final moment of consciousness, he fell toward my mother and died peacefully in her arms.

Very few people fully comprehended the depth of my dad's love of learning. When he died, he left a book beside his big chair, opened to a description of the molecular structure of deoxyribonucleic acid and the process by which hereditary characteristics are transmitted from one generation to the next. Beside it was a list (in his handwriting) of the twenty essential amino acids in humans, and how they are genetically coded. (He called them "God's four-letter words.") My dad had an insatiable desire *to know*, alternating regularly between biology, physics, astronomy, ecology, theology, politics, medicine and the arts. He left a half-finished painting of a mountain stream in his basement, with a photograph propped to its right. A palette of oils still rests where he placed them on that final Saturday night. Yes, my dad loved *everything* God made, and it is thrilling to contemplate the learning process that must be occurring right now on the other side!

Finally, my dad also loved me. I've known that from my earliest moments of awareness. I'm told that when I was a small child, perhaps three years of age, we lived in a one-bedroom apartment. My little bed was located beside the bed of my parents. Dad said it was not uncommon during that time for him to awaken at night and hear a little voice whispering, "Daddy? Daddy?"

He would answer quietly, "What, Jimmy?"

Then I would reply, "Hold my hand!"

My dad would reach across the darkness and grope for my little hand, finally engulfing it in his. He said the instant he encompassed my hand, my arm would become limp and my breathing deep and regular. I had gone back to sleep. You see, I only wanted to know that he was *there!* I have been reaching for him throughout my forty-one years, and he has always been there. And now for the first time in my life, he's gone.

So where do we go from here? Do we leave this church today in despair and discouragement? Certainly not, although our sorrow is incalculable. But my dad is not in that casket before us. He is *alive*, and we will soon see him again. He has achieved the pearl of eternal life, which is our heritage, too. I now understand that the death of my dad was not an isolated tragedy that happened to one unfortunate man and his family. In a real sense, this is the human condition which affects us all. Life will soon be over for everyone in this sanctuary . . . and for everyone whom we love.* Therefore, I have determined to live each day as Christ would dictate, keeping in mind the temporal nature of everything which now seems so permanent. Even in death, you see, my dad has taught me about life.

Thank you for allowing me to share my deepest feelings and emotions, today. I must acknowledge, in closing, that James Dobson was not a perfect man. It would be unfortunate to eulogize him in a way that would embarrass him if he were sitting among us. My father had a generous assortment of flaws, even as you and I. But I loved him. Perhaps . . . as much as any son ever loved his dad.

Danae and Ryan [addressed to my children], you had a great man for a grandfather. Not because he was President or because he will be remembered in the history books. He was great because of his uncompromising dedication to the Christian faith. And if I can be half the father to you that he was to me, you will be fortunate children, indeed.

"A sudden death is God's kiss upon the soul!"
—Anonymous

---

*Seven members of our family have died in the past eighteen months: my father, Shirley's grandmother (Mrs. Hassie Wisham), my uncle (Dr. James McGraw), my aunt (Mrs. Naomi Dobson), my great uncle and aunt (Rev. and Mrs. R. M. Parks) and Shirley's uncle (Mr. Al Frasher).

4

The Revelation

Two years before my father's death, he shared an experience that occurred while he had been praying and reading the Bible. He seemed almost embarrassed to reveal the details, but I coaxed him to tell me the story. It involved an overwhelming impression, almost a divine decree, that he and I were going to cooperate on a very important project. He hastened to say that he didn't want me to think he was trying to "ride on my coattail." In fact, his first impulse was to tell no one about the revelation for fear that his motives would be misunderstood.

His apprehension was unfounded. I learned very early in life that when God "speaks" to Dad, I had better pay attention. This man and his Lord had a very unusual relationship. It often involved sessions of prayer and communion, lasting from four to six hours, focusing especially on his ministry and on those whom he loved. He was known in the small town where I spent my preschool years as "the man with no leather on his shoes." He spent so much time on his knees that he wore out the toes of his shoes before the soles. Thus, James Dobson, Sr. and the Lord had a very unique relationship. When God revealed His purpose to His faithful servant, the outcome was an absolute certainty.

But what task would we accomplish together? Neither of us knew the answer to that question, nor did we pursue it further. We did join forces to work on a conference book entitled *Family under Fire*, but that didn't seem to be related to the revelation. The months rolled by and the matter was filed under the broad heading "Things I don't understand about the Lord."

Then came my father's initial heart attack while I was in San Antonio. That devastating telephone conversation reverberated in my head. "Your dad is dying. He has developed both arhythmia and congestion, which is usually a fatal combination following a myocardial infarction. We don't expect him to live through the night. Come as quickly as you can get here!"

Two friends rushed me to the airport, where Shirley was already waiting. But as we drove through the San Antonio traffic, the Lord spoke to me. His voice was not audible, nor was it accompanied by smoke and fire. I can't even tell you how the message was conveyed. All I know is that God reminded me of His revelation to my dad, and then said, "You are going to write a book for husbands and fathers, based on the life of your dad. The inspiration will be derived from his values, his dedication, his walk with Me. This is the joint venture of which I spoke two years ago."

As we made that long plane ride from San Antonio to Kansas City, Shirley and I knew that my dad's condition would be obvious instantly as we stepped into the terminal. If my mother was there to meet us, that would mean he was gone. But if she were not present, then she would still be with him at the hospital. Upon disembarking from the plane, we scanned the crowd breathlessly and to our great relief, Mother was not there. Instead, we were greeted by the wife of the president of the college where my father served as a professor. And she was smiling.

"Your dad is remarkably better," she said. "In fact, he's waiting to see you at the hospital."

I will always be thankful for having the priceless opportunity to see him alive, again—to express those words of appreciation and love that we seldom convey before it is too late. I stood by his bed in that intensive care unit. There amidst beeping oscilloscopes and bottles of glucose, I patted those delicate artistic hands that I have loved since my earliest awareness. He was entirely calm and coherent, revealing no hint of his brush with death.

Then I told him about the Lord's message to me on the way to the airport. I explained that his part of the project was already completed: it involved sixty-six years of integrity and devotion and love. I had watched him at home throughout my childhood, where it was impossible to hide his true nature. But never one time did I see him compromise with evil or abandon the faith by which he had lived. His character had been like a beacon for me, illuminating my way and steering me past the snares that entrapped so many of my friends.

"Thank you, Dad," I said, with deep emotion.

He smiled knowingly, and I quietly slipped out of his room. Though the months have passed and he is now gone, that conversation lingers as I begin my part of the joint venture. Today, May 24, would have been his sixty-eighth birthday, and it is fitting that I use this occasion to describe the values for which he stood.

But this book is not intended as a biography of my dad's life, by any means. In fact, its primary theme actually originated three years before his death. I had asked the Lord, as a special favor, to reveal His message to the Christian family.

I prayed, "As long as I'm going to be speaking and writing and attempting to influence husbands and wives and children, I would like to know what *you* want me to convey. Why should I depend on my own puny insight and wisdom, when I can tap the resources of the Creator of families? Give me, then, the concepts that you want me to communicate."

Again, I experienced one of those quiet moments of awareness when I knew the Lord had spoken. It should be emphasized that for me, at least, these examples of unmistakable leadership from God are relatively infrequent events. More typically, I learn of His will through providential circumstances, doors that open or close, and so on. But on a few occasions, His desires have been communicated directly from His heart to mine.

Such was the case in response to my prayer for wisdom and insight (although it sounds terribly pompous and self-important to relate now). But this was God's reply, translated into my own words: "If America is going to survive the incredible stresses and dangers it now faces, it will be because husbands and fathers again place their families at the highest level on their system of priorities, reserving a portion of their time and energy for leadership within their homes!"

I have been dutifully conveying that message at every opportunity for the past twenty years. I've said it on the radio, on television, on audio cassettes and on film. The time has come, at last, to put it in writing, where the concept can be explored in its many dimensions. That brings us to this day.

Having described the background for this book, let me be honest about what it means to me. I suspect that authors often write a new manuscript in the same spirit that General Motors brings out a new model. It merely takes its place in a long line of creations, having no more significance than the one before or after. However, I feel that my message to men is the most critical topic I have ever addressed, and as such, may be the task for which I was born. The Western world stands at a great crossroads in its history. And it is my opinion, based on the experience I shared, that our very survival as a people will depend on the presence or absence of masculine leadership in millions of homes.

Why do I place such importance on the involvement of *men* in determining the survival of a culture? Because no modern society can exceed the stability of its individual family units, and women seem more aware of that fact than their husbands. Consider the evidence. Who read the books on family living? Eighty percent are known to be women. Who attend seminars on meaningful family life? The majority are women. Who enroll in Bible study classes devoted to Scriptural underpinnings of the family? Women outnumber men by an incredible margin. Who listen to family radio programs and cassette tapes on marriage and parenthood? Once again, they are likely to be female.

What I'm saying is that Christian women, to a large extent, are already motivated to preserve their families. And though I hate to admit it, women often know more than their husbands about the role God has ordained for men. One of the most common letters I receive is sent by hundreds of women who ask the same question:

> My husband won't assume spiritual leadership in our family. He doesn't seem to be aware of my needs and the requirements of our children. How can I get his attention?

That's why I believe, with everything within me, that husbands hold the *keys* to the preservation of the family. If we can get men to slow down long enough to look at the issues, some will make the changes necessary for survival. And I'm certain that their wives will follow suit.

Derek Prince expressed his view that the major problems facing the Western world can be traced to what he called "renegade males." A renegade is defined as "one who reneges." It is a harsh indictment, but there is validity in the assessment. God has charged men with the responsibility for providing leadership in their homes and families: leadership in the form of loving authority; leadership in the form of financial management; leadership in the form of spiritual training; and leadership in maintaining the marital relationship. Husbands are instructed to "love [their] wives, just as Christ loved the Church and gave himself up for her" (Eph. 5:25, NIV). That is not a casual suggestion to Christian men; it is God's *commandment* to husbands and fathers. This book, then, is a call to arms . . . an urgent plea for men to recommit themselves to this divinely ordered responsibility.

My father exemplified what I believe to be God's concept of masculinity. And, as might be expected, he learned it from *his* father. We'll discuss the life of R. L. Dobson, my paternal grandfather, in a subsequent chapter.

5

The Heritage

During the Christmas season 1969, my father's two surviving brothers and his sister gathered in California for a family reunion. And on that happy occasion, they spent the better part of five days reminiscing about their childhood and early home life. One of the grandchildren had enough initiative to record the discussions on cassette tapes, and I was privileged to obtain a complete set. What a rich heritage this provided, granting insight into my grandparents' home and the early experiences of my dad.

While all the conversations were of interest to me, there was a common thread that was especially significant throughout the week. It focused on the *respect* with which these four siblings addressed the memory of their father (my grandfather). He died in 1935, a year before my birth, yet they spoke of him with an unmistakable awe more than thirty-four years later. He still lived in their minds as a man of enormous character and strength.

I asked them to explain the qualities that they admired so greatly, but received little more than vague generalities.

"He was a tower of strength," said one.

"He had a certain dignity about him," said another, with appropriate gestures.

"We held him in awe," replied the third.

It is difficult to summarize the subtleties and complexities of the human personality, and they were unable to find the right words. Only when we began talking about specific remembrances did the personality of this patriarch become apparent. My dad provided the best evidence by writing his recollection of Grandfather Dobson's death, which I've reproduced below. Flowing throughout this narrative is the impact of a great man on his family, even three decades after his demise.

The Last Days of R. L. Dobson

The attack that took his life occurred when he was sixty-nine years of age, and resulted ultimately in the breakup of the family circle. For many years after his death, I could not pass Tri-State Hospital without noting one particular window. It stood out from the rest, hallowed because it represented the room where he had suffered so much. The details of those tragic days and nights remain in my memory, unchanged by the passage of time.

We had been three days and three nights practically without sleep, listening to him struggle for breath, hearing the sounds of approaching death, smelling the smells of death. Dad lay in a deep coma. His heavy breathing could be heard up and down the corridor. We walked the halls of that old hospital for hours listening to the ceaseless struggle which now was becoming fainter and fainter. Several times the nurse had called us in and we had said the last "good-bye"—had gone through the agony of giving him up, only to have his heart rally, and then the endless vigil would begin all over again. Finally, we had gone into an adjoining room not prepared for sleep, but some in the chairs and some across the beds, we had fallen into the sleep of utter exhaustion.

At five minutes to four o'clock the nurse came in and awakened one of my twin brothers. Robert roused with a start. "Is he gone?" he asked.

"No, but if you boys want to see your dad one more time while he is alive, you'd better come, now."

The word quickly passed around and we filed into the room to stand around his bed for the last time. I remember that I stood at his left side: I smoothed back the hair from his forehead, and laid my hand on his big old red hand, so very much like my own. I felt the fever that precedes death: 105. While I was standing there a change came over me. Instead of being a grown man (I was twenty-four at the time) I became a little boy again. They say this often happens to adults who witness the death of a parent. I thought I was in the Union Train Station in Shreveport, Louisiana, in the late afternoon, and I was watching for his return. The old Kansas City Southern passenger train was backing into the station and I saw it come 'round the curve. My heart swelled with pride. I turned to the little boy standing next to me and said, "You see that big man standing on the back of the train, one hand on the air brake and the other on the little whistle with which he signals the engineer? That big man is my dad!" He set the air brakes and I heard the wheels grind to a stop. I saw him step off that last coach. I ran and jumped into his arms. I gave him a tight hug and I smelled the train smoke on his clothes. "Daddy, I love you," I said.

It all comes back. I patted that big hand and said "Goodbye, Dad," as he was sinking fast, now. "We haven't forgotten how hard you worked to send five boys and one girl through college: how you wore those old conductor uniforms until they were slick—doing without—that we might have things that we didn't really need. . . ."

At three minutes to four o'clock, like a stately ship moving slowly out of time's harbor into eternity's sea, he breathed his last. The nurse motioned us to leave, and pulled the sheet over his head, a gesture that struck terror to my heart, and we turned with silent weeping to leave the room. Then an incident occurred that I will never forget. Just as we got to the door, I put my arm around my little mother and said, "Mama, this is awful."

Dabbing at her eyes with her handkerchief, she said, "Yes, Jimmy, but there is one thing Mother wants you to remember, now. We have said 'good night' down here, but one of these days we are going to say 'good morning' up there."

I believe she did say "good morning" too, eleven years later, and I know he met her "just inside the Eastern gate."

His death was marked by quietness and dignity, just like the life he had lived. Thus came to an end the affairs of R. L. Dobson, and thus ended, too, the solidarity of the family. The old home place was never the same again. The old spirit that we had known as children was gone forever!

Though this illustration reveals few of the specific characteristics that made R. L. Dobson such a powerful influence in his family, it does tell us how his son felt about him. I happen to know some of the other details. He was a man of absolute integrity and honesty. Though not a Christian until shortly before his death, he lived by an internal standard that was singularly uncompromising. As a young man, for example, he invested heavily in a business venture with a partner whom he later discovered to be dishonest. When he learned of the chicanery, he virtually gave the company to the other man. That former partner built the corporation into one of the most successful operations in the South, and became a multimillionaire. But my grandfather never looked back. He took a clean conscience with him to his grave.

There were other admirable traits, of course, and many of them were transmitted to my dad. These two men personified much of what I'm trying to convey in this examination of masculinity. My father added the dimension of *vulnerability* to the pattern, which is beautifully captured in the drawing by Ray Craighead (his art student) reproduced on the dedication page of this book.

Having looked superficially at the image of two strong fathers and their influence at home, let's turn now to the specifics. We'll discuss the interaction of a man with his children, his wife, his work, and his God, among related subjects. And as we do, may I make a suggestion for those who enjoy a personal relationship with the Lord? You might pause to ask him, *prior* to reading those chapters, what new understandings He wishes to convey through the pages of this book. It is my desire that He speak to each family (and especially to each man) in the terms we need to hear.

A MAN AND HIS CHILDREN

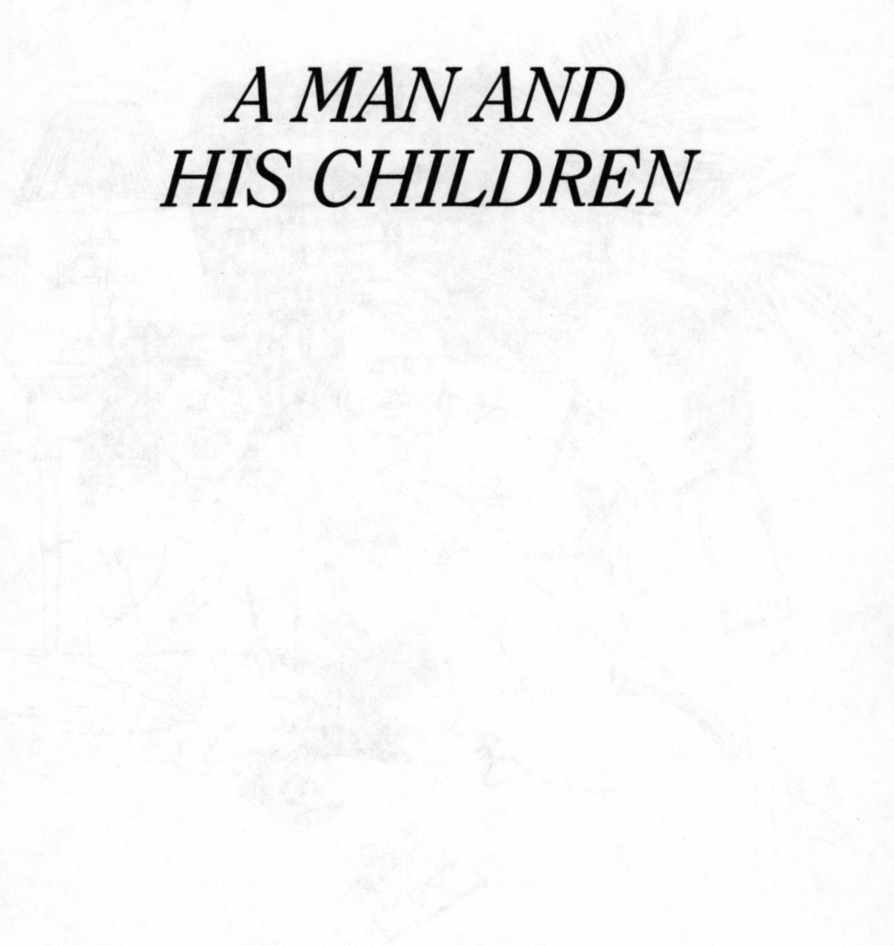

6

A Man and His Children

I was walking toward my car outside a shopping center a few weeks ago, when I heard a loud and impassioned howl.

"Auggghh!" groaned the masculine voice.

I spotted a man about fifty feet away who was in great distress (and for a very good reason). His fingers were caught in the jamb of a car door which had obviously been slammed unexpectedly. Then the rest of the story unfolded. Crouching in the front seat was an impish little three-year-old boy who had apparently decided to "close the door on dad."

The father was pointing frantically at his fingers with his free hand, and saying, "Oh! Oh! Open the door, Chuckie! They'recaught . . . hurry . . . Chuckie . . . please . . . open . . . OPEN!"

Chuckie finally got the message and unlocked the door, releasing Dad's blue fingers. The father then hopped and jumped around the aisles of the parking lot, alternately kissing and caressing his battered hand. Chuckie sat unmoved in the front seat of their car, waiting for Pop to settle down.

I know this incident was painful to the man who experienced it, but I must admit that it struck me funny. I suppose his plight symbolized the enormous cost of parenthood. And yes, Virginia, it is expensive to raise boys and girls today. Parents give the best they have to their children, who often respond by slamming the door on their "fingers"—especially during the unappreciative adolescent years. Perhaps that is why someone quipped, "Insanity is an inherited disease. You get it from your kids."

But there are other things that we get from our kids, including love and meaning and purpose and an opportunity to give. They also help us maintain our sense of humor, which is essential to emotional stability in these stressful days. I'm reminded of Anne Ortlund's eleven-year-old son whom she described in her book *Disciplines of a Beautiful Woman*. She had taken this rambunctious boy to their pediatrician for a routine physical examination. Before seeing the doctor, however, the nurse weighed and measured the child and attempted to obtain a medical history.

"Tell me, Mrs. Ortlund," said the nurse, "how is he sleeping?"

Nels answered on his own behalf, "I sleep very well." The nurse wrote that down.

"How's his appetite, Mrs. Ortlund?"

"I eat everything," said Nels. She wrote that down.

"Mrs. Ortlund, how are his bowels?"

The boy responded, "A, E, I, O and U."*

Those memories are priceless to the parent who isn't too tired to notice. Let me share one more true story. A father told me recently about a five-year-old boy who was sitting on the toilet at the precise instant an earthquake rocked Los Angeles County on February 9, 1971. The jolt was so severe that it knocked this lad off the potty. But never having been in an earthquake before, he thought the rumble had been caused by his *own* bathroom activity. "What did I do, Mom?" he asked, with childlike wonder.

---

*Waco, Tex.: Word Books, 1977, p. 92.

A family is literally a "museum of memories" to those who have been blessed by the presence of children. Although my kids are now grown, I can recall ten thousand episodes that are carefully preserved in my mind. The "videotapes" of their early years are among my most valued possessions: even now, I see a six-year-old girl coming home from school. Her hair is disheveled and one sock is down around her ankle. It is obvious that she's been spinning upside down on the playground bars. She asks for a glass of milk and sits down at the kitchen table, unaware of the tenderness and love that I feel for her at that moment. Then she runs out to play.

Another "tape" begins to roll. I see a four-year-old boy with a Band-aid on his knee and bread crumbs on his face. He approaches my chair and asks to sit on my lap.

"Sorry," I said. "Only one boy in the world can climb on me when he chooses."

"Whoizzat?" he replies.

"Oh, you wouldn't know him. He's a kid named Ryan."

"But my name is Ryan!"

"Yes, but the boy I'm talking about has blond hair and blue eyes."

"Don't you see my blond hair? And my eyes are blue."

"Yes, but many kids have those. The only boy who can get on my lap is my son . . . my only son . . . whom I love."

"Hey, that's me! I'm your son. My name is Ryan! And I'm coming up!"

That little game was played for seven years, and it still has meaning.

But I can hear my readers saying, "You're just a sentimentalist."

"You bet I am!" I reply. I'm not ashamed to admit that *people* matter to me, and I'm most vulnerable to those people within my own family. I've enjoyed every stage in the lives of our two kids and wished that they (we) could remain young forever.

Not only have Shirley and I enjoyed the developmental years, but Danae and Ryan have apparently shared that appreciation. Our daughter, especially, has loved every aspect of childhood and has been most reluctant to leave it. Her phonograph records and her stuffed animals and her bedroom have been prized possessions since toddlerhood. Likewise, she sat on Santa's lap for four years after she knew he was a phony. But, alas, she turned thirteen years old and began hearing a new set of drums. About a year later, she went through her toys and records, stacking them neatly and leaving them in front of Ryan's bedroom door. On the top was a note which Shirley brought to me with tears in her eyes. I read:

> Dear Ryan:
>
> These are yours now.
> Take good care of them like I have.
>
> Love,
> Danae

That brief message signaled the closing of the door called "Childhood." And once it shut, no power on earth could open it again. That's why the toddler and elementary school years should be seen as fleeting opportunities. Yet this priceless period of influence often occurs at a time when fathers are the least accessible to their kids. They are trying to establish themselves in their occupations, racing and running and huffing and puffing, dragging home a briefcase crammed to the brim with night work, scurrying to the airport to catch the last plane to Chicago, moonlighting to pay those vacation bills, and finally collapsing in bed in a state of utter exhaustion. Another day has passed with no interchange between Dad and his teachable little boy or girl.

One mother told me of hearing her preschool son talking to another four-year-old boy on the front steps.

"Where is your daddy?" he asked. "I've never seen him."

"Oh, he doesn't *live* here," came the reply. "He only *sleeps* here."

Without wanting to heap guilt on the heads of my masculine readers, I must say that too many fathers only *sleep* at their homes. And as a result, they have totally abdicated their responsibilities for leadership and influence in the lives of their children. I cited a study in my previous book *What Wives Wish Their Husbands Knew About Women* that documented the problem of inaccessible fathers. Let me quote from that source.

> An article in *Scientific American* entitled "The Origins of Alienation," by Urie Bronfenbrenner best describes the problems facing today's families. Dr. Bronfenbrenner is, in my opinion, the foremost authority on child development in America today, and his views should be considered carefully. In this article, Dr. Bronfenbrenner discussed the deteriorating status of the American family and the forces which are weakening its cohesiveness. More specifically, he is concerned about the circumstances which are seriously undermining parental love and depriving children of the leadership and love they must have for survival.
>
> One of those circumstances is widely know as the "rat-race." Dr. Bronfenbrenner described the problem this way, "The demands of a job that claim mealtimes, evenings and weekends as well as days; the trips and moves necessary to get ahead or simply to hold one's own; the increasing time spent commuting, entertaining, going out, meeting social and community obligations . . . all of these produce a situation in which a child often spends more time with a passive babysitter than with a participating parent."
>
> According to Dr. Bronfenbrenner, this rat race is particularly incompatible with fatherly responsibilities, as illustrated by a recent investigation which yielded startling results. A team of researchers wanted to learn how much time middle-class fathers spend playing and interacting with their small children. First, they asked a group of fathers to estimate the time spent with their one-year-old youngsters each day, and received an average reply of fifteen to twenty minutes. To verify these claims, the investigators attached microphones to the shirts of small children for the purpose of recording actual

> parental verbalization. The results of this study are shocking: The average amount of time spent by these middle-class fathers with their small children was thirty-seven seconds per day! Their direct interaction was limited to 2.7 encounters daily, lasting ten to fifteen seconds each! That, so it seems, represents the contribution of fatherhood for millions of America's children.*

Let's compare the thirty-seven-second interchanges between fathers and small children with another statistic. The average preschool child watches between 30 and 50 hours of television per week (the figures vary from one study to another). What an incredible picture is painted by those two statistics. During the formative years of life, when children are so vulnerable to their experiences, they're receiving thirty-seven seconds a day from their fathers and thirty or more hours a week from commercial television! Need we ask where our kids are getting their values?

Someone observed, "Values are not *taught* to our children; they are *caught* by them." It is true. Seldom can we get little Johnny or Mary to sit patiently on a chair while we lecture to them about God and the other important issues of life. Instead, they are equipped with internal "motors" which are incapable of idling. Their transmissions consist of only six gears: run, jump, climb, crawl, slide and dive. Boys and girls are simply not wired for quiet conversations about heavy topics.

How, then, do conscientious parents convey their attitudes and values and faith to their children? It is done *subtly*, through the routine interactions of everyday living.** We saw this fact illustrated in our own home when Danae was ten years old and Ryan was five. We were riding in the car when we passed a porno theater. I believe the name of the particular movie was "Flesh Gordon," or something equally

---

*James C. Dobson, *What Wives Wish Their Husbands Knew About Women* (Wheaton, Ill: Tyndale House, 1975), pp. 157–58.

**See Deut. 6:4–9.

sensuous. Danae, who was sitting in the front seat, pointed to the theater and said,

"That's a dirty movie, isn't it, Dad?"

I nodded affirmatively.

"Is that what they call an X-rated movie?" she asked.

Again, I indicated that she was correct.

Danae thought for a moment or two, then said, "Dirty movies are really bad, aren't they?"

I said, "Yes, Danae. Dirty movies are very evil."

This entire conversation lasted less than a minute, consisting of three brief questions and three replies. Ryan, who was in the back seat, did not enter into our discussion. In fact, I wondered what he thought about the interchange, and concluded that he probably wasn't listening.

I was wrong. Ryan heard the conversation and apparently continued thinking about it for several days. But amusingly, Ryan did not know what a "dirty movie" was. How would a five-year-old boy learn what goes on in such places, since no one had ever discussed pornography with him? Nevertheless, he had his own idea about the subject. That concept was revealed to me four nights later at the close of the day.

Ryan and I got down on our knees to say his bedtime prayer, and the preschooler spontaneously returned to that conversation earlier in the week.

"Dear Lord," he began in great seriousness, "help me not to go see any dirty movies . . . where everyone is spitting on each other."

For Ryan, the dirtiest thing he could imagine would be a salivary free-for-all. That *would* be dirty, I had to admit.

But I also had to acknowledge how *casually* children assimilate our values and attitudes. You see, I had no way of anticipating that brief conversation in the car. It was not my deliberate intention to convey my views about pornography to my children. How was it that they learned one more dimension of my value system on that morning? It occurred because we happened to be together . . . to be talking to one another. Those kinds of subtle, unplanned interactions account for much of the instruction that passes from one generation to the next. It is a powerful force in shaping young lives, *if! If* parents are occasionally at home with their kids; *if* they have the energy to converse with them; *if* they have anything worthwhile to transmit; *if* they care.

My point is that the breathless American lifestyle is particularly costly to children. Yet 1.8 million youngsters come home to an empty house after school each day. They are called "latchkey" kids because they wear the keys to their front doors around their necks. Not only are their fathers overcommitted and preoccupied, but now, their mothers are energetically seeking fulfillment in the working world, too. So who is at home with the kids? More commonly, the answer is *nobody.*

A popular song beautifully portrays the cost of overcommitment in family life. It was written by Sandy and Harry Chapin, who titled it "Cat's in the Cradle." I've obtained permission to reproduce the lyrics, as follows, specifically for the fathers who are reading this book:

Cat's in the Cradle

By Sandy and Harry Chapin

My child arrived just the other day
he came to the world in the usual way—
But there were planes to catch and bills to pay
he learned to walk while I was away
and he was talkin fore I knew it and as he grew
he'd say

I'm gonna be like you, Dad
you know I'm gonna be like you.

and the cat's in the cradle and the silver spoon
Little boy blue and the man in the moon
when you comin' home, Dad

I don't know when
but we'll get together then—
you know we'll have a good time then

My son turned 10 just the other day
he said, Thanks for the ball, Dad, com'on let's play
Can you teach me to throw?
I said not today, I got a lot to do
He said, That's okay
and he walked away but his smile never dimmed
it said I'm gonna be like him, yeah
you know I'm gonna be like him

and the cat's in the cradle and the silver spoon
Little boy blue and the man in the moon
when you comin' home, Dad

I don't know when
but we'll get together then—
you know we'll have a good time then

Well he came home from college just the other day
so much like a man I just had to say
Son, I'm proud of you, can you sit for awhile
He shook his head and said with a smile—
what I'd really like, Dad, is to borrow the car keys
see you later, can I have them please?

When you comin' home, Son?
I don't know when
but we'll get together then
you know we'll have a good time then

I've long since retired, my son's moved away
I called him up just the other day
I said I'd like to see you if you don't mind
He said, I'd love to, Dad—if I can find the time

You see my new job's a hassle and the kids have the flu
but it's sure nice talkin to you, Dad
It's been nice talking to you

And as I hung up the phone, it occurred to me—
he'd grown up just like me; my boy was just like me

and the cat's in the cradle and the silver spoon
Like boy blue and the man in the moon
when you comin' home, Son?
I don't know when
but we'll get together then, Dad,
we're gonna have a good time then

Do those words strike home to anyone but me? Have *you* felt the years slipping by with far too many unfulfilled promises to your children? Have you heard yourself saying,

> Son, we've been talking about that wagon we were going to build one of these Saturdays, and I just want you to know that I haven't forgotten it. But we can't do it this weekend 'cause I have to make an unexpected trip to Indianapolis. However, we *will* get to it one of these days. I'm not sure if it can be next weekend, but you keep reminding me and we'll eventually work together. And I'm going to take you fishing, too. I *love* to fish and I know a little stream that is jumping with trout in the Spring. But this just happens to be a very busy month for your mom and me, so let's keep planning and before you know it, the time will be here.

Then the days soon become weeks, and the weeks flow into months and years and decades . . . and our kids grow up and leave home. Then we sit in the silence of our family rooms, trying to recall the precious experiences that escaped us there. Ringing in our ears is that haunting phrase, "We'll have a good time . . . then . . ."

Oh, I know I'm stirring a measure of guilt into the pot with these words. But perhaps we need to be confronted with the important issues of life, even if they make us uncomfortable. Furthermore, I feel *obligated* to speak on behalf of the millions of children around the world who are reaching for fathers who aren't there. The names of specific boys and girls come to my mind as I write these words, symbolizing the masses of lonely kids who experience the agony of unmet needs. Let me acquaint you with two or three of those children whose paths I have crossed.

I think, first of the mother who approached me after I had spoken some years ago. She had supported her husband through college and medical school, only to have him divorce her in favor of a younger plaything. She stood with tears in her eyes as she described the impact of his departure on her two sons.

"They miss their daddy every day," she said. "They don't understand why he doesn't come to see them. The older boy, especially, wants a father so badly that he reaches for every man who comes into our lives. What can I tell him? How can I meet the boy's needs for a father who will hunt and fish and play football and bowl with him and his brother? It's breaking my heart to see them suffer so much."

I gave this mother a few suggestions and offered my understanding and support. The next morning I spoke for the final time at her church. Following the service, I stood on the platform as a line of people waited to tell me good-bye and extend their greetings. Standing in the line was the mother *with* her two sons.

They greeted me with smiles and I shook the older child's hand. Then something happened which I did not recall until I was on my way back to Los Angeles. The boy did not let go of my hand! He gripped it tightly, preventing me from welcoming others who pressed around. To my regret, I realized later that I had unconsciously grasped his arm with my other hand, pulling myself free from his grip. I sat on the plane, realizing the full implications of that incident. You see, this lad *needed* me. He needed a man who could take the place of his renegade father. And I had failed him, just like all the rest. Now I'm left with the memory of a child who said with his eyes, "Could you be a daddy to me?"!

Another child has found a permanent place in my memory, although I don't even know her name. I was waiting to catch a plane at Los Angeles International Airport, enjoying my favorite activity of "people watching." But I was unprepared for the drama about to unfold. Standing near me was an old man who was obviously waiting for someone who should have been on the plane that arrived minutes before. He examined each face intently as the passengers filed past. I thought he seemed unusually distressed as he waited.

Then I saw the little girl who stood by his side. She must have been seven years old, and she, too, was desperately looking for a certain face in the crowd. I have rarely seen a child more anxious than this cute little girl. She clung to the old man's arm, who I assumed to be her grandfather. Then as the last passengers came by, one by one, the girl began to cry silently. She was not merely disappointed in that moment; her little heart was broken. The grandfather also appeared to be fighting back the tears. In fact, he was too upset to comfort the child, who then buried her face in the sleeve of his worn coat.

"Oh, God!" I prayed silently. "What special agony are they experiencing in this hour? Was it the child's mother who abandoned her on that painful day? Did her daddy promise to come and then change his mind?"

My great impulse was to throw my arms around the little girl and shield her from the awfulness of that hour. I wanted her to pour out her grief in the protection of my embrace, but I feared that my intrusion would be misunderstood. So I watched helplessly. Then the old man and the child stood silently as the passengers departed from two other planes, but the anxiety on their faces had turned to despair. Finally, they walked slowly through the terminal and toward the door. Their only sound was the snuffing of the little girl who fought to control her tears.

Where is this child now? God only knows.

If the reader will bear with me, I must introduce you to one other child whose family experience has become so common in the Western world. I was waiting at Shawnee Mission Hospital for word on my dad's heart condition, after he was stricken in September. There in the waiting room was an *American Girl* magazine which caught my attention. (I must have been desperate for something to read to have been attracted to the *American Girl.*)

I opened the cover page and immediately saw a composition written by a fourteen-year-old girl named Vicki Kraushaar. She had submitted her story for publication in the section of the magazine entitled "By You." I'll let Vicki introduce herself and describe her experience.

That's the Way Life Goes Sometimes

When I was ten, my parents got a divorce. Naturally, my father told me about it, because he was my favorite. [Notice that Vicki did not say, "I was *his* favorite."]

"Honey, I know it's been kind of bad for you these past few days, and I don't want to make it worse. But there's something I have to tell you. Honey, your mother and I got a divorce."

"But, Daddy—"

"I know you don't want this, but it has to be done. Your mother and I just don't get along like we used to. I'm already packed and my plane is leaving in half an hour."

"But, Daddy, why do you have to leave?"

"Well, honey, your mother and I can't live together anymore."

"I know that, but I mean why do you have to leave town?"

"Oh. Well, I got someone waiting for me in New Jersey."

"But, Daddy, will I ever see you again?"

"Sure you will, honey. We'll work something out."

"But what? I mean, you'll be living in New Jersey, and I'll be living here in Washington."

"Maybe your mother will agree to you spending two weeks in the summer and two in the winter with me."

"Why not more often?"

"I don't think she'll agree to two weeks in the summer and two in the winter, much less more."

"Well, it can't hurt to try."

"I know, honey, but we'll have to work it out later. My plane leaves in twenty minutes and I've got to get to the airport. Now I'm going to get my luggage, and I want you to go to your room so you don't have to watch me. And no long good-byes either."

"Okay, Daddy. Good-bye. Don't forget to write."
"I won't. Good-bye. Now go to your room."
"Okay. Daddy, I don't want you to go!"
"I know, honey. But I have to."
"Why?"
"You wouldn't understand, honey."
"Yes, I would."
"No, you wouldn't."
"Oh well. Good-bye."
"Good-bye. Now go to your room. Hurry up."
"Okay. Well, I guess that's the way life goes sometimes."
"Yes honey. That's the way life goes sometimes."
After my father walked out that door, I never heard from him again.*

Vicki speaks eloquently on behalf of a million American children who have heard those shattering words, "Honey, your mother and I are getting a divorce." Throughout the world, husbands and wives are responding to the media blitz which urges and goads them to do their own thing, to chase impulsive desires without regard for the welfare of their families.

"The kids will get over it," goes the rationalization.

Every form of mass communication seemed mobilized to spread the "me first" philosophy during the 1970s and early 1980s. Frank Sinatra said it musically in his song, "I did it *my* way." Sammy Davis, Jr., echoed the sentiment in "I've gotta be me." Robert J. Ringer provided the literary version in *Looking Out for Number One*, which became the best-selling book in America for forty-six weeks. It was flanked by *Open Marriage, Creative Divorce*, and *Pulling Your Own Strings*, among hundreds of other dangerous best sellers. The est program then sold the same sickness under the guise of psychological health.

It all sounded so noble at the time. It was called "the discovery of personhood," and if offered an intoxicating appeal

*Reprinted by permission from *American Girl*, a magazine for all girls published by Girl Scouts of the U. S. A.

to our selfish lusts. But when this insidious philosophy had wormed its way into our system of values, it began to rot us from within. First, it encouraged an insignificant flirtation with sin (perhaps with a man or woman from New Jersey) followed by passion and illicit sexual encounters, followed by camouflaging lies and deceit, followed by angry words and sleepless nights, followed by tears and anguish, followed by crumbling self-esteem, followed by attorneys and divorce courts and property settlements, followed by devastating custody hearings. And from deep within the maelstrom, we can hear the cry of three wounded children—two girls and a boy—who will never fully recover. "Then when lust hath conceived, it bringeth forth sin; and sin, when it is finished, bringeth forth death" (James 1:15, KJV).

Lest I sound self-righteous and "preachy," let me focus the glaring spotlight on my own inadequacies. While I have never been involved in an affair, *nor will I ever,* there have certainly been times when I have permitted overcommitment to rob my children of my involvement. I'll reveal the details in the following chapter for those who have the inclination to continue.

My father often quoted Eugene Field's "Little Boy Blue" to me when I was a child. This poem has always been a favorite, but it has assumed new meaning since the birth of my children.

Little Boy Blue

The little toy dog is covered with dust,
  But sturdy and staunch he stands;
And the little toy soldier is red with rust,
  And his musket moulds in his hands.
Time was when the little toy dog was new,
  And the soldier was passing fair;
And that was the time when our Little Boy Blue
  Kissed them and put them there.

"Now, don't you go till I come," he said,
  "And don't you make any noise!"

So, toddling off to his trundle-bed,
  He dreamt of the pretty toys;
And, as he was dreaming, an angel song
  Awakened our Little Boy Blue—
Oh! the years are many, the years are long,
  But the little toy friends are True!

Ay, faithful to Little Boy Blue they stand,
  Each in the same old place—
Awaiting the touch of a little hand,
  The smile of a little face;
And they wonder, as waiting the long years through
  In the dust of that little chair,
What has become of our Little Boy Blue
  Since he kissed them and put them there.

Eugene Field
1850–1895

7

A Man and His Ultimate Priority

It occurred first in 1969, when *Dare to Discipline* was being written. I was running at an incredible speed, working myself to death like every other man I knew. I was Superintendent of Youth for my church, and labored under a heavy speaking schedule. Eight or ten "unofficial" responsibilities were added to my full-time commitment at USC School of Medicine and Children's Hospital of Los Angeles. I once worked seventeen nights straight without being home in the evening. Our five-year-old daughter would stand in the doorway and cry as I left in the morning, knowing she might not see me until the next sunrise.

Although my activities were bringing me professional advancement and the trappings of financial success, my dad was not impressed. He had observed my hectic lifestyle and felt obligated to express his concern. While flying from Los Angeles to Hawaii one summer, he used that quiet opportunity to write me a lengthy letter. It was to have a sweeping influence on my life. Let me quote one paragraph from his message which was especially poignant:

> Danae [referring to our daughter] is growing up in the wickedest section of a world much farther gone into moral decline than the world into which you were born. I have observed that the greatest delusion is to suppose that our children will be devout Christians simply because their parents have been, or that any of them will enter into the Christian faith in any other way than through their parents' deep travail of prayer and faith. But this prayer demands time, time that cannot be given if it is all signed and conscripted and laid on the altar of career ambition. Failure for you at this point would make mere success in your occupation a very pale and washed-out affair, indeed.

Those words, written without accusation or insult, hit me like the blow from a hammer. It contained several themes which had the ring of eternal truth. First, it *is* more difficult to teach proper values today than in years past because of the widespread rejection of Christian principles in our culture. In effect, there are many dissonant voices which feverishly contradict everything for which Christianity stands. The result is a generation of young people who have discarded the moral standards of the Bible.

Numerous studies have documented the steady increase in promiscuity occurring among teenagers and college-aged young people. For example, the *American Journal of Diseases of Children** reported that of 677 seventh, eighth, and ninth graders in a mostly white, lower middle class junior high in Indianapolis, 55 percent had had sex. More than 50 percent of the boys had intercourse by age thirteen, and more than 50 percent of the girls had intercourse by sixteen.

Quoting from Josh McDowell's book, *The Myth of Sex Education*, "A 1987 study by the National Academy of Science discovered, 'the attitude shift has been best documented

*"Teens Are Starting to Have Sex Earlier," *USA Today*, January 17, 1989.

among girls. From 1971 to 1982, the proportion of unmarried girls aged 15-19 who had had sexual intercourse at least once increased from 28 percent to 44 percent.'" *

This is the world in which our children are being raised. We need all the help we can get to lead them through the mine fields of adolescence.

The second concept in my dad's letter was the one that ended my parental complacency. He helped me realize that it is possible for mothers and fathers to love and revere God while systematically losing their children. You can go to church three times a week, serve on its governing board, attend the annual picnic, pay your tithes and make all the approved religious noises, yet somehow fail to communicate the real meaning of Christianity to the next generation.

I have since talked to dozens of parents whose children are grown and married.

"We thought our kids had accepted our faith and beliefs," they say, "but somehow, we failed to get it across."

For those younger parents whose children are still at an impressionable age, please believe the words of my dad, "The greatest delusion is to suppose that our children will be devout Christians simply because their parents have been, or that *any* of them will enter into the Christian faith in any other way than through their parents' deep travail of prayer and faith."

If you doubt the validity of this assertion, may I suggest that you read the story of Eli in 1 Samuel 2–4. Here is the account of a priest and servant of God who failed to discipline his children. He was apparently too busy with the "work of the church" to be a leader in his own home. The two boys grew up to be evil young men on whom God's judgment fell.

It concerned me to realize that Eli's service to the Lord was insufficient to compensate for his failure at home. Then I read farther in the narrative and received confirmation of the

*Lena Williams, "Teen-Age Sex: New Codes Amid the Old Anxiety," *New York Times*, February 27, 1989, B11, as quoted in Josh McDowell, *The Myths of Sex Education* (San Bernadino, Calif.: Here's Life Publishers, 1990), 8–9.

principle. *Samuel,* the saintly man of God who stood like a tower of spiritual strength throughout his life, grew up in Eli's home. He watched Eli systematically losing his children, yet Samuel proceeded to fail with his family, too! That was a deeply disturbing truth. If God would not honor Samuel's dedication by guaranteeing the salvation of his children, will He do more for *me* if I'm too busy to do my "homework"?

Having been confronted with these spiritual obligations and responsibilities, the Lord then gave me an enormous burden for my two children. I carry it to this day. There are times when it becomes so heavy that I ask God to remove it from my shoulders, although the concern is not motivated by the usual problems or anxieties. Our kids are apparently healthy and seem to be holding their own emotionally and academically. (Update: Danae finished college in 1990 and Ryan was entering his junior year at the time of the revision.) The source of my burden derives from the awareness that a "tug of war" is being waged for the hearts and minds of every child on earth, including these two precious human beings. Satan would deceive and destroy them if given the opportunity, and they will soon have to choose the path they will take.

This mission of introducing one's children to the Christian faith can be likened to a three-man relay race. First, your father runs his lap around the track, carrying the baton, which represents the gospel of Jesus Christ. At the appropriate moment, he hands the baton to you, and you begin your journey around the track. Then finally, the time will come when you must get the baton safely in the hands of your child. But as any track coach will testify, *relay races are won or lost in the transfer of the baton.* There is a critical moment when all can be lost by a fumble or miscalculation. The baton is rarely dropped on the back side of the track when the runner has it firmly in his grasp. If failure is to occur, it will likely happen in the exchange between generations!

According to the Christian values which govern my life, my most important reason for living is to get the baton—the gospel—safely in the hands of my children. Of course, I want to place it in as many other hands as possible, and I'm deeply devoted to the ministry to families that God has given me. *Nevertheless, my number one responsibility is to evangelize my own children.* In the words of my dad, everything else appears "pale and washed out" when compared with that fervent desire. Unless my son and daughter grasp the faith and take it with them around the track, it matters little how fast they run. Being first across the finish line is meaningless unless they carry the baton with them.

The urgency of this mission has taken Shirley and me to our knees since before the birth of our first child. Furthermore, since October 1971 until early 1978, I designated one day a week for fasting and prayer specifically devoted to the spiritual welfare of our children. (Shirley then accepted the responsibility and continues it to this day.) This commitment springs from an intense awareness of our need for divine assistance in the awesome task of parenthood. There is not enough knowledge in the books—not enough human wisdom anywhere on earth—to guarantee the outcome of parenting. There are too many factors beyond our control—too many evil influences—that mitigate against the Christian message. That is why we find ourselves in prayer, week after week, uttering this familiar petition:

> Lord, here we are again. You know what we need even before we ask, but let us say it one more time. When You consider the many requests we have made of You through the years . . . regarding our health and my ministry and the welfare of our loved ones . . . please put this supplication at the *top* of the list: keep the circle of our little family unbroken when we stand before You on the Day of Judgment. Compensate for our mistakes and failures as parents, and counteract the influences of an evil world that would undermine the faith of our children. And especially, Lord, we ask for Your involvement when our son and daughter stand at the crossroads, deciding whether or not to walk the Christian path. They will be beyond our care at that moment, and we humbly ask You to *be there*. Send a significant friend or leader to help them

choose the right direction. They were yours before they were born, and now we give them back to You in faith, knowing that You love them even more than we do. Toward that end, we dedicate this day of fasting and prayer.

Not only has God heard this prayer, but He has blessed it in ways that we did not anticipate in the beginning. First, it has represented a project which Shirley and I have enjoyed *together*, drawing us closer to one another as we drew closer to God. Secondly, this act of fasting each week serves to remind us continually of our system of priorities. It is very difficult to forget your highest values when one day out of seven is spent concentrating on them. Finally, and most importantly, the children have seen this act of discipline every Tuesday, and have been influenced by it. Conversations similar to the one below occurred throughout the critical years of childhood.

"Why are you not eating dinner with us tonight, Dad?"

"This is Tuesday and I'm fasting today."

"Oh, yeah—what did you say 'fasting' meant?"

"Well, some Christians go without food during a short time of special prayer. It's a way of asking God for a blessing, or of expressing love to Him."

"What are you asking for?"

"Your mother and I are praying for you and your brother, today. We're asking God to lead and direct your lives; we want Him to help you choose a profession and to find the right person to marry, if that is His will. We're also asking Him to walk with you every day of your lives."

"You must love us a lot to fast and pray like that."

"We *do* love you. And God loves you even more."

I suppose there's another explanation behind my concern for the spiritual welfare of our two children. I'm told that George McCluskey, my great-grandfather on the maternal side, carried a similar burden for his children through the final decades of his life. He invested the hour from eleven to twelve o'clock each morning to intercessory prayer for his family. However, he was not only asking God to bless his children; he extended his request to generations not yet born! In effect, my great-grandfather was praying for *me.*

Toward the end of his life, the old man announced that God had made a very unusual promise to him. He was given the assurance that *every* member of four generations of our family would be Christians, including those yet to be born. He then died and the promise became part of the spiritual heritage that was passed to those of us in George McCluskey's bloodline.

Since I represent the fourth generation subsequent to the one that included my great-grandfather, his promise assumes added significance. It has, in fact, been fulfilled in a fascinating way. McCluskey and his wife were ministers and charter members in their church denomination. They brought two daughters into the world, one eventually becoming my grandmother and the other my great-aunt. Those two girls married men who were ministers in the same denomination as their parents. Between them, they produced a boy and four girls, one becoming my mother. The girls all married ministers in the same denomination and the boy became one. Then came my generation. My cousin H. B. London and I were the first two members to reach the age for college, where we were roommates. During the first semester of our sophomore year, he announced that God had called him to be a minister in (you guessed it) the same denomination as his great-grandfather. And believe me, I began to get very *nervous* about the entire proposition!

I now represent the first, though not the only, member of four generations from the time of my great-grandfather who has not felt specifically "called" into the ministry. But considering the hundreds of times I have stood before audiences, talking about the gospel of Jesus Christ and its application to family life, I have to ask, "What's the difference?"! God has marvelous methods of implementing His purposes in our lives. There have been times as I have sat on the platform of a large church, waiting to speak, that I have felt the presence of the old man . . . and it seemed as though he was smiling mischievously from the beyond.

Though my great-grandfather is long dead, having died a year before my birth, he still provides the richest source of inspiration for me. It staggers the mind to realize that the prayers of this one man, spoken more than fifty years ago, reach across four generations of time and influence developments in my life today. That is the power of prayer and the source of my hope and optimism. Don't tell me God is dead . . . or that He doesn't honor His commitments. George McCluskey and I know that He lives!

The men in my family have transmitted a spiritual heritage that is more valuable than any monetary estate they could have accumulated. And I am determined to preserve it on behalf of my children. There is no higher calling on the face of the earth.

Are All the Children In

I think at times as the night draws nigh
  of an old house on the hill
And of a yard all wide and blossomed-starred
  where the children play at will
And when the night at last came down hushing
  the merry din
Mother would look around and ask—
  are all the children in
Oh, it's many, many a year since then
  and the old house on the hill
No longer echoes to childish feet and the
  yard is still, so still
But I see it all as the shadows creep
  and though many the year since then
I can hear Mother ask—are all the children in
I wonder if when the shadows fall on the last short
  earthly day
When we say good-bye to the world outside
All tired with our childish play
When we step out into the other land where
  Mother so long has been
Will we hear her ask just as of old
  are all the children in

—Anonymous

8

A Man and His Authority

The following "Letter to the Editor" appeared in *Moody Monthly,* dated February 1979:

> The other day I was sitting in a muffler shop, waiting for a new muffler to be put in our car. A young Mommi came in with Mark, about five years old, and plopped down two seats away from mine. After three minutes, Mark began to demand "a dwink," pointing to the pop machine.
>
> "No, Mark," the Mommi said. But Mark knew, and I knew, by the way she said "no" that she really meant "keep pushing me and I'll give in." So Mark began his campaign. He threatened to hit her. He got on the floor and screamed. He accused her of not loving him. And he said some things that little Maxis or Marks should not say. It was too much.
>
> I turned to the Mommi and said, "Please, for Mark's sake, discipline him! He will thank you for it later. Buy a copy of Dr. James Dobson's book, *Dare to Discipline* (Tyndale) for Mark's sake and yours."
>
> Did she? I don't know. Will you? I hope so.

The letter was unsigned, so I have no way of thanking the writer for her generous recommendation. I know how she feels, however, for I have also watched little Maxis and Marks do their thing in airports and restaurants and muffler shops across the country. And as you might guess, it is incredibly difficult for me to remain silent when I see a 40-pound child intimidate and outmaneuver his 150-pound parent. I'm rarely as blunt as the writer of the letter above, although I once asked the mother of a four-year-old spitfire named Tara if her child's name was spelled Terror. Mother did not reply.

In the absence of parental leadership, some children become extremely obnoxious and defiant, especially in public places. Perhaps the best example was a ten-year-old boy named Robert, who was a patient of my good friend Dr. William Slonecker. Dr. Slonecker and his pediatric staff dreaded the days when Robert was scheduled for an office visit. He literally attacked the clinic, grabbing instruments and files and telephones. His passive mother could do little more than shake her head in bewilderment.

During one physical examination, Dr. Slonecker observed severe cavities in Robert's teeth and knew that the boy must be referred to a local dentist. But who would be given the honor? A referral like Robert could mean the end of a professional friendship. Dr. Slonecker eventually decided to send him to an older dentist who reportedly understood children. The confrontation that followed now stands as one of the classic moments in the history of human conflict.

Robert arrived in the dental office, prepared for battle.

"Get in the chair, young man," said the doctor.

"No chance!" replied the boy.

"Son, I told you to climb onto the chair, and that's what I intend for you to do," said the dentist.

Robert stared at his opponent for a moment and then replied, "If you make me get in that chair, I will take off all my clothes."

The dentist calmly said, "Son, take 'em off."

The boy forthwith removed his shirt, undershirt, shoes and socks, and then looked up in defiance.

"All right, son," said the dentist. "Now get on the chair."

"You didn't hear me," sputtered Robert. "I said if you make me get on that chair, I will take off *all* my clothes."

"Son, take 'em off," replied the man.

Robert proceeded to remove his pants and shorts, finally standing totally naked before the dentist and his assistant.

"Now, son, get in the chair," said the doctor.

Robert did as he was told, and sat cooperatively through the entire procedure. When the cavities were drilled and filled, he was instructed to step down from the chair.

"Give me my clothes now," said the boy.

"I'm sorry," replied the dentist. "Tell you mother that we're going to keep your clothes tonight. She can pick them up tomorrow."

Can you comprehend the shock Robert's mother received when the door to the waiting room opened, and there stood her pink son, as naked as the day he was born? The room was filled with patients, but Robert and his mom walked past them and into the hall. They went down a public elevator and into the parking lot, ignoring the snickers of onlookers.

The next day, Robert's mother returned to retrieve his clothes, and asked to have a word with the dentist. However, she did not come to protest. These were her sentiments: "You don't know how much I appreciate what happened here yesterday. You see, Robert has been blackmailing me about his clothes for years. Whenever we are in a public place, such as a grocery store, he makes unreasonable demands of me. If I don't immediately buy him what he wants, he threatens to take off all his clothes. You are the first person who has called his bluff, doctor, and the impact on Robert has been incredible!"

No great insight is required to recognize the need for discipline in the lives of Robert, Tara, and Mark, among thousands of their peers. Common sense would reveal as much. Children who are permitted to rule their bewildered parents are among the most frustrated creatures in God's universe, as they scream and protest and pound on the floor. Nevertheless, the humanistic theorists of our day have somehow concluded that what these kids need is freedom from adult leadership. Authority, even when it is permeated with love, is perceived as harmful to children.

That incredible concept has given birth to a powerful political force operating within the Children's Rights Movement (CRM). Their objectives are outlined in a Child's Bill of Rights, originally written by Dr. Richard Farson,* and paraphrased below:

1. Children should have the right to make *all* their own decisions. CRM advocates consider this to be the fundamental right on which all others stand. As such, it proposes the annihilation of parental leadership.
2. Children of any age should have the right to live where they choose. For example, if a three-year-old boy decided to move in with a candy-buying neighbor, his parents would be legally prohibited from bringing him home. No kidding!
3. Children of any age should have the right to vote and be involved in any decisions that affect their lives (whether governmental, ecclesiastical, educational, medical or familial.)
4. Children should have access to any information that is available to adults. No pornography or violence could be shielded from a child, nor could his medical or school records be withheld.
5. Children should be permitted to engage in any sexual activity that is legal for their parents. If a fifteen-year-old boy elected to bring home a playmate to spend the night, his parents could only step aside and watch them shut the bedroom door. An eight-year-old girl could

*Richard Farson, *Birthrights: A Child's Bill of Rights* (New York: Macmillan, 1974).

pleasure an adult male with no legal implication for either generation, provided the consent was "mutual."

6. Children of any age should be totally responsible for their own educational pursuits, being free to quit school or attend only when convenient. Compulsory education would be eliminated at all grade levels.
7. Children should have their physical environment constructed to fit their size, instead of asking them to adapt to the world of adults. The meaning of this item is unclear; I'm assuming it would be illegal to build adult-sized furniture or put drinking fountains at their present height.
8. Children should never be spanked under any circumstances, whether at school or at home.
9. Children should be guaranteed the same system of justice that now applies to adults. No minor disciplinary action could occur at school, for example, until the child was tried, faced by his accusers, informed of the evidence against him, and pronounced guilty by a jury of his peers.
10. Children of any age should be permitted to join a labor union, seek employment, receive equal pay for equal work, sign legal contracts, manage all of their own money, and be financially independent. The scrawled signature of a seven-year-old would be legally binding. It has even been suggested by John Holt and others that children should receive a guaranteed income, although it is unclear whom he intended to provide it.

Can there be any doubt about the objective of these extreme "Children's Rights" advocates? They do not wish merely to *weaken* parental authority; they want to *kill* it, once and for all. Their stated goals represent, in essence, a series of prohibitions for parents and teachers. No, sir, you can't require your eight year old to go to school, or live at home, or feed the dog, or attend church, or take his medicine, or speak respectfully to parents, or be home by midnight, or clean his room, or return the stolen toy, or avoid X-rated movies, or stop playing "doctor" with the child next door, or quit drinking liquor. No, sir, you will go to jail if you deprive you child of his rights in this fashion. You are the "peer" of your son, not his leader.

"Talk is cheap," I can hear a few readers saying. "Just because a kookie psychologist offers some way-out proposals for children is no reason to believe those restrictions will be imposed on *my* family."

I'm not so confident. The first major triumph for CRM was achieved in Sweden, 1979, when it became illegal for parents to spank or otherwise punish their children. The law, which the Swedish Parliament passed by a vote of 259–6, prohibits "*any* act which, for the purpose of punishing, causes the child injury or pain, even if the disturbance is mild and passing." The intent also prohibits psychological punishment such as scoldings, sending the child to the bedroom, withdrawing television rights, and similar humiliations. An emergency telephone service is provided twenty-four hours a day so that youngsters can report parental violations directly to an ombudsman.

Following this incredible development, American psychologists took to the airways, advocating passage of a similar law in this country. The elimination of punishment is merely a small part of what the *Los Angeles Times* called "The Mounting March for Children's Rights." Accordingly, we can expect the other nine objectives to become increasingly volatile in the years ahead. In Sweden, again, where the Movement has found the most fertile ground, a prominent professor of law at Stockholm University has proposed that the Swedish constitution be amended to provide numerous rights to minors. One component that he hopes to include is the right of kids to "divorce" their parents. (Since writing the statement above, Sweden *has* passed the proposed law.)

Of broader concern, the United Nations adopted a disturbing document in 1989 entitled "The United Nations Convention on the Rights of the Child." While it contained many worthy provisions designed to protect the children of the world from exploitation and deprivation, it also included seven articles that would undermine the authority of parents. Indeed, they conform entirely to the spirit of the Children's Rights Movement. They are:

- Article 13 grants freedom of expression and the right to "seek, receive and impact information and ideas of all kinds . . . either orally, in writing or in print, in the form of art, or through any other media of the child's choice." No allowance is made for possible parental restrictions based on family standards of decency.
- Article 14 guarantees children freedom of "thought, conscience and religion." The parental role is only "to provide direction."
- Article 15 prohibits any restrictions on a child's freedom of association except as necessary for national security, public safety or order, public health or morals, or to protect the rights and freedoms of others. No parental right to oppose undesirable friendship is mentioned.
- Article 16 prohibits arbitrary interference with a child's privacy, family, home, or correspondence.
- Article 17 entrusts to the mass media the responsibility for providing children with information and material for their "social, spiritual and moral well-being and physical and mental health." The media also should protect them from "information and material injurious to his or her well-being."
- Article 18 grants the children of all working parents "the right of benefit from child-care services and facilities."
- Article 19 requires the state to legislate and educate against all forms of abuse of children in the care of their parents, guardians or others, in order to stamp out "all forms of physical or mental violence." Observers are left wondering precisely what this means and how much farther such legislation might go.*

*Jim Sclater, "The Child Rights Sham," *British Columbia Report*, September 10, 1990, 21–22.

It does not require a public policy analyst to recognize the thrust of this United Nations Convention or its potential impact on parent leadership. Most significantly, the documentation functions like a treaty. In other words, it becomes legally binding on individuals living in countries which ratify it. So far, ratification has occurred in seventy-one nations, including France, Sweden, Spain, Australia, Germany, the Soviet Union, and even the Vatican.

Canada reportedly stands on the verge of adoption as I write in 1991. The United States has not officially considered ratification only because the president has not sent the convention to Congress for a vote. There is good reason to believe it will pass if that opportunity occurs. On September 11, 1990, the U.S. Senate formally asked President Bush to send the document to Capitol Hill for consideration. On September 17, 1990, the House passed a similar resolution. By the time you read this book, the provisions of the United Nations Convention on the Rights of the Child could be the law of the land, superseding the U.S. Constitution and being legally binding on every citizen in this country.

My point is that the Children's Rights Movement is international in scope, and that it has scored significant victories in the past twenty years. Ultimately, its adherents wish to replace the ancient wisdom of the Judeo-Christian system of values with the humanistic notions of the twentieth century. We must not let them succeed. Parental authority and family stability simply must not be undermined if we are to raise healthy children and maintain the heritage handed to us by our forefathers.

In a brilliant monograph entitled "Children's Rights: The Ideological Road to Sweden," Professor William Donahue expressed this concern:

> It is one of the great tragedies of our day that those who professionally claim to represent the best interest of children . . . the self-described child advocates . . . often do more to contribute to the problem then resolve it. Specifically,

> it is those children's rights advocates who have pushed for positive rights (as opposed to those who wish to stem child abuse) that have done, and are continuing to do, great damage to the psychological well-being of children. Their motives may be benign, but that is of little consequence in the end. They think the number one problem facing children is the lack of freedom. Having made the wrong diagnoses, they double their mistake by holding a flawed definition of freedom. Strike three is their solution to the problem.*

Donahue concludes, "If children were granted the same rights as adults, the very seat of parental authority would collapse. Absent that social base, all the individual attributes that freedom is predicated on would never develop. Society, and the liberty that inheres it, would self destruct" (p. 5).

I should emphasize that I am not opposed to the many worthwhile organizations that are working to secure a better life for children. Physical abuse, sexual exploitation, and psychological trauma are being inflicted on helpless boys and girls across this country, and I certainly do not wish to discredit the efforts of those who seek to ameliorate their suffering. However, within this body of concerned individuals is a smaller constituency which I have described. They seek to impose a new way of life . . . a new parental ethic . . . on families everywhere. They have been remarkably successful in this effort during the past decade.

The extreme element of the Children's Rights Movement is now shifting its emphasis from a philosophical level to the courtroom. I received a letter from an attorney several years ago who sought my help in defending a father who was threatened with the loss of his child. The details are difficult to believe. It appears that the Department of Social Service in his community is attempting to remove a six-year-old girl from her home

*William Donahue, "Children's Rights: The Ideological Road to Sweden." Published by the Rockford Institute, Center on the Family in America. Vol 2, No. II, 1988, 1–2.

because her father will not permit her to attend movies, listen to rock music or watch certain television programs. This child is well adjusted emotionally and is popular with her friends in school. Her teacher reports that she ranks in the top five students in her class, academically. Nevertheless, the courts are being asked to remove her from her home because of the intolerable "abuse" she is experiencing there.

Few matters make me angry during this tranquil phase of my life, but you've just read one of them. When humanists are permitted to impose their naive idealism on the composition and functioning of the basic family unit, including yours and mine, then we are in serious trouble as a nation. In this instance, they are undermining the right of parents to instill moral values in their children, which is a responsibility ordained by God, Himself. I have written these words before, but feel compelled to repeat their beleageured message: authority is the glue that holds human organizations together, whether in a government, military, school, business . . . or home. Without leadership in human relationships, chaos soon reigns supreme.

Three principles relative to authority are vitally important to the family, and to the continuation of our way of life. Let me discuss them briefly:

1. The primary responsibility for the provision of authority in the home has been assigned to men.

It will not be popular to restate the age-old Biblical concept that God holds *men* accountable for leadership in their families. Nevertheless, that's the way I interpret the Scriptures. 1 Timothy 3:4–5 (PHILLIPS) states:

> He [the father] must have proper authority in his own household, and be able to control and command the respect of his children.

Whether it seems out of date or not, a Christian man is obligated to lead his family to the best of his ability. This assignment does not justify iron-fisted oppression of children or the disregard of a woman's needs and wishes, of course. But God apparently expects a *man* to be the ultimate decision maker in his family. Likewise, he bears heavier responsibility for the outcome of those decisions. If his family has purchased too many items on credit, then the financial crunch is ultimately his fault. If the family never reads the Bible or seldom goes to church, God holds the man to blame. If the children are disrespectful and disobedient, the primary responsibility lies with the father . . . not his wife. (I don't remember Eli's wife being criticized for raising two evil sons; it was her husband who came under God's wrath. See 1 Samuel 3:13.)

From this perspective, what happens to a family when the designated leader doesn't do his job? Similar consequences can be seen in a corporation whose president only pretends to direct the company. The organization disintegrates very quickly. The parallel to leaderless families is too striking to be missed. In my view, America's greatest need is for husbands to begin guiding their families, rather than pouring every physical and emotional resource into the mere acquisition of money. That belief motivated the book you are reading.

2. Children naturally look to their fathers for authority.

When my son Ryan was five years old, he overheard a reference to my childhood.

"Daddy, were you ever a little boy?" he asked.

"Yes, Ryan, I was smaller than you," I replied.

"Were you ever a *baby*?" he inquired with disbelief.

"Yes. Everyone is a tiny baby when he is born."

Ryan looked puzzled. He simply could not comprehend his 6-foot 2-inch, 190-pound father as an infant. He thought for a minute and then said, "Were you a *daddy*-baby?"

It was impossible for Ryan to imagine me without the mantle of authority, even if I were a tiny newborn. His nine-year-old sister reacted similarly the first time she was shown home movies of me when I was only four. There on the screen was a baby-faced, innocent lad on a horse. Danae had to be assured that the picture was of me, whereupon she exclaimed, "*That* kid spanks me?!"

Danae and Ryan both revealed their perception of me . . . not as a man who had been given authority . . . but as man who *was* authority. Such is the nature of childhood. Boys and girls typically look to their fathers, whose size and power and deeper voices bespeak leadership. That's why, despite numerous exceptions, men teachers are likely to handle classroom discipline more easily than soft ladies with feminine voices. (A woman teacher once told me that the struggle to control her class was like trying to keep thirty-two Ping-Pong balls under water at the same time.)

That is also why mothers need the disciplinary involvement of their husbands. Not that a man must handle every act of disobedience, but he should serve as the frame on which parental authority is constructed. Furthermore, it must be clear to the kids that Dad is in agreement with Mother's policies and he will defend her in instances of insurrection. Referring to 1 Timothy again, this is what is meant by a father having the "proper authority in his own household."

3. Authority *will* be tested.

Deeply ingrained in the human temperament is a self-will that rejects external authority. This spirit of rebellion manifests itself during the first year of life and dominates the personality during the second. The "terrible twos" can be summarized by this barbed question, "By what right do you or anyone else try to tell me what to do with my life!?" That same question will be bellowed during the adolescent years, along with sweet little comments such as, "I didn't ask to be born, you know!" Johnny Carson once said that if his teenager ever said that to him he'd reply, "It's a good thing you didn't ask. I'd have said *no*."

My point is that human beings at all ages are inclined to test the limits of authority. At its most basic level, this resistance is an expression of mankind's spiritual rebellion against God. Anyone who doubts this stubborn nature need only observe the sheer power of a toddler's self-will. Have you ever seen an angry three year old hold his breath until he becomes unconscious? It happens. Consider the child whose mother wrote me the following note:

> My husband and I realized our two-year-old daughter was a strong-willed child the night she was introduced to green peas. Julie took one bite and then refused to swallow. But she also refused to spit out the peas, no matter what we tried to do. We attempted to pry open her jaws, then threatened to spank her. Finally, we pleaded with Julie to cooperate, but she wouldn't budge. There was nothing left to do but put her to bed. Twelve hours later she awoke bright and cheery with no peas in her mouth. We found them in a little pile down at the foot of her bed. Her father and I were very relieved that those green peas did not remain in her mouth all night long!

Could it be that a two-year-old girl is actually capable of outmaneuvering and outlasting the adults in her world? It certainly is. And if there is one blind spot in twentieth-century psychology, it is the failure to recognize this pugnacious human temperament and the importance of responding appropriately when willful defiance occurs.

But what is the appropriate action to take in moments of rebellion? I will permit a Certified Public Accountant, William Jarnagin, to answer that question. He wrote me the following letter which speaks volumes about parent-child relationships.

> Dear Dr. Dobson:
>
> This is a note of thanks for your work in strengthening the American family. My wife and I have recently read four of your books and we have profited very much from them.
>
> Please permit me to relate a recent experience with our six-year-old son, David. Last Friday night, my wife, Becky, told him to pick up some orange peelings he had left on the carpet, which

he knows is a "no-no." He failed to respond, and as a result received one slap on his behind, whereupon he began an obviously defiant temper tantrum.

Since I had observed the whole episode, I then called for my paddle and applied it appropriately, saw to it that he picked up and properly disposed of the orange peelings, and sent him straight to bed, since it was already past his bedtime. After a few minutes, when his emotions had had a chance to settle down, I went to his room and explained that God had instructed all parents who truly love their children to properly discipline them, etc., and that we truly love him and therefore would not permit such defiant behavior.

The next morning, after I had gone to work, David presented his mother with the following letter, together with a little stack of ten pennies:

From David and Deborah
To Mom and Dad

Ross Dr. 3d house
Sellmer, Tennasse
39718

Dear Mom and Dad

here is 10 Cints for
Pattelling me when I
really neded and that
gos for Deborah to
I love you

Love yur son David
and yur Doter Deborah

Oh, incidentally, Deborah is our one-year-old daughter whose adoption should be final sometime in June.

Keep up your good work and may God bless you.

Sincerely,
William H. Jarnagin

Mr. William Jarnagin understands the appropriate response of a father to a child's defiance. It is neither harsh nor insulting nor dangerous nor whimsical. Rather, it represents the firm but loving discipline that is required for the best interest of the child. How fortunate is the boy or girl whose father still comprehends that timeless concept.

Summary

Men in Western nations have experienced a severe crisis of identity in recent years, similar to the confusion that their wives have encountered. It has been brought on by persistent challenges to everything traditionally masculine, just as the women's movement has mocked traditionally female behavior and mores. Masculine leadership, especially, has been ridiculed as "macho" and invariably self-serving. But the purpose of this chapter has been to reaffirm the importance of authority in a family—first, in the provision of gentle direction and guidance, and second, in raising healthy children. Both objectives appear to be part of the Creator's blueprint for a successful home.

9

Questions Pertaining to Children

We have dealt exclusively with the relationship between a man and his children to this point. Before turning to other aspects of masculine involvement, perhaps we should devote a remaining chapter to questions and answers relevant to boys and girls. This approach will permit me to clarify the views presented, while anticipating additional questions that might have been raised. Of special concern will be the matter of man's "ultimate priority"—winning children to Christ.

We'll begin with an issue that is especially troubling to Christian women, today. It is, in fact, a question that is often asked whenever I speak on the subject of fatherhood.

1. *I agree with your belief that the father should be the spiritual leader in the family, but it just doesn't happen that way at our house. If the kids go to church on Sunday, it's because I wake them up and see that they get ready. If we have family devotions, it's done at my insistence, and I'm the one who prays with the*

children at bedtime. If I didn't do these things, our kids would have no spiritual training. Nevertheless, people keep saying that I should wait for my husband to accept spiritual leadership in our family. What do you advise in my situation?

That's an extremely important question, and a subject of controversy right now. As you indicated, some Christian leaders instruct women to wait passively for their husbands to assume spiritual responsibility. Until that leadership is accepted, they recommend that wives stay out of the way and let God put pressure on the husband to assume the role that He's given to men. I strongly disagree with that view when small children are involved. If the issue focused only on the spiritual welfare of a husband and wife, then a woman could afford to bide her time. However, the presence of boys and girls changes the picture dramatically. Every day that goes by without spiritual training for them is a day that can never be recaptured.

Therefore, if your husband is not going to accept the role of spiritual leadership that God has given him, then I believe you must do it. You have no time to lose. You should continue taking the family to church on Sunday. You should pray with the children and teach them to read the Bible. Furthermore, you must continue your private devotions and maintain your own relationship with God. In short, I feel that the spiritual life of children (and adults) is simply too important for a woman to postpone for two or four or six years, hoping her husband will eventually awaken. Jesus made it clear that members of our own family can erect the greatest barriers to our faith, but must not be permitted to do so. He says, "Do not think that I have come to bring peace on earth; I have not come to bring peace, but a sword. For I have come to set a man against his father, and a daughter against her mother, and a daughter-in-law against her mother-in-law; and a man's foes will be those of his own household. He who loves father or mother more than me is not worthy of me; and he who loves son or daughter more than me is not worthy of me" (Matt. 10:34–38, RSV).

I mentioned my grandfather, R. L. Dobson, earlier in this book. He was a moral man who saw no need for the Christian faith. His spiritual disinterest placed my grandmother, Juanita Dobson, under great pressure, for she was a devout Christian who felt she must put God first. Therefore, she accepted the responsibility of introducing her six children to Jesus Christ. There were times when my grandfather exerted tremendous pressure on her, not to give up her faith, but to leave him out of it.

He said, "I am a good father and provider, I pay my bills, and I am honest in dealing with my fellow man. That is enough."

His wife replied, "You are a good man, but that is *not* enough. You should give your heart to God." This he could not comprehend.

My ninety-seven-pound grandmother made no attempt to force her faith on her husband, nor did she treat him disrespectfully. But she quietly continued to pray and fast for the man she loved. For more than forty years she brought this same petition before God on her knees.

Then at sixty-nine years of age, my grandfather suffered a stroke, and for the first time in his life he was desperately ill. One day his young daughter came into his room to clean and straighten. As she walked by his bed, she saw tears in his eyes. No one had ever seen him cry before.

"Daddy, what's wrong?" she asked.

He responded, "Honey, go to the head of the stairs and call your mother."

My grandmother ran to her husband's side and heard him say, "I know I'm going to die and I'm not afraid of death, but it's so dark. There's no way out. I've lived my whole life through and missed the one thing that really matters. Will you pray for me?"

"Will I pray?" exclaimed my grandmother. She had been hoping for that request throughout her adult life. She fell to her knees and the intercessions of forty years seemed to pour out through that bedside prayer. R. L. Dobson gave his heart to God that day in a wonderful way.

During the next two weeks, he asked to see some of the church people whom he had offended and requested their forgiveness. He concluded his personal affairs and then died with a testimony on his lips. Before descending into a coma from which he would never awaken, my grandfather said, " . . . Now there is a way through the darkness."

The unrelenting prayers of my little grandmother had been answered.

Returning to the question, I would like to caution women not to become "self-righteous" and critical of their husbands. Let everything be done in a spirit of love. However, there may be some lonely years when the burden of spiritual leadership with children must be carried alone. If that is the case, the Lord has promised to walk with you through these difficult days.

2. *Parents have been commanded in the Bible to "train up a child in the way he should go." But this poses a critical question: What way should he go? If the first seven years represent the "prime time" for religious training, what should be taught during this period? What experiences should be included? What values should be emphasized?*

It is my strong belief that a child should be exposed to a carefully conceived, systematic program of religious training. Yet we are much too haphazard about this matter. Perhaps we would hit the mark more often if we more clearly recognized the precise target.

Listed below is a "Checklist for Spiritual Training"—a set of targets at which to aim. Many of the items require maturity which children lack, and we should not try to make adult Christians out of our immature youngsters. But we can gently urge them toward these goals—these targets—during the impressionable years of childhood.

Essentially, the five scriptural concepts which follow should be consciously taught, providing the foundation on which all future doctrine and faith will rest. I encourage every Christian parent to evaluate his child's understanding of these five areas:

CONCEPT I: "And thou shalt love the Lord thy God with all thy heart" (Mark 12:30, KJV).

1. Is your child learning of the love of God through the love, tenderness, and mercy of his parents? (most important)
2. Is he learning to talk about the Lord, and to include Him in his thoughts and plans?
3. Is he learning to turn to Jesus for help whenever he is frightened or anxious or lonely?
4. Is he learning to read the Bible?
5. Is he learning to pray?
6. Is he learning the meaning of faith and trust?
7. Is he learning the joy of the Christian way of life?
8. Is he learning the beauty of Jesus' birth and death?

CONCEPT II: "Thou shalt love thy neighbor as thyself" (Mark 12:31, KJV).

1. Is he learning to understand and empathize with the feelings of others?
2. Is he learning not to be selfish and demanding?
3. Is he learning to share?
4. Is he learning not to gossip and criticize others?
5. Is he learning to accept himself?

CONCEPT III: "Teach me to do thy will; for thou art my God" (Ps. 143:10, KJV).

1. Is he learning to obey his parents as preparation for later obedience to God? (most important)
2. Is he learning to behave properly in church—God's house?
3. Is he learning a healthy appreciation for both aspects of God's nature: love and justice?
4. Is he learning that there are many forms of benevolent authority outside himself to which he must submit?
5. Is he learning the meaning of sin and its inevitable consequences?

CONCEPT IV: "Fear God, and keep his commandments: for this is the whole duty of man" (Eccles. 12:13, KJV).

1. Is he learning to be truthful and honest?
2. Is he learning to keep the Sabbath day holy?
3. Is he learning the relative insignificance of materialism?
4. Is he learning the meaning of the Christian family, and the faithfulness to it which God intends?
5. Is he learning to follow the dictates of his own conscience?

CONCEPT V: "But the fruit of the Spirit is . . . self-control" (Gal. 5:22–23, RSV).

1. Is he learning to give a portion of his allowance (and other money) to God?
2. Is he learning to control his impulses?
3. Is he learning to work and carry responsibility?
4. Is he learning the vast difference between self-worth and egotistical pride?
5. Is he learning to bow in reverence before the God of the universe?

In summary, your child's first seven years should prepare him to say, at the age of accountability, "Here am I, Lord. Send me!"

3. *It is very difficult for us to have meaningful devotions as a family because our young children seem so bored and uninvolved. They yawn and squirm and giggle while we are reading the Bible. On the other hand, we feel it is important to teach them to pray and study God's word. Can you help us deal with this dilemma?*

The one key word to family devotions is *brevity*. Children can't be expected to comprehend and appreciate lengthy adult spiritual activities. Four or five minutes devoted to one or two Bible verses, followed by a short prayer, usually represents the limits of attention during the preschool years. To force young children to comprehend eternal truths in an eternal devotional can be eternally dangerous.

4. *My wife and I are new Christians, and we now realize that we raised our kids by the wrong principles. They're grown now, but we continue to worry about the past, and we feel great regret for our failures as parents. Is there anything we can do at this late date?*

Let me deal, first, with the awful guilt you are obviously carrying. There's hardly a parent alive who does not have some regrets and painful memories of their failures as a mother or a father. Children are infinitely complex, and we cannot be perfect parents any more than we can be perfect human beings. The pressures of living are often enormous, and we get tired and irritated; we are influenced by our physical bodies and our emotions, which sometimes prevent us from saying the right things and being the model we should. We don't always handle our children as unemotionally as we wish we had, and it's very common to look back a year or two later and see how wrong we were in the way we approached the problem.

All of us experience these failures! *No one does the job perfectly!* That's why each of us should get alone with the Creator of parents and children, saying,

> "Lord, you know my inadequacies. You know my weaknesses, not only in parenting, but in every area of my life. I did the best I could, but it wasn't good enough. As You broke the fishes and the loaves to feed the five thousand, now take my meager effort and use it to bless my family. Make up for the things I did wrong. Satisfy the needs that I have not satisfied. Wrap Your great arms around my children, and draw them close to You. And be there when they stand at the great crossroads between right and wrong. All I can give is my best, and I've done that. Therefore, I submit to You my children and my self and the job I did as a parent. The outcome now belongs to You."

I know God will honor that prayer, even for parents whose job is finished. The Lord does not want you to suffer from guilt over events you can no longer influence. The past is the past. Let it die never to be resurrected. Give the situation to God, and let Him have it. I think you'll be surprised to learn that you're no longer alone!

5. *My wife and I are extremely busy during this period of our lives. My job takes me on the road several days a week, and my wife has become very successful as a real estate agent. Quite honestly, we are not able to spend much time with our three children, but we give them our undivided attention when we are together. My wife and I wish we had more family time, but we take comfort in knowing that it's not the* quantity *of time between parents and child that really matters; it's the* quality *of time that makes the difference. Would you agree with that statement?*

Permit me to respond to your question by a back-door approach which may seem irrelevant, at first. As a person who earns part of his living by use of the King's English, I often find myself examining the validity of folk wisdom and clichés which have been accepted prima facie within our culture. While discussing the legal ramifications of pornography with a friend, for example, he confidently uttered that familiar phrase, "Well, you can't legislate morality, you know." I nodded in agreement, but later asked myself, "Why not?"

It is immoral to kill, rape, slander, defraud, and plunder, yet we have managed to legislate against these behaviors, haven't we? Is not all criminal law based on the prohibition of certain inherently evil acts? Indeed, we would be in a mess if our lawmakers truly believed, "You can't legislate morality, you know."

Returning to the question of quantity versus quality in parent-child relationships, we confront yet another widely quoted cliché that is equally porous. Without intending disrespect for the father who asked the above question, this phrase is bandied about by overcommitted and harassed parents who feel guilty about the lack of time they spend with their children. Their boys and girls are parked at child care centers during the day and with baby-sitters at night, leaving little time for traditional parenting activities. And to handle the discomfort of neglecting their children, Mom and Dad cling to a catchphrase that makes it seem so healthy and proper: "Well, you know, it's not the *quantity* of time that matters, it's the *quality* of your togetherness that counts."

There is a grain of truth in most popular notions, and this one is no exception. We can all agree that there is no benefit in being with our children seven days a week if we are angry, oppressive, unnurturing and capricious with them. But from that point forward, the quantity versus quality issue runs aground. Simply stated, *that dichotomy will not be tolerated in any other area of our lives; why do we apply it only to children?* Let me illustrate.

Let's suppose you are very hungry, having eaten nothing all day. You select the best restaurant in your city and ask the waiter for the finest steak on his menu. He replies that the filet mignon is the house favorite, and you order it charcoal-broiled, medium rare. The waiter returns twenty minutes later with the fare and sets it before you. There in the center of a large plate is a lonely piece of meat, one inch square, flanked by a single bit of potato.

You complain vigorously to the waiter. "Is this what you call a steak dinner?"

He then replies, "Sir, how can you criticize us before you taste that meat? I have brought you one square inch of the finest steak money can buy. It is cooked to perfection, salted with care, and served while hot. In fact, I doubt if you could get a better piece of meat anywhere in the city. I'll admit that the serving is small, but after all, sir, everyone knows that it isn't the quantity that matters; it's the quality that counts in steak dinners."

"Nonsense!" you reply, and I certainly agree. You see, the subtlety of this simple phrase is that it pits two necessary virtues in opposition to one another and invites us to choose between them. If quantity and quality are worthwhile ingredients in family relationships, then why not give our kids *both?* It is insufficient to toss our "hungry" children an occasional bite of steak, even it if is prime, corn-fed filet mignon.

My concern is that the quantity versus quality cliché has become, perhaps, a rationalization for giving our kids *neither!*

6. *I want to ask you a very personal question. Your books deal with practical aspects of everyday living. They offer solutions and suggestions for handling the typical frustrations and problems of parenthood and marriage. But that makes me wonder about* your *own family. Does your home always run smoothly? Do you ever feel like a failure as a father? And if so, how do you deal with self-doubt and recrimination?*

I have been asked this question many times, although the answer should surprise no one. Shirley and I experience the same frustrations and pressures that others face. Our behavior is not always exemplary, nor is that of our children. And our household can become very hectic at times.

Perhaps I can best illustrate my reply by describing the day we now refer to as "Black Sunday." For some reason, the Sabbath can be the most frustrating day of the week for us, especially during the morning hours. I've found that other parents also experience tensions during the "get 'em ready for church" routine. But Black Sunday was especially chaotic. We began that day by getting up too late, meaning everyone had to rush to get to church on time. That produced emotional pressure, especially for Shirley and me. Then there was the matter of the spilt milk at breakfast, and the black shoe polish on the floor. And, of course, Ryan got dressed first, enabling him to slip out the back door and get himself dirty from head to toe. It was necessary to take him down to the skin and start over with clean clothes once more. Instead of handling these irritants as they arose, we began criticizing one another and hurling accusations back and forth. At least one spanking was delivered, as I recall, and another three or four were promised. Yes, it was a day to be remembered (or forgotten). Finally, four harried people managed to stumble into church, ready for a great spiritual blessing, no doubt. There's not a pastor in the world who could have moved us on that morning.

I felt guilty throughout the day for the strident tone of our home on that Black Sunday. Sure, our children shared the blame, but they were merely responding to our disorganization. Shirley and I had overslept, and that's where the conflict originated.

After the evening service, I called the family together around the kitchen table. I began by describing the kind of day we had had, and asked each person to forgive me for my part in it. Furthermore, I said that I thought we should give each member of the family an opportunity to say whatever he or she was feeling inside.

Ryan was given the first shot, and he fired it at his mother.

"You've been a real grouch today, Mom!" he said with feeling. "You've blamed me for everything I've done all day long."

Shirley then explained why she had been unhappy with her son, trying not to be defensive about his charges.

Danae then poured out her hostilities and frustrations. Finally, Shirley and I had an opportunity to explain the tensions that had caused our overreaction.

It was valuable time of ventilation and honesty that drew us together once more. We then had prayer as a family and asked the Lord to help us live and work together in love and harmony.

My point is that *every* family has moments when they violate all the rules—even departing from the Christian principles by which they have lived. Fatigue itself can damage all the high ideals which have been recommended to parents in seminars and books and sermons. The important question is, how do mothers and fathers reestablish friendship within their families when the storm has passed? Open, nonthreatening discussion offers one solution to that situation.

Returning to the question, let's acknowledge that a psychologist can no more prevent all emotional distress for his family than a physician can circumvent disease in his. We live in an imperfect world which inflicts struggles on us all. Nevertheless, Biblical principles offer the most healthy approach to family living—even turning stress to our advantage. (Someday I'll tell you about Black Monday.)

7. *You've indicated that seven deaths have occurred in your family during an eighteen-month period. We have also had several tragic losses in our family in recent years. My wife died when our children were five, eight, and nine. I found it very difficult to explain death to them during that time. Can you offer some guidelines regarding how a parent can help his children cope with the stark reality of death—especially when it strikes within the immediate family?*

Some years ago, I attended a funeral at the Inglewood Cemetery-Mortuary in Inglewood, California. While there, I picked up a brochure written by the president of the mortuary, John M. McKinley. Mr. McKinley had been in the funeral business for fifteen years before writing this valuable pamphlet entitled "If It Happens to Your Child." He gave me permission to reproduce the content here in answer to your question.

> I knew Tommy's parents because they lived in the neighborhood and attended the same church. But I knew Tommy especially well because he was one of the liveliest, happiest five-year-olds it had ever been my pleasure to meet. It was a shock, therefore, when his mother became a client of mine at the death of her husband.
>
> As a doctor must learn to protect himself from the suffering of his patients, so a funeral director must protect himself from grief. During the course of the average year I come in direct contact with several thousand men and women who have experienced a shattering loss, and if I did

not isolate myself from their emotions, my job would be impossible. But I have not been able to isolate myself from the children.

"I don't know what I would have done if I had not had Tommy," his mother told me when I visited her in her home the morning she called me. "He has been such a little man—hasn't cried, and is doing everything he can to take his daddy's place." And it was true. Tommy was standing just as he imagined a man would stand, not crying, and doing his best to take his daddy's place.

I knew it was wrong. I knew I should tell her so—that Tommy was not a man; that he needed to cry; that he needed comfort probably far more than she. But I am not a psychologist, and I said nothing.

In the two years since then I have watched Tommy. The joy has not come back in his face, and it is clear even to my layman's mind that he is an emotionally sick child. I am sure it began when his mother, unknowingly, made it difficult—impossible—for him to express his grief, and placed on him an obligation he could not fulfill; that of "taking daddy's place."

There have been few examples so clear cut as Tommy's, but I have seen so much that made me wince, and I have been asked so often: "What should I tell Mary?" or Paul, or Jim, that I finally decided to do something about it. I went to the experts, the men who know how a child should be treated at such moments of tragedy, and I asked them to lay down some guidelines that parents could understand and follow. I talked to several psychologists and psychiatrists and pediatricians, but principally to Dr. A. I. Duvall, a psychiatrist, and Dr. James Gardner, a child psychologist. Translated into my layman's language, here is the gist of what I learned:

—When a child, like any other human being, experiences a deeply painful loss, not only should he be permitted to cry; he should be encouraged to cry until the need for tears is gone. He should be comforted while the tears are flowing, but the words "don't cry" should be stricken from the language.

—The need to cry may be recurrent for several days, or at widening intervals, several months; but when the need is felt, no effort should be made to dam the tears. Instead, it should be made clear that it is good to cry, and not "babyish," or "sissy" or anything to be ashamed of.

—At times, the child may need to be alone with his grief, and if this feeling comes, it should be respected. But otherwise physical contact and comfort will be almost as healing as the tears.

—The child should be told the truth; that death is final. "Mommy has gone on vacation," or "Daddy has gone on a trip" only adds to the confusion and delays the inevitable. Children—particularly young children—have a very imperfect time sense. If "Mommy has gone on a vacation," they are going to expect her back this afternoon or tomorrow. And when tomorrow and tomorrow comes and she does not reappear, not only will the hurt be repeated, endlessly, the child will lose faith in the surviving parent just at the time when faith and trust are needed most. It is hard to say "never" when you know it will make the tears flow harder, but it is the kindest word in the long run.

—It is not necessary to explain death to a young child. It may even be harmful to try. To the five-year-old, "death" is absence, and explanations may only confuse him. If he has seen a dead bird or a dead pet, it may be helpful to make a comparison; but the important fact which the child must accept is absence. If he can be helped to accept the fact that father or mother or brother or sister is gone and will never return, then through questions and observations he will gradually build his own picture of "death" and its meaning.

—A child should not be unduly shielded from the physical appearance and fact of death. If a father dies, the child should be permitted to see the body, so that with his own eyes he can see the changes, the stillness, the difference between the vital strength which was "daddy" and this inanimate mask which is not "daddy" at all. Seeing with his own eyes will help.

—A child should be protected, however, from any massed demonstrations of grief, as from a large group of mourners at a funeral. Rather, the child should be taken in privately before the funeral to say good-bye.

—If the child is very young—say two to five or six—great care should be used in explaining death in terms which are meaningful to adults, but which may be very puzzling to children. For example, to say that "Mommy has gone to Heaven" may make perfect sense to a religious bereaved father, but it may leave a five-year-old wondering why mommy has deserted him. At that answer, "Heaven" is simply a far place, and he will not be able to understand why his mother stays there instead of coming home to take care of him.

—Along with tears, a child is quite likely to feel sharp resentment, even anger at the dead parent, or the brother or sister who has "gone." This feeling is the result of the child's conviction that he has been deserted. If this feeling does arise the child should be permitted to express it freely, just as in the case of tears.

—More common, and frequently more unsettling to a child is its guilt feelings when a death occurs. If he has been angry at his sister, and the sister dies, he is likely to think it is his fault, that his anger killed her. Or if his mother dies, and he is not told honestly and simply what has happened, he is likely to believe that his misbehavior drove her away. Guilt feelings in young children, reinforced by death, can lead to neurotic patterns which last throughout life.

But if a child is encouraged to cry until the need for tears is gone; if he is comforted enough; if he is told the simple truth; if he is permitted to see for himself the difference between death and life; if his resentment or guilt is handled in the same straightforward way as his tears, his sense of loss will still be great, but he will overcome it.

There is a positive side, too. If death is treated as a natural part of human experience, it is much easier for a loved one to live in memory. When the initial impact of grief is gone, it is a natural thing to remember and re-tell stories which evoke vivid recollections of the personality and habits which made the loved one a special person. Children take great delight in this, for in their rich world of imagination they can make the absent one live again. Such reminiscing does not renew or increase their sorrow. To the extent that it makes them free to remember, the cause for sorrow is removed.

Mr. McKinley's advice is excellent, as far as it goes. However, it has not included any references to the Christian message, which provides the *only* satisfactory answer to death. Obviously, I disagree with Mr. McKinley's reservations about heaven. We can say, "Your mother is gone for now, but thank God we'll be together again on the other side!" How comforting for a grieving child to know that a family reunion will someday occur from which there will never be another separation! I recommend that Christian parents begin acquainting their children with the gift of eternal life long before they have need of this understanding.

8. *A note from the author: One of the great privileges of my life has been the receipt of personal mail from people who have read my books or heard my broadcasts. We receive nearly 200,000 letters each month, which represent a source of continual enlightenment and encouragement to me. (I read them while riding an exercycle every morning.) Of this mail, the portion I enjoy most comes from children and teenagers. I've reproduced below three letters from kids, because of the unique messages they contain. The final two are examples of many wherein children express frustration regarding their parents' overcommitted schedules.*

Dear Sir:

In your last Newsletter you asked me to help support your television project. I'm writing to let you know why I won't. First, we don't even have a T.V. Second, we send our extra money to Missionaries. Third, I'm only eleven years old and I don't have any money.

Now I want to go back to the first reason, because it is the most important one. In Psalms 101:3 it says: "I will set no wicked thing before my eyes . . . " I have never lived with a television. My parents never bought one. But from reading and hearing other people talk, I understand there are people shown on television who don't have enough clothes on. People who steal, kill, lie and cheat and swear. My parents have taught me, and the Bible says, those things are wicked.

Maybe this doesn't make sense to you, but it does to me. I don't think I'm missing anything, because we get to travel a lot and read lots and lots of books.

Yours truly,
Tanya

Dear Tanya:

Your letter makes plenty of sense to me! Your parents are absolutely right in saying that television is an evil force in our society, and I respect them for having the courage not to own a set.

But I respect *you* even more. At only eleven years of age, you already know what you believe and are committed to the Christian way of life. I only wish most adults had the faith that you revealed in your letter.

God has a purpose for your life, Tanya. It will be fun watching His plan unfold. He loves you very much, and so do I.

James Dobson

Dear Dr. Dobson:

I feel like I've known you all my life after reading *Preparing for Adolescence.* You answered all my questions in it.

I would like to tell you something about my experiences. When I was only seven, we had to move from our town because my dad felt God calling him to the pastorate.

I had always been close to my parents. Then we moved and everything changed. My mom worked longer hours than before. Sometimes I would go a whole week without seeing her. And that's no lie. She would come home crabby and then everybody would go to bed crabby.

My dad was going to seminary, so he had the same schedule as my sister [five years old] and I. But he was studying during his wakeful hours. I thank God for keeping his hand on my sister's and my life during those tender years.

When I was nine years old, my dad was called to be a pastor of a church. Now, three years later, I still have a communication gap with my parents. But not my Heavenly Father.

The first year we were in our new town, I began having severe pains in my legs. Then I couldn't walk. I have juvenile rheumatoid arthritis. Two months later, I was able to walk again, only because of treatments and prayers.

Now I'm starting the seventh grade in September. I still have arthritis but I'm "Learning to Lean."

Please pray for me, Dr. Dobson, as I'm entering adolescence and coping with my arthritis. It still gives me problems with my walking.

Yours in Christ,
Charlotte

Dear Charlotte:

How special it was for you to write me. I receive thousands of letters each year from parents and teachers who have read my books, but fewer young people like you take the time to write. I appreciated your comments about *Preparing for Adolescence,* and I'm glad you found it helpful.

You are obviously a *very* courageous girl and I admire the way you have faced difficult experiences. Remain true and faithful to God's laws, Charlotte, regardless of what the rest of the world does. He will lead and guide you in the important days ahead.

Thanks again for taking time to write and share with me. I know God will continue to bless you as you grow in His love.

Sincerely,
James Dobson

Dear Dr. Dobson

I have a working mom and a working dad and I would like to know what us kids can do.

Brian

I will permit parents to respond to Brian's question. They are, after all, the only ones who *can* provide a satisfactory answer to it.

A MAN AND HIS WIFE

10

A Man and His Wife

We turn our attention now to the relationship between husbands and wives, which reminds me of a telephone call I received recently from a man who had read my previous book *The Strong-Willed Child.* It did not answer his questions. Furthermore, he said he had read my earlier book *What Wives Wish Their Husbands Knew About Women,* and it didn't satisfy his needs, either.

"What I want you to write," he continued, "is a combination of those two books on the subject 'How to Live with a Strong-Willed Woman'!"

I told him I wouldn't touch that topic with a shovel, yet here I am about to wade into an equally volatile matter. I want to discuss the characteristic of women that men complain about most, and vice versa. In fact, I plan to speak more bluntly in this chapter than in any statement on the subject I've ever written. That should be enough to win me some enemies among both sexes, but the time has come for straight talk to husbands and wives.

Perhaps you know that the divorce rate in America is now higher than in any other civilized nation in the world. That is tragic. Even more distressing to me is knowledge that the divorce rate for *Christians* is only slightly lower than for the population at large. How could that possibly be true? Jesus taught his followers to be loving, giving, moral, responsible, self-disciplined, honest, and respectful. He also explicitly prohibited divorce except for radical circumstances of infidelity. With these instructions, He provided an unshakable foundation for a stable and loving relationship between husband and wife. How can it be, then, that those who claim to have accepted Jesus' teaching and devoted their lives to Christian principles are hardly more successful in maintaining harmonious families than those who profess nothing? There's an enormous contradiction tucked within those words. As Howard Hendrix said, "If your Christianity doesn't work at home, it doesn't work. Don't export it!"

The truth is, the *same* circumstances that destroy non-Christian marriages can also be deadly in the homes of believers. I'm not referring to alcoholism or infidelity or compulsive gambling. The most common marriage killer is much more subtle and insidious. Let me explain.

Suppose I have a counseling appointment at four o'clock tomorrow afternoon with a person whom I've never met. Who is that person and what will be the complaint that brings him or her to me? First, the counselee will probably be Mrs. Jones, not her husband. A man is seldom first to seek marriage counseling, and when he does, it is for a different motive than his wife seeks it. She comes because her marriage is driving her crazy. He comes because his *wife* is driving him crazy.

Mrs. Jones will be, perhaps, between twenty-eight and forty-two years of age, and her problem will be *extremely* familiar to me. Though the details will vary, the frustration she communicates on that afternoon will conform to a well-worn pattern. It will sound something like this.

"John and I were deeply in love when we got married. We struggled during the first two or three years, especially with financial problems, but I knew he loved me and he knew I loved him. But then, something began to change. I'm not sure how to describe it. He received a promotion about five years ago, and that required him to work longer hours. We needed the money, so we didn't mind the extra time he was putting in. But it never stopped. Now he comes home late every evening. He's so tired I can actually hear his feet dragging as he approaches the porch. I look forward to his coming home all day 'cause I have so much to tell him, but he doesn't feel much like talking. So I fix his dinner and he eats it alone. (I usually eat with the kids earlier in the evening.) After dinner, John makes a few phone calls and works at his desk. Frankly, I like for him to talk on the telephone just so I can hear his voice. Then he watches television for a couple of hours and goes to bed. Except on Tuesday night he plays basketball and sometimes he has a meeting at the office. Every Saturday morning he plays golf with three of his friends. Then on Sunday we are in church most of the day. Believe me, there are times when we go for a month or two without having a real, in-depth conversation. You know what I mean? And I get so lonely in that house with three kids climbing all over me. There aren't even any women in our neighborhood I can talk to, because most of them have gone back to work. But there are other irritations about John. He rarely takes me out to dinner and he forgot our anniversary last month, and I honestly don't believe he's ever had a romantic thought. He wouldn't know a rose from a carnation, and his Christmas cards are signed, just "John." There's no closeness or warmth between us, yet he wants to have sex with me at the end of the day. There we are, lying in bed, having had no communication between us in weeks. He hasn't tried to be sweet or understanding or tender, yet he expects me to become passionate and responsive to him. I'll tell you, I can't do it. Sure, I go along with my duties as a wife, but I sure don't get anything out of it. And after the two-minute trip is over and John is asleep, I lie there resenting him and feeling like a cheap prostitute. Can you believe that? I feel *used* for having sex with my own husband! Boy, does that depress me! In fact, I've been awfully depressed lately. My self-esteem is rock bottom right now. I feel like nobody loves me . . . I'm a lousy mother and a terrible wife. Sometimes I think that God probably doesn't love me, either. Well, now I'd better tell you what's been going on between John and me more recently. We've been arguing a lot. I mean *really* fighting. It's the only way I can get his attention, I guess. We had an incredible battle last week in front of the kids. It was awful. Tears. Screaming. Insults. Everything. I spent two nights at my mother's house. Now, all I can think about is getting a divorce so I can escape. John doesn't love me anyway, so what difference would it make? I guess that's why I came to see you. I want to know if I'll be doing the right thing to call it quits."

Mrs. Jones speaks as though she were the only woman in the world who has ever experienced this pattern of needs. But she is not alone. It is my guess that 90 percent of the divorces that occur each year involve at least some of the elements she described—an extremely busy husband who is in love with his work and who tends to be somewhat insensitive, unromantic, and noncommunicative, married to a lonely, vulnerable, romantic woman who has severe doubts about her worth as human being. They become a matched team: he works like a horse and she nags.

In the hopes of making husbands aware of the universality of their wives' complaints, let me illustrate the point further, only this time, we'll deal with real people instead of a fictitious prototype. Reproduced below is an actual letter (modified to protect the identity of the writer) which represents a thousand others I've received.

Dear Dr. Dobson:

I have read your book *What Wives Wish Their Husbands Knew About Women*. It hit right where I live. Especially the part about low self-esteem. In today's world where so many women have jobs, it is sometimes hard to feel you are worth much if you aren't employed. I mean, some people look down upon a mother like myself who devotes full time to her children and family. But I know Christ doesn't see it that way, and that's what counts.

Unfortunately, I couldn't get my husband to read your book, which brings me to my problem. It is really hard to communicate with my husband when I have to compete with the television, kids and work. At mealtimes, which should be a time for talking, he has to listen to Paul Harvey news on the radio. He's not home for the evening meal because he works the 3 to 11 p.m. shift. I really would like him to listen to your "Focus on the Family" program, but he won't.

I'm not permitted to go to Bible Study now (I attended for one year) because he says the kids will pick up diseases from the other children. Of course, I know that's not the real reason. I have a 2½-year-old son and a 3-month-old baby and feel I need to get out among adults. Oh well, I guess I'll keep on praying.

Keep broadcasting your good shows. It would be nice for you to devote another program to husband-wife relationships, mainly communication. Thank you for listening to me.

Another woman handed me the following note after hearing me speak. It says in a few words what others conveyed with many.

Will you *please* discuss this. Dad arrives home, reads the newspaper, eats dinner, talks on the phone, watches T.V., takes a shower and goes to bed. This is a *constant daily routine.* It never changes. On Sunday we go to church, then come home. We take a nap and then it's back to work again on Monday morning. Our daughter is nine, and we are not communicating, and life is speeding by in this monotonous routine.

I can hear masculine readers saying, "If women want a slower lifestyle, less materialism, and more romantic activities with their husbands, why don't they just tell them so?"

They *do* tell them so, in fact. But men find it very difficult to "hear" this message, for some reason.

I'm reminded of the night my father was preaching in an open tent service which was attended by more cats and dogs than people. During the course of his sermon, one large alley cat decided to take a nap on the platform. Inevitably, my father took a step backward and planted his heel squarely on the tail of the tom. The cat literally went crazy, scratching and clawing to free his tail from my father's 6-foot 3-inch frame. But Dad could become very preoccupied while preaching, and he didn't notice the disturbance. There at his feet was a panicky animal, digging holes in the carpet and screaming for mercy, yet the heel did not move. Dad later said he thought the screech came from the brakes of automobiles at a nearby corner. When my father finally walked off the cat's tail, still unaware of the commotion, the tom took off like a Saturn rocket.

This story typifies many twentieth-century marriages. The wife is screaming and clawing the air and writhing in pain, but the husband is oblivious to her panic. He is preoccupied with his own thoughts, not realizing that a single step to the right or left could alleviate the crisis. I never cease to be amazed at just how deaf a man can become under these circumstances.

I know of a gynecologist who is not only deaf, but blind as well. He telephoned a friend of mine who is also a physician in the practice of obstetrics and gynecology. He asked for a favor.

"My wife has been having some abdominal problems and she's in particular discomfort this afternoon," he said. "I don't want to treat my own wife and wonder if you'd see her for me?"

My friend invited the doctor to bring his wife for an examination, whereupon he discovered (are you ready for this?) that she was five months pregnant! Her obstetrician husband was so busy caring for other patients that he hadn't even noticed his wife's burgeoning pregnancy. I must admit wondering how in the world this woman ever got his attention long enough to conceive!

There's another aspect of the male-female relationship that should also be discussed for the man who wants to understand his wife. Appreciation is expressed to the well-known author Dr. Dennis Guernsey for calling to my attention the research by Rollins and Cannon* and others which reveals a contrasting pattern of "personal satisfaction" by husbands and wives. A woman's satisfaction with her home (which represents the primary job for a homemaker) is never higher than at the time she gets married. But alas, her attitude is likely to slide. It typically deteriorates with the birth of her first baby and continues to sink through the child-rearing years. It reaches a low point in conjunction with the empty-nest syndrome—when the kids leave home. Her satisfaction then rebounds considerably and remains stable during the retirement years.

The husband's job satisfaction follows an opposite pattern. His low point occurs during the early years of marriage, when he accepts a poorly compensated, nonstatus position. But as he works his way up the ladder, he draws greater emotional rewards (and more money) from his work. This increasing job satisfaction may continue for twenty years or longer, with his work encompassing ever more of his time and energy.

The chart on page 127 will illustrate this contrasting job satisfaction by men and women. Obviously the point of greatest danger occurs in the late thirties and forties, when the wife is most dissatisfied with her assignment and the husband is most enthralled with his. That combination is built for trouble, especially if the man feels no responsibility to help meet his wife's needs and longings. (Please remember that these studies merely reflect *trends* and statistical possibilities. Individuals may respond very differently.)

---

*Boyd C. Rollins and Kenneth L. Cannon, *Journal of Marriage and the Family,* May 1974, p. 271.

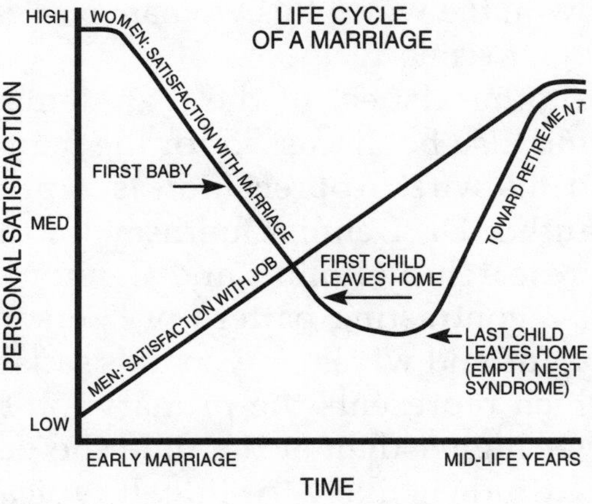

In the absence of strong and loving support from husbands, how do women cope with the circumstances I've described? We all know that behavior does not occur in a vacuum; it is motivated by powerful emotional currents running deep within the personality. Thus, I've observed eight avenues of response that may be taken by a depressed and frustrated wife. They are nonexclusive; in other words, more than one approach can occur simultaneously, or one can lead to others. The eight are as follows:

1. A woman can detach herself from home and family, reinvesting her emotional energy in an outside job. The "back to work" phenomenon by Western women is, in part, a product of this coping mechanism (combined with the pressures of inflation).
2. She can become very angry at men and society for their perceived insults and disrespect. This source of hostility helped to power the now defunct women's liberation movement and gave it an aggressive character. Fortunately, both men and women quickly recognized that *that* was not the answer.
3. She can remain at home in an atmosphere of great depression or despair. Depression is "anger turned inward," and is usually related to low self-esteem. This woman often becomes a classic nagger.

4. She can attempt to meet her pressing needs by getting into an illicit affair. This disastrous avenue usually becomes a dead-end street, leaving her more depressed and lonely than before. We'll discuss its implications in greater detail in chapter 13.
5. She can turn to alcohol and drugs as a temporary palliative. Many homemakers are yielding to this alternative, as evidenced by the rising rate of alcoholism among American women.
6. She can commit suicide (or make a suicidal attempt as a call for help).
7. She can denounce the responsibilities of mothering, by either remaining childless, or by failing to meet the needs of her kids at home. Or she can run away and let Dad take over.
8. The depressed woman can, of course, seek a divorce in the hope of starting afresh with someone more understanding and loving. Today, more than ever, this final alternative looms as *the* accepted method of coping with marital frustration.

None of these coping mechanisms is very productive. In fact, each of the eight has specific negative consequences. Not even attempted suicide is certain to attract the attention of a mate. I counseled with one woman approximately two weeks after she was released from the hospital. Having made every possible attempt to make contact with her husband, she slid deeper into depression and despair. Finally, she resorted to the ultimate decision. In full view of her husband, she brought all available prescription drugs from the medicine cabinet and proceeded to swallow 206 assorted pills. Her husband stood watching in disbelief. She then went to the bedroom to lie down and die. But she didn't want to leave this earth, of course. It was a desperate method of dramatizing her condition to the man whose love she needed. Unfortunately, he did not respond. When she realized that he had no intention of rescuing her, she pulled herself together and drove to a nearby hospital. After pumping her stomach, the hospital staff telephoned her husband who came to her bedside. He held her hand for two hours without ever asking why she hadn't wanted to live! In fact, the day he brought her to my office, more than two weeks later, he made his first comment about the event. As he walked around the car to open her door, he said, "I want you to know that you nearly scared me to death a couple of weeks ago!"

Readers might find it difficult to believe that this man loved his wife, but it's true. His lack of attention to her needs was related to a potential business failure that made it difficult for him to "give" to his wife—or even hear her cries. He was facing a crisis of his own, which often occurs in disintegrating marriages.

If the usual coping mechanisms fail to deliver viable solutions to the problems of marital conflict, what *is* the answer? That brings us back to the promise, made in the beginning of this chapter, that I would offer some *straight talk* to husbands and wives. Never before have I abandoned diplomacy in dealing with family issues, but I beg your tolerance in this instance. The current crisis in marriage demands a bold approach that is equal to the magnitude of the danger. You can't kill a dragon with a pop-gun, as they say. Therefore, I'll first take a few shots at men and then turn my guns on the ladies.

A message to the husbands of Christian homemakers:

It is *high* time you realized that your wives are under attack today! Everything they have been taught from earliest childhood is being subjected to ridicule and scorn. Hardly a day passes when the traditional values of the Judeo-Christian heritage are not blatantly mocked and undermined.

—The notion that motherhood is a worthwhile investment of a woman's time suffers unrelenting bombardment.

—And the idea that wives should yield to the leadership of their husbands, as commanded in Ephesians 5:21–33 is considered almost medieval in its stupidity.

—And the concept that a man and woman should become one flesh, finding their identity in each other rather than as separate and competing individuals, is said to be intolerably insulting to women.

—And the belief that divorce is an unacceptable alternative has been abandoned by practically everybody. (Have you heard about Sue and Bob?)

—And the description of the ideal wife and mother, as offered in Proverbs 31:10–31 is now unthinkable for the modern woman. (She's come a long way, baby.)

—And the role of the female as help-meet, bread-baker, wound-patcher, love giver, home builder, and child-bearer is nothing short of disgusting.

All of these deeply ingrained values, which many of your wives are trying desperately to sustain, are continually exposed to the wrath of hell itself. The Western media—radio, television and the press—are working relentlessly to shred the last vestiges of Christian tradition. And your wives who believe in that spiritual heritage are virtually hanging by their thumbs! They are made to feel stupid and old-fashioned and unfulfilled, and in many cases, their self-esteem is suffering irreparable damage. They are fighting a sweeping social movement with very little support from anyone.

Let me say it more directly. For the man who appreciates the willingness of his wife to stand against the tide of public opinion—staying at home in her empty neighborhood in the exclusive company of jelly-faced toddlers and strong-willed adolescents—it is about time you gave her some help. I'm not merely suggesting that you wash the dishes or sweep the floor. I'm referring to the provision of emotional support . . . of conversation . . . of making her feel like a lady . . . of building her ego . . . of giving her one day of recreation each week . . . of taking her out to dinner . . . of telling her that you love her. Without these armaments, she is left defenseless against the foes of the family—the foes of *your* family!

But to be honest, many of you husbands and fathers have been thinking about something else. Your wives have been busy attending seminars and reading family literature and studying the Bible, but they can't even get you to enter a discussion about what they've learned. You've been intoxicated with your work and the ego support it provides.

What better illustration can I give than the letter quoted on page 122. It came from a desperate woman whose husband is rarely at home, and even when he's there he has nothing to say. He prefers the company of Paul Harvey, who asks no questions and expects no answers. Furthermore, he's a first-class "punkin eater." You know the story.

> Peter, Peter, Punkin Eater
> Had a wife and couldn't keep her
> Put her in a punkin shell
> And there he kept her very well. . . .

Yeah, Old Pete has got his little woman right where he wants her. She's cooped up in a house with two children under three years of age, changing diapers and wiping noses and cooking meals for him and Mr. Harvey. That's some existence for a living, breathing female with deep needs to be loved and respected. Not only does Peter not intend to meet those needs, but he forbids her to take them elsewhere. He doesn't even want her to go to a Bible study class because, would you believe, he fears his kids will catch a disease. Never mind the disease that is choking the life out of his wife—the disease called *loneliness.* To the wives of all the world's punkin eaters, I say, "Go to the Bible study class anyway!" Submission to masculine leadership does not extend, in my opinion, to behaviors that will be unhealthy for the husband, the wife, and the marriage. Nor should a woman tolerate child abuse, child molestation, or wife-beating.

The message could not be more simple or direct to a Christian man: the Lord has commanded you to "love your wives, even as Christ loved the church, giving His life for it." She needs you now. Will you fit her into your plans?

A message to the wives of busy and unresponsive men:

There are two sides to every coin, and it's time now that we flipped this one over. This chapter has been dominated by the feminine perspective, not because that point of view is more valid or significant, but because it is so poorly understood by the majority of men. I wrote an entire book entitled *What Wives Wish Their Husbands Knew About Women*, for the purpose of conveying some of those frustrations to men. Nevertheless, husbands have their own legitimate complaints to make, too. So brace yourselves, ladies. I'm coming your way.

My strongest words are addressed to the wife of a good man, whom we will call Fred. He loves Barbara and the kids. Honest! He would literally lay down his life for them if required. He doesn't drink. He has never smoked. He has no compulsion to gamble. He wouldn't touch another woman under any imaginable circumstances. He gets up every morning and plods off to work, perhaps holding down a boring, menial job for forty-five years. He brings his salary home and does his best to stretch it through the month. He lives by a moral code that is remarkable for this dishonest era. His income tax return is scrupulously accurate, and he's never stolen so much as a paper clip from his boss. He doesn't beat the kids or kick the dog or flirt with the widow next door. He is as predictable as the sunrise, and I'm sure that God has a special place for him on the other side.

But Steady Freddie has a serious flaw. He was raised in a day when little boys were taught to withhold their thoughts and feelings. "Children are to be seen and not heard," said his parents. He can't remember being hugged or praised, and everybody knows that boys don't cry. So Fred learned his lessons well. He became as tough as nails and as silent as the night, but in so doing, he lost touch with his emotions. Now, he *cannot* be spontaneous and affectionate, no matter how hard he tries. It just isn't within him. And most of his thoughts remain unspoken and private.

One would hope that Barbara would accept Fred as he is, since she knew his nature before they were married. In fact, it was his quiet reserve that made Fred attractive to her when they were courting. He always seemed so strong, so in control, compared to her impulsive flightiness. But now Barbara is fed up with her unromantic husband. She is deeply angry because he won't communicate with her, and she nags him incessantly about his alleged "failures" as a husband. He can do n*othing* right and she makes them both miserable year after year.

Let's bring the illustration closer to home. Fred and Boiling Barbara do not represent an unusual combination of personality characteristics. I have seen hundreds of husbands and wives who share their conflict. Many men—not just those who were taught to be inexpressive—find it difficult to match the emotions of their wives. They *cannot* be what their women want them to be. But instead of looking at the *whole* man, assessing his many good qualities as they counterbalance this "flaw," the wife concentrates on the missing elements and permits it to dominate their relationship. She's married to a good man . . . but he's not good enough!

Only men who are married to such women fully understand just how wretched life can be. King Solomon had at least one malcontent in his harem, for he wrote "It is better to dwell in the wilderness, than with a contentious and an angry woman" (Prov. 21:19, KJV). He later referred to her dissatisfaction as resembling "a continual dropping in a very rainy day" (Prov. 27:15, KJV). He is right! An agitated woman rants and raves and cries and complains. Her depression is perpetual, destroying vacations, holidays, and the months in between. She may, in retaliation, refuse to cook or clean or take care of the kids. The husband then has the great thrill of coming home to a shattered house and a bitterly angry woman five days a week. And the sad part of the story is that he is often *unable* to become what she wants him to be. He has seriously attempted to rearrange his basic nature on five or six occasions, but to no avail. A leopard can't change its spots, and an unromantic, noncommunicative man simply cannot become a sensitive talker. The marital impasse is set in concrete.

Churning in the mind of the depressed wife is the possibility of divorce. Day and night she contemplates this alternative, weighing the many disadvantages against the one major attraction: *escape*. She worries about the effect of divorce on the kids and wonders how she'll be able to support them and wishes she didn't have to tell her parents. Round and round go the positives and negatives. Should I or shouldn't I? She is both attracted and repelled by the idea of a dissolution.

This contemplative stage reminds me of a classic documentary film which was shot during the earliest days of motion pictures. The cameraman captured a dramatic event that took place on the Eiffel Tower. There, near the top, was a naive "inventor" who had constructed a set of birdlike wings. He had strapped them to his arms for the purpose of using them to fly, but he wasn't totally convinced that they would work. The film shows him going to the rail and looking downward, then pacing back and forth. Next he stood on the rail trying to get enough courage to jump, then returned to the platform. Even with the primitive camera of those days, film has captured the internal struggle of that would-be-flier. "Should I or shouldn't I? If the wings work, I'll be famous. If they fail, I'll fall to my death." What a gamble!

The man finally climbed on the rail, turned loose of the nearby beam, and weaved back and forth for a breathless moment of destiny. Then he jumped. The last scene was shot with the camera pointed straight downward, as the man fell like a rock. He didn't even bother to flap his wings on his way to the ground.

In some respects, the depressed homemaker is like the man on the ledge. She knows that divorce is a dangerous and unpredictable leap, but perhaps she will soar with the freedom of a bird. Does she have the courage to jump? No, she'd better stay on the safety of the platform. On the other hand, this could be the long-sought escape. After all, everyone else is doing it. She wavers back and forth in confusion . . . and often takes the plunge.

But what happens to her then? It's been my observation that her "wings" do not deliver the promised support. After the wrenching legal maneuvers and custody fight and property settlement, life returns to a monotonous routine. And what a routine. She has to get a job to maintain a home, but her marketable skills are few. She can be a waitress or a receptionist or a sales lady. But by the time she pays a baby sitter (*if* she can find one) there is little money left for luxuries. Her energy level is in even shorter supply. She comes home exhausted to face the pressing needs of her kids, who irritate her. It's a rugged existence.

Then she looks at her ex-husband who is coping much better. He earns more money than she and the absence of kids provides him more freedom. Furthermore (and this is an important point), in our society there is infinitely more status in being a divorced man than a divorced woman. He often finds another lover who is younger and more attractive than his first wife. Jealousy burns within the mind of the divorcee, who is lonely and, not surprisingly, depressed again.

This is no trumped-up story just to discourage divorce. It is a characteristic pattern. I've observed that many women who seek divorce for the same reasons indicated (as opposed to infidelity) will live to regret their decision. Their husbands, whose good qualities eventually come into view, begin to look very attractive again. But these women have stepped off the ledge . . . and they must yield to the forces of nature.

Divorce is *not* the answer to the problem of busy husbands and lonely wives. Just because the secular world has liberalized its attitudes toward the impermanence of marriage, no such revision has occurred in the Biblical standard. Would you like to know *precisely* what God thinks of divorce? He has made His view abundantly clear in Malachi 2:13–17, especially with reference to husbands who seek a new sexual plaything:

> Yet you cover the altar with your tears because the Lord doesn't pay attention to your offerings anymore, and you receive no blessing from him. "Why has God abandoned us?" you cry. I'll tell you why; it is because the Lord has seen your treachery in divorcing your wives who have been faithful to you through the years, the companions you promised to care for and keep. You were united to your wife by the Lord. In

> God's wise plan, when you married, the two of you became one person in his sight. And what does he want? Godly children from your union. Therefore guard your passions! Keep faith with the wife of your youth. For the Lord, the God of Israel, says he hates divorce and cruel men. Therefore control your passions—let there be no divorcing of your wives. You have wearied the Lord with your words. "Wearied him?" you ask in fake surprise. "How have we wearied him?" By saying that evil is good, that it pleases the Lord! Or by saying that God won't punish us—he doesn't care (TLB).

If divorce is not the solution, then what can be said on behalf of the emotionally starved woman? First, it will be helpful for her to recognize the *true* source of her frustration. Granted, her husband is not meeting her needs, but I doubt if men have ever responded as women preferred. Did the farmer of a hundred years ago come in from the fields and say, "Tell me how it went with the kids today"? No, he was as oblivious to his wife's nature as Fred is of Barbara's. Then why did the farmer's wife survive while Barbara is climbing the walls? The difference between them can be seen in the *breakdown in the relationship between women!* A century ago, women cooked together, canned together, washed clothes at the creek together, prayed together, went through menopause together, and grew old together. And when a baby was born, aunts and grandmothers and neighbors were there to show the new mother how to diaper and feed and discipline. Great emotional support was provided in this feminine contact. A woman was never really alone.

Alas, the situation is very different today. The extended family has disappeared, depriving the wife of that source of security and fellowship. Her mother lives in Connecticut and her sister is in Texas. Furthermore, American families move every three or four years, preventing any long-term friendships from developing among neighbors. And there's another factor that is seldom admitted: American women tend to be economically competitive and suspicious of one another.

Many would not even consider inviting a group of friends to the house until it was repainted, refurnished, or redecorated. As someone said, "We're working so hard to have beautiful homes and there's nobody in them!" The result is isolation—or should I say insulation—and its first cousin: loneliness.

Depriving a woman of all meaningful emotional support from outside the home puts enormous pressure on the husband-wife relationship. The man then becomes her primary source of conversation, ventilation, fellowship, and love. But she's not his only responsibility. He is faced with great pressure, both internal and external, in his job. His self-esteem hangs on the way he handles his business, and the status of the entire family depends on his success. By the time he gets home at night, he has little left with which to prop up his lonely wife . . . even if he understands her.

Let me speak plainly to the wife of the busy but noncommunicative husband: *you cannot depend on this man to satisfy all your needs*. You will be continually frustrated by his failure to comply. Instead, you must achieve a network of women friends with whom you can talk, laugh, gripe, dream, and recreate. There are thousands of homemakers around you who have the same needs and experience. They'll be looking for you as you begin your search for them. Get into exercise classes, group hobbies, church activities, Bible studies, bicycle clubs—whatever. But at all costs, resist the temptation to pull into the four walls of a house, sitting on the pity pot and waiting for your man to come home on his white horse.

Many times a man's most irritating characteristic is a byproduct of the quality his wife most respects. Perhaps his frugality and stinginess, which she hates, have made him successful in business, which she greatly admires. Or perhaps his attentiveness to his mother's needs, which his wife resents, is another dimension of his devotion to his own family. Or in Fred's case, his cool stability in the face of crisis, which drew Barbara to him, is related to his lack of spontaneity and exuberance during their tranquil days. The point is, *God gave your husband the temperament he wears, and you must accept those characteristics that he cannot change. After all, he must do the same for you.* "For I have learned, in whatsoever state I am, therewith to be content. I know both how to be abased, and I know how to abound: every where and in all things I am instructed both to be full and to be hungry, both to abound and to suffer need. I can do all things through Christ which strengtheneth me" (Phil. 4:11–13, KJV).

Conclusion

There is nothing so ugly as a husband or wife who bitterly attacks and demeans his mate. But nothing is so beautiful as a loving relationship that conforms to God's magnificent design. We'll conclude with a brilliant example of this divinely inspired love. It was written by the surgeon who experienced it. Perhaps you will be deeply moved by his words, as was I.

> I stand by the bed where a young woman lies, her face postoperative, her mouth twisted in palsy, clownish. A tiny twig of the facial nerve, the one to the muscles of her mouth, has been severed. She will be thus from now on. The surgeon had followed with religious fervor the curve of her flesh; I promise you that. Nevertheless, to remove the tumor in her cheek, I had cut the little nerve.
>
> Her young husband is in the room. He stands on the opposite side of the bed, and together they seem to dwell in the evening lamplight, isolated from me, private. Who are they, I ask myself, he and this wry-mouth I have made, who gaze at and touch each other so generously, greedily? The young woman speaks.
>
> "Will my mouth always be like this?" she asks.
>
> "Yes," I say, "it will. It is because the nerve was cut."
>
> She nods, and is silent. But the young man smiles.
>
> "I like it," he says. "It is kind of cute."
>
> All at once I *know* who he is. I understand, and I lower my gaze. One is not bold in an encounter with a god. Unmindful, he bends to kiss her crooked mouth, and I so close I can see

how he twists his own lips to accommodate to hers, to show her that their kiss still works. I remember that the gods appeared in ancient Greece as mortals, and I hold my breath and let the wonder in.*

* Richard Selzer, M.D., *Mortal Lessons: Notes in the Art of Surgery* (New York: Simon & Schuster, 1976), pp. 45–46.

11

A Man and the Straight Life

I received a classic letter recently from a woman who described an event that occurred during her first year of marriage. She and her husband became aware that a mouse was cohabiting their apartment—a concept which the woman found intolerable. Her husband set a trap to catch the furry little rodent, and soon did so. However, the type of cage that he constructed permitted them to capture the creature alive, presenting the question, "What do we do with him now?" Neither husband nor wife had the courage to murder the mouse in cold blood, but they didn't want to let him go, either. They finally settled on a solution. They would drown him.

The husband filled a bucket with water and carefully placed the cage, mouse included, into the liquid. The couple then left home for two hours, so as not to witness the final struggle. But when they returned, they found that the water didn't quite cover the tope of the cage. The mouse had made the same discovery, and managed to keep the tip of his nose above the surface by standing on one toe.

I never learned how the final execution was administered. You see, the wife told me the story not to acquaint me with the plight of her mouse, but to illustrate her *own* difficulties. She said that the rodent, standing on one aching toe, came to symbolize her first year of marriage. She survived, but only by stretching to keep her nose above water.

Alas, the illustration applies to millions of other husbands and wives as well. Only by stress and strain are they able to avoid drowning in a sea of never-ending responsibilities. I want to devote the remainder of this chapter to such people, who are coping with the pressures of the "straight life." Let me begin by defining my terms.

The straight life for a homemaker is washing dishes three hours a day; it is cleaning sinks and scouring toilets and waxing floors; it is chasing toddlers and mediating fights between preschool siblings. (One mother said she had raised three "tricycle motors," and they had worn her out.) The straight life is driving your station wagon to school and back twenty-three times per week; it is grocery shopping and baking cupcakes for the class Halloween party. The straight life eventually means becoming the parent of an ungrateful teenager, which I assure you is no job for sissies. (It's difficult to let your adolescent find himself—especially when you know he isn't even looking!) Certainly, the straight life for the homemaker can be an exhausting experience, at times.

The straight life for a working man is not much simpler. It is pulling your tired frame out of bed, five days a week, fifty weeks out of the year. It is earning a two-week vacation in August, and choosing a trip that will please the kids. The straight life is spending your money wisely when you'd rather indulge in a new whatever; it is taking your son bike riding on Saturday when you want so badly to watch the baseball game; it is cleaning out the garage on your day off after working sixty hours the prior week. The straight life is coping with head colds and engine tune-ups and crab grass and income-tax forms; it is taking your family to church on Sunday when you've heard every idea the minister has to offer; it is giving a portion of your income to God's work when you already wonder how ends will meet. The straight life for the ordinary, garden-variety husband and father is everything I have listed and more . . . much more.

The straight life for the woman employed outside the home is another breathless assignment. She "gives at the office," but comes home to most of the responsibilities carried by the full-time homemaker. Exhaustion is her constant companion, as she careens from one task to another. Especially if she has two or more young children, the "working mother" must have a strong constitution simply to survive.

Perhaps the most difficult role, however, is played by single parents having custody of children. They deserve our sincere admiration. These individuals, who are usually women, must complete the tasks ordinarily assigned to husbands *and* wives, without the support and love of a partner. The straight life for them runs not on level ground but uphill seven days a week. Occasionally I meet a man or woman whose journey seems almost unbearable. I will never forget the telephone conversation I had with a young mother some years ago. We were broadcasting live on the radio, and I was attempting to answer questions of callers who sought my advice. The program was recorded, permitting me to reflect on that emotional conversation. The soft, feminine voice of a girl, perhaps twenty-three years of age, still echoes in my mind.

She was the mother of two preschool children, the youngest being a thirteen-month-old son with cerebral palsy. He could neither talk nor walk nor respond in the manner of other children his age. The older brother, then three years of age, apparently resented the attention given the baby, and constantly tested the limits of his mother's authority. As we conversed, however, I learned of additional difficulties. Her husband had been unable to withstand these pressures and had departed a few months earlier. So there was this young woman, burdened by the guilt and trials of a sick baby and a rebellious toddler, also confronted by abandonment and rejection from her husband. My heart ached for her.

After broadcasting this conversation, we received dozens of letters from listeners who requested the mother's name and address. People wanted to pray for her and offer financial aid. But I couldn't help them. I only knew her as a voice—a voice which conveyed sadness and pain and fear and courage and faith. Obviously, this young woman walks the straight life day by day . . . alone.

My point is that the straight life eventually gets heavy . . . for all of us who are walking that line. There are times when we ask, "What am I doing here? Is this all there is to life? Am I destined to plod through my remaining years with this never-ending responsibility?"

Until thirty years ago, only one socially acceptable answer was offered in response to those weary questions: "Keep plugging! You have mouths to feed, backs to clothe, a boss to please, and a home to maintain. Clench your fists, and get back to work." It may not have been a comforting conclusion, but it produced *stability* in families and in society.

Today, a new answer is being offered. It says, "I wouldn't take it any more. You're a dope for being everybody's grubby slave. Why don't you chuck it all and start a new life? The kids will adjust, somehow. They don't appreciate you anyway. Maybe you can find a new lover, someone who really cares. C'mon, baby. Grab all the gusto you can get, 'cause you'll only go around once in life!"

What I'm saying is that for all of us who walk the straight life today, there are *voices* that continually invite us to leave it. Examine any magazine or turn on the television set and you're likely to encounter these opponents of self-discipline and responsibility. Let's examine four of the voices that are most influential in encouraging people to abandon the straight life.

The first is the voice of *pleasure*. To the person who has worked seventy hours a week for a period of years, the possibility of enjoyment can become a major attraction. I consulted with one man who left his wife and married his secretary. I asked him what motivated this dramatic decision, and he answered immediately.

"I am the father of four kids," he said. "I have been a full-time husband and father for ten years, putting up with constant noise and bickering and financial pressures at home. I have rarely had any time to myself, and my life has been one long obligation. Then Martha came onto the scene, and I went with her, because, quite frankly, fun and games looked good to me."

This man was obviously "pulled" off the straight life by the voice of pleasure.

The second voice that influences more women than men can be called the *lure of romanticism*. Wives, especially those married to busy husbands, crave the excitement of romantic encounters. They long for "Some enchanted evening, across a crowded room"! Another song that gives expression to these needs is entitled "The Dreams of the Everyday Housewife." Its lyrics describe a lonely woman in a tattered housedress, thumbing through the pages of an old scrapbook. She finds a crushed and dried flower, given to her so long ago on the night of the high school prom. She was so charming that evening, and the boys were stunned by her beauty. Then just for a moment, her housedress becomes an evening gown, and she twirls before the mirror in ecstasy. She is beautiful again and the object of desire and envy. But it is just a passing fantasy, and the vision fades. Now she hungers for a small measure of that romantic excitement in her life. She is not alone. This craving for a Cinderella-type encounter is a very common yearning among wives and mothers. That is why the *lure of romanticism* entices so many women off the straight life.

The third voice calling adults off the path of responsibility is the *desire for extramarital sexual relation*s. Dr. Robert Whitehurst, from the Department of Sociology at the University of Windsor, Ontario, was once asked this question: "Do most men, at some point, have extramarital desires?" His reply, published in the journal *Sexual Behavior* included these comments: ". . . *All* men from the first day of marriage onward *think* about this possibility. . . ." ". . . *Although* these tendencies toward extramarital sexual activity diminish in later middle age and beyond, they never entirely vanish or disappear in normal men."

These strong statements leave little room for exceptions, but I agree that it is *not uncommon*, at least, for married men to think about an extramarital affair. The lure of infidelity has incredible power to influence human behavior. Even Christian men, who are committed to God and their wives, must deal with the same sexual temptations. Nevertheless, the Apostle Peter wrote in unmistakable terms about people who yield to these pressures: "With eyes full of adultery, they never stop sinning; they seduce the unstable; they are experts in greed—an accursed brood! *They have left the straight way* and wandered off to follow the way of Balaam son of Beor, who loved the wages of wickedness" (2 Pet. 2:14–15, NIV, emphasis added).

This brings us to the fourth voice, which is even more influential than those considered to this point. I've called it *ego needs*. Both men and women appear equally vulnerable to this powerful desire to be admired and respected by members of the opposite sex. Therefore, those who become entangled in an affair often do so because they want to prove that they are still attractive to women (or men). The thrill comes from knowing "someone finds me sexy, or intelligent, or pretty, or handsome. That person enjoys hearing me talk . . . likes the way I think . . . finds me exciting." These feelings emanate from the core of the personality—the ego—and they can make a sane man or woman behave in foolish and dishonorable ways.

I'm reminded of the seventh chapter of Proverbs, wherein King Solomon is warning young men not to patronize prostitutes. These are the words of Israel's wisest king:

> I was looking out the window of my house one day, and saw a simple-minded lad, a young man lacking common sense, walking at twilight down the street to the house of this wayward girl, a prostitute. She approached him, saucy and pert, and dressed seductively. She was the brash, coarse type, seen often in the streets and markets, soliciting at every corner for men to be her lovers.

> She put her arms around him and kissed him, and with a saucy look she said, "I've decided to forget our quarrel! I was just coming to look for you and here you are! My bed is spread with lovely, colored sheets of finest linen imported from Egypt, perfumed with myrrh, aloes and cinnamon. Come on, let's take our fill of love until morning, for my husband is away on a long trip. He has taken a wallet full of money with him, and won't return for several days."
>
> So she seduced him with her pretty speech, her coaxing and her wheedling, until he yielded to her. *He couldn't resist her flattery*. He followed her as an ox going to the butcher, or as a stag that is trapped, waiting to be killed with an arrow through its heart. He was as a bird flying into a snare, not knowing the fate awaiting it there.
>
> Listen to me, young men, and not only listen but obey; don't let your desires get out of hand; don't let yourself think about her. Don't go near her; stay away from where she walks, lest she tempt you and seduce you. For she has been the ruin of multitudes—a vast host of men have been her victims. If you want to find the road to hell, look for her house (Prov 7:6–27, TLB, emphasis added).

Notice that Solomon did not say that the young man could not withstand the sexual enticement of this woman. It was her *flattery* that he found irresistible. She made him think she admired him, and that was the fatal blow. I only wish Solomon had acknowledged that millions of *women* have been caught in the same snare, set by sweet-talking men. Both males and females are equally vulnerable to ego needs and flattery.

Let me diagram this path of responsibility and the voices that call to us from the world of folly.

PLEASURE ROMANTICISM

STRAIGHT LIFE

SEX EGO NEEDS

I've found it interesting to observe men and women who decide to leave the straight life in pursuit of alien voices. Rarely do they make a sudden left or right turn and plunge into an affair or a differing lifestyle. Instead, they make very small, safe departures from that line, and then return for a time of evaluation. (See diagram.)

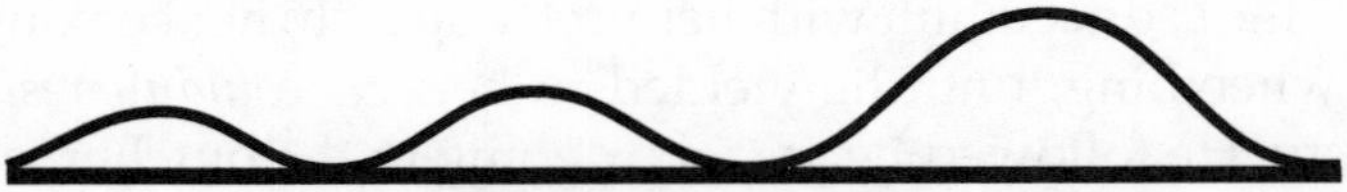

STRAIGHT LIFE

In the early stages, an observer might not even recognize the behavior as an illicit response. It may represent a luncheon with a secretary that lasts only thirty minutes longer than usual. Both the man and woman could justify their actions, if pressed. They were talking about business most of the time. But both of them know that their business conversation is not responsible for the excitement they feel inside. They are flirting with a departure from the straight life. Later in the day she hands him a sheet of paper, and as he accepts it, he allows his hand to pass gently over hers. It's no big deal. They have done nothing wrong. But both of them are making tiny "blips" off the path of responsibility. If they don't check their inclinations at that point, the blip will become a bulge, and the illicit relationship will grow. Such matters are almost always progressive unless deliberately quenched. Finally, the love affair that began with a long lunch becomes a flaming passion that is incompatible with the straight life. Then the break occurs dramatically.

Perhaps it *appears* that Tom or Marge suddenly abandoned their homes, marriages, kids and jobs . . . but you can be sure that they've contemplated and "tested" the break for weeks.

But now we come to a very important question. What happens to the person who chases after the exciting voices?

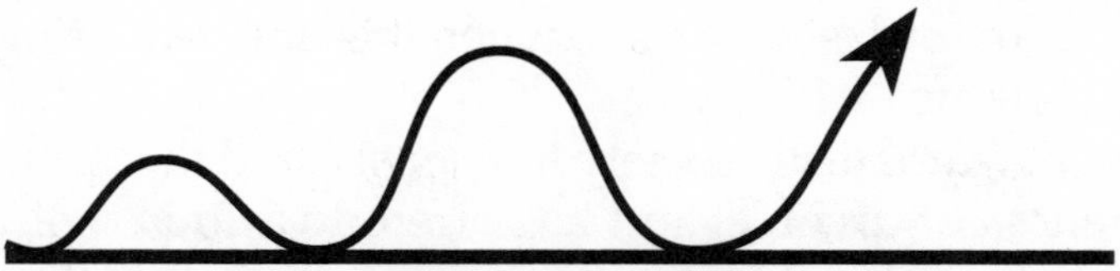

Do they really live happily ever after? Hardly! I have watched those who departed from the world of responsibility, and an interesting phenomenon invariably occurs: they eventually establish another straight life! The grass is greener on the other side of the fence, but it still has to be mowed. Sooner or later, the pleasure of an illicit affair has to come to an end. Folks have to get back to work. Nor can the fantastic romantic feeling last forever. In fact, the new lover soon becomes rather commonplace, just like the former husband or wife. His or her flaws come into focus, and the couple has their first fight. That takes the edge off the thrill. And the sexual relationship gradually loses its breathtaking quality because it's no longer new. There are times when it doesn't appeal at all. But most significantly, the man and woman eventually turn their thoughts to earning a living and cooking and cleaning and paying taxes again, permitting ego needs to accumulate as before. Alas, after the emotions have been on a moon-shot, they are destined to come back down to earth once more.

Then what does our amorous couple do when they conclude for the second time that the straight life has become intolerably heavy? I am acquainted with men and women, and so are you, who have ripped from one straight life to another in vain search of prolonged pleasure and sex- and ego-gratification. In so doing, they leave in their wake former husbands or wives who feel rejected and bitter and unloved. They produce little children who crave the affection of a father or mother . . . . but never find it. All that is left on the march toward old age is a series of broken relationships and shattered lives and hostile children. A scriptural principle foretells the inevitable outcome: "Then when lust hath conceived, it bringeth forth sin; and sin, when it is finished, bringeth forth death" (James 1:15, KJV).

Our humanistic society has considered these painful consequences of divorce, and has offered various "solutions" to troubled families. One of those suggestions, which must rank as the most ridiculous idea in the history of marriage, is that we should bring infidelity *into* the straight life. This concept of nonexclusive marriage was described by Nina and George O'Neill, in their best-selling book from fifteen years ago, *Open Marriage*. They proposed that husbands and wives permit one another to bed down with whomever they please, without so much as a tip of the hat to the spouse. Even the O'Neills admitted a few years later that their idea didn't work. It seems that they overlooked the presence of jealousy in the relationship. Who would have thought it?

Dick Hobson said it better, writing in the *Los Angeles Magazine*,

> . . . our character structure is built in, and we can't get free that easily. Changing the externals—the social mores—can give the dangerous illusion that something has really changed. So now you're telling us that sex is good and we should have lots of it; then why are we not? Because we're still being run by an internal standard that never heard of the Sexual Revolution (April, 1977, p. 197).

Back to the drawing boards. If we can't bring infidelity into marriage, maybe we can make it easier to escape from the straight life. Toward this end, John F. Whitaker, M.D., has written "A Personal Marriage Contract" which is almost as foolish as *Open Marriage*. It was published in *Woman's Day*, of all places, and bore this headline: "A set of contemporary guidelines for the young couple who are contemplating marriage today." Whitaker then provided a contract to be signed, witnessed, and dated by the parties involved. If you can read the conditions of the contract without becoming indignant, you're made of different stuff than I. Let me quote a few of the items:

> I understand that nothing is forever; that there are no absolute guarantees, and that NOW is the only real forever.
>
> I cannot make you happy or unhappy, but I can make myself happy. My happiness will be an invitation for you to join me in happiness, joy and love.
>
> I will set my own standards and ultimately depend upon myself for approval.
>
> I give up the myth that there is a "one and only" who will make me happy.
>
> When I make commitments to do what I want to do, then I am being free. . . . There is no freedom without responsibility.
>
> Since I understand that we cannot be everything to each other, I will respect and value the importance of your having separate play and work activities with separate friends and co-workers.
>
> I understand that there will be pain as well as joy, and I accept the risk of a brief period when we part. [Notice that the author does not say "if we part."] I know that I must ultimately give up everyone I love unless he dies first.
>
> I will love, honor, respect (but not obey or subjugate myself to you) until either of us changes his mind and maintains a change of attitude for a period of one year or until the termination date of the contract.
>
> Don't expect me to accept you as you are when you fail to maintain mental attractiveness and fail to take care of your mind.

> Don't expect me to accept you as you are when you fail to maintain physical attractiveness and fail to take care of your body.
>
> I will put myself first. By keeping myself full, satisfied, and not hungry, I will have an abundance of joy, love, and caring to give you.
>
> I will own my separate money and property, and enjoy sharing ownership with you of our common money and property.
>
> Whenever we are confronted with a problem, I will resolve my feelings first, and then, with a cool mind, rationally solve any mutual problems with you.
>
> While I reserve the right to have private areas of my life that I will not share with you, I will not lie to you either by word or action or by failure to share relevant information that affects our relationship.
>
> I will not give come-on signals to others for sexual relations when I see that you feel threatened. I will count on you to recognize, admire and stroke me for my sexuality and attractiveness as a man or woman.*

A place is provided on the contract for the designated term of the agreement. The instructions read, "On the date of termination, we will reconfirm or renegotiate the contract; or we will cease being WITH each other, will part in a friendly manner and will go on with our lives separately."

Isn't that a sweet basis on which to build a marriage? The author is proposing that a straight life be established, but that the newlyweds agree in advance not to stay on it very long. And you can be assured that they won't. One basic flaw runs through the easy-out concept: it underestimates the power of

---

*From the book *Personal Marriage Contract* by John F. Whitaker, M.D., Copyright 1976, by John F. Whitaker, M.D., published by OK Street, Inc., Dallas, Texas, 1976.

sex and marriage to make us "one flesh," and fails to anticipate the ripping and tearing of that flesh at the moment of disintegration. Like *Open Marriage,* it will only bring pain to those who apply its godless philosophy.

Then what *is* the answer to a straight life that oppresses its family members? What solutions are consistent with the Christian faith? The remedy, as I have been attempting to say throughout this book, is to bring those external voices *into* the straight life. You see, the greater the frustration on the path of responsibility, the louder are the voices that call us from it. To lessen their appeal, we must simply meet the same needs within the context of marriage. First, every couple should reserve time specifically for pleasure. Husbands and wives should go on a date at least once a week, leaving children at home. Likewise, some form of sports or recreational activity should be enjoyed as a family whether it be tennis, golf, swimming, skiing, or some other option.

Second, every husband and wife should seek to keep the romantic fires aglow in the relationship, by the use of love notes and surprises and candlelight dinners and unexpected weekend trips, among other possibilities.

Third, couples *must* reserve some of their time and energy for meaningful sexual activity. Tired bodies make for tired sex. The physical aspect of the relationship can be approached creatively, and indeed, must be.

Fourth, most successful marriages are those where both husband and wife seek to build the self-esteem of the other. How tragic it is when a destructive relationship prevails. It makes me uncomfortable even to be in the company of a man and woman who are taking verbal swats at each other, attempting to insult and debase the partner. Ego needs *can* be met within the bonds of marriage, and nothing contributes more to closeness and stability than to convey respect for the personhood of the spouse.

But who will invest the necessary effort to bring these amenities into marriage? Again, my observation is that most women are merely waiting for their husbands to assume leadership in this objective. They are more than willing to follow suit, but they can't do the job alone. It's a game only two can play.

Readers who are facing the greatest marital difficulties might want to consult my book, *Love Must Be Tough*. It was written specifically to those in a state of marital crisis.

A MAN AND HIS WORK

12

A Man and His Work

Having discussed the straight life in general terms, it is appropriate now that we examine the specific responsibility of a man's work. This topic has great relevance to the central theme of this book, which has focused on a man's priorities and the importance he gives to his family. In twentieth-century America, it is almost inevitable that a vigorous competition arises between a man's job and his home. Achieving a balance between two areas of responsibility requires constant vigilance, and, quite frankly, most men tip the scales dramatically in the direction of their employment.

I have already admitted that I have also struggled to achieve a proper perspective between my profession and my family. Just when I think I have conquered the dragon of overcommitment, I say "yes" a few times when I should have said, "no, thanks," and the monster arises to maul me again. I know of no easier mistake to make, nor one that has such devastating implications for the family.

In chapter 7, I described an extremely hectic period of my life occurring in 1969, and how my father helped me rearrange my priorities for the better. Nevertheless, the *worst* siege of overcommitment I've ever experienced came years later. I went through six weeks of incredible pressure, involving obligations that should have been spread over six months. I still don't know what wave of stupidity caused me to yield to such nonsense. I wasn't forced. No one threatened my life. I was not financially pressed. I can recall having *no* excuse. I simply relaxed my guard for a few weeks and found myself in a race for survival.

I had agreed to speak at various functions around the country on five out of six consecutive weekends. That, in itself, was ridiculous, meaning I would not see my children on a Saturday for more than a month. But at the same time, I was facing deadlines on a new book, three new tape albums, a weekly radio broadcast, and a random IRS audit (lucky me). To compound matters, the San Antonio trip and near death of my dad, mentioned earlier, occurred in the middle of this period. Fatigue mounted week by week as I ran to catch planes and write speeches and search for tax receipts.

The climax occurred in early October when I flew to Cincinnati to participate in a Praise Gathering, sponsored by Mr. Bill Gaither. I lost a night of sleep going in, due to the time change, and then spent two days standing before crowds ranging from two hundred to eight thousand people. It was an exhilarating time of teaching and sharing and counseling, but it squeezed the last drop of energy from my frame. I staggered toward the airport in a state of utter exhaustion. One thought pulsed through my head as the plane headed west: *"It's over!"*

For six weeks I had had no time to myself. My great desire was to crawl through the front door of my house and remain in isolation for at least seven days. Above all, I wanted to watch the USC-Alabama football game on television the next day. That, to me, is therapy at its best (provided USC wins!).

Let's leave that westbound plane for a moment and journey to a home in Arcadia, California, where my wife, Shirley, is also approaching the end of a siege. For six long weeks she has run the home without benefit of a man. It has been her task to discipline and train and guide and feed and medicate and bathe two rambunctious kids. Needless to say, she is *also* nearing the point of exhaustion. Furthermore, Shirley has hardly seen her husband since the first of September, and her emotional needs have been on a prolonged "hold." One thought gives her strength to continue: "At last, Jim is coming home and he'll take over!"

It takes no great analyst to observe that Shirley and I approached that final weekend on a collision course! An explosion was just a matter of time, because each of us was too exhausted to consider the needs of the other.

I should pause to explain the relationship that Shirley and I enjoy as husband and wife. God has blessed our marriage in such a beautiful way. Shirley is, truly, my very best friend on the face of the earth. In fact, if I had one free evening that I could spend with any person of my choice, there is no one in the world who would outrank my own wife. It is amazing that two people could live together for thirty-one years and yet find so much to talk about and share day by day. We have also grown in mutual understanding so that it is rarely necessary to quarrel and argue at this stage in our lives. The "power struggle" of earlier years is largely over. Nevertheless, I'm here to tell you that Shirley and I had a dandy fight on the weekend following the Praise Gathering.

I arrived home on Friday night, and Shirley greeted me warmly at the door. We chatted about recent events and the kids and routine matters before sleep overtook us. The next morning went smoothly enough . . . at least until breakfast was over. We ate on the patio in the back yard. But as we were finishing the meal, our attitudinal differences suddenly blew up in our faces.

"Uh, Jim," said Shirley, "as you know, seventy-five members from the Singles Department at our church will be using our house tonight, and I need you to help me get ready for them. First, I want you to wash down the patio umbrella for me."

My blood pressure immediately shot up to about 212, and steam began to curl from my ears. Didn't Shirley know how hard I had worked? What kind of a slave driver is this woman? Doesn't she understand how badly I need this day? Well, I'll tell you something! I'm watching that football game, and if Shirley doesn't like it she can just lump it!

I don't recall what words I used to convey these thoughts, but I must have gotten the idea across. Shirley stood startled for a moment, then went in the house and slammed the door. I sat under the dirty umbrella for a few minutes, filled with righteous indignation. I never felt so justified in my life. "After all, you know, I'm not an iron man. I need rest, too, and I'm gonna have it!"

So I had my way. I watched the USC-Alabama game in my study, but the tension around me was incredible. Silence prevailed between husband and wife. Not a word had been spoken since our terse interchange in the back yard. Then our anger began to turn into mutual hurt, which is even more damaging to communication.

The seventy-five church members came that evening and were served refreshments on the patio. They didn't seem to notice the dirty umbrella. They eventually departed, leaving me in the company of a mute female who still acted like the entire episode was my fault. Isn't that just like a woman?!

Then came the awkward time of day called bedtime. I climbed into my side of the king-sized bed and parked as close to the edge as possible without plunging over the precipice. Shirley did likewise, clinging tenaciously to her "brink." At least eight feet of mattress separated us. No words were spoken. There were, however, frequent sighs from both parties, accompanied by much rolling and tossing. Shirley finally got up to take two aspirin and then returned to bed. Fifteen minutes later I turned on the light to put some nose drops in my nostrils. What followed was one of the worst nights of sleep in my life.

The next morning was Sunday, which presented more uncomfortable moments. We dressed and went to our adult class, still bearing deep wounds and resentment. And wouldn't you know, the teacher chose that morning to talk about marital harmony and God's plan for husbands and wives. Shirley and I nodded and smiled in agreement, but we felt like kicking each other under the table. It made me suspect that many other couples were also putting on a good front to hide their real feelings. (I later told this story to the same class and found that my suspicions were accurate.)

I wish I could say that the problem was resolved on Sunday afternoon, but such was not the case. Nor did it end on Monday or Tuesday. By Wednesday morning, we were sick to death of this silent warfare. We were both more rested by that time, and the issue began to lose some of its fire. I told Shirley I wanted her to join me for breakfast at a restaurant, and announced my intention of going to work late.

What occurred was a beautiful time of communication and love. I began to see that Shirley was in the same state of need that I had been. She began to understand the depths of my fatigue. We talked it out and reestablished the closeness that makes life worth living. Not only did we survive the crisis, but we learned several valuable lessons and grew from the experience.

I have not written the details of this conflict for the purpose of entertaining you. Rather, it is my conviction that *most* couples have fought over the same issue, and the lessons that Shirley and I learned from it can be helpful to others. Three distinct concepts emerged which may assist you in handling a similar episode in your marriage. Let me enumerate them.

1. All miscommunication results from differing assumptions.

It is now clear that my battle with Shirley resulted entirely from our differing assumptions about the approaching weekend, and our failure to clarify those attitudes before they collided. I assumed that my responsibilities as husband and father would not resume until I had been given a chance to rest and recuperate. That was a reasonable expectation, but it happened to differ with Shirley's assumption. She felt that her lonely tour of duty at home was to end with my return from the wars, and that I would accept the burden from her weary shoulders with the rise of the Saturday sun. It was a reasonable supposition, but not in harmony with mine. We could have avoided the conflict by a five-minute conversation prior to the umbrella incident.

I should have said, "Shirley, I know you've had it rough here at home these past six weeks, and I intend to help you pull things together. But I'm going to ask you to understand me for a few more days. I'm more tired than I ever remember being, and I find it difficult to even engage in conversation. If you'll let me hole up for a few days . . . watch some football games on television and sleep a lot . . . I'll pick up my domestic responsibilities the first part of next week."

Shirley would have understood this request and honored it. That's the kind of woman she is. Likewise, if she had said to me, "Jim, these past six weeks have been extremely hectic here at home. I know you couldn't help it, but we've missed your presence here. Just as soon as possible, I need you to get involved with the kids, and for that matter, I want to be with you, too. And besides, there's *one* task I can't do that I would appreciate your handling Saturday morning. You see, the umbrella is dirty and—"

The brief explanation would have helped me understand Shirley's situation. But in reality, we allowed our differing assumptions to remain unspoken . . . and you know the rest of the story.

Bad marriages are saturated with differing assumptions between husbands and wives. He assumes that he has met his marital responsibilities by earning a living for the family. She assumes that he should also meet her romantic needs and occasionally help with the kids. Constant friction occurs where those diverse views collide. He assumes that sexual intercourse is his prerogative, whenever and wherever he desires it. She assumes that sexual intercourse is to occur after they've enjoyed a time of communication, love, and mutual respect. Great conflict occurs between those contrasting perspectives. He assumes that their money belongs primarily to him, since he earned it. She assumes that she's entitled to half the resources as the law implies. The list of these commonly differing assumptions is virtually endless, and the havoc they inflict is apparent in every divorce court.

One of the purposes of marriage counseling, at least as I perceive it, is to work through those differing points of view in search of compromise and harmony.

2. *The hostility in many marriages is a direct expression of deep hurt between husband and wife.*

Returning to my conflict with Shirley, remember that neither of us sought to hurt the other person. Our initial anger was not motivated by malice or vindictiveness, but by a sense of having been wronged. That situation often underlies marital conflict. Being wounded in spirit gives birth to anger and resentment, leading to destructive words between husbands and wives.

Let's quietly visit a newlywed couple who is in the midst of a terrible battle. She is screaming insults at him and he hurls the meanest concoctions back at her. They stand red-faced in their apartment, disassembling one another's ego. Observers might be surprised to learn that their *basic* problem is not one of mutual anger. They both have been *hurt* by the behavior of the other. The accusations they sling back and forth are merely reactions to the pain inside. Nevertheless, their words serve to deepen the original wounds and intensify the pain. It becomes a vicious cycle that can quickly destroy a relationship.

That cycle could be broken if *one* of the combatants could muster the courage to talk about his own pain, rather than increasing the discomfort of his partner.

"John, I cooked this delicious meal . . . spent three hours in the kitchen trying to please you. Then you didn't even call to say you'd be late. Frankly, it hurt my feelings and made me feel that you don't respect me."

John can receive that message without having to say hurtful things in response. But if Mary calls him "irresponsible, uncaring, heartless and just like your mother," then the battle lines are drawn. Understanding these dynamics of personal conflict can help lessen the hostility when disagreements occur.

3. *Overcommitment is the Number One Marriage Killer.*

This third lesson growing out of our conflict is the most important, and reiterates a concept presented throughout this book. Not only are fatigue and time pressure destructive to parent-child relationships, but they undermine even the healthiest of marriages. How can a man and woman communicate with each other when they're too worn out even to talk? How can they pray together when every moment is programmed to the limit? How can they enjoy a sexual relationship when they are exhausted at the end of every day? How can they "date" one another or take walks in the rain or sit by a fire when they face the tyranny of an unfinished "to do" list?

From this vantage point, I have to admit that my fight with Shirley was primarily *my* fault. Not that I was wrong in wanting to rest after arriving home. But I was to blame for foolishly overcommitting my time during that period. The conflict would never have occurred if I had not scheduled myself wall to wall for six weeks. My lack of discipline in my work caused Shirley and me to become exhausted, which brought a chain reaction of negative emotions: irritability, self-pity, petulance, selfishness, and withdrawal. Few marriages can survive a long-term dose of that bitter medicine.

I mentioned earlier that I shared this story with my adult Sunday school class a few weeks after it occurred. My comments happened to have been recorded that day, and a cassette tape package is now being marketed under the title *How to Save Your Marriage*. It has produced some interesting correspondence from those who have heard the message. One of those letters is reproduced below with permission from the writer.

> Dear Dr. Dobson:
>
> It is one o'clock in the morning—I have just finished listening to your tape "How to Save Your Marriage." In addition to my regular job as treasurer/general manager of a major corporation, I carry an untold number of responsibilities with church, Christian, and community organizations.
>
> I have listened to your tape only one time but am left with a sense of absolute frustration and guilt. I am the prototype of the man you have described so aptly. And, I don't know how to extricate myself from this situation. Practically everything which you point out applies to my case—overscheduling, economic need, etc., etc.

I have three children: second-year college, fourth-year high school, first-year high school—and I know that they will never look back on times with me as the best days of their childhood. This really hurts.

I know that something must be done. I know that the Lord is able. I am not sure that I can change. I guess my purpose in writing this letter—at this hour—is somewhat therapeutic: to acknowledge my condition, to take a concrete first step in that same direction, and to ask your prayers on my behalf.

I have two of your books which I have glanced at or skimmed through. Your taped message, however, was listened to while working. I don't recall ever hearing a more honest and practical message in my twenty years as a Christian.

Thanks for your sharing in such a practical way. My present thought is to let my wife listen to the tape and then let it serve as a basis for an in-depth discussion. It occurs to me that perhaps I should ask the kids to listen, also, and perhaps this can serve as a beginning of new relationships with them. I don't know.

Again, thinking of the "concrete step," I'll mail this letter on the way home.

Thanks for your honesty,

Sincerely in Christ,

I've included this letter to illustrate what men already know: it isn't easy to implement a slower lifestyle. Prior commitments have to be met. Financial pressures must be confronted. The employer seldom *asks* if you want to accept a new assignment. Your business would fail without your supervision. Your patients have no other physician to whom they can turn. Several of your church members are in the hospital and awaiting your ministerial visit. There seems to be no place to stop. Also, we must not overlook that ever-present masculine need to succeed . . . to push . . . to strive . . . to accomplish.

Besides, isn't everyone else doing the same thing? Sure they are. I don't even know any men who aren't running at a breathless pace. My physician, my lawyer, my accountant, my handyman, my mechanic, my pastor, my next-door neighbor. There is symbolic sweat on the brow of virtually every man in North America. Most of these husbands and fathers will admit that they're working too hard, but an interesting response occurs when this subject is raised. They have honestly convinced themselves that their overcommitment is a *temporary* problem.

"Well, this is a difficult year, you see, because I'm going to night school and trying to earn a living at the same time. But it won't always be so hectic at our house. I figure I'll have the degree by a year from June. Then pressure will ease up."

or . . .

"My wife and I just bought this new business, and it's gonna take us a year to get it rolling. Then we can hire the help we need. Until then, though, we're having to work ten to twelve hours a day. That cuts into our family life quite a bit, but it won't last very long."

or . . .

"We just moved into a new house, and I've had to put in all the yards and build on a room in back. Every Saturday and most evenings are invested in that project. My son keeps asking me to fly a kite with him and go fishing and stuff, and I wish I could. I keep telling him if he can wait 'til next summer we'll have a lot of time to do those things."

or . . .

"My wife had a baby two weeks ago and he's not sleeping through the night, so our schedule is all haywire now. I figure it'll be kinda difficult until we get him in kindergarten."

Most people can tell you with a straight face that the pressures they feel are the result of temporary circumstances. Their future will be less hectic. A slower day is coming. A light shines at the end of the dark tunnel. Unfortunately, their optimism is usually unjustified. It is my observation that the hoped-for period of tranquility rarely arrives. Instead, these short term pressures have a way of becoming sandwiched back to back, so that families emerge from one crisis and sail directly into another. Thus, we live our entire lives in the fast lane, hurtling down the road toward heart failure. We have deluded ourselves into believing that circumstances have forced us to work too hard for a short time, when, in fact, we are driven from *within*. We lack the discipline to limit our entanglements with the world, choosing instead to be dominated by our work and the materialistic gadgetry it will bring. And what is sacrificed in the process are the loving relationships with wives and children and friends who give life meaning.

Conclusion

I, for one, have examined America's breathless lifestyle and find it to be *unacceptable*. At fifty-four years of age (I would be fifty-five but I was sick a year), I have been thinking about the stages of my earthly existence and what they will represent at its conclusion. There was a time when all of my friends were graduating from high school. Then I recall so many who entered colleges around the country. And alas, I lived through a phase when everyone seemed to be getting married. Then a few years later, we were besieged by baby shower announcements. You see, my generation is slowly but relentlessly moving through the decades, as have 2400 generations that preceded it. Now, it occurs to me that a time will soon come when my friends will be dying. ("Wasn't it tragic what happened to Charles Painter yesterday?")

My aunt, Naomi Dobson, wrote me shortly before her death in 1978. She said, "It seems like every day another of my close friends either passes away or is afflicted with a terrible disease." Obviously, she was in that final phase of her generation. Now she is also gone.

What does this have to do with my life, today? How does it relate to yours? I'm suggesting that we stop and consider the brevity of our years on earth, perhaps finding new motivation to preserve the values that will endure. Why should we work ourselves into an early grave, missing those precious moments with loved ones who crave our affection and attention? It is a question that every man and woman should consider.

Let me offer this final word of encouragement for those who are determined to slow the pace: once you get out from under constant pressure, you'll wonder why you drove yourself so hard for all those years. *There is a better way!*

13

A Man and His Money

WOULD YOU LIKE to know what Americans think of money and the junk it will buy? Turn on a television set any day at 10:00 A.M., and watch the contestants as they compete for prizes and cash. Observe the coo-coo birds as they leap in the air, frothing at the mouth and tearing at the clothes of the moderator. Notice that their eyes are dilated and their ears are bright pink. It's an unfortunate condition known as *gameshow greed,* and it renders its victims incapable of rational judgment.

> Yes, BETTY MOLINO. YOU have won a NEW WASHING MACHINE, a year's supply of CHEWY candy bars, and this marvelous new doll, WANDA WEE-WEE, that actually soaks your daughter's lap. CONGRATULATIONS, Betty, and thanks for playing "GRAB BAG" (frantic applause).

How do I know so much about gameshow greed? Because I've been there! Back in 1967, my lovely wife managed to drag me to the "Let's Make a Deal" show. Shirley put toy birds all over her head and blouse, and I carried a dumb sign that said, "My wife is for the birds." Really funny, huh? It was good enough for Monty Hall, however, and we were selected as lucky contestants. They placed us in the two front seats near the cameras, but began the program by "dealing" with other suckers.

I kept thinking as I sat in contestants' row, "What in the world am I doing here with this stupid sign?" I couldn't have been more skeptical about the proposition. Finally, Monty called our names and we awaited the verdict.

"Here behind Door #1 is . . . A NEW CAR!" (the audience went crazy with excitement.)

Suddenly, I was gripped by a spasm in the pit of my stomach. My mouth watered profusely and my heart began knocking on the sides of my chest. There on that stage was the car of my dreams—a brand-new Camaro. Desire came charging up my throat and stuck in the region of my Adam's apple. My breathing became irregular and shallow, which was another unmistakable clue. I had been struck by gameshow greed.

To understand this reaction, you would have to know that I have owned several of the worst cars in automotive history. Throughout my college years I drove a 1949 Mercury convertible that had power seats, power windows, power top, power everything . . . but no power to run them. I put the windows up in the winter and down in the summer. There they remained, despite fluctuating temperatures. Shirley, who was then my girlfriend, must have loved me tremendously to have tolerated that car. She *hated* it. The front seat had a spring with a bad temper that tore her clothes and punctured her skin. Nor did Ol' Red always choose to run. Shirley spent more than one evening guiding that hunk of scrap iron slowly down the road while I pushed from behind. Talk about hurting your college pride!

The crowning blow occurred shortly after our graduation from college. We were invited to appear for important job interviews and we put on our Sunday best for the occasion. There we were, suit and tie, heels and hose, going sixty miles an hour down the road in Ol' Red, when the top suddenly blew off. Strings and dust flapped us in the face as the canvas waved behind the car like Superman's cape. The ribs of the top protruded above our heads, reminiscent of undersized roll-over bars. And can you believe that Shirley got mad at *me* for letting that happen! She crouched on the floorboard of the car, criticizing me for driving such a beat-up automobile. It is a miracle that our relationship survived that emotional afternoon.

Although Ol' Red had been put to sleep long before the "Let's Make a Deal" experience, I still had never owned a new car. Every available dollar had gone to pay school bills at the University of Southern California in my pursuit of a doctorate, which was earned just two months prior to the television venture.

This explains my reaction to the beautiful automobile behind Door #1.

"All you have to do to win the car," said Monty, "is tell us the prices of these four items." Shirley and I guessed the first three, but the deck was stacked on number four. It was a Hoover portable vacuum cleaner, whose price turned out to be $53.00. We had to guess within $3.00, as I recall. We consulted each other during the commercial break and took a wild shot at $108.00.

"Sorry," said Monty Hall. "You've been zonked. But here, take the vacuum cleaner (wow!) and the $3 you won on the other mystery items. And thanks for playing 'Let's Make a Deal.'"

On the way home, Shirley and I talked about how our emotions had been manipulated in that situation. We had both experienced an incredible greed, and the feeling was not comfortable. I have since learned a very valuable lesson about lust and how it operates in a spiritual context. It has been my observation that *whatever* a person hungers for, Satan will appear to offer it in exchange for a spiritual compromise. In my case, a new automobile was the perfect enticement to unleash my greed. But if illicit sex is your desire, it will eventually be made available. Don't be surprised when you are beckoned by a willing partner. If your passion is for fame or power, that object of lust will be promised (even if never delivered). Remember that Jesus was offered bread following His forty-day fast in the wilderness. He was promised power and glory after He had been contemplating His upcoming road to the cross. My point is that Satan uses our keenest appetites to destroy us. Let me repeat the Scripture: "Then when lust hath conceived, it bringeth forth sin: and sin, when it is finished, bringeth forth death" (James 1:15, KJV).

Likewise, if you hunger and thirst after great wealth—beware! Satan's objective is half accomplished already: this materialistic passion is paramount in Western culture. Someone recently handed me a brochure published by Security Bank in California, which was designed to appeal to a gadget-minded culture. It asked the question, "What do you want to make you happy?" The remaining pages of the pamphlet listed the great sources of joy—a boat, a car, a stove, a television set, and a refrigerator. I wonder if the executives at Security Bank actually believe that happiness can be purchased in the form of an appliance or a vehicle? If so, they should review the words of Jesus, who said, "Take heed, and beware of covetousness: for a man's life consisteth *not* in the abundance of the things which he possesseth" (Luke 12:15, KJV, emphasis added).

Of all the values transmitted to me by my father, none made a more lasting impression than his attitude toward money. As an evangelist, he could never depend on the amount of money he would be given. The local church would collect a free will offering for my father, but many times the gifts were barely sufficient to pay his traveling expenses. Furthermore, he would usually stay with the pastor during a ten-day revival; while there he often observed that the children needed shoes or books or medication. On the final night of the meeting when the modest offering was given to him, my dad would take enough money to get home and then donate the balance to meet the needs of the pastor's family.

Then my dad would return to be greeted by my mother and me. I can still hear the conversations between my good parents.

"Did you have a successful revival?" my mother would ask.

"The Lord was with us," replied my dad.

"How much did they pay you?" she continued.

"Well, I need to talk to you about that," grinned my father.

"I know," said Mom. "You gave it all away, didn't you?"

"Yes, the pastor's kids were so needy and I wanted to help them," he explained.

My mother would invariably sanction his decision, saying if my dad felt that way it was all right. God had always taken good care of us and would continue to do so.

A few days later when the bills began to accumulate, our little family would gather on our knees before the Lord. Dad would pray first.

"Lord, you know we've been faithful with the resources you've given us. We've tried to be responsive to the needs of others when you laid them on our hearts. Now, Lord *my* family is in need. You've said, 'Give and it shall be given unto you.' So we bring to you our empty meal barrel and ask you to fill it."

As a child, I listened intently to these prayers and watched carefully to see how God responded. I tell you without exaggeration that money invariably arrived in the next few days. God did not make us rich, as some ministers promise today. But He never let us go hungry. On one occasion, $1200 arrived in the mail the day after family prayer. My childlike faith grew by leaps and bounds at this demonstration of trust and sacrifice by my father and mother. I regret that my own children have never seen their parents forced to depend on God in the way I experienced as a boy.

It is interesting to me that Jesus had more to say in the Bible about money than any other subject, which emphasizes the importance of this topic for my family and yours. He made it clear that there is a direct relationship between great riches and spiritual poverty, as we are witnessing in America today. And as I mentioned earlier, it is my belief that excessive materialism in parents has the power to inflict enormous spiritual damage on our sons and daughters. If they see that we care more about *things* than people . . . if they perceive that we have sought to buy their love as a guilt reducer . . . if they recognize the hollowness of our Christian testimony when it is accompanied by stinginess with God . . . the result is often cynicism and disbelief. And more importantly, when they observe Dad working fifteen hours a day to capture ever more of this world's goods, they *know* where his treasure is. Seeing is believing.

Fathers, it is your responsibility to teach your children Christian attitudes toward possessions and money. It is accomplished not with words, but by the way you handle your own resources. Dr. Mark Lee stated in his book *Creative Christian Marriage,* "A family's value system can be determined from the way they spend money." He is right. It can also be determined from the way the family *doesn't* spend money, since miserliness is also a form of greed.

As a final thought, it can accurately be said that everything you own will eventually own you. I remember experiencing the truth of this proverb when I moved into a new office some years ago. An interior designer came by and suggested that I spread a few decorator items around for effect. Among his ideas was the proposal that I buy a chime clock for the wall. The cost was nearly $200, and I declined. But he talked to Shirley and together, they convinced me that I couldn't possibly live without that clock. So what was I to do?

The interior designer purchased the clock for me and hung it in a conspicuous spot on the wall. It functioned properly for a couple of months, and then suddenly lost its mind. The chime didn't know the time of day and began gonging wildly at odd hours. Thus irritated, I dug through the files to find the guarantee. Then the clock had to be boxed and transported to the repair shop. It was retrieved five days later and hung on the wall, again.

A month later, the chime went haywire once more. The entire process of repairing the clock had to be repeated. And so it went. It has now been thirteen years since I purchased that piece of junk, and it has never worked for more than six months at a time. Over and over I have been through the "fix-it" routine. I tell you honestly that that Regulator clock hangs silently on my wall today. It still looks nice, but it no longer keeps time. I've given up on the repairman.

Do you understand what ownership of this timepiece has cost me? I'm only allotted a specific number of days on this earth. Whatever that finite lifespan turns out to be, I have spent a certain percentage of those precious days in slavery to that stupid clock. That is what material possessions do to us. To all of you boat lovers or car buffs or apartment owners out there . . . whatever it is that you possess . . . you have traded your time to buy those items and now you must sweat to maintain them. That is the price of ownership. That is our way of life. I regret it.

Let me conclude this discussion by listing fifteen quotations which focus on the subject of money. Two are from my pen and others are Scripture verses or adaptations from various sources. Perhaps you will find them helpful in reinforcing your own system of values.

1. "The amount of a man's wealth consists in the number things he can do without."—Ralph Waldo Emerson.
2. "The best way to live happily ever after is not be after too much."—Anonymous.
3. "Desire is like a river. As long as it flows within the banks of God's will—be the current strong or weak—all is well. But when it flows over those boundaries and seeks other channels, then disaster lurks in the rampage."—James Dobson, Sr.
4. "For what shall it profit a man, if he shall gain the whole world, and lose his own soul?"—Jesus, Mark 8:36, KJV.
5. "The only thing you can take to heaven with you is your children (and others you have told about Christ)."—Anonymous.
6. "The love of money is the root of all evil."—1 Timothy 6:10, KJV.

7. "The greatest secret of life is to spend it on something that will outlast it."—Anonymous.
8. "God is entitled to a portion of our income, not because He needs, but because we need to give it."—James Dobson, Jr.
9. "Why spend your money on foodstuffs that don't give you strength? Why pay for groceries that don't do you any good? Listen and I'll tell you where to get good food that fattens up the soul!"—Isaiah 55:2, TLB.
10. "But they that will be rich fall into temptation and a snare, and into many foolish and hurtful lusts, which drown men in destruction and perdition."—1 Timothy 6:9, KJV.
11. "Such is the human race. Often it does seem a pity that Noah and his party didn't miss the boat."—Mark Twain.
12. "A person brings nothing into this world, and takes nothing out of it. Considering the kind of world it is, he's lucky to break even."—Anonymous.
13. There are said to be seven ages of man.
    First age: A child sees the earth.
    Second age: He wants it.
    Third age: He hustles to get it.
    Fourth age: He decides to be satisfied with about half of it.
    Fifth age: He would be satisfied with less than half of it.
    Sixth age: He is now content to possess a two by six foot section of it.
    Seventh age: He gets it.—Anonymous
14. Lee Iacocca is reported to have said that he has never seen a businessman say at his retirement that he wished he had spent more time in his work. It is his *family* that is finally seen as most important .
15. "I have concluded that the accumulation of wealth, even if I could achieve it, is an insufficient reason for living. When I reach the end of my days, a moment or two from now, I must look backward on something more meaningful than the pursuit of houses and land

and machines and stocks and bonds. Nor is fame of any lasting benefit. I will consider my earthly existence to have been wasted unless I can recall a loving family, a consistent investment in the lives of people, and an earnest attempt to serve the God who made me. Nothing else makes much sense."—James Dobson, Jr., *What Wives Wish Their Husbands Knew About Women*.

A MAN AND HIS MASCULINITY

14

A Man and a Woman and Their Biological Differences

Chapter 2 was devoted to the importance of maintaining male and female sex roles as separate entities. In other words, I attempted to explain why men and women should *behave* differently. Returning to that general subject, I would like to offer some evidence to show that men and women are biologically unique. The women's movement, in its assault on traditional sex roles, has repeatedly asserted that males and females are identical except for the ability to bear children. Nothing could be farther from the truth.

Let's begin by discussing the human brain, where maleness and femaleness are rooted. Careful research is revealing that the basic differences between the sexes are neurological in origin, rather than being purely cultural as ordinarily presumed. As Dr. Richard Restak stated in his book, *The Brain: The Last Frontier:*

> Certainly, anyone who has spent time with children in a playground or school setting is aware of the differences in the way

> boys and girls respond to similar situations. Think of the last time you supervised a birthday party attended by five-year-olds. It's not usually the girls who pull hair, throw punches, or smear each other with food. Usually such differences are explained on a cultural basis. Boys are expected to be more aggressive and play rough games, while girls are presumably encouraged to be more gentle, nonassertive, and passive. After several years of exposure to such expectations, so the theory goes, men and women wind up with widely varying behavioral and intellectual repertoires. As a corollary to this, many people believe that if the child-rearing practices could be equalized and sexual-role stereotypes eliminated, most of these differences would eventually disappear. As often happens, however, the true state of affairs is not that simple.
>
> Recent psychological research indicates that many of the differences in brain function between the sexes are innate, biologically determined, and relatively resistant to change through the influences of culture.*

Dr. Restak presents numerous studies that document this statement, and then concludes this chapter by quoting Dr. David Wechsler, creator of the most popular intelligence test for use with adults.

> ". . . our findings do confirm what poets and novelists have often asserted, and the average layman long believed, namely, that men not only behave but 'think' differently from women." (p. 206)

Both Drs. Restak and Wechsler are right. Males and females differ anatomically, sexually, emotionally, psychologically, and biochemically. We differ in literally every cell of our bodies, for each sex carries a unique chromosomal pattern. Much is written today about so-called sex-change operations, whereby males are transformed into females or vice versa. Admittedly, it is possible to alter the external genitalia by surgery, and silicone can be used to pad the breasts or round

---

*Richard Restak, *The Brain: The Last Frontier* (Garden City, N.Y.: Doubleday & Company, 1979), 197.

out a bony frame. Hormones can then be injected to feminize or masculinize the convert. But nothing can be done to change the assignment of sex made by God at the instant of conception. That determination is carried in each cell, and it will read "male" or female" from the earliest moment of life to the point of death. The Bible says emphatically, "Male *and* female created he them" (Gen. 1:27, KJV, emphasis added). Not one sex, but *two!*

Furthermore, it is my deep conviction that each sex displays unique emotional characteristics that are genetically endowed. Cultural influences cannot account for these novelties. Few psychologists have had the courage to express this view in recent years, because some people perceived it to be insulting. But to be *different* from men does not make women *inferior* to men. Males and females are original creations of God, each bearing strengths and weaknesses that counterbalance and interface with one another. It is a beautiful design that must not be disassembled.

Just how do female emotions differ from those of males? Let's consider first the importance of the menstrual cycle. I'm reminded of the late 1960s when hairy young men and women became almost undistinguishable from each other. Two of these hippies, a male and female, were involved in a minor traffic accident and were taken to a local hospital for treatment. The nurse who was completing the intake forms could not determine from their clothing and appearance which sex they represented. After considering the dilemma for a moment she asked, "Okay, which one of you has a menstrual cycle?"

The hippie with the bass voice looked at her through his bangs and said, "Not me, man. I gots a Honda."

The question was more significant than merely determining the sex of the patients. Included in this matter of menstruation are many implications for the way females feel about life during the course of the month. It has been said, quite accurately, that the four weeks of the menstrual cycle are characteristic of the four seasons of the year. The first week after a period can be termed the springtime of the physiological calendar. New estrogens (female hormones) are released each day and a woman's body begins to rebound from the recent winter.

The second week represents the summertime of the cycle, when the living is easy. A woman during this phase has more self-confidence than during any other phase of the month. It is a time of maximum energy, enthusiasm, amiability, and self-esteem. Estrogen levels account for much of this optimism, reaching a peak during mid-cycle when ovulation occurs. The relationship between husband and wife is typically at its best during these days of summer, when sexual desire (and the potential for pregnancy) are paramount.

But alas, the fall must surely follow summer. Estrogen levels steadily dwindle as the woman's body prepares itself for another period of menstruation. A second hormone, called progesterone, is released, which reduces the effect of estrogen and initiates the symptoms of premenstrual tension. It is a bleak phase of the month. Self-esteem deteriorates day by day, bringing depression and pessimism with it. A bloated and sluggish feeling often produces not only discomfort but also the belief that "I am ugly." Irritability and aggression become increasingly evident as the week progresses, reaching a climax immediately prior to menstruation.

Then come the winter and the period of the menstrual flow. Women differ remarkably in intensity of these symptoms, but most experience some discomfort. Those most vulnerable even find it necessary to spend a day or two in bed during the winter season, suffering from cramping and generalized misery. Gradually, the siege passes and the refreshing newness of springtime returns.

How can anyone who understands this cyclical pattern contend that there are no genetically determined psychological differences between males and females? No such system operates in men. The effect of the menstrual cycle is not only observable clinically, but it can be documented statistically.

The incidences of suicides, homicides, and infanticides perpetrated by women are significantly higher during the period of premenstrual tension than any other phase of the month. Consider also the findings of Alec Coppen and Neil Kessel, who studied 465 women and observed that they were more irritable and depressed during the premenstrual phase than during the mid-cycle. "This was true for neurotic, psychotic and normal women alike. Similarly Natalie Sharness found the premenstrual phase associated with feelings of helplessness, anxiety, hostility, and yearning for love. At menstruation, this tension and irritability eased, but depression often accompanied the relief, and lingered until estrogen increased."*

I doubt that these facts will come as a great revelation to men or women. Both sexes know that behavior and attitudes are related to the monthly pattern. I receive interesting letters from men who ask, "How can I cope with my wife's irrita-bility during this phase?" Their question reminds me of an incident shared with me by my late friend Dr. David Hernandez, who was an obstetrician and gynecologist in private practice. The true story involves Latin men whose wives were given birth control pills by a pharmaceutical company. The Federal Drug Administration in America would not permit hormonal research to be conducted, so the company selected a small fishing village in South America which agreed to cooperate. All the women in the town were given the pill on the same date, and after three weeks the prescription was terminated to permit menstruation. That meant, of course, that every adult female in the community was experiencing premenstrual tension at the same time. The men couldn't take it. They all headed for their boats each month and remained at sea until the crisis passed at home. They knew, even if some people didn't, that females are different from males . . . especially every twenty-eight days.

But there are other ways women are unique. Female emotions are also influenced by two other exclusively feminine functions, lactation and pregnancy. Furthermore, the hypothalamus, which is located at the base of the brain and has been called the "seat of the emotions," is apparently wired

**Psychology Today*, February 1972.

very differently for males than females. For example, a severe emotional shock or trauma can be interpreted by the hypothalmus, which then sends messages to the pituitary by way of neurons and hormones. The pituitary often responds by changing the body chemistry of the woman, perhaps interrupting the normal menstrual cycle for six months or longer. Female physiology is a finely tuned instrument, being more vulnerable and complex than the masculine counterpart. Why some women find that fact insulting is still a mystery to me.

How do these differences translate into observable behavior? Medical science has not begun to identify all the ramifications of sexual uniqueness. Some of the implications are extremely subtle. For example, when researchers quietly walked on high school and college campuses to study behavior of the sexes, they observed that males and females even transported their books in different ways. The young men tended to carry them at their sides with their arms looped over the top. Women and girls, by contrast, usually cradled their books at their breasts, in much the same way they would a baby. Who can estimate how many other sex-related influences lie below the level of consciousness?

Admittedly, some of the observed differences between the sexes *are* culturally produced. I don't know how to sort out those which are exclusively genetic from those which represent learned responses. Frankly, it doesn't seem to matter a great deal. The differences exist, for whatever reason. At the risk of being called a sexist, or a propagator of sexual stereotypes (or worse), let me delineate a few of the emotional patterns typical of women as compared with men.

1. As stated in Chapter 2, the reproductive capacity of women results in a greater appreciation for stability, security, and enduring human relationships. In other words, females are more *future*-oriented because of their concern for children.

2. Related to the first item is a woman's emotional investment in her home, which usually exceeds that of her husband. She typically cares more than he about the minor details of the house, family functioning, and such concerns.

To cite a personal example, my wife and I decided to install a new gas barbecue unit in our backyard. When the plumber completed the assignment and departed, Shirley and I both recognized that he had placed the appliance approximately six inches too high. I looked at the device and said, "Hmmm, yes sir, he sure made a mistake. That post is a bit too high. By the way, what are we having for dinner tonight?" Shirley's reaction was dramatically different. She said, "The plumber has that thing sticking up in the air and I don't think I can stand it!" Our contrasting views represented a classic difference of emotional intensity relating to the home.

3. Anyone who doubts that males and females are unique should observe how they approach a game of Ping Pong or Monopoly or dominoes or horseshoes or volleyball or tennis. Women often use the event as an excuse for fellowship and pleasant conversation. For men, the name of the game is *conquest*. Even if the setting is a friendly social gathering in the host's backyard, the beads of sweat on each man's forehead reveal his passion to win. This aggressive competitiveness has been attributed to cultural influences. I don't believe it. As Richard Restak said, "At a birthday party for five-year-olds, it's not usually the girls who pull hair, throw punches, or smear each other with food."

4. Males and females apparently differ in the manner by which they develop self-esteem. Men draw the necessary evidence of their worthiness primarily from their jobs—from being respected in business, profession or craft. Women, however, *especially those who are homemakers*, depend primarily on the romantic relationship with their husbands for ego support. This explains why the emotional content of a marriage is often of greater significance to women than men and why tokens of affection are appreciated more by wives, who obtain esteem from these expressions of love and generosity.

5. A maternal instinct apparently operates in most women, although its force is stronger in some than others. This desire to procreate is certainly evident in those who are unable to conceive. I receive a steady influx of letters from women who

express great frustration from their inability to become mothers. Although culture plays a major role in these longings, I believe they are rooted in female anatomy and physiology.

6. Perhaps the most dramatic differences between males and females are evident in their contrasting sexual preferences. He is more visually oriented, caring less about the romantic component. She is attracted not to a photograph of an unknown model or by a handsome stranger, but to *particular* man with whom she has entered into an emotional relationship. This differing orientation is merely the tip of the iceberg in delineating the sexual uniqueness of males and females.

These items are illustrative and are not intended to represent a scientific delination of sexual differences. The reader is invited to add his own observations to the list and to make his own interpretations.

Conclusion

By way of summary to these chapters dealing with male and female identities, let me offer two *opinions* with regard to masculine leadership. They are as follows:

1. Because of the fragile nature of the male ego and a man's enormous need to be respected, combined with female vulnerability and a woman's need to be loved, I feel it is a mistake to tamper with the time-honored relationship of husband as loving protector and wife as recipient of that protection.

2. Because two captains sink the ship and two cooks spoil the broth, I feel that a family must have a leader whose decisions prevail in times of differing opinions. If I understand the Scriptures, that role has been assigned to the man of the house. However, he must not incite his crew to mutiny by heavyhanded disregard for their feelings and needs. He should, in fact, put the best interests of his family above his own, even to the point of death, if necessary. Nowhere in Scripture is he authorized to become a dictator or slave-owner.

Other combinations of husband-wife teamwork have been successful in individual families, but I've seen many complications occurring in marriages where the man was passive, weak, and lacking in qualities of leadership. None of the modern alternatives have improved on the traditional, masculine role as prescribed in the Good Book. It was, after all, inspired by the Creator of mankind.

If this be macho, sexist, chauvinist, and stereotypical, then I'm guilty as charged. (Please address all hate mail to my secretary, who has a special file prepared for it.)

15

Whatever Happened to the Women's Liberation Movement?

I've referred several times to the now-defunct Women's Liberation Movement, which was in its heyday when this manuscript was first written. It left its mark before disappearing from the scene, but the general public quickly realized that anger between the sexes and lesbian ideologies, even the Equal Rights Amendment, were not in society's best interests. Unfortunately, many gullible people were sucked into the web before their eyes were opened. Some are still paying the price for mistakes made during that era.

The best testimonial I have read to this effect was written by Kay Ebeling and published in the "My Turn" section of *Newsweek* magazine (November 19, 1990). I will let her speak from the vantage point of the nineties.

The Failure of Feminism

The other day I had the world's fastest blind date. A Yuppie from Eureka penciled me in for 50 minutes on a Friday and met me at a watering hole in the rural northern California town of Arcata. He breezed in, threw his jammed daily planner on the table and shot questions at me, watching my reactions as if it were a job interview. He eyed how much I drank. Then he breezed out to his next appointment. He had given us 50 minutes to size each other up and see if there was any chance for romance. His exit was so fast that as we left he let the door slam back in my face. It was an interesting slam.

Most of our 50-minute conversation had covered the changing state of male-female relationships. My blind date was 40 years old, from the Experimental Generation. He is "actively pursuing new ways for men and women to interact now that old traditions no longer exist." That's a real quote. He really did say that, when I asked him what he liked to do. This was a man who'd read Ms. Magazine and believed every word of it. He'd been single for 16 years but had lived with a few women during that time. He was off that evening for a ski weekend, meeting someone who was paying her own way for the trip.

I too am from the Experimental Generation, but I couldn't even pay for my own drink. To me, feminism has backfired against women. In 1973 I left what could have been a perfectly good marriage, taking with me a child in diapers, a 10-year-old Plymouth and Volume 1, Number One of Ms. Magazine. I was convinced I could make it on my own. In the last 15 years my ex has married or lived with a succession of women. As he gets older, his women stay in their 20s. Meanwhile, I've stayed unattached. He drives a BMW. I ride buses.

Today I see feminism as the Great Experiment That Failed, and women in my generation, its perpetrators, are the casualties. Many of us, myself included, are saddled with raising children alone. The resulting poverty makes us experts at cornmeal recipes and ways to find free recreation on weekends. At the same time, single men from our generation amass fortunes in CDs and real-estate ventures so they can breeze off on ski weekends. Feminism freed men, not women. Now men are spared the nuisance of a wife and family to support.

After childbirth, if his wife's waist doesn't return to 20 inches, the husband can go out and get a more petite woman. It's far more difficult for the wife, now tied down with a baby, to find a new man. My blind date that Friday waved good-bye as he drove off in his RV. I walked home and paid the sitter with laundry quarters.

The main message of feminism was: woman, you don't need a man; remember, those of you around 40, the phrase: "A woman without a man is like a fish without a bicycle?" That joke circulated through "consciousness raising" groups across the country in the '70s. It was a philosophy that made divorce and cohabitation casual and routine. Feminism made women disposable. So today a lot of females are around 40 and single with a couple of kids to raise on their own. Child-support payments might pay for a few pairs of shoes, but in general, feminism gave men all the financial and personal advantages over women.

What's worse, we asked for it. Many women decided: you don't need a family structure to raise your children. We packed them off to day-care centers where they could get their nurturing from professionals. Then we put on our suits and ties, packed our briefcases and took off on this Great Experiment, convinced that there was no difference between ourselves and the guys in the other offices.

'Biological thing': How wrong we were. Because like it or not, women have babies. It's this biological thing that's just there, these organs we're born with. The truth is, a woman can't live the true feminist life unless she denies her child-bearing biology. She has to live on the pill, or have her tubes tied at an early age. Then she can keep up with the guys with an uninterrupted career and then, when she's 30, she'll be paying her own way on ski weekends too.

The reality of feminism is a lot of frenzied and over-worked women dropping kids off at day-care centers. If the child is sick, they just send along some children's Tylenol and then rush off to underpaid jobs that they don't even like. Two of my working-mother friends told me they were mopping floors and folding laundry after midnight last week. They live on five hours of sleep, and it shows in their faces. And they've got husbands! I'm not advocating that women retrogress to the brainless housewives of the '50s who spent afternoons baking macaroni sculptures and keeping Betty Crocker files. Post-World War II women were the first to be left with a lot of free time, and they weren't too creative in filling it. Perhaps feminism was a reaction to that bored housewife, especially as she was portrayed in the media. In that respect, feminism has served a purpose.

Women should get educations so they can be brainy in the way they raise their children. Women can start small businesses, do consulting, write freelance out of the home. But women don't belong in 12-hour-a-day executive office positions, and I can't figure out today what ever made us think we would want to be there in the first place. As long as that biology is there, women can't compete equally with men. A ratio cannot be made using disproportionate parts. Women and men are not equal, we're different. The economy might even improve if women came home, opening up jobs for unemployed men, who could then support a wife and children, the way it was, pre-feminism.

Sometimes on Saturday nights I'll get dressed up and go out club-hopping or to the theater, but the sight of all those other women my age, dressed a little too young, made up to hide encroaching wrinkles, looking hopefully into the crowds, usually depresses me. I end up coming home, to spend my Saturday night with my daughter asleep in her room nearby. At least NBC Saturday-night lineup is geared demographically to women at home alone.

A former editor-in-chief and government public information officer, Kay Ebeling is now a single mother of a three-year-old daughter. Her eighteen-year-old son has lived with his father since age five, when Ebeling went to work full time. "It was really ironic," Ebeling says. "I gave up custody of my son so I could pursue the feminist dream of an 'unfettered' career. Then I became a workaholic, trying to find the gratification on the job that I lost by giving up my son." She now writes freelance out of her home and does occasional child-care so she can earn a living and still be a full-time "stay-at-home" mother.

A MAN AND HIS EMOTIONS

16

A Man and His Mid-Life Years

You'll recall that we began our discussion in the first chapter by looking at my own mid-life "reassessment" and some of the reactions of my friends during this unsettling period. We have not, as yet, examined the experience known as a mid-life crisis or the forces that unleash it. The question we must answer is, why do so many men have to bump their heads on the same old rock?

To explain the meaning of mid-life crisis, let's first consider a child at the moment of birth. Though he has just arrived on the scene, a great deal can be anticipated about his next twenty years. We can predict, with a high degree of accuracy, that he will experience most of the same periods of stress and conflict that other boys and girls have encountered. He'll toddle through the terrible twos, then glide into the more tranquil elementary school years before being besieged by puberty. The period of early adolescence is likely to be stormy, followed a few years later by the frightening experience of leaving home. This perilous journey from birth to adulthood has been studied exhaustively and mapped inch by inch. There are very few surprises within the science of child development today.

However, we have only recently begun to recognize that *adulthood* is also characterized by predictable periods of tranquility and stress. The journey is not as well charted for men and women as it has been for children, of course, but the map is beginning to take shape. It is now apparent that the mature years continue to be characterized by alternating periods of equilibrium and disequilibrium, and that the human experience offers remarkable similarities from person to person. The Apostle Paul referred to this commonality when he wrote, "There hath no temptation taken you but such as is common to man" (1 Cor. 10:13, KJV).

Other books have attempted to map the entire journey from youth to old age, (i.e., *Passages* by Gail Sheehy, and *Stages* by John Claypool). Our concern here will be limited to that brief stretch of road known as the mid-life years, which can be particularly bumpy for everyone on board. Both males and females can expect to be jostled and jarred while traveling that unpaved section of the highway. Women experience these stresses during the disequilibrium of menopause, when reproductive activity is waning.

For this discussion, however, our emphasis will be on the *male* in mid-life crisis. It is a vitally important topic, especially to those men who are approaching their third and fourth (or possibly fifth) decades on this earth. Lee Stockford reported the findings of three studies involving more than 2100 persons and concluded that 80 percent of the executives between 34 and 42 years of age experience a mid-life trauma of some variety. This estimate is consistent with my own observations, especially among highly motivated, successful business and professional men.

To men and their wives who want a better understanding of the stresses I've described, I enthusiastically recommend Jim Conway's excellent book, *Men in Mid-Life Crisis*. Dr. Conway is a minister who went through his own mid-life nightmare and survived to tell the story. His book is the best

I have read on the subject and will be helpful to those who have reached that stage of their journey.

After Conway's book came to my attention, I devoted several radio programs to its theme. A literal avalanche of mail and phone calls poured into my office the following month. Men wrote to say, "I am there," and wives asked, "How can I help my husband through this awful experience?"

With Dr. Conway's permission, I have chosen to review the major concepts from his book* and then add my own suggestions and interpretations. Let's begin with the basic question, "What is a mid-life crisis?" It is a time of intense personal evaluation when frightening and disturbing thoughts surge through the mind, posing questions about who I am and why I'm here and what it all matters. It is a period of self-doubt and disenchantment with everything familiar and stable. It represents terrifying thoughts that can't be admitted or revealed even to those closest to us. These anxieties often produce an uncomfortable separation between loved ones at a time when support and understanding are desperately needed.

Conway identifies four major "enemies" which plague a man entering his mid-life years. The first is his own body. There is no doubt about it; that guy who thought he would be perpetually young is now growing older. His hair is falling out, despite desperate attempts to coddle and protect every remaining strand. "Me, bald?" he shudders. Then he notices he doesn't have the stamina he once had. He begins getting winded on escalators. Before long, words assume new meanings for him. "The rolling stones" are in his gall bladder and "speed" (which once referred to amphetamines or fast driving) is his word for prune juice. He takes a business trip and the stewardess offers him "coffee, tea, or milk of magnesia." The cells in his face then pack up and run south for the winter, leaving a shocked and depressed man standing two inches from the mirror in disbelief.

---

*The following discussion excerpted from *Men in Mid-Life Crisis* by Jim Conway, © 1978 David C. Cook Publishing Co., Elgin, Ill. 60120. Used by permission.

I'm kidding, of course, but not much. If you think only women get depressed over evidence of aging, then you know little about the male of the species. It is also disturbing to most men to realize they will soon lose their appeal to the opposite sex . . . that physical power and vitality are declining . . . that the golden age of youth has come and gone. This awareness becomes undeniable during the period between thirty-five and forty years of age. Until then, an athletic man can still compete in basketball or tennis or baseball with his younger friends. But suddenly, for reasons which I can't explain, the deterioration becomes more noticeable in this Valley of the Shadow. Those who disagree have simply been too busy to recognize the decline. Even the best and most durable of professional athletes usually end their careers in their thirty-sixth or thirty-seventh years, not by choice but by the onset of huffing and puffing.

Consider the record of Muhammad Ali, who was the world heavyweight boxing champion at thirty-five, but had been whipped by a boy (Leon Spinks) at thirty-six and was retired at thirty-seven. Jerry West and John Havlicek, who at thirty-five were two of the best guards in NBA history, were both out of business at thirty-seven. John McEnroe and Jimmy Connors went the way of all flesh, too, as did Sugar Ray Leonard and Marvelous Marvin Hagler. The pattern is repeated dozens of times every year. A superstar who consistently wowed the fans *suddenly* gets too old to compete. And another jock waves good-bye to the crowd.

Those of us who earn our living in nonathletic pursuits are less vulnerable to aging, but deep inside we also know things are changing. Our fathers often experience their first cardiac problems when we are in our middle decades, which makes us nervous about the time bombs ticking within our own chests. A deodorant commercial asks, "Where will you be when it stops working?" Every middle-aged man has posed that question about his heart. Some, like myself, have experienced "The Attack."

To summarize this first great concern of the mid-life years, a man approaching forty is forced to admit (1) he is getting older; (2) the changes produced by aging are neither attractive nor convenient; (3) in a world that equates human worth with youth and beauty, he is about to suffer a personal devaluation; and (4) old age is less than two decades away, bring eventual sickness and death. When a man confronts this package for the first time, he is certain to experience an emotional reverberation of *some* type.

The second enemy facing a man in his mid-life years is his work. He typically resents his job and feels trapped in the field he has chosen. Many blue- and white-collar workers wish they'd had the opportunity to study medicine or law or dentistry. Little do they realize that physicians and attorneys and orthodontists often wish they had selected less demanding occupations . . . jobs that didn't impose the constant threat of malpractice suits . . . jobs that could be forgotten on evenings and weekends . . . jobs that left time for recreation and hobbies. This occupational unrest at all socioeconomic levels reaches a peak of intensity in the middle years, when a new awareness of life's brevity makes men reluctant to squander a single day that remains. But, on the other hand, they have little choice. The financial needs of their families demand that they keep pressing . . . so the kids can go to college . . . so the house payment can be met . . . so the lives they have known can continue . . . so they can support their aging parents. Thus, their emotions are caught in an ever-tightening vise.

A man's common reaction to this frustration is to seek an escape. Some husbands run away without telling their loved ones where they're going. Others make a radical change in employment, perhaps losing years of retirement benefits or seniority. But the majority hang tough. They just complain and get depressed and threaten to quit . . . but they'll be on the job tomorrow morning. If you listen closely you'll hear them mutter, "I don't wanna but I gotta!"

We should consider one other aspect of a man's work during his mid-life years, relating to his dreams. When he was young, he fully expected to be the President, or at least a millionaire by the time he was thirty. But as time begins to run out, he realizes not only that he'll never achieve his fantasy, but that his *present* accomplishment probably represents the high-water mark for his life. Yes, Virginia, *this* is it! We can easily see why Conway identified a man's work as his enemy during this period of transition.

The third enemy that rises to confront a middle-aged man is believe or not, his own family. These stormy years of self-doubt and introspection can be devastating to marriage. Such a man often becomes angry and depressed and rebellious toward those closest to him. He resents the fact that his wife and kids need him. No matter how hard he works, they always require more money than he can earn, and that agitates him further. At a time when he is in a selfish mood, wanting to meet his own needs, it seems that every member of the family is pulling on him. Even his parents have now become his financial and emotional responsibility. Again, he is seized by the urge to run.

At this delicate point in a man's life, Satan reaches into his ugly bag of tricks and retrieves the most foul of all his suggestions: adultery. What a vile alternative to plant in the troubled mind of a husband and father at this time of disenchantment. That pretty little secretary, who has serious emotional needs of her own, possesses enormous power to soothe his wounds and patch his pride. She offers the ultimate escape from the entrapment of mid-life. But what a price she and her lover will pay for their illicit adventure. When their fling has run its course, they must face the spouses they have betrayed and the children they have abandoned and the God they have disobeyed. The consequences of their sin will reverberate through eternity, hurting the innocent as certainly as the guilty.

Conway informs us that King David's affair with Bathsheba, leading ultimately to the murder of her husband, actually began with a severe mid-life crisis. Indeed, David's writings do reveal the classic struggles of a middle-aged man. He wrote in Palms: "for my days disappear like smoke. . . . My life is passing swiftly as the evening shadows. I am withering like grass. . . . He has cut me down in middle life, shortening my days" (Ps. 102:3, 11, 23, TLB).

At this point of vulnerability, David, who was on the roof, happened to see Bathsheba as she bathed. The rest of the sordid story is history. It was to be the one black mark on David's record, according to the unflinching assessment written in 1 Kings 15:5 (TLB): "For David had obeyed God during his entire life except for the affair concerning Uriah the Hittite" (Uriah was Bathsheba's husband whom David murdered after learning of her pregnancy).

It is important to understand that David and Bathsheba fell into this sin because they were *ripe* for an affair. David, who had literally hundreds of wives and concubines, was entitled to possess any unmarried woman in the land. Instead, he wanted Uriah's wife—not because *she* was different, but because *he* was different. His damaged ego needed what she could offer at that precise time. And as for Bathsheba, remember that her husband was away at war. She was probably lonely and depressed on that night of passion. Why else was she bathing in full view of the king?

Conway's point, which is undeniable, is that a man and woman commit adultery when they are emotionally *ready* for it. As he said, "Invariably, a set of circumstances sets them up, like David, and they think of the affair as a way to satisfy the discontent they feel." Let the reader beware.

The fourth and final enemy of a man in mid-life crisis appears to be God Himself. Through a strange manipulation of logic, man blames the Creator for all his troubles, approaching Him with rebellion and anger. In return, he feels condemned and abandoned and unloved by God. The consequence is a weakened faith and a crumbling system of beliefs. This explains, more than any other factor, the radical changes in behavior that often accompany the struggles of middle life.

Let me give this latter point the strongest possible emphasis. One of the most common observations made by relatives and friends of a man in mid-life crisis reflects this sudden reversal of personality and behavior.

"I don't understand what happened to Loren," a wife will say. "He seemed to change overnight from a stable, loving husband and father to an irresponsible rogue. He quit going to church. He began openly flirting with other women. He lost interest in our sons. Even his clothing became modish and flamboyant. He started combing his hair forward to hide his baldness and he bought a new sports car that we couldn't afford. I just can't figure out what suddenly came over my dependable husband."

This man has obviously experienced the changes we have described, but his *basic* problem is spiritual in nature. As his system of beliefs disintegrated, then his commitment to related Biblical concepts was weakened accordingly. Monogamy, fidelity, responsibility, life after death, self-denial, Christian witnessing, basic honesty, and dozens of other components of his former faith suddenly became invalid or suspect. The result was a rapid and catastrophic change in lifestyles which left his family and friends in a state of confusion and shock. This pattern has occurred for thousands of families in recent years.

Let's turn our attention now from a description of the problem to a few suggestions for those who have experienced these difficulties. Returning to my prior recommendation, I would urge everyone (male and female) to read Conway's book. He devoted a 300-page manuscript to a topic I could only address in a chapter or two. In the final pages of *Men in Mid-Life Crisis,* Conway lists ten suggestions under the heading "What seemed to help me." There he discusses the therapeutic value of exercise, new challenges, music, talking, rest, Bible reading and prayer in reestablishing one's equilibrium. I will not repeat those concepts here, choosing instead to emphasize two factors which Conway may have understated.

First, I want to give *hope* directly to the man in mid-life crisis. Just as behavioral scientists were able to predict that you would journey into this troubling era, we can also anticipate your emergence from it. An analogy to adolescence is helpful at this point: both periods are relatively short-term, age-related times of transition which produce intense anxiety, self-doubt, introspection, and agitation. Fortunately, however, neither adolescence nor the mid-life years represent permanent traps which hold victims captive. Rather, they can be thought of as doors through which we must all pass and from which we will all emerge. What I'm saying is that *normality will return* (unless you make some disruptive mistakes in a desperate attempt to cope).

Second, I feel the need to stress what I consider to be *the* fundamental cause of a mid-life crisis. It results from what the Bible refers to as "building your house upon the sand." It is possible to be a follower of Jesus Christ and accept His forgiveness from sin, yet still be deeply influenced by the values and attitudes of one's surrounding culture. Thus, a young Christian husband and father may become a workaholic, a hoarder of money, a status-seeker, a worshiper of youth, and a lover of pleasure. These tendencies may not reflect his conscious choices and desires; they merely represent the stamp of society's godless values on his life and times.

Despite his unchristian attitudes, the man may appear to "have it all together" in his first fifteen years as an adult, especially if he is successful in early business pursuits. But he is in considerable danger. Whenever we build our lives on values and principles that contradict the time-honored wisdom of God's Word, we are laying a foundation on the sand. Sooner or later, the storms will howl and the structure we have laboriously constructed will collapse with a mighty crash.

Stated succinctly, a mid-life crisis is more likely to be severe for those whose values reflect the temporal perspectives of this world. A man does not mourn the loss of his youth, for example, if he honestly believes that his life is merely a preparation for a better one to follow. And God does not become the enemy of a man who has walked and talked with Him in daily communion and love. And the relationship between a man and his wife is less strained in the mid-life years if they have protected and maintained their friendship since they were newlyweds. In short, the mid-life crisis represents a day of reckoning for a lifetime of wrong values, unworthy goals, and ungodly attitudes.

Perhaps this explains my observation that most men in the throes of a mid-life crisis are long-term workaholics. They have built their mighty castles on the sandy beach of materialism, depending on money and status and advancement and success to meet all their needs. They reserved no time for wife, children, friends or God. Drive ! Push! Hustle! Scheme! Invest! Prepare! Anticipate! Work! Fourteen-hour days were followed by weekends at the office and forfeited vacations and midnight oil. Then after twenty years of this distorted existence, they suddenly have cause to question the value of it all. "Is this really what I want to do with my life?" they ask. They realize too late that they have frantically climbed the ladder of success, only to discover that it was leaning against the wrong wall.

Perhaps the reader now understands why I have attacked this overcommitted lifestyle throughout my book. In Western custom, it is the villain that destroys marriage, Christian devotion, emotional health, and the well-being of children. In my opinion, overwork is the sour note in the symphony of American values. It can even make a forty-year-old man want to run and hide.

Across the fields of yesterday
He sometimes come to me
A little lad just back from play
The boy I used to be

He smiles at me so wistfully
When once he's crept within
It is as though he had hoped to see
The man I might have been

Author unknown

17

A Man and His Emotions

Have you ever stood outdoors near the end of a day and heard the whining sound of a mosquito flying past your ear?

"I'll bet I'm about to get punctured," you think.

Just then, you feel the creature light on your forearm and you immediately glance downward. But to your surprise, the insect is not there. You merely imagined that you had been invaded.

Or in another context, have you ever awakened after a frightening dream, lying breathless in your bed? You listened to the sounds of the night, wondering if the dream was based on reality. Then suddenly, just as you expected, there was a "bump" coming from the dark side of the house. An hour later you concluded that no one was actually there.

Emotions are powerful forces within the human mind. Fear, especially, has a remarkable way of generating evidence to support itself. Physicians and psychologists in clinical practice spend a large portion of their time convincing people that their self-diagnoses are not accurate, that their symptoms are imaginary or psychosomatic.

Even the young and the brave experience such deception. My good friend Steve Smith won a bronze star for courage in Vietnam combat. However, the first night his unit arrived in the war-torn country was not to be remembered for remarkable valor. His company had never seen actual combat, and the men were terrified. They dug foxholes on a hill and nervously watched the sun disappear beyond the horizon. At approximately midnight, the enemy attacked as anticipated. Guns began to blaze on one side of the mountain, and before long all the soldiers were firing frantically and throwing hand grenades into the darkness. The battle raged throughout the night and the infantry appeared to be winning. Finally, the long-awaited sun came up and the body count began. But not one single dead Viet Cong lay at the perimeter of the mountain. In fact, not one enemy soldier had even participated in the attack. The company of green troops had fought the night in mortal combat . . . and won.

Permit me one further example of emotions that overruled reason. The city of Los Angeles was paralyzed with fear in 1969, when Charles Manson and his "family" murdered Sharon Tate and her friends and then butchered Leno and Rosemary La Bianca in cold blood. Residents wondered who would be next. My mother was quite convinced that she was the prime candidate. Sure enough, Mom and Dad heard the intruder as they lay in bed one night. "Thump!" went the sound from the area of the kitchen.

"Did you hear that?" asked my mother.

"Yes, be quiet," said my father.

They lay staring at the darkened ceiling, breathing shallowly and listening for further clues. A second "thump" brought them to their feet. They felt their way to the bedroom door, which was closed. At this point, we are shown a key difference between how my mother and my father faced a crisis. Mom's inclination was to hold the door shut to keep the intruder from entering the bedroom. Thus, she propped her foot against the bottom of the door and threw her weight against the upper section. My father's approach was to confront the attacker head on. He reached through the darkness and grasped the doorknob, but his pull met the resistance from my mother.

My father assumed someone was holding the door shut from the other side. My terrified mother, on the other hand, could feel the killer trying to force the door open. My parents stood there in the pitch blackness of midnight, struggling against one another and imagining themselves to be in a tug of war with a murderer. Mother then decided to abandon ship. She released the door and ran to the window to scream at the top of her lungs. She took a great breath of air with which to summon the entire city of Pasadena, when she realized a light was on behind her. Turning around, she saw that my dad had gone into the other part of the house in search of their attacker. Obviously, he was able to open the door when she released it. In reality, there was no prowler. The thumps were never identified and Charles Manson never made his anticipated visit.

Let me personalize the issue at hand. What imaginary fears are *you* supporting with contrived evidence? What role do rampant, uncontrolled emotions play in your life? It is likely that what you feel, right or wrong, is a powerful force in determining your behavior day by day. Emotional experience in the Western world has become *the* primary motivation of values and actions and even spiritual beliefs. Furthermore, (and this is the point), we are living in a day when we are being encouraged to release our emotions . . . to grant them even greater power in ruling our destinies. Even in the nineties, we still see the evidences of the selfishness of prior decades, urging us to "go for it" . . . to give free reign to the urges within. Debbie Boone's popular song for the seventies, "You Light Up My Life," carried this phrase, "It can't be wrong, 'cause it *feels* so right." (Hitler's murder of the Jews probably felt right to the Nazis at the time.) Most love songs, in fact, make it clear that a commitment to one another is based on the excitement the couple shares. Thus, when the thrill evaporates, so does the relationship. By contrast, the greatest piece of literature ever written on the subject of love, the 13th chapter of 1 Corinthians, includes not a single reference to feelings: "Love is very patient and kind, never jealous or envious, never boastful or proud, never haughty or selfish or rude. Love does not demand its own way. It is not irritable or touchy. It does not hold grudges and will hardly even notice when others do it wrong" (1 Cor. 13:4–5, TLB).

One of the most destructive and foolish social movements of this century was the so-called Discovery of Personhood, which sought to free our emotions from restraint and inhibition. This pop-psyche movement, so prevalent in San Francisco and other California cities in the past, encourages us to get in touch with our feelings . . . to open up . . . to tell it like it is. We've come through an emphasis on "encounter groups," where participants were urged to attack one another and cry and scream and remove their clothes and even whack each other with foamy "encounter bats." Great stuff.

I have no desire to return our culture to the formality of the nineteenth century, when father was a marble statue and mother couldn't smile because her corset was too tight. But if our grandparents represented one extreme of emotional repression, contemporary man has become a temperamental yo-yo at the other.We live and breathe by the vicissitudes of our feelings, and for many, the depression of the "lows" is significantly more prevalent than the elation of the "highs." Reason is now *dominated* by feelings, rather than the reverse, as God intended. "But when the Holy Spirit controls our lives he will produce this kind of fruit in us: love, joy, peace, patience, kindness, goodness, faithfulness, gentleness and *self-control*" (Gal. 5:22, TLB, emphasis added).

This need for *self-control* is emphasized by the difficulties and stresses that occur in the lives of virtually every human being on earth. As Mark Twain said, "Life is just one darn thing after another." It's true. At least once every two weeks, someone gets a chest cold or the roof springs a leak or the car throws a rod or an ingrown toenail becomes infected or a business crisis develops. Those minor frustrations are inevitable. In time, of course, more significant problems develop. Loved ones die and catastrophic diseases appear and life slowly grinds to a conclusion. This is the nature of human experience, whether we like it or not. That being true, nothing could be more dangerous than to permit our emotions to rule our destinies. To do so is to be cast adrift in the path of life's storms.

It is possible not only to survive in a crisis, but actually to thrive on it. No better example exists than in the person of Dr. Stephen Hawking, an astrophysicist at the University of Cambridge in England. He is generally believed to be the most brilliant scientist since Einstein, and certainly, the most gifted theoretical astronomer now living. What may not be known, however, is that Dr. Hawking has a progressive neuromuscular disease called amyotrophic lateral sclerosis. (ALS is the disease that took the life of Yankee baseball player Lou Gehrig.) Hawking is confined to a wheelchair and can no longer move his arms or legs. His body has deteriorated to where he can "speak" only with the aid of a computer. His attempts to communicate have become so labored that those who don't know him think he has expressed an entire thought, when in fact, he's only spoken a few words. He is too weak to write, feed himself, comb his hair, or fix his glasses. *Omni Magazine* said this about him: "Hawking . . . can do little but sit and think. His mind is a blackboard. He memorizes the long strings of equations that give life to his ideas, then dictates the results to his colleagues or secretary—a feat that has been compared to Beethoven's writing an entire symphony in his head."

The article in *Omni Magazine* then quoted Dr. Hawking as he assessed his reaction to the illness. I can't forget his words. He said that before he was stricken with the disease, he was bored with his profession and with life in general. Nothing interested or motivated him. He drank too much and did little work. Then came the catastrophic illness and his attitudes changed dramatically. The privilege of living became especially precious to him. Speaking of this awakening, Dr. Hawking said, "When one's expectations [for life] are reduced to zero, one really appreciates everything that one does have."*

What a tremendous insight! The human emotional apparatus is constructed so as to disregard that which is taken for granted. Good health, delicious food, pleasant entertainment, peaceful circumstances, and beautiful homes are of little consequence to those who have had them since birth. Can you recall seeing a healthy teenager get up in the morning and express appreciation because his joints didn't hurt, or his vision was excellent, or because he breathed with ease or he felt so good? Not likely. He has never known the meaning of prolonged pain or sickness, and he accepts his good health without even considering it. But when those greatest of life's blessings begin to vanish, our appreciation for them increases accordingly. For a man like Stephen Hawking, who now faces continued physical deterioration and premature death, the whole world assumes new significance: the beauty of a tree, the privilege of watching a sunset, the company of loved ones—it all takes on meaning.

Let's apply this concept to the American way of life, which will explain many of the emotional problems and psychiatric symptoms which beset us. We have been taught to anticipate the finest and best from our existence on this earth. We feel almost entitled, by divine decree, to at least seventy-two years of bliss, and anything less than that is a cause for great agitation. In other words, our *level of expectation* is incredibly high.But life rarely delivers on that promise. It deals us disappointment and frustration and disease and pain and loneliness, even in the best of circumstances. Thus, there is an inevitable gap between life as it is and life as it ought to be.

The result is a high incidence of depression, especially among women, and an unacceptable rate of suicide, especially among the young, and a general anxiety among the rest

*Dennis Overbye, *Omni Magazine*, February 1979, p. 46.

of us. I have watched men develop ulcers over relatively insignificant business reverses. I have seen women suffer daily agitation over the most minor inconveniences, such as having too small a house or a cranky neighbor, when every other dimension of their lives was without a blemish.

Compare the instability of such individuals with the attitudes of German families near the close of World War II. Every night, a thousand British bombers would unload their destructive cargo over Hamburg and Berlin and Munich. By day, the American planes would do the same. Loved ones were dying on all sides. Neighborhoods were shattered and burned. Little children were maimed and killed. There was not enough food to eat and the water was polluted. The fabric of their lives was shredded. Yet historians tell us that their morale remained intact until the end of the war. They did not crack. They went about the business of reordering their homes and making the best of a horrible situation.

How can we account for this courage in the face of disaster, as compared with affluent North Americans who, though they have everything, are wringing their hands in the offices of psychiatrists? The difference, in the words of Stephen Hawking, is in our level of expectations. The Germans expected to sacrifice and experience suffering. They were, therefore, prepared for the worst when it came. But we are vulnerable to the slightest frustration, because we have been taught that troubles could be avoided. We have permitted our emotions to rule us, and in so doing, we have become mere slaves to our feelings.

Even Christian ministers have contributed to this distortion. "Become a follower of Christ and end your troubles," goes the sales pitch. "You can prosper in your business . . . and, in fact, if you'll utter the right noises to God, He'll make you rich. You can avoid all sickness and all injury and all physical malfunctions." It's quite a package, when you think about it.

Unfortunately, the promise is unscriptural. Jesus said, "In the world, ye *shall* have tribulation: but be of good cheer; I have overcome the world" (John 16:33, KJV, emphasis added).

Christianity has always been *future*-oriented. "And God shall wipe away all tears from their eyes; and there shall be no more death, neither sorrow, nor crying, neither shall there be any more pain: for the former things are passed away" (Rev. 21:4, KJV). Nowhere does the Bible promise such ease and bliss in this life, however. In fact, the Scripture indicates just the opposite—that trials are sent our way so that we can grow and become stronger. Those who hold tenaciously to the other point of view—that God is obligated to remove every source of stress—must explain why He permitted John the Baptist to be falsely accused and beheaded, and why the Apostle Paul spent so much time in dungeons. They must also interpret the following Scripture written in Hebrews 11:35–39, TLB:

> But others trusted God and were beaten to death, preferring to die rather than turn from God and be free—trusting that they would rise to a better life afterwards.
>
> Some were laughed at and their backs cut open with whips, and others were chained in dungeons. Some died by stoning and some by being sawed in two; others were promised freedom if they would renounce their faith, then were killed with the sword. Some went about in skins of sheep and goats, wandering over deserts and mountains, hiding in dens and caves. They were hungry and sick and ill-treated—too good for this world. And these men of faith, though they trusted God and won his approval, none of them received all that God had promised them.

I am reminded of Job, in the Old Testament, who lost all his possessions and his children. Then his health deteriorated. There he was, sitting on the ground, covered with boils, lonely for his family, impoverished, rejected by his friends, and wondering whatever happened to God. But in that hour of blackness when every imaginable misfortune had befallen him, his faith did not falter. His spirit did not break. Instead, he looked upward from his misery and said, "Though he slay me, yet will I trust him" (Job 13:15, KJV). That, for all times, is the classic example of a man's intellect and his will refusing to capitulate to emotion and circumstances.

Summary

Much has been written about the need for men to get in touch with their feelings—to be willing (and able) to cry and love and hope. These suggestions are valid. As we will see in a subsequent chapter, my father, who symbolized masculinity for me, was a very tender man who was not ashamed to weep. I certainly am not suggesting that men display a phony cheerfulness when they are dying inside. Nevertheless, there are dangers in permitting emotions to rule our minds. Feelings must not dominate rational judgment, especially in times of crisis, not should we allow the minor frustrations of living to produce depression and despair.

Though I hope never to experience the measure of sorrow suffered by Job and the biblical martyrs, I want to adopt their steadfastness when trouble, such as a heart attack, comes my way. Likewise, as the head of my family, I want to lower our level of expectations in anticipation of the winter. As Dr. Hawking indicated, life will take on new meaning if we are successful in that endeavor.

Footprints

> One night a man had a dream. He dreamed he was walking along the beach with the Lord. Across the sky flashed scenes from his life. For each scene, he noticed two sets of footprints in the sand: one belonging to him and the other to the Lord.
>
> When the last scene of his life flashed before him, he looked back at the footprints in the sand. He noticed that many times along the path of his life there was only one set of footprints. He also noticed that it happened at the very lowest and saddest times in his life.
>
> This really bothered him and he questioned the Lord about it. "Lord, you said that once I decided to follow you, you'd walk with me all the way. But I have noticed that during the most troublesome times in my life, there is only on set of footprints. I don't understand why when I needed you the most you would leave me."

The Lord replied, "My son, my precious child, I love you and I would never leave you. During your times of trial and suffering, when you see only one set of footprints, it was then that I carried you."

Author unknown

18

A Man and His Animals

Proverbs 12:10 says "A righteous man cares for his animal(s), but the kindest acts of the wicked are cruel." It makes sense, doesn't it? Anyone who would care about the welfare of a helpless dog or cat or cow is likely to have a soft spot for hurting people, as well. My dad was such a man. He loved everything God made, especially furry little canines called toy terriers.

Penny was a brilliant representative of that breed. We adopted him into our family when I was thirteen years of age, and the two of us grew up together. By the time I left for college, he was established as a full-fledged member of the Dobson household, with all the rights and privileges thereof. He and my dad had a special understanding for one another, like two old friends who could communicate deep feelings without uttering a word. Only dog lovers will fully comprehend what I mean.

But alas, Penny grew old and decrepit. At seventeen years of age, he was afflicted with a terminal case of cancer and was obviously experiencing severe pain. He would walk the fence and moan hour after hour. My dad knew the time had come to put his little friend to sleep, but he couldn't bring himself to do it.

"How can I kill my dog?" he would ask.

But it was more cruel to let Penny suffer. So Dad made an appointment with the veterinarian at the humane society to discuss the matter. The doctor was a perceptive man and recognized how painful this event was for my father. He shared a similar situation with reference to his own dog, and these two grown men sat and wept together.

The decision was made to end Penny's life, and the day was chosen. Throughout the prior afternoon, a man and a dog sat together under the vine-covered arbor in their backyard. Neither spoke. (Penny communicated his thoughts with his ears and eyes and tail.) I suspect they both cried. Then they said good-bye for the final time.

When the moment came, Penny was given five barbituarates to prevent him from recognizing the despised smell of the animal hospital. My mother handed him to the attendant and then hurried back to the car. Dad was visibly shaken. For nearly a week, he sat alone under the arbor, going there immediately after fulfilling his teaching responsibilities at the college each day. He continued to grieve for Penny for several years.

During this time, we encouraged my father to get another dog, but he was reluctant to expose himself to another painful loss. Nine years passed before he considered trying to replace the memory of Penny.

But wait, why don't I let him tell you the story in his own words. The following narrative was written by my dad, shortly before his death.

Guaranteed Healthy

I like dogs. Some of my best friends are dogs! I sometimes think that I can communicate better with dogs than I can with people. At least I have never had a dog misunderstand me to the point of breaking up a friendship once it was established! I had grieved for my little toy terrior, Penny, for nine years. I said I would never get another dog. Some of this was due to the Judas Iscariot kind of guilt I was carrying. You see, I was forced by my very love for him to end his hopeless agony. I, his trusted keeper, betrayed him to his executioner! Penny, so gentle, so obedient, so intelligent! Gone was my constant companion of seventeen years! I miss him still and always will but "Nine years is enough," I told my wife. "I will get me another dog."

"You are just asking for more pain," she said. "A dog's life usually averages about eight to ten years—then you will have to go through this sorrow again."

"Maybe not," I said. "I have thought a lot about this decision. I will soon be over the hill myself. It could be that we will arrive at the Golden Gate at about the same time."

I decided to take great care in selecting this new pet. I wanted the same kind of dog, a toy terrier, but he would have to be pedigreed. Penny had been a lucky accident—a throwback more like his fox terrier ancestors. I know the breed and know, too, that beyond the AKC papers, you have to select the individual dog for intelligence and other desirable qualities. You have to get a pup by six weeks of age, to be sure he hasn't been ruined by someone else. Then he would have to be in perfect health, having had the necessary shots, etc.

All these thoughts were getting settled in my mind as I started watching the papers for dog advertisements. No luck. Someone would always beat me to the best dogs, since I wouldn't answer an ad on Sunday, and that's when thoroughbreds were offered. Finally, I saw a notice from a pet shop about a toy terrier, but I didn't take it seriously.

"There's something funny about this," I told my wife. "The ad says the dog is a nine-month-old thoroughbred, but he has no papers. Nine months in a pet shop and nobody wants him! It doesn't sound good to me. I wouldn't buy an unregistered dog anyway!" But later, I said, "Let's just drive out and see him."

We found the shop in a run-down section of the city. My wife was almost afraid to get out of the car. The business was in one room of an old abandoned house. When I stepped through the front door, the stench almost overwhelmed me. I spotted the dog in question at once. He was crowded into a cubicle with other larger puppies who were bumping him and stepping on his tiny body. They were a motley assortment of mongrels of various kinds, all yapping and defecating; some were trying to sleep away their misery, curled up on the wire bottom of their filthy enclosure!

When the saleslady brought the little toy terrier out and put him down on the floor he seemed to be in a wall-eyed trance.

"This dog has been through some traumatic emotional experience," I thought. He looked up at me with pitiful glazed eyes that reflected unspeakable sadness. Far from considering him, I couldn't believe anyone would offer an animal for sale in this condition. His skinny little frame, all four pounds of it, was trembling, and every few seconds he would cough and gag from some kind of chest infection. I thought I recognized this as a case of the dreaded distemper. Between coughs, he would dig frantically at his ears, which were infested with mites. He would follow me about the room, meekly, his tiny tail clamped tightly down—a picture of dejection.

"Nobody knows what other disease he has got—maybe incurable," I thought. "Oh, no! I'm not getting into that!" But in spite of myself I wanted to cry. He seemed to be saying, "You look like a nice man, but I know you will be like all the rest." He was so little and helpless and hopeless. While I was hardening myself to his unhappy fate with such reasoning as "It's not my fault . . . I can't turn my home into a dog hospital," he put out his warm pink tongue and licked my hand, as much to say, "Thanks, anyway, for coming to see me." I had to get out of there quick!

We were silent as we drove away. When we had gone a few blocks I made an instant decision. I guess it was the effect of that lick on the hand—the intuitive longing it expressed!

Wheeling the car around, I started back. I turned stone deaf to the neatly logical reasoning my wife poured into my ear. In a split second, instead of a nameless wart of a dog in a rotten pet shop, that had become my little dog in there, suffering and lonely and sick! I was bursting with compassion that should rightfully have been expended on a more worthy object: I know, God, please forgive me. I wrote the check and received in exchange a receipt for the money. On it were the incredible words, *"Guaranteed Healthy!"*

I folded the shivering form into my arms, stink and all. A warm bath soon removed the nauseating smell; then I took him to the best veterinarian I could find. He took one look and shook his head.

"I'll try, but I can't promise he will make it," he said. It was days of antibiotics for the cough, weeks of application of drops for the ear mites, worm medicine, shots of various kinds, a tonic to regulate that wildly beating little heart, and love made warm and tender by years of grieving for Penny. And to the astonishment of the doctor, most of all, we have a dog to be proud of, fit and sound.

And talk about gratitude! My pup, whom we named Benji, expresses it in the blasphemous, idolatrous way he worships me. He thinks I am God Almighty when he comes to meet me in the morning, twisting and wiggling like he will tear himself in two. It is as though he will never allow himself to forget his private hell in the pet shop!

Three years after this happy beginning, Benji was to lose his beloved master. He had seen my mother and father leave in the car one morning, but only one of them returned. No one could explain to him the meaning of death, of course. So Benji sat waiting month in and out, straining to hear the sound of that familiar voice. The shutting of a car door would bring him hope and excitement . . . followed by obvious disappointment. Wrong person, again.

I visited my mother several months after the funeral to help pack my father's possessions and give away his clothes.

As I busily folded coats and pants and placed them in a suitcase, Benji jumped on the bed. He reverently approached the clothes and sniffed them carefully on all sides. He climbed into the suitcase and curled up within one of my father's most familiar coats. Then he looked up at me.

"I understand, Benji. I miss him, too," I said.

Conclusion

Why have I included a story about a dog in a book about men? I guess I wanted to illustrate that husbands and fathers are entitled to feel and love and enjoy. Those like my father who can permit themselves the experience of deep emotions are much more vulnerable to the vicissitudes of life, admittedly, but their sensitivity is worth the price they pay for it.

A MAN AND HIS GOD

19

A Man and His God

One of my colleagues died during my last year at Children's Hospital, having served on our university medical faculty for more than twenty-five years. During his tenure as a professor, he had earned the respect and admiration of both professionals and patients, especially for his research findings and contribution to medical knowledge. This doctor had reached the pinnacle of success in his chosen field, and enjoyed the status and financial rewards that accompany such accomplishment. He had tasted every good thing, by the standards of the world.

At the next staff meeting following his death, a five-minute eulogy was read by a member of his department. Then the chairman invited the entire staff to stand, as is our custom in situations of this nature, for one minute of silence in memory of the fallen colleague. I have no idea what the other members of the staff contemplated during that sixty-second pause, but I can tell you what was going through my mind.

I was thinking, "Lord, is this what it all comes down to? We sweat and worry and labor to achieve a place in life, to impress our fellow men with our competence. We take ourselves so seriously, overreacting to the insignificant events of each passing day. Then finally, even for the brightest among us, all these experiences fade into history and our lives are summarized with a five-minute eulogy and sixty seconds of silence. It hardly seems worth the effort, Lord."

But I was also struck by the collective inadequacy of that faculty to deal with the questions raised by our friend's death. Where had he gone? Would he live again? Will we see him on the other side? Why was he born? Were his deeds observed and recorded by a loving God? Is that God interested in *me*? Is there meaning to life beyond investigative research and professorships and expensive automobiles? The silent response by two hundred and fifty learned men and women seemed to symbolize our inability to cope with these issues.

Then a wave of relief spread over me as I thought about the message of Christianity and the meaning of the cross. This Good News provides the *only* satisfactory explanation for why we're here and where we're going. The final heartbeat for the Christian is not the mysterious conclusion to a meaningless existence. It is, rather, the grand beginning to a life that will never end. That's why we can proclaim, even at the graveside of a loved one, "O death, where is thy sting? O grave, where is thy victory?" (1 Cor. 15:55, KJV).

How extremely important it is for the man of the home to know the answers to these perplexing questions, and be able to lead his family in the paths of righteousness. When he accepts that spiritual responsibility as God intends, the entire family is likely to follow his example. "And they said, Believe on the Lord, Jesus Christ, and thou shalt be saved, *and thy house*" (Acts 16:31, KJV, emphasis added). This issue is of such significance that I feel compelled to devote the balance of this chapter to the basic plan of salvation. Perhaps someone will comprehend the Christian message for the first time through reading these pages, which is my prayer.

I used to ponder a difficult theological question that appeared unanswerable at the time. It seemed strange that God would send His only Son, Jesus, to die in agony on the cross at Mount Calvary. I reasoned that God, as Creator of the universe, was in charge of everything. That entitled Him to make His own rules and establish His own boundaries. Therefore, it seemed to me that God could have provided *any* plan of salvation He chose—anything that suited His fancy.

It was illogical that God would create a system that would ultimately require the suffering and death of His own Son on the cross. I could not comprehend why He would put Himself through such grief and sorrows on our behalf when He could have offered a less costly plan of salvation. I struggled with this issue as a young Christian and was perplexed by the questions it raised. I knew all the pat answers given to me in Sunday school, and I could quote the Scriptures. But none of the interpretations satisfied me.

It is interesting to look back on the things that troubled us in earlier days. I now have a better understanding of God's plan of salvation and what motivated it. And the explanation is of great significance for me, because it deals with the very essence of Christianity.

Before reading my conclusion about God's plan, you should know that I am neither a minister nor a pastor nor a theologian. I can make no claims to theological expertise. I do, however, know a little Greek and a little Hebrew. The Greek owns a gas station in Los Angeles, and the Hebrew runs a delicatessen in San Diego. That's a very bad joke, but it illustrates the fact that I am admittedly unqualified to speak as a Biblical authority. However, this lack of theological training may help me communicate with other nontheologians in everyday language. If my explanation becomes a gross oversimplification for some people, I hope they'll forgive me.

Here, then, is my concept of the plan of salvation and why Jesus' death was necessary: It begins, as it should, with an understanding of God's nature. Throughout Scripture, the Almighty is represented by two uncompromising characteristics: *his love and His justice.* Both of these aspects are reflected in everything God does, and none of His actions will ever contradict either component.

The love and justice of God were especially evident when He created Adam and Eve. Obviously, He could have "programmed" them to love Him and obey His laws. This could have been accomplished by creating them as highly sophisticated robots or puppets. He did, in fact, program the brains of lower animals, causing birds to build a certain kind of nest and wolves to kill wounded elk. They have no choice in the matter.

Shirley and I used to have a wonderful little Dachshund named Siggie, who displayed an assortment of wired-in behavior about which *neither* of us had a choice. For example, he couldn't help barking when the front doorbell rang, even if I threatened to kill him for waking the baby. Nor could he keep from gobbling his food as though he would never get another meal. God had imposed instinctual behavior in Siggie (some of which I wanted to eliminate) which operated automatically and without learning.

But the Lord elected to put no instinctual behavior in mankind, leaving us free to learn. This explains the utter helplessness of human infants, who are the most dependent of all creatures at birth. They lack the initial advantages of unlearned responses but will later run circles around the brightest animals with "locked-in" reactions. Such is the nature of our humanness.

By granting us freedom of choice, therefore, God gave meaning to our love. He sought our devotion but refused to demand it. However, the moment He created this choice, it became inevitable that He would eventually be faced with man's sin. I've heard Christians speculate on what might have happened if Adam and Eve hadn't disobeyed God. The answer seems obvious. If they had not sinned, a subsequent generation would have. After all, if no one ever made the wrong choice, then there was no true choice to be made.

But Adam and Eve *did* sin, as we know, and thereby confronted God with the most serious dilemma of all time. His love for the human race was unlimited, which required that He forgive His disobedient children. The Bible says, "As a father pitieth his children, so the Lord pitieth them that fear him" (Ps. 103:13, KJV). That is an analogy I can comprehend. I know how I pity my children when they've done wrong. My inclination is to forgive them.

But in spite of God's great love, His justice required complete obedience. It demanded repentance and punishment for disobedience. So herein was a serious conflict with God's nature. If He destroyed the human race, as His justice would require in response to our sinful disobedience, His love would have been violated: but if He ignored our sins, His justice would have been sacrificed. Yet neither aspect of His nature could be compromised.

But God, in His marvelous wisdom, proposed a solution to that awful dilemma. If He could find one human being who wasn't worthy of damnation—just one individual in the history of mankind who had never sinned, a man or a woman who was not guilty—then the sin of every other person on earth could be laid upon that One and He could suffer for all of us. So God, being timeless, looked across the ages of man from Adam to Armageddon, but He could not find anyone who was innocent. "For all have sinned, and come short of the glory of God" (Rom. 3:23, KJV) it would later be written. There wasn't a person who was worthy of assuming the guilt, blame, and punishment for the rest of us. Therefore, the only alternative was for God to send His own Son to bear the sins of the entire human family. And herein we see the beauty of God's plan and the reason Jesus had to die. When He was crucified here on earth, Jesus harmonized the conflict between God's love and justice and provided a remedy for fallen mankind.

Thus, Jesus said as He was dying, "It is finished!" meaning, "I have carried out the plan of salvation that God designed for sinful man." And that's why God turned His back on Jesus when He was on the cross, prompting Him to cry in anguish, "My God, my God, why hast thou forsaken me?" (Matt. 27:46, KJV). In that moment, Jesus was bearing the punishment for all human sins down through the ages, including yours and mine.

This understanding of the plan of salvation is not based on guesses and suppositions, of course. It is drawn from the literal interpretation of God's Word. This message is, in fact, the primary theme of all Scripture. The Old Testament says, "Jesus is coming!" and the New Testament proclaims, "Jesus is here!" But if I had to select one passage to represent the concept I've presented, it would be the 53rd chapter of Isaiah (my favorite chapter in the Bible). It was written seven hundred years before the birth of Christ and provides an incredible prophecy of His mission. The summary of God's entire plan is presented in this one chapter. Let me quote it from *The Living Bible:*

> But oh, how few will believe it! Who will listen? To whom will God reveal his saving power? In God's eyes he was like a tender green shoot, sprouting from a root in dry and sterile ground. But in our eyes there was no attractiveness at all, nothing to make us want him. We despised him and rejected him—a man of sorrows, acquainted with bitterest grief. We turned our backs on him and looked the other way when he went by. He was despised and we didn't care.
>
> Yet it was *our* grief he bore, *our* sorrows that weighed him down. And we thought his troubles were a punishment from God, for his *own* sins! But he was wounded and bruised for *our* sins. He was chastised that we might have peace; he was lashed—and we were healed! *We* are the ones who strayed away like sheep! *We,* who left God's paths to follow our own. Yet God laid on *him* the guilt and sins of every one of us!
>
> He was oppressed and he was afflicted, yet he never said a word. He was brought as a lamb to the slaughter; and as a sheep before her shearers is dumb, so he stood silent before the ones condemning him. From prison and trial they led him away to his death. But who among the people of that day realized it was their sins that he was dying for—that he was suffering their punishment? He was buried like a criminal in a rich man's grave; but he had done no wrong, and had never spoken an evil word.

> Yet it was the Lord's good plan to bruise him and fill him with grief. But when his soul has been made an offering for sin, then he shall have a multitude of children, many heirs. He shall live again and God's program shall prosper in his hands. And when he sees all that is accomplished by the anguish of his soul, he shall be satisfied; and because of what he has experienced, my righteous Servant shall make many to be counted righteous before God, for he shall bear all their sins. Therefore I will give him the honors of one who is mighty and great, because he has poured out his soul unto death. He was counted as a sinner, and he bore the sins of many, and he pled with God for sinners (Isa. 53, TLB).

Isn't that a beautiful explanation of Jesus' purpose here on earth? It makes clear why God's plan necessarily involved His own Son—His grief and sorrow and death. Only by paying this incredible price could He harmonize the potential contradiction between love and justice, and provide a "way of escape" for mankind. It also explains why there is no other name by which we are saved and why we cannot escape if we neglect so great a salvation (Heb. 2:3).

One important question remains to be answered: Just how does a person proceed, now, to accept this plan and follow the risen Lord? I believe there are two basic steps in that process (although some churches emphasize only one). The first is to believe in the name of Jesus Christ. John 3:16 (KJV) says, "For God so loved the world, that he gave his only begotten Son, that whosoever believeth in him should not perish, but have everlasting life." Romans 10:13 (TLB) says it another way: "Anyone who calls upon the name of the Lord will be saved." So the first obligation for anyone is to accept what Christ did as being for him, personally.

But as I understand the Scripture, and from my own theological perspective, there's a second responsibility which is often underemphasized. James expressed it like this: "Are there still some among you who hold that 'only believing' is enough? Believing in one God? Well, remember that the demons believe this too—so strongly that they tremble in terror!

When will you ever learn that 'believing' is useless without *doing* what God wants you to do? Faith that does not result in good deeds is not real faith" (2:19, TLB). So something else is required. While it's true that you can't "work" your way into salvation—you cannot do enough good deeds to earn it—*repentance* is still an important part of the process.

"Repentance" is a word that's often misunderstood. What does it really mean? Billy Graham defined repentance as having three parts to it. The first is conviction. You have to know what is right before you can do what is right; and you have to know what is wrong in order to avoid those misbehaviors. Repentance also involves a deep awareness that you stand guilty before the Lord. I've seen people who call themselves Christians and say, "Yes, I believe in Jesus," but they seem to have no real comprehension or awareness of their own sin and guilt. They have no "contriteness" of heart. From the Scripture in James we see that even demons "believe and tremble"; *yet many individuals believe and do not tremble.*

But where does this spirit of repentance originate? It must come through the teaching of the Holy Spirit. Deuteronomy 4:29 says, "But if from thence [from this point forward] thou shalt seek the Lord thy God, thou shalt find him, if thou seek him with all thy heart and with all thy soul" (KJV). So you must want this relationship with God. He must be so important that you will allow Him to turn your life around and change your behavior. In summary, then, repentance includes conviction, knowing right from wrong; then contrition, being aware of your guilt and sin; and finally, a resulting change of mind and heart and behavior.

Time and space limitations make it impossible to discuss other important theological issues of relevance to salvation, including *confession* (Rom. 10:9–10) and *baptism* (Acts 22:16 and 2:38). Entire volumes have been written on a topic I have attempted to address in a single chapter. Perhaps I have, at least, provided a foundation from which the new believer can launch his own study of the Bible.

I think it would be helpful, in conclusion, to give an example of the kind of prayer that a person might pray if he understands what I've been writing and wants to accept Jesus Christ as his own Lord and Savior. Let me express it in this way:

> Lord, I bring you my sinful nature as you've revealed it to me. I know I don't have anything valuable to offer except myself and my love. I can't earn your forgiveness but you've offered it as a free gift from your Son, Jesus Christ. I accept your control of my life, and intend to serve You, obey You, and follow You from this moment forward. You have my past, my present, my future, my family, my money and my time. *Nothing* will I withhold. Thank you for loving me and forgiving me and making me your own. Amen.

Sanctuary

Through the mesquite brush in the evening hush
  Down a road that is dimly described
Past the dead cow's bones and the blackened stones
  Where the ghost of an Indian hides

Like a wild thing to drink at the windmill tank
  Winds the trail now disguised of intent
Down the dry gulch bed to the rise up ahead
  Where the wolf seeks the jackrabbit's scent

Yonder beck'ning spire is the windmill's tower
  Far away in the shimmering haze
Both cathedral and shrine is this derrick of mine
  Like my heart, lifting high, full of praise

See those galloping steeds, the tumbleweeds
  How they fret 'neath the barbed wire fence
Fastly hitched for this hour, they are shorn of their
    power
  Till the night wind shall call them hence.

Heaven's vesper song seems to call me along
  Through the purple and violet and blue
Congregation of one, to my God I have come

And the top of this tower is my pew

Up the weathered flank on the ladder's plank
To my perch near the wheel and the vane
Nor regret that my rest's taken hard by the nest
Of the hawk circling wide o'er the plain

Now the mill's rumbling throat yields a pipe-organ
note
Though some say it creaks and it scolds
To the wheel's waving palms, there's a giving of alms
As the sun turns the green into gold

Limpid waters outspill, with a lyrical rill
From the rusty old pipes down below
And my soul stands enawed, for the presence of God
Heavy rides on the evening glow

James C. Dobson, Sr.

20

A Man and His Death

How does a good man die? We are given numerous examples in the Scriptures which serve as inspiration to those who call themselves Christians. My favorite is the account of King David's final hours, when he asked that his beloved son Solomon be brought to his chambers. There, in the presence of witnesses, a father offered his concluding words of advice to the young man he had designated to succeed him. We can be certain that the statements made on that occasion carried great significance, for David was obviously conveying eternal truths to his son. A man is seldom casual or frivolous when staring death in the face. Thus, these words represent a summation of all that David believed and loved:

> And thou, Solomon my son, *know thou the God of thy father,* and serve him with a perfect heart and with a willing mind: for the Lord searcheth all hearts, and understandeth all the imaginations of the thoughts: *if thou seek him, he will be found of*

thee; but if thou forsake him, he will cast thee off forever (1 Chron. 28:9, KJV, emphasis added).

Every son should be so fortunate as to receive such profound advice from his father. Those sixty words contain all that a young man or woman should know to live a successful and meaningful life. Notice the precision of David's words. He did not instruct Solomon to get to know *about* God. He told him to become acquainted directly *with* God. The distinction is vital (I may know *about* Jimmy Carter and George Washington and Albert Einstein but I have never met them face to face). I am also impressed by David's reference to God's judgment for those who disobey His commandments: "But if thou forsake Him, He will cast thee off forever." That warning has eternal implications for you and me, as well.

We've seen how King David approached the benediction of his life on earth. Let me, now, offer a more contemporary example of how a good man dies. It is fitting that I devote these concluding words to my own father. He provided the inspiration for the entire book, as you must know by this point.

The last chapter in the life of my dad begins at Eastertime 1977, when my parents came to visit Shirley and me in California. I took several days off work and spent that time in pleasant conversation with our loved ones. At one point, I turned to my dad and asked spontaneously, "What do you want for an epitaph at the close of your life?"

He thought briefly and then replied, "Only two words: 'He prayed.'" I can think of no phrase that better summarized his devotion to God and the daily communion he maintained with Him. It is fitting that his final act on earth was to ask for God's blessing on the meal that had been prepared. Accordingly, those two words, "He prayed," appear on his footstone today.

I then turned to my mother and asked, "What epitaph do you want on your tombstone?" She had a rich sense of humor and immediately responded, "I told you I was sick!"

Her remark reminded me of the eighty-year-old man who said, "If I'd have known I was gonna live so long I'd have taken better care of myself!"

We enjoyed that week of laughter and fellowship with my parents, having no idea, of course, that this was to be the last trip my father would take. The clock was ticking down toward zero, with only eight months remaining.

Later in the year, as death approached, my dad was to experience two concluding revelations from God that moved him deeply. I learned about the first in a telephone conversation in September. We were talking about my upcoming television series and various topics of mutual interest. Then suddenly Dad said, "Well, there's one thing I know. God is going to take care of your mother."

I replied, "Yes, I'm sure He will," but wondered why he had chosen that occasion to make such a statement. Five days later, he suffered his near-fatal heart attack.

As my mother and I sat in the hospital waiting for news of his progress, I remembered his strange comment on the telephone. I shared his words with my mother and asked if she understood why he had chosen to tell me about her secure future.

"I know what he meant," she replied. She then told me that two weeks earlier, my dad had been resting on the bed while she worked around the room. She glanced at him and noticed that there were tears in his eyes.

"What's the matter?" she asked.

He paused for a few seconds and then said, "The Lord just spoke to me."

"Do you want to tell me about it?" she continued.

"It was about you!" replied my dad.

"Then you'd *better* tell me!" she said.

"It was a strange experience," said my dad. "I was just lying here thinking about many things. I wasn't praying or even thinking about you when the Lord spoke to me and said, 'I'm going to take care of Myrtle.'" They looked at each other in awe, wondering what it meant.

Five days later, they experienced the most severe trauma of their lives, and eighty-four days hence, my mother learned the meaning of widowhood.

Although many years have passed since the death of my father on that cold December day, the Lord's promise was not forgotten. I won't impose all the details on you. Let it simply be known that the God of my father comforted, provided for, and sustained the woman he left behind.

Of course, she continued to grieve for the man she loved. There is *no* painless way to lose a constant companion and friend of forty-three years. The early evening hours were especially lonely, and my mother used them to write poetry to the memory of her husband. I especially appreciated the following piece which she permitted me to share with you:

I Thought I Saw You Today

I thought I saw you today.
Standing with your hands in your pockets.
Laughing, the wind playing mischievously
    with your hair.
My heart lunged toward you as
You disappeared, leaving a total stranger
    standing there.
How could I have imagined the
    man to be my darling . . .
My precious darling.

Myrtle Dobson

It is the nature of things that *most* married women will eventually become widows. Thus, I'm sure that millions of women would understand perfectly the heartache my mother was conveying with these brief words.

I learned of my dad's second revelation on October 2, 1977, after he had been hospitalized for two weeks. I flew to Kansas City for a brief visit, which was to be the final time I would see him alive. He was brimming over with effervescence on that Sunday morning. He had so much he wanted to say to me. His medical progress appeared encouraging and he was anticipating being released from the hospital in a few days. Among weightier subjects, we discussed his little dog, Benji, who anxiously awaited the return of his master.

Then my dad became very serious. "There's something I want to try to describe to you," he said. "I had the most incredible experience the morning after my heart attack." He began weeping as he spoke.

I was concerned that his emotional state would affect his heart, and I asked him to wait and tell me later. He agreed and we let the matter drop. I had to leave the following day, and he died before our planned rendezvous at Christmas.

My dad did reveal the details of his experience to my mother and to a friend, Dr. Dean Baldwin, the week prior to his death. Furthermore, in going through his writings after death, I discovered a partially completed description of the event, in his own handwriting. The narrative that follows was taken from those three sources, describing a dramatic vision that he saw the morning after his heart attack. (Remember that his physicians had predicted he wouldn't live through that night.) These are his approximate words.

"It happened in the early morning hours when I was neither awake nor asleep. I was lying there in my quiet hospital room, when I suddenly saw the most beautiful person I'd ever seen. His identity was not immediately revealed, but I now believe Him to have been Jesus. This was no dream, in the classic sense. I was conscious of my circumstances, and the figure was extremely vivid. It was apparent that I was being permitted to observe a kind of courtroom scene—a divine proceeding—but my being there was as an onlooker. No word was addressed to me directly. The 'person' was seated and he was writing in a book. It seemed that he was considering an extremely important issue. Then I realized it was *my* case he was evaluating. The details of my life were being reviewed carefully. He stopped writing and began to plead my case directly to God. I have never heard such eloquent language as he described my circumstances, calling me by name repeatedly. Then he continued to write until he came to the bottom of the page, at which time he completed the last sentence and thrust his hand outward in a sudden gesture. Though no words were spoken, his motion and his countenance revealed his conclusion about my life. It said, 'For time and eternity, he is *acceptable!*'"

Dr. Baldwin reports that my father was weeping openly as he described this dramatic experience. Then he explained, with great feeling, that he was given a concluding message of major significance, but it was too personal to disclose. He could not even reveal it to my mother, with whom he shared everything. We can only guess that his impending death was foreseen in that incredible moment.

The vision then disappeared, leaving my dad in the gray, early morning light of the hospital room. He was so deeply affected by the experience that he made no attempt to tell anyone about it until my visit two weeks later. Even to the time of his death, he couldn't talk of the matter without crying.

Some would claim that my dad experienced a drug-induced dream in that hour. I don't believe it. My father, who was not given to mystical exaggeration, was emphatic that the vision had not been a hallucination or imaginary event. I will leave it for the reader to decide. There is one fact, however, of which I am certain. This man *was* found "acceptable" by his Maker. He had lived by an uncompromising standard of devotion to Jesus Christ. He had fought a good fight and kept the faith until the end.

The twenty-third Psalm promises the righteous that God will walk with them through the valley of the shadow of death. He certainly fulfilled that covenant on behalf of my father. And the life of this good man came to an end, only to continue in greater glory on the other side.

The passing of my dad has changed my own view of death. I still have an instinctual desire to live—especially since my work at home is incomplete—but I no longer perceive the end of life as the greatest of all tragedies. Now, I know I will be welcomed across the threshold by my old friend. I'm sure he will be so excited to show me the stars and planets and the heavenly city. I also expect him to introduce me, face to face, to the Lord I've tried to serve since I was three years old.

But for now, he is gone, and *I* am the one who is on trial in that divine courtroom. I am left with this prayer:

> Heavenly Father, I yearn to be the kind of husband and father that you desire of me. My highest ideal on this earth is to earn those words of approval, "Well done, thou good and faithful servant." Yet I feel so inadequate to discharge my responsibility properly. I know that my children's concept of you will be greatly influenced by how they perceive me, and that thought is terrifying. But I know you only expect me to do the best I can, and that thought is comforting. Thank you for the model you gave me in my father. Help me now to perpetuate that example before the children whom you have loaned to Shirley and me. And though I've said it before, keep the circle unbroken when we stand before Your throne.
>
> Finally, Lord, would you also give my dad a brief message for me. Tell him that I love him. No son ever owed his father more!

